T0302273

COMPENSATION AND REWARD MANAGEMENT

This book presents a comprehensive account of the intricacies related to compensation and reward management in Indian organizations—a vital strategic feature of HR management. It presents a blend of theoretical concepts, definitions, approaches, methods and techniques related to compensation practices being followed/likely to be followed in organizations. Starting with a conceptual framework, it discusses wage determination and wage fixation practices in India, salary reviews and reward management policies, and processes and procedures, in addition to international remuneration with special reference to expatriates and the remuneration of third country nationals. In addition to examining the designing and monitoring of salary grade structures including salary progression curves, it spells out divergent systems and institutions for wage determination/ wage fixation practices in Indian organizations.

Rich in pedagogical features, including learning objectives, discussion questions, individual and group activities, the volume also has numerous case studies. This book will be useful to students of human resource management, business economics, corporate finance, corporate governance, organizational studies, strategic management, finance, business and industry, public administration, social work and other allied fields.

R.C. Sharma is Founder Vice Chancellor of Amity University Gurugram (AUG) and Ex-Professor Emeritus, Amity Business School, AUG. Besides being honoured with the Lifetime Achievement Award, Dr Sharma has also been felicitated with several prestigious awards including a Gold Medal for securing a First Class in PGDPM (Kurukshetra University). Having more than five decades of experience in corporate, teaching and research, he has authored several textbooks in the area of management, the last two volumes being *Industrial Relations and Labour Legislation* in 2016 (PHI Learning) and *Human Resource Management: Theory* *and Practice* in 2018 in addition to around 200 research papers/articles already published in leading journals and periodicals. He has also been Editor-in-Chief of *Amity Management Analyst*, a very popular biannual journal, for more than a decade.

Sulabh Sharma is Head, Model Line Commuters; Senior General Manager, Research and Development, Centre for Innovation and Technology, Hero MotoCorp Limited; and Ex-Senior Vice President, Head—R&D, PP&IDS, QA, SS&SC, PE, Revolt Intellicorp. He has published around 20 research papers on HR-related topics in leading journals and has filed 10 design patents. He has over 27 years of rich hands-on cross-functional experience and has worked as a platform leader for more than 100 mobility models for NPD with some of the most known research centres of automotive giants and design houses spread across Asia (Japan and Thailand), Europe (Italy, Germany and Spain) and North America (the United States). He has also been trained by some of the best institutes and agencies in the field of design and project management, such as IIT Delhi, PMAC, Boston Consulting Group, Project Management Institute, FranklinCovey, Business Experts Network and Dale Carnegie to name a few.

COMPENSATION AND REWARD MANAGEMENT

Wage & Salary Administration and Benefits

R. C. Sharma and Sulabh Sharma

Routledge
Taylor & Francis Group

LONDON AND NEW YORK

First published 2024
by Routledge
4 Park Square, Milton Park, Abingdon, Oxon OX14 4RN

and by Routledge
605 Third Avenue, New York, NY 10158

Routledge is an imprint of the Taylor & Francis Group, an informa business

British Library Cataloguing-in-Publication Data
A catalogue record for this book is available from the British Library

ISBN: 978-1-032-62609-3 (hbk)
ISBN: 978-1-032-62611-6 (pbk)
ISBN: 978-1-032-62612-3 (ebk)

DOI: 10.4324/9781032626123

Typeset in Times New Roman
by Deanta Global Publishing Services, Chennai, India

CONTENTS

FIGURES

TABLES

PREFACE

Say whatever some critics may like to, the fact remains that 'compensation' and 'reward' matter. These matter to employees because these are the only source of their income, and these matter to employers as well because labour costs, exceptions apart, generally constitute 50–70 per cent of the total costs of production. These matter to other stakeholders also. Wherever there exist activities related to the production of goods and services, the issues of compensation and reward will also exist. Compensation and reward are, thus, two of the major pillars supporting the realm of the economic world.

All the same, there is a lack of uniformity in the perception of different stakeholders about compensation and reward, and the related matters, because of which compensation and reward have emerged as grey areas demanding pragmatic research and in-depth studies. It is keeping the aforesaid scenario in view that the present textbook was envisaged. Hence, both the theoretical foundations and practices pursued in the corporate sector to manage compensation and reward have been deliberated upon in the present volume to enable the decision-makers to formulate appropriate policies, processes and procedures related to the arena of compensation and reward, and issues related thereto.

With their decades of experience in corporate, teaching and research, the authors have discussed, analyzed and interpreted the various concepts, theories, practices, tools and techniques, approaches, methods, pertinent regulations, interventions and other related mechanisms relevant to compensation and reward, and allied issues in the present text.

In the aforesaid attempt, many exhibits, tables, case studies, practical examples, recent developments, probable management strategies, individual and group exercises, authentic facts and figures, references, discussion questions, explanations of various terms and so on have been used extensively and meaningfully to make the reading of the present textbook more factual, realistic, illustrative, meaningful and interesting.

The book commences with a conceptual framework and moves to compensation management, to divergent systems and institutions for wage determination and wage fixation in practice in Indian organizations, and further to contingent pay comprising pay for performance, pay for competence, pay for skills and so on. Thereafter, the book moves to administering and controlling salary costs and salary review, designing and operating fringe benefits and non-financial benefits, and then to reward management policy, processes and procedures, followed by a comprehensive discussion on tax planning, Income Tax Act, 1961, and ultimately reaching its final destination, namely international remuneration.

The book is intended to be extremely useful not only to the postgraduate students and faculties of HRM, public administration, social work, business economics and other allied fields but also to professionals and researchers to gain conceptual clarity and information on various topics and to understand the current problems in the arena of HRM, which require pragmatic research and realistic solutions. It is expected that this textbook will meet the requirements of all concerned in the field of HRM.

The authors look forward to receiving feedback, including suggestions and recommendations, from all the stakeholders at rcsharma25544@gmail.com to add more value to the present volume.

ACKNOWLEDGEMENTS

The authors gratefully acknowledge the inspiration, guidance and support that they were fortunate to receive from a good number of intellectuals, learned authors and experts, legal luminaries, corporate and government authorities, universities, peers, students, secretarial staff, various journals, periodicals, newspapers, government and private publications, and so on.

The authors feel indebted to all the authors of various texts, research papers and articles published in books, journals, periodicals and newspapers, which have been referred to or quoted from in the present text.

Dr Ashok K. Chauhan, Founder President, Ritnand Balved Education Foundation (RBEF), and Dr Aseem Chauhan, Chancellor, Amity University Gurugram (AUG), and Additional President, RBEF—the two distinguished intellectuals and superb educational planners and administrators—genuinely deserve a deep sense of gratitude from the authors. The authors are also thankful to Professor (Dr) Padmakali Banerjee, President and Vice Chancellor SPS University, Udaipur, and Professor (Dr) Vikas Madhukar, Pro Vice Chancellor, Dean, Faculty of Management Studies and Director, ABS, (AUG); Ms. Misha Sharma, a student, Psychology Hons. Flame University for her secretarial assistance; and Dr. Nipun Sharma, CEO, Jeeves and F1, Flipkart, who was instrumental in providing the authors with very useful inputs from the corporate scenario, also deserves thanks for his contribution.

The authors would like to put on record their special thanks to the entire team of Routledge—the renowned international publisher—for completing the whole job of publication of this book very efficiently and effectively within the stipulated period.

In the end, the authors are thankful to all the visible and invisible forces that have been helpful to them directly or indirectly, though the same could not be named here due to paucity of space.

ABBREVIATIONS

BARS	Behaviourally Anchored Rating Scales
BLS	Bureau of Labour Statistics
BPO	Business Process Outsourcing
CBP	Competency-Based Pay
CBDT	Central Board of Direct Taxes
CBT	Central Board of Trustees
CIRM	Central India Relations Machinery
CPI	Consumer Price Index
DA	Dearness Allowance
DPSP	Deferred Profit-Sharing Plan
EPFO	Employees' Provident Fund Organisation
EPS	Employees' Pension Scheme
ESIA	Employees' State Insurance Act
ESIC	Employees' State Insurance Corporation
ESOP	Employees Stock Option Plan
EXPAT	Expatriate
GC	Global Corporation
GOI	Government of India
GST	Goods and Services Tax
HCN	Host-Country National
HR	Human Resources
HRS	Human Resource Secretariat
ILO	International Labour Organization
IT	Information Technology
ITA	Income Tax Act

LCN	Local Country National
MBO	Management By Objectives
MNC	Multinational Corporation
NDA	National Democratic Alliance
OI	Optimism Index
PCN	Parent Country National
PRP	Performance-Related Pay
PSUs	Public Sector Undertakings
SBP	Skill-Based Pay
TCN	Third Country National
TCS	Tata Consultancy Services
TQM	Total Quality Management
TV	Television
VRS	Voluntary Retirement Scheme

DECLARATION

All material reproduced in the volume is original and clearly cited and the chapters have not been published elsewhere in an earlier publication, as articles, or as personal blogs, and if it has, has necessary permission clearances for re-use.

Prof (Dr) R.C. Sharma

1

CONCEPTUAL FRAMEWORK

Introduction

Labour costs and rewards constitute a significant part of the total cost of production on which depends, to a great extent, the profitability of an organization. Hence, labour costs need to be managed appropriately; otherwise not only the profitability of the organization will be jeopardized but also there will be a question mark on

DOI: 10.4324/9781032626123-1

the very sustainability of the organization. It is here that compensation and reward management comes into vogue.

Compensation and Reward Management

Compensation and reward management is concerned with the design, development, implementation, maintenance, communication and evaluation of compensation processes which deal with working out the relative worth of all the jobs in an organization, designing and monitoring of pay structures, paying for skills, competence or performance, performance management, employee benefits, reward management procedures and the like. Compensation management allows to control bottom-line expenditures and simultaneously offers competitive and motivating compensation whether it is fixed pay, variable pay, merit increases, or stock options, that is, total compensation. The purpose of compensation management is to make the most of company money in a manner that rewards employees for their work. Broadly speaking, compensation management is related to the formulation and implementation of strategies and policies that aim at rewarding employees fairly, equitably and consistently as per their worth to the enterprise. Compensation and reward management analyses and controls employee compensation and other benefits. The overall aim of the whole exercise is to improve individual, group and organizational performance and increase employee motivation. Compensation and reward management is a broad term and includes under its ambit a lot of issues as discussed in the subsequent pages of this chapter.

The concept of compensation management got impetus from a number of writers. For example, in his work, Lawler[1] introduced the concept of 'strategic pay' desiring compensation policies to focus on the enterprise's goals, values and culture as well as the challenges posed by a competitive global economy.

Around the same time, Schuster and Zingheim[2] initiated the concept of the 'new pay', pointing out that pay is a positive force to bring about organizational change and suggested the idea of variable pay. They further suggested that the total compensation programme should be designed in such a manner that results as well as behaviours which are instrumental in accomplishing the key goals of the enterprise are appropriately rewarded. In 1996, Flannery, Hofrichter and Platten[3] came forward with the concept of 'dynamic pay', suggesting certain principles for making a pay strategy successful and effective, the main principles being the alignment of compensation with the enterprise's strategic business goals, its culture and values, and that compensation should be linked to other changes, and further that compensation should be refined, refined again and refined some more. Later on, in his other work, *Treat People Right!*, in 2003, Lawler suggested the concept of 'treating the people right', stating that the reward systems should be so designed that it may be effective in motivating people to work, satisfying them and also contributing to the effectiveness of the enterprise.

Of late, the extraordinary growth sectors like IT, ITES, BPOs, Telecom and Finance have led to huge demand for talent at all levels, and therefore, HR professionals as well as HR consultants have already started studying the paradigm shift of concepts, perceptions and the necessity for revising the compensation systems and thus adding to the importance of compensation management. Today the paradigm shift from standard wage and salary to compensation or cost to company (CTC) is distinctly visible in companies' hiring practices. The increasing realization that the application of a systematic and scientific approach to compensate employees for their work in a fair, equitable and logical manner is of paramount importance and has enabled compensation management to occupy a distinct place in the arena of human resource management.

The main objective of compensation management is to reward personnel fairly, equitably and consistently in proportion to their worth to the enterprise. It also aims at creating not only a reward structure for an enterprise and to operate it efficiently and effectively but also intends to motivate personnel of the enterprise to work towards accomplishing strategic goals of the enterprise.

Compensation

Employee compensation is important to the employees because monetary compensation that they get as a reward for their contribution to the process of production is the only means of economic survival besides determining their social status. It is also significant for the employer as it usually constitutes the greatest single component of the cost of production.[4] Employee compensation is important not only to the employees and the employers but also to society because it plays a substantial role in determining the prices of products which the members of the society must pay—thus affecting the cost of their living. Hence, the determination of employee compensation assumes added significance in human resource management (HRM) and, therefore, needs to be well planned and administered as it affects all the stakeholders in an organization.[5]

The 3-Ps of the compensation concept include pay for person, pay for position and pay for performance. A compensation philosophy is simply a formal statement documenting an organization's position regarding employee compensation. In other words, it is an organization's formalized explanation of its employee payment structures. It tells the 'why' behind employee pay and gives rise to a framework for consistency. The compensation philosophy is used by an organization to attract, retain and motivate its employees. Broadly speaking, market pay, equal pay, flexible pay or tailored pay are the four basic compensation philosophies. For example, with a philosophy of market pay, compensation is decided by breaking down jobs into various elements that are graded in terms of value.

Meaning and Definition

'Compensation' does not mean the same thing to everyone. Different stakeholders, such as employees, managers and society, have different perspectives on compensation. However, here we shall confine to employees' perspective about compensation. 'Employees may see compensation as a return in an exchange between their employer and themselves, as an entitlement for being an employee of the company, or as a reward for a job well done'.[6] Compensation is a sort of return to the employees on their investment in their education and training and the contribution they make in terms of their time and energy at their workplace.

Compensation also indicates the value the employer attaches to his employee's skills, abilities, expertise, experience, education, training and so on. Besides, for an employer, since employee compensation is a major constituent of the total cost of production, it needs to be judiciously determined so that it enables the organization to be competitive and to sustain itself meaningfully with good prospects.[7]

In simple words, compensation includes all those things that an organization pays its employees in return for their talent and time.

Employers not only treat compensation as a major expense (labour cost) but also a tool to influence work behaviour as well as to improve the performance of the enterprise because adequate compensation is instrumental in affecting the attitude, keenness to learn new skills and creativity of the workers in the positive direction. Some people use the word 'reward' instead of 'compensation'. In Japan, the term *kyuyo* is used for compensation which means 'giving something'. In China, it is the term *daikyus* that is used for compensation, which implies how the receiver is treated in terms of his wages, benefits, training and development opportunities and so on. Thus, the basic idea behind the term 'compensation' remains the same though expressed in different words by different authors or at different places. As a matter of fact, all forms of financial returns and tangible services and benefits received by an employee as part of his employment relationship together constitute compensation.

Whether compensation is a hygiene factor or motivational factor has also been a controversial matter. In this regard, it may be mentioned that compensation is a hygiene factor if the salary paid on a monthly basis is fixed. Compensation will be considered as a motivational factor if it is variable. It should vary proportionally to the results, goals or targets determined mutually for the purpose. Thus, compensation is a strategic matter.

Difference between Pay and Compensation

While 'pay' is the money or the other compensation given in exchange for goods or services, 'compensation' is the act or principle of compensating. 'Compensation' is broader than pay as the compensation includes all of the benefits and perks that an organization offers to its employees on top of income. Compensation, therefore, relates to all of the pay types and benefits that employers provide to their employees.

Difference between Wages and Income

Wages are normally paid by the hour; i.e., wages are a kind of income that is earned by the hours per week. As against this, income is the sum of all the wages, profits, salaries, rents and other forms of earnings.

Difference between Payroll and Compensation and Benefits

While 'payroll' is the HR function of managing, processing and distribution of periodic paycheques to employees and, therefore, typically involves payment of regular salary and wages, commissions and bonuses, 'compensation' is a broader term than pay as it includes all of the benefits and perks that an organization provides to its employees on top of income.

Difference between Salary and Wages

Though in day-to-day talks, most people don't differentiate between salary and wages, yet according to academicians a 'salary' is a fixed amount paid at regular intervals usually to white-collar employees such as managers, directors or highly skilled and licensed professionals; it is being dependent on skillsets they offer and also what value they add to the organization. Wages, on the other hand, are hourly or daily-based payments given to manual labour for the amount of work finished in an hour or a day.

Total Compensation/Rewards and Its Components and Types

In addition to compensation and benefits which are tangible, there are intangible rewards also such as appreciation, recognition, work-life balance, development opportunities and so on, all (tangible and intangible) taken together constitute total compensation. As a matter of fact, total compensation/reward includes under its ambit both monetary (extrinsic) and non-monetary (intrinsic) rewards available to an employee in an organization (see Figure 1.1).

1. **Monetary (extrinsic) rewards:** These include the following:
   a. **Base/basic wage:** Basic wage is a stable wage paid over a period of time which could be on a monthly, weekly or daily basis. This wage is the normal rate for a given level of output.[8] Thus, given a certain job, with all its attendant requirements of education, skills, training and expertise, it is the price to be paid to get it done. It is usually progressive over time, that is, it progresses more evenly over time if there is a running grade, otherwise it remains fixed with no changes. It is the basic wage that provides a stable base to the wage structure.[9] Basic pay/compensation is the basic cash compensation paid by the employer for the work performed by the

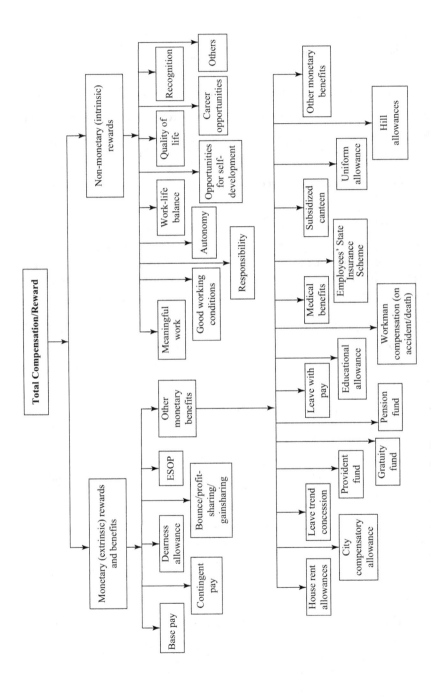

FIGURE 1.1 Components of Total Compensation/Reward

employee. It tends to reflect the value of the work itself and ignore differences in individual contribution. The fixation of basic wage is affected by the prevailing market salary level paid by other employers for that type of job, statutory minimum wage, recommendations of the Indian Labour Conference, patterns set by the industrial tribunals, directives of the Pay Commissions, collective bargaining, wage settlements, periodic job evaluation and so on. The basic wage may differ from job to job depending on minimum educational and professional qualifications, training, skills, expertise, experience, skills and so on required by a particular job. It may also differ based on mental and physical requirements, responsibilities assigned, stress involved and so on.

b. **Contingent pay/variable pay/differential pay:** Contingent pay consists of payments related to individual performance, contribution, competence or skill or to team or organizational performance.[10] It is a non-fixed monetary reward that is contingent on performance, results achieved or even discretion. It is paid through various types of different pay plans such as sales commissions or incentives and overtime pay.

c. **Dearness allowance:** Starting from the First World War, the system of payment of dearness allowance (DA) aims at neutralizing the impact of price rise on the wages and salaries of employees. DA protects the wage earners' real income by neutralizing the increased cost of living due to increase in prices. However, some of the issues involved in this regard include: whether the payment of DA should be automatic as soon as there is rise in the cost of living, and if it is so, what part of price should be compensated, that is, whether fully or partially and whether the 'capacity to pay' of the industry is to be kept into consideration while deciding the payment of DA or increasing it. There are various methods of DA payment. For example, DA may be linked to consumer price index (CPI) in each region. As per this system, payment of DA is regulated on the basis of actual price movement in a particular region/sector or industry. The system may have two methods: (a) a specified rate of DA is fixed for every point rise in the CPI irrespective of the income group an employee belongs to, and (b) the DA is based on income groups and cost of living brackets or slabs. As per this system, the absolute amount of DA goes up with each higher income group. In it, DA does not change with every point in the cost-of-living index. Another example is that of the flat-rate system which provides a lump sum payment to the employees over a period of time to neutralize the impact of inflation.

d. **Bonus:** Since some authors consider bonus as a deferred wage, it may be considered as a constituent of wage structure. In our country, payment of bonus is regulated as per the provisions of the Payment of Bonus Act, 1965. Bonus is a lump sum payment to an employee in recognition of good achievement. Some people consider it as an ex gratia payment, some others view it as a deferred wage, and yet some others consider it as a statutory payment.

e. **Profit-sharing (see Chapter 5).**
f. **Gainsharing (see Chapter 5).**
g. **Employee stock option plan (ESOP)/equity-based compensation (see Chapter 3).**
h. **Other monetary benefits:** These may include the following:
   I.   House rent allowance.
   II.   City compensatory allowance.
   III.   Provident fund.
   IV.   Gratuity fund.
   V.   Pension fund.
   VI.   Leave with pay/paid holiday trips.
   VII.   Life insurances.
   VIII. Company car.
   IX.   Club membership.
   X.   Free residential accommodation.
   XI.   Educational allowance.
   XII.   Workmen compensation.
   XIII. Medical benefits.
   XIV.   Employees' State Insurance (ESI) Scheme.
   XV.   Subsidized canteen facilities.
   XVI.   Uniform allowance.
   XVII. Others.

2. **Non-monetary (intrinsic) rewards:** Non-monetary rewards usually emerge from the work itself as well as from the work environment. Such rewards provide psychic satisfaction and help in maintaining a work-life balance. These rewards may include:
   a. Meaningful work.
   b. Good working conditions.
   c. Mentorship.
   d. Desirable work schedule.
   e. Opportunities to travel or to meet other people in the same field.
   f. Responsibility.
   g. Autonomy.
   h. Work-life balance.
   i. Opportunities for self-development.
   j. Quality of life.
   k. Career opportunities.
   l. Recognition.
   m. Others.

In normal course, especially in developing economies, it is the monetary reward that is valued more, but simply throwing money at the workers is not enough. There is no doubt that money matters, but it is not everything. Cash is a weak tactic in the overall reward strategy; it is too easily replicated. Intrinsic reward is more difficult to emulate.[11] An employee is a human being first. His psychic requirements too are to be taken care of if he is expected to give his best. Intrinsic or non-monetary rewards play a vital role in motivating an employee and making him more productive because a total reward strategy which allots the required space to non-monetary reward helps better in creating a work experience that meets the requirements of employees. It enthuses employees to contribute extra effort. Creating a fun and challenging work environment is more difficult. But once created, it continues motivating the workers to improve their performance for a long time.

The total compensation thus comprises 'compensation', 'benefits' and 'the work experience'. Of course, some authors such as Duncan Brown and Michael Armstrong[12] have prescribed total compensation in the form of 'transactional rewards' which are monetary in nature and 'relational rewards' such as learning and developmental opportunities and work experience which add to the value of transactional rewards. Hence, both are important in their own place. In addition to transactional and relational elements, the Hay Group Engaged Performance Model, which was developed in the late 1990s, laid emphasis on a compelling and high-performance workplace for total compensation to be meaningful.

Relational rewards comprise (a) inspiration and values which include quality of leadership, recognition, organizational values and behaviours, risk sharing, communication and reputation of the organization; (b) future growth and opportunities which may consist of career advancement, learning and development, and performance improvement; (c) enabling environment which may include physical work environment, job training, tools and equipment, safety, security, and information and processes and so on; (d) quality of work which may be concerned with perception about the worth of work, achievement, challenges involved, work load, interest, quality of work relationship, freedom and autonomy; and (e) work-life balance which may involve flexibility, job security, social environment, recognition of lifecycle requirements, helping environment and so on.

Importance of the Total Compensation Approach

The total compensation approach has several benefits. It gives greater satisfaction to the employee and keeps him motivated which, in turn, results in higher productivity of the employee. Besides, it provides greater opportunities for the beneficiary to meet his individual needs. It is also helpful in attracting and retaining talent and also instrumental in improving employment relationships. Relational rewards give an emotional touch and result in better bonding and motivation. As a matter of fact, it results in building relationship capital. The combined effect of monetary and non-monetary compensation is deeper and is likely to leave its impact for a longer duration. It also involves employees in various compensation processes whereby they feel more empowered and prouder of their organization. In the US, about 18,700 people are compensation managers, and the role is growing around 4% a year.

Wages/Salaries

The term 'wages' is used to denote payments to hourly rated production workers or wages are the remuneration paid for the labour of unskilled, semi-skilled or skilled operative workforce. In this type of labour, the element of corporal labour is much more in comparison to mental efforts and capabilities. International Labour Organization (ILO) defined the term wage as 'the remuneration paid by the employer for the services of the hourly, daily, weekly and fortnightly employees'.[13] So far as the term 'salary' is concerned, it is used to denote payments to clerical, supervisory and managerial employees on a monthly or annual basis. Such employees usually contribute their mental labour to the organization. Again, salaries are usually paid on a monthly basis, whereas wages may be paid on a daily or hourly basis. However, for our purpose, the distinction between the two carries no meaning because, broadly speaking, the same issues are involved in the administration of both wage and salary policies, and all types of employees are treated as human resources (HR).

Other Terms

Other terms related to wage and salary are as follows:

1. **Nominal/money wage:** Nominal or money wage refers to the monetary form of wage payment.
2. **Real wage:** Real wage represents the actual exchange value of money wage, that is, the purchasing power of money wage.
3. **Take-home salary:** It refers to the amount of salary left to the employee after making authorized deductions such as income tax, provident fund and life insurance premium.
4. **Statutory minimum wage:** It is the amount of remuneration fixed according to the provisions of the Minimum Wages Act, 1948.
5. **Minimum wages:** In the context of our country, minimum wages mean that minimum amount which the labour thinks necessary not only for the bare sustenance of life but also for the preservation of the efficiency of the worker. In other words, minimum wages are the amount or remuneration 'which may be sufficient to enable a worker to live in reasonable comforts, having regard to all obligations to which an average worker would ordinarily be subjected to'.[14]

6. **Living wage:** It represents the highest level of wages including all amenities which a citizen living in the modern civilized society is entitled to and expects when the economy of the country is sufficiently advanced and the employer is able to meet the expanding aspirations of his workers. (The present level of our national income does not permit the payment of a living wage or standards prevalent in advanced countries of the world.)

7. **Fair wage:** According to the Fair Wages Committee, a fair wage is above the minimum wage but somewhat below the living wage, depending on the capacity of the organization to pay.

8. **Basic compensation:** It is the basic compensation that an employee receives for the work performed by him. It tends to reflect the value of the work and ignores differences in individual contribution. It is also known as basic pay.

9. **Supplementary compensation:** These are benefits for time not worked, such as vacation and holiday pay and sick pay.

10. **Variable compensation:** It ties pay to productivity or profitability, usually as one-time lump sum. It keeps fluctuating depending on the productivity or performance of an employee.

Theories of Wages

The main theories of wages can be categorized under the following two heads:

Economic Theories

1. **Subsistence theory:** Originating from the Physiocratic school of French economists, it is Ricardo (1772–1823) whose name is associated with this theory of wages. According to this theory, wages tend to settle at the level just sufficient to maintain the worker and his family at the minimum subsistence. In case wages rise above the subsistence level, the population will increase, and, therefore, due to increase in the supply of labour, wages will come down to the subsistence level. It was the Malthusian theory of population from which Ricardo took his inspiration. The subsistence theory was called the *iron law of wages* or the brazen law of wages by the German economist Lassalle. However, the subsistence theory of wages is no more popular.

2. **Wage–fund theory:** The next approach of wage fixation is the wage–fund theory which emerged because of the weakness in the subsistence theory of wages. According to this theory, a fixed amount of wage fund is available for distribution at any one time and the level of wages depends on the number of labour seeking employment. It is because if in any industry, the wages of workers go above the available amount of the wage fund, the workers from

other industries will feel attracted towards the industry where the rates of wages are higher giving rise to the supply of labour in that industry, and, therefore, the rates of wages will come down. However, the theory suffers from many shortcomings. For example, there is no reason to assume that the available wage fund will remain constant. Hence, such shortcomings gave rise to some other theories. All classical theories of wage rates come to the forefront when demand and supply are equated. The term 'equilibrium' is appropriate because if wages happen to have been fixed above this level, economic forces will operate and push them down to the equilibrium level, and if they happen to fall below this figure, similar forces will drive them up to that level again.[15] These theories assume that the available supply of labour is, for the time being, fixed and similar in the case with the number of potential employees. It is because of these assumptions that the term 'equilibrium' seems to be appropriate. However, the wage–fund theory has also lost its relevance because there is no justification to assume that the available wage fund will remain constant.

3. **Marginal productivity theory:** The third approach to wage fixation is marginal productivity theory which emerged in pursuance of the approach based on equilibrium rates of wages. As per this theory, the main regulators of wages are the demand for and supply of labour and compensation. The theory states that any industry would continue employing additional labour as long as it pays to employ them, that is, the addition of labour must cause an increase in production, otherwise at a certain stage, additional employment will become counterproductive. In other words, the cost of employing an additional labour should result in, at least, equal amount of return.

4. **Surplus value theory:** Karl Marx stated that as per a special feature of the capitalist wage system, the supply of labour is always tended to be kept in surplus, that is, more than the demand for it. In the capitalist form of production, there is the rate of exploitation, that is, the rate of surplus value, which is the ratio of surplus labour to necessary labour.[16] But the institution of collective bargaining and some other mechanisms can restrict this tendency to a great extent.

5. **Bargaining theory:** Propagated by John Davidson, the theory states that there is always an upper limit on wage rates above which the employers will not pay, otherwise they would run into loss due to increased labour costs. In the same way, there is also a lower limit on wages which may be either because of legal requirements or the subsistence level below which it will be difficult to get labour. Between these two limits, wage rates are determined depending on the bargaining power of the workers or their trade union and the employer or their association.

6. **Purchasing power theory:** Lord J.M. Keynes in his book, *The General Theory of Employment, Interest and Money*, mentioned that in case wage rates are high, the workers will have more purchasing power which will cause an increase in the aggregate demand for goods and services and output activity

will tend to go up and demand for labour will also shoot up and so on. Reverse will happen if the purchasing power is low.

7. **Modern theories of wages:** As a result of shortcomings in the classical and other wage theories, some modern theories of wages came up which have some improvement over the earlier ones. Modern theories postulate that wages are determined by the laws of demand and supply on the one hand, and by the various external factors and constraints, on the other hand. The traditional theories of wages are, by and large, individualistic. They either do not take into account the role of workers' trade unions and collective bargaining in the wage determination or do not attach the required weightage to the aforesaid institutions. It should be kept in view that trade unions as well as collective bargaining play a very important role in wage determination, and, therefore, no theory of wage determination should ignore these two agencies.

Behavioural Theories

As per behavioural theories, wages act both as a dissatisfier and a motivator. Since money, valence, equity, contingencies and internal and external relativities are critical factors in impacting employee behaviour, they deserve to be taken care of while determining wages. Some of the main behavioural theories in this respect are as follows:

1. **Equity theory:** The theory states that both internal and external equities should be maintained while determining wage rates, otherwise it will be difficult to attract and retain employees. While internal equities refer to differentials in pay due to differences in skills or responsibilities and so on, external equities indicate how wage levels for similar type of skills level in one organization compare with those in other organizations in the same or similar industry and locators and regions.
2. **Herzberg's two-factor theory:** According to Herzberg, the propounder of this theory, rewards can be categorized into two parts, namely (a) hygiene factors and (b) motivation factors. While the rewards which are external to the job such as pay and perks are hygiene factors, autonomy, job enrichment, job enlargement, recognition, appreciation and so on are motivators and related to job context. The absence of hygiene factors is a dissatisfier, and the availability of motivational factors induces the employees to put in their best efforts. Hence, while determining wages, the role of both the hygiene and the motivation factors should also be taken into consideration.
3. **Vroom's expectancy theory:** The process model of employee motivation, presented by Victor Vroom in 1964,[17] is known as expectancy theory, according to which motivation is a product of the value the employee seeks and his expectation of probability that a certain action will lead to those values. Keith Davis[18] has also pointed out that whenever an individual performs any action, he conducts

a cost-benefit analysis. If the expected benefit is enough to justify the cost of effort, he is likely to put in effort, that is, before undertaking a given level of effort, the employee seeks an answer to the question that if he makes a stronger effort on his job, will a better level of performance be achieved, and further that if he achieves such an outstanding level of performance, what type of rewards or negative outcomes will happen. Not only this, he would also need to know how valuable the outcome or performance level is to him. In other words, it can be said that the motivation of an employee depends on his expectations about his ability to perform a task and receive the desired awards, the formula being:

$$\text{Motivational Force} = \text{Valence} \times \text{Expectancy}$$

Where Valence = Strength (of motivation). However, this theory despite its theoretical excellence in providing an accurate description of the motivation process contributes little towards actually motivating employees.[19] Whatever is said above can be put as shown in Figure 1.2.

In this way, the motivation of force behind a specific level of work performance is the function of (a) employee's perception that the probability or perceived likelihood that certain outcomes will result from the employee's efforts and (b) the valence (value or utility) of such outcomes to him.

Does Compensation Motivate Behaviour?

Monetary rewards, a significant component of compensation, play a very important role in motivating an employee, and behaviour is the outcome of motivation.

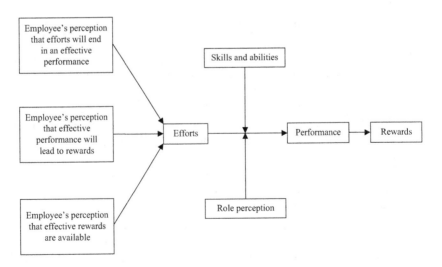

FIGURE 1.2   Expectancy Model

Hence, it is obvious that compensation motivates behaviour. This fact is also supported by various theories of motivation, one of the latest being Vroom's expectancy theory. Extrinsic motivation is affected a great deal by compensation which an employee receives from his employer for the services he renders for him. In case such compensation is not appropriate, the employee is likely to be less motivated or not motivated at all, which will reflect upon his work behaviour and, in all probabilities, he is likely to be less productive. On the other hand, if compensation is adequate or duly rewarding, the employee is likely to be proud of it and will be far more motivated which is likely to prompt him to put his heart and soul into his work.

Thus, compensation is a very powerful instrument to motivate behaviour. Of course, a few exceptions are always there.

Compensation Philosophy

A compensation philosophy of an organization is a formal statement that spells out the organization's stand or position with regard to employee compensation. Such a policy is a sort of commitment of the organization towards compensation of its employees. While explaining the 'why' behind employee pay, it also creates a framework for consistency. As such, the foundation of all compensation decisions is based on the compensation philosophy of the organization. Compensation philosophy expresses what the enterprise values are and is prepared to reward employees for it.

A compensation philosophy should be transparent as the transparency of the commitment of the organization towards employee compensation is beneficial to both the employee and the organization, especially at the time of formulation of pay strategy or salary negotiations between the employer and the employees or their respective associations.

All the same, it is a complex job to develop a compensation philosophy. It needs thoughtful consideration and care while developing a compensation philosophy. It should be developed through teamwork between the executives and non-executives. All concerned should be involved in the exercise, and all key factors such as objectives of the organization, size of the organization, financial position of the organization, type of industry, salary being offered by competitors and status of talent already existing in the organization and required in future should be taken into consideration. The basic objective of developing a compensation philosophy is that it should be instrumental in accomplishing the goals of the organization, and it is necessary to explore certain issues related to compensation philosophy. The first and foremost is to identify the purpose of compensation philosophy, whether its objective is to attract, retain and motivate people or something else, so that it may focus on the desired objectives. In case the objective is to attract, retain and motivate people, then having conducted salary survey in the market, it should mix base pay, incentives pay and benefits keeping in view the resources available at the disposal of the organization. For instance, while developing a pay philosophy at the level of a public sector undertaking, it may lay due emphasis on work-life balance in addition to a more rounded philosophy, whereas in case of developing a pay philosophy for a private organization, the focus may be on competitive pay and the like. As such, pay philosophy may vary from organization to organization and from time to time within the same organization, depending on the circumstances prevailing in the organization or during a particular period of time.

The next issue with regard to compensation philosophy is the frequency at which it should be reviewed. Though most organizations conduct salary reviews once a year, there may be a few which may go for it biannually. Hence, the frequency of compensation philosophy review should be decided by the compensation team. Sometimes, the organization may require new college recruits at different periods of time in a year, or in any extraordinary situation, recruitment is made at a different time than the usual recruitment season. For all such eventualities, the organization will have to take personal decisions regarding the review of compensation philosophy, that is, whether it needs review or not.

Another issue is related to consistency in the compensation philosophy. It has been observed in a good number of organizations that employee seniors in terms of length of service period in the same rank in the same organization get less salary than the ones recruited recently or a few months or a year or two earlier. Such issues should be taken care of by the compensation philosophy.

Whatever be the pay philosophy of the organization, it should be well communicated to all the employees across the organization. It is good to spell out the pay philosophy while the pay is being negotiated at the time of appointment and the candidate be told why he is being offered more or less than the market rate. The candidate may appreciate it, whether the rate being offered to him is more or less, because of the transparency of the pay philosophy. It may not be very convincing to him if the pay philosophy comes to his notice or if he is told about it at a later stage.

Next, the pay philosophy should be of quality. It should be perceived as fair by the employees of the organization whether it meets all the legal requirements, appears to be equitable, is fiscally appropriate, can be defended if the situation demands at any juncture, the individual programmes are aligned with the overall compensation philosophy, or can be easily communicated and is easily understandable by all concerned.

A good compensation philosophy should be able to withstand challenging situations whenever they emerge and the organization has to confront them. It should take care not only of organizational needs but also individual needs. So far as organizational needs are concerned, the philosophy should be such that it may be helpful in accomplishing organizational goals. It is possible only when the compensation philosophy encourages reinforcement of good performance and performance enhancement. Simultaneously, it should also ensure elimination or, at least, substantial reduction in absenteeism/cost of production. It should also be able to sustain cultural changes and be able to maintain balance between performance pay and individual performance pay. It should also take a balanced view of both short-term and long-term requirements of compensation arrangements. Coming to the individual needs met by the compensation philosophy, it may be pointed that compensation philosophy should be able to take care of all those factors which affect motivation of individuals and what is it that impacts employee satisfaction.

All good companies have well-defined compensation philosophy. For example, in IBM, the compensation philosophy focuses on contribution pay, that is, it is what you do that matters. The compensation philosophy of ICL emboldens the performance culture. The company rewards those employees who develop capabilities that meet the company's business requirements.

Compensation Strategy

Meaning and Definition

A compensation strategy is a budget and employee compensation plan for rewarding, developing and creating incentives for the people working in an organization. While defining compensation strategy, Michael Armstrong and Helen Murlis[20] state: Rewards strategy provides specific directions on how the organization will develop and design programmes that will ensure that it rewards the behaviour and performance outcomes that support the achievement of its business goals. A comprehensive compensation strategy is the foundation for evolving an environment that not only rewards employee performance but also duly recognizes it and can be instrumental in creating and sustaining a sound culture of employee engagement. According to Milkovich, Newman and Venkata Ratnam, a strategic perspective focuses on those compensation choices that help the organization gain and sustain competitive advantage.[21] Managers should tailor their pay systems to align with the business strategy of the organization.[22]

It is through the compensation strategy that efforts of the entire organization are made to aim at accomplishing the organization's strategic objectives. The deliberate utilization of the pay system as an essential integrating mechanism through which the efforts of various sub-units and individuals are directed towards the achievement of the organization's strategic objectives is necessary. The compensation strategy should be based on the premise that it is the employees who are the ultimate source of values. Hence, compensation processes should take care of the needs of the employees and also of the enterprise. It should also be based on the organization's requirements for performance. It should be able to not only reinforce and validate the thrust of the business but also support change.

Characteristics of Compensation Strategy

A compensation strategy aims at making a significant contribution towards the accomplishment of an organization's goals. It also integrates compensation policies and processes with the key strategies of the organization meant for enhancing performance. It aims at attracting and retaining high performers so as to meet organizational objectives. It fits the culture of the organization and helps in adapting to change. It helps in balancing rewards for individual, team and organizational performance. It aims not only at extracting the desired employee behaviour but also helping in doing that. It focuses on the established values of the organization such as encouraging innovation, promoting teamwork, maintaining the quality of the product and serving the customer appropriately.

It should also meet the compensation needs and expectations of the employees both as individuals and in groups. It should be flexible so that it may take care of future changes. It should also be indicative of the organization's expectations of its employees and what are the values that the organization stands for. It should also be instrumental in aligning the core competence of the organization and individual competence. It should also be capable of preparing the best mix of monetary and non-monetary rewards and benefits.

In case compensation policies and processes are to be aligned with business and HR goals, it is advisable to develop a compensation strategy whose foundation comprises the business and HR strategies, the kind of employees, statutory obligations, old and current reward practices and so on. However, for an effective compensation strategy, there are seven keys which include: budget allocation, that is, how much percentage of the total compensation budget will be utilized for salary. Obviously, the remaining percentage of the total compensation budget will be spent on benefits and incentives; developing salary ranges internally so that average salaries in a specific geographic region may be determined; salary audits so as to ensure that the salary ranges are competitive; working out benefit packages which suit individual requirements as it helps in retaining people; having structured performance management processes which ensure that corporate objectives are being met by employees and other things are moving as desired; statutory obligations are met; and finally, there should be structured administration, failing which the other steps taken may not yield the desired results.

Different Strategies

It is also to be understood that there is necessarily no uniformity in the strategies of all organizations. Strategies differ widely from industry to industry and also within the same industry. Not only this, even within the same organization the strategies may differ from unit to unit if it has more than one unit or from department to department or even from time to time within the same department or unit and so on. Much depends on the external environment, especially in the context of competitors. Internal environment too plays its own role while the strategy is formulated because internal factors like the work culture and technology being used during a particular period, the raw material or quality of employees available during a period, may also play an important role and, therefore, should be taken into consideration while strategy is being formulated. As a matter of fact, strategy refers to the fundamental directions that an organization chooses.[23]

Developing a Total Compensation Strategy

Developing a compensation strategy is a complex task. Anyway, Milkovich et al.[24] have suggested the following four simple steps for developing a compensation strategy, namely (a) assess total compensation implications, (b) map a total compensation strategy, (c) implement and (d) reassess.

As far as assessing total compensation implications is concerned, first of all, factors should be identified which have led to the success of the organization and which of them are likely to be critical in the future. Such factors may include understanding the specific industry of which the organization is a part and what steps the organization is envisaging to withstand the challenges of the competitive environment in future and whether the strategy of the organization is good enough to be successful, and whether there is perfect alignment of compensation strategy with the strategies of other departments of the organizations. If need be, competitive dynamics may be viewed globally. Then comes culture and values which are reflected in the compensation system. The compensation strategy should reflect the values and culture it stands for. For example, it should spell out security, ESOP, incentives, work-life programmes, advance opportunities, personal satisfaction in work performance and the like, if these are there in the organization. Thereafter comes social, political and legal contexts. Since compensation choices are affected a great deal by the social, political and legal contexts, these should find enough space in the compensation strategy. Besides, as employees have individual differences and preferences, these things should also be taken care of while formulating compensation strategy so that all individuals despite their differences with regard to so many things find adequate satisfaction. For example, there can be different benefit programmes so that an individual employee may choose a benefit programme that suits him most to satisfy his and his family's needs. In many industries, unions play a vital role. Hence, a compensation strategy should include and attach due weightage to the unions' viewpoints. Next, the pay strategy should also fit with the overall HR strategy. Only then, the compensation strategy may prove effective.

The second major step in developing a compensation strategy involves mapping the total compensation strategy, that is, offering a complete picture of the compensation strategy and clarifying that the organization means business in developing its compensation strategy. It should specify the importance given in it to the objectives, internal alignments, external competitiveness, employee contributions, transparency and so on. The third step in developing a compensation strategy relates to its implementation which should be through the design and execution of the compensation system which translates compensation strategy into practice. The fourth step in developing a compensation strategy involves follow-up, that is, depending on feedback, it should be reassessed, realigned and taking other remedial steps.

Source of Competitive Advantage

There is no doubt the compensation strategy is helpful in accomplishing the objectives of an organization, but not all compensation decisions are a source of competitive advantage and similarly not all compensation decisions are strategic. Milkovich et al.[25] have suggested three tests that determine whether a pay strategy is a source of competitive advantage. These are: (a) alignment, that is, alignment of the competitive strategy with the business strategy, economic and sociopolitical conditions and the overall HR system; (b) differentiation, that is, it should be different, not easily replicable by others; and (c) value addition, that is, instead of calculating return on investment (ROI) on account of compensation paid, it should be found out whether there is any value addition. It may be in terms of attracting and retaining talent and the like.

Compensation Strategy: Internal Alignment

Internal alignment means maintenance of internal equity with regard to pay relationships among different jobs or competencies or skills or all taken together. In other words, internal alignment addresses pay relationships inside the enterprise. According to Milkovich et al.,[26] the relationships form a pay structure that should support the organization's strategy, workflow and motivational behaviour towards its objectives. It is always desirable to keep into consideration the goals of the entire organization when thinking about internal pay structures as the same impact not only employees' attitudes but also their work behaviour.

Compensation Strategy: External Alignment

While formulating compensation strategy, not only the internal alignment should be made but also the external alignment should be addressed, especially the pay structures worked out by your competitors for different skills, jobs, competencies and so on. In case external alignment is not attempted, the organization may not be able to attract and retain talent.

Integrating Business and Compensation Strategy

It has been observed that a strategy impacts an organization's design and management style, both of which should drive the design of reward systems[27] because these systems, in turn, help to drive performance by influencing important individual and organizational behaviour. The compensation strategy should be linked with the business strategy, that is, the broad statements and strategic intentions of the compensation strategy should be in line with those of the business strategy.

Result Obtained

Though there is no hard and fast rule, it has been observed that organizations whose compensation strategy has perfect (a) alignment with business and HR strategy, (b) is externally competitive, that is, paying slightly more than the competitors and (c) pay is performance based and so on have yielded better results.

Compensation Policy

Compensation policy is one of the most vital and critical HR policies. Traditionally, compensation processes. The compensation policy is guided, to a great extent, by the compensation philosophy of the organization. Compensation policy is all the more important because it takes care of not only the levels of compensation but also plays a vital role in attracting and retaining talent in the organization. It spells out the approach of the organization towards internal equities and external equities as also what is it that the organization wants to emphasize upon. It indicates the organization's approach towards total compensations. It also clarifies as to what extent the employees of the organization will be involved in the design of compensation systems and to what extent transparency will be there with regard to information on compensation structure and other related issues. Another important issue is with regard to the scope for use of contingent reward for promoting performance, competence, skills, contribution and the like. It will also spell out the extent to which the flexibility is feasible and in what respect.

As a matter of fact, compensation policies are the collection of rules that are concerned with the calculation of salary and benefits entitlement for all individuals employed in the organizations. There can be several compensation policies such as determination of salary and benefits for new recruits, supervisory salary adjustment policy, adjustment of salary and benefits on account of transfer policy, promotion policy, increment policy, position rating policy, re-employment after lay-off policy, red circle policy, overtime policy, contractual employment policy, market adjustment policy, pay bands policy, gratuity policy, retroactive salary adjustment policy and progression policy. For example, there are 24 compensation policies for individuals employed by the Government of Newfoundland and Labrador which are found in the *Compensation Policy and Procedure Manual* (CPPM) in the Strategic Human Resource Division. The government policies in Newfoundland and Labrador are updated by the Human Resource Secretariat (HRS). New policies are approved by the Treasury Board and uploaded on the relevant website and deleted from the CPPM.

Compensation policies may have four varieties or a combination of two or more. First, there can be a policy relating to internal alignment which is concerned with pay relationships within the organization. It refers to comparisons among job or skill levels within the organization. Under it, jobs and skills of employees are compared with regard to their relative contributions to the business objectives of the enterprise. This is a very important aspect because internal pay relationships impact an employee's decision whether to continue in the organization or not. It also affects an employer's decision whether to get more flexible by investing in additional training and so on. Second, there can be a compensation policy relating to external alignment which is concerned with pay comparisons with competitive enterprises. There can be a comparison of pay mix that the competitors use and the pay mix that our organization uses, the basic purpose being to identify where our pay is positioned and what forms are used, and thus how far it is creating an advantage over our competitor firms. It is said that usually pay systems are market driven. Thus, decisions related to external competitiveness may keep attracting and retaining the desired talent and also controlling labour costs. Third, there can be a compensation policy that lays more emphasis on 'paying for contribution or performance'. It may spell out which programmer be paid differently from another, if one has made better contribution and so on. The policy may also point out whether the organization will share any profit with the personnel of the organization. Paying for contribution is an important phenomenon as it influences an employee's attitude and work behaviour in the organization. Fourth, the compensation policy may be related to management of the pay system which may ensure that the right people get the right pay for achieving the right objectives in the right way.[28] The aforementioned policies may not yield the desired results unless they are well-managed and administered.

Compensation policies should be reviewed periodically by competent authorities. It will be better if necessary feedback is taken from workers and their trade unions. Managers should ensure that employees are aware of compensation policies that affect their salary and benefit entitlement. The employees too should ensure that they are aware of compensation policies of their organization. It will become easier if compensation policies are accessible to all employees, managers and strategic human resource management (SHRM) division. There should be strict adherence to compensation policies by all concerned.

Again, if in the course of implementation of compensation policies, there appears any inconsistency with these policies it should be pointed out to the authorities concerned and the inconsistency should be reconciled and remedied. The employees too should also notify the inconsistency, if any, they come across or experience during the course of implementation of compensation policies.

Base of Compensation Management

The base of compensation management is correlated with its objectives. In addition to rewarding employees of the organization fairly, equitably and consistently as per the worth of individuals to the enterprise, the compensation management aims at motivating employees to work in the direction of accomplishing strategic goals of the organization. That is why compensation management developed on the basis of psychologists' behavioural research which started in the early 1900s. Psychologists, including Sigmund Freud and his successors, worked on how employees react to rewards and what motivates them to work and in the process several theories of motivation came into existence which are closely related to compensation management.

The Psychological Contract

The Concept and Definition

The concept of psychological contract was developed by Denise,[29] a contemporary research scholar. Psychological contract represents the mutual beliefs, perceptions and informal obligations between an employer and an employee. As a matter of fact, the concept of psychological contract was first initiated by Argris in 1960, though it is only during the last two to three decades that it has become popular and more research has been done in this area. The employees are likely to maintain high production, low grievances and so on in case their foremen assure, guarantee and respect the norms of the employee informal culture. Thus, psychological contracts refer to the relationship between an employer and an employee where there exist unwritten and mutual expectations from each other. Managing compensation is largely about managing expectations—what employees expect from their employers in return for their contribution and what employers expect from their employees in return for their pay and the opportunities to work and develop their skills.[30] It can, therefore, be stated that a psychological contract is a philosophy rather than a formula or a devised plan. It involves compassion, respect, trust, objectivity and so on.

Today, employees are expected to contribute more in terms of effort, time, skills and flexibility, though they get less in terms of job security, lifetime employment and so on. Therefore, any violation of psychological contract is likely to cause buyout as it eliminates the notion of reciprocity, and it is well known that reciprocity is critical in maintaining well-being.

A psychological contract not only sets the dynamics for the employment relationship but also defines the detailed practicality of the work to be carried out. A psychological contract can be differentiated from the formal written contract of employment which, by and large, only identifies mutual duties and responsibilities in a general way. Armstrong and Murlis[31] state that there are two types of contracts which define employment relationship, namely (a) 'transactional contracts' which are called 'economic contracts'. These contracts contain well-described terms of exchange. Based on law, these are normally expressed in monetary terms with specified performance requirements. These focus more on the explicit elements of the contract without accounting much for intrinsic qualities of an employee or a prospective employee. These contracts are related to careerism, lack of trust in employers and greater resistance to change, which is why these are usually in writing, and (b) 'relational contracts'—these are formed by beliefs regarding exchange agreements. As such, these define workplace relationship between employer and employee. It is a type of social exchange relationship. These may be less well-defined or not defined at all. These have more abstract terms and refer to an open-ended membership of the organization. Performance requirements attached to membership may be ambiguous or incomplete.[32]

A psychological contract is normally implied rather than stated. It is not subject to agreement, that is, the arrangement is only in the minds of the two parties concerned, namely the employer and the employee, that is, it is not agreed between them. It simply refers to all those aspects of employment relationship which are neither well-defined nor clearly understood. And such aspects of employment relationship have a great bearing on the commitment, motivation, job satisfaction and morale of the employees.

Having discussed the concept of psychological contract from different angles, we may define it as the combination of beliefs held by any employee and his employer about what they expect from each other. Falling in line with this sort of thinking, Sims[33] also says that a psychological contract is a set of expectations held by the individual employee that specify what the individual and organization expect to give and receive from one another in the course of their working relationship.

Characteristics

The main characteristics of a psychological contract are as follows:

1. It is a system of beliefs.
2. It encompasses the actions employees believe are expected of them and what they expect in return from their employers.
3. It implies what behaviour employers expect from their employees.
4. It is normally unwritten.
5. It involves abstract terms.
6. It is related to those employment relationships which are neither well-defined nor clearly understood.
7. It is implicit.
8. It is dynamic.

Thus, from the employer's point of view, a psychological contract may embrace aspects of employment relationship such as effort, commitment, competence and loyalty. Similarly, from the viewpoint of employees, a psychological contract may cover aspects of employment relationship such as security of job, career expectations, fair treatment, consistency, equity, scope for exhibiting their competence, trust in the enterprise and leadership style.

Importance

Some of the main points that illustrate the significance of psychological contract may be as follows:

1. It creates emotions which impact work behaviour of an employee.
2. It creates attitudes which also affect work behaviour of an employee.
3. It leads to a prolonged harmonious relationship between the employer and the employee.
4. It promotes trust between the two parties, namely the employer and the workers.

A psychological contract serves a great purpose if both the employer and the employee meet each other's expectations and have trust in each other.

Developing and Maintaining

In order to develop and maintain a productive psychological contract, it is necessary that at the time of the employment interview itself, both favourable and unfavourable aspects of the job be made known to the candidates. Once selected, during the course of their induction programmes, the inductees be made aware of HR policies of the company and the standards of performance expected of them. Performance management processes be appropriately developed and personal development plans be evolved and used. Similarly, during training and development programmes,

performance expectations should be spelt out and the core values of the organization be highlighted. There should be increased interaction between managers and their teams and transparency be assured. HR procedures such as discipline handling, grievance handling and promotions be developed. HR policies related to employment, development, rewards and so on be duly communicated to all concerned.

Compensation and Legal Issues in Compensation Management

It is obvious that government is a key stakeholder in compensation decision-making which is a vital component of compensation management. It is for various reasons, for example, it is one of the vital concerns of the government that there is no pay discrimination. Hence, the government has to ensure that procedures for determining pay are fair. Again, the government has to protect employees from exploitation by the employers. Hence, it has to form rules for overtime pay and prohibit employment of child labour. The government has to also provide safety nets for the unemployed and disadvantaged groups through unemployment insurance (especially during lay-off period), minimum wages and so on. Since the government is a big employer, it tries to monitor the demand for labour through its purchase and financial policy decisions. Similarly, the supply of labour is also regulated by government to a great extent, for example, through immigration policy. It also regulates contract labour through monitoring wages of contract labour. It also ensures that no unreasonable deductions are made from the salary of employees and further that payment of wages is made well in time. The government also regulates hours of work and equal pay for equal work. It also prohibits discrimination in all employment practices on the basis of race, sex, colour, religion, gender or nationality. Protection during pregnancy period for female workers is to be ensured by the government. Sharing of extra earnings with the employees in the form of bonuses is also ensured by the government so that there is no industrial dispute on this count. It has to be seen that wage differentials are there, but the same should be reasonable. Government has to also see if the provisions for provident fund, gratuity, state insurance and so on are made appropriately.

The compensation management has to make necessary arrangements to take care of the aforesaid issues. For example, in our country, the government has enacted the following Acts in this regard:

1. Employees' Compensation Act, 1923.
2. Payment of Wages Act, 1936.
3. Industrial Disputes Act, 1947.
4. Minimum Wages Act, 1948.
5. ESI Act, 1948.
6. Employees Provident Funds and Miscellaneous Provisions Act, 1952.
7. Maternity Benefit Act, 1961.
8. Payment of Bonus Act, 1965.
9. The Contract Labour (Regulation and Abolition) Act, 1970.
10. Payment of Gratuity Act, 1972.
11. Equal Remuneration Act, 1976.
12. Labour Codes viz., Code on Wages, 2019, Industrial Relations Code 2020, Social Security Code 2020, Occupational Safety, Health and Working Conditions Code 2020.
13. Others.

Since labour is on the Concurrent List, the state governments have also passed some Acts in this direction depending on the requirements of the state concerned.

Factors Affecting Employee Compensation/Wage Rates/ Wage Structure/Levels of Pay

There are several factors affecting employee compensation, the main being the following:

1. Demand for and supply of labour.
2. Status of trade unions.

3. Cost of living.
4. Labour productivity.
5. Collective bargaining.
6. Company's wage policy.
7. Prevailing wage rates/external relativities.
8. Job requirements and intrinsic value of the jobs.
9. Company's ability to pay.
10. Wage legislation and government's wage policy.
11. Wage boards.
12. Region-cum-industry settlements.
13. Internal pricing through job evaluation/internal relativities.
14. Business performance.
15. Tribunal/court awards.
16. Competition.
17. Financial circumstances of the company.
18. Business performance.
19. Trade unions.
20. Others.

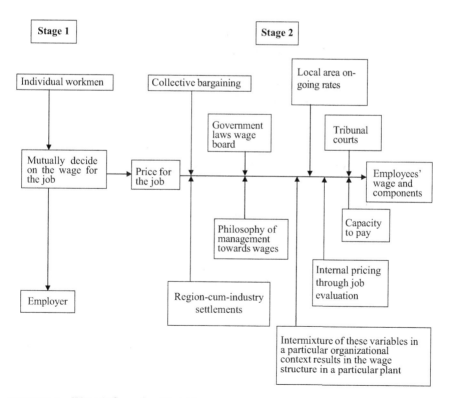

FIGURE 1.3   Wage Influencing Variables

Intermixture of the above-mentioned variables in a particular organizational context results in the wage structure/wage rates/employee compensation.

Monappa[34] developed a model of wage influencing variables wherein he divided these into two stages. Whereas Stage 1 is the self-contained model where external influence is marginal, Stage 2 depicts the interplay of external and internal influence. In Stage 1, it is the mutual negotiation
between the individual worker and the employer through which wages are decided. It is the price for the job which may be influenced by collective bargaining (unions push), region-cum-industry settlements, government laws, wage boards, philosophy of management towards wages and so on. Stage 2 comprises interplay of external and internal influences such as local area on-going rates, capacity of the organization to pay and job evaluation. Intermix of these variables in a particular organizational context results in the wage structure in a particular plant reflecting the employee's wage and components. This is presented in Figure 1.3.

Chapter Review

1. 'Compensation and reward management' is concerned with the design, development, implementation, maintenance, communication and evaluation of compensation processes which deal with working out the relative worth of all the jobs in an organization, designing and monitoring pay structures, paying for skills, competence or performance, performance management, employee benefits, reward management procedures and the like.

2. Compensation and reward management analyses and controls employee compensation and other benefits. The overall aim of the whole exercise is to improve the individual, group and organizational performance through rewarding people fairly, equitably and consistently in proportion to their worth to the enterprise.

3. 'Compensation', in simple words, includes all those things that an organization pays to its employees in return for their talent and time. Total compensation/reward includes under its ambit both monetary (extrinsic) and non-monetary (intrinsic) rewards. While the former includes base wage, contingent or variable pay, DA, bonus, profit-sharing, gainsharing, ESOP/equity-based compensation and lots of other monetary benefits, the latter includes mostly intangible benefits such as meaningful work, mentorship, good working environment, desirable work schedule, praise, recognition and responsibility.

4. There are several theories of wages which may be grouped under two categories, namely:
   (a) economic theories such as subsistence theory, wage–fund theory, marginal productivity theory, surplus value theory, purchasing power theory and modern theories of wages and
   (b) behavioural theories such as equity theory, Herzberg's two-factor theory and Vroom's expectancy theory.

5. Compensation is a very powerful motivator. A compensation philosophy of an organization is a formal statement that spells out the organization's stand or position with regard to employee compensation. While explaining the 'why' behind employee pay, it also creates a framework for consistency. It should, therefore, be transparent and be instrumental in accomplishing the goals of the organization.

6. So far as 'compensation strategy' is concerned, it is a budget and employee compensation plan for rewarding, developing and creating incentives for employees. It provides specific directions on how the organization will develop and design programmes that will ensure that it rewards the behaviour and performance outcomes that support the achievement of its business goals. It should also meet the compensation needs and expectations of the employees. It should be flexible so as to accommodate changes whenever required. An effective compensation strategy should have seven keys like how much percentage of the total compensation budget will be utilized for salary and so on. Strategy may differ from one organization to another organization. The steps involved in developing a compensation strategy include: assessing total compensation implications, mapping a total compensation strategy, and implementing and reassessing. There are three tests that determine whether a pay strategy is a source of competitive advantage, namely alignment, differentiate and add value. The compensation policy should be integrated with the business strategy.

7. Coming to compensation policy, it provides guidelines for the implementation of compensation strategy as also for working out the design and management of compensation processes. The compensation policy itself is guided by the compensation philosophy of the organization. It also helps in attracting and retaining the desired talent in the organization. It should be reviewed periodically by competent authorities.

8. As far as the 'psychological contract' is concerned, it represents the mutual beliefs, perceptions and informal obligations between an employer and an employee. It refers to the relationship between an employer and an employee where there exist unwritten and mutual expectations from each other. There are two types of contracts which define employment relationship, namely (a) transactional contracts, usually in writing, define terms of employment and are legal in nature and (b) relational contracts which have more abstract terms and refer to an open-ended membership of the organization. These are normally implied rather than stated. These are a system of beliefs, dynamic in nature and unwritten.

    In order to develop and maintain a productive psychological contract, it is necessary that at the time of the employment interview itself, both favourable and unfavourable aspects of the job be made known to the candidates.

9. There are several legal issues in compensation management such as there should not be any pay discrimination, no exploitation by the employers,

minimum wages and prohibition of child labour. Besides, there are several labour/employment/social security/welfare-related acts already passed by the government, which have to be complied with.

10. There are several factors affecting employee compensation such as wage rates, wage structure, levels of pay, demand and supply of labour, cost of living, trade unions, collective bargaining, productivity, wage policy, company's ability to pay, wage boards, business performance and competition.

DISCUSSION QUESTIONS

1. Discuss the meaning and definition of compensation management.
2. Discuss the concept of total compensation/reward. Also, distinguish between extrinsic and intrinsic rewards, quoting suitable examples.
3. Discuss the difference between money wages and real wages and also how fair wages differ from minimum wages and living wages.
4. Discuss the various economic and behavioural theories of wages.
5. Discuss the difference between compensation philosophy and compensation policy.
6. Discuss the allied issues related to compensation strategy.
7. Discuss the meaning and definition of psychological contract. Also, discuss its importance and how to maintain it.
8. Discuss the legal issues involved in compensation in our country.
9. Discuss the factors affecting employee compensation/wage rates/wage structure/level of pay.
10. Discuss how to develop a total compensation strategy.

APPLICATION CASE

Mr S. Banerjee who has been working as HR manager in a car tyre manufacturing company for about last three months is wondering why the employees are not happy with the compensation policy of the organization. He talked to a number of employees and most of them appeared to be dissatisfied with the compensation policy. He was all the more surprised to find that the average total compensation/reward being given per employee was almost as much as was being given by the competitive organizations in the market, still most employees felt aggrieved. Mr Banerjee, therefore, constituted a committee comprising Mr A. Sharma, production manager; Mr G.B. Gupta, finance manager; and Mr Banerjee himself as the chairman of the committee to review the compensation policy of the company. Having a number of sittings and examining various relevant documents, the committee made a number of observations and recommendations as follows:

It was pointed out by the committee that the compensation policy does not provide explicit guidelines for the implementation of compensation strategy as also for working out the design and management of compensation processes. Not only that, the compensation policy did not reflect the compensation philosophy of the company. There appeared to be a mismatch between the two. It was also observed by the committee that the compensation policy does not spell out the company's approach towards internal and external equities which was one of the major factors responsible for dissatisfaction among the employees. It appeared that the representatives of employees were not involved, while the policy was formulated. Besides, the criteria for contingent reward for good performance or acquiring new/additional skills and so on were not clear. Flexibility was missing. Guidelines on determination of salary and benefits for new recruits, supervising salary adjustment policy, benefits accruing due to promotion or on transfer, pay bands policy, salary progression policy, red circle policy, overtime policy and so on left much to be desired. Another major cause of employee dissatisfaction emerged from the fact that there was an imbalance between the financial benefits and non-financial benefits. Not only this, there were no cafeteria packages. Amount was being spent on certain benefits which were not appreciated by many employees.

The committee further observed that it was three years back that the compensation policy was reviewed, whereas in the last three years several changes, both inside and outside the company, have taken place and, therefore, policy review is overdue.

The committee, in particular, stressed on the immediate review of relational benefits being extended to the employees. It was pointed out in the report submitted by the committee that since expenditure incurred on relational benefits is minimal and its impact is great, these benefits which are intrinsic and have a great impact on motivational level of the employees need immediate review. Based on the observations and recommendations made by the committee, the HR manager prepared a final report and submitted it to the top management recommending a complete overhaul of the compensation policy of the company.

Questions

1. Why was the compensation policy not proving effective in keeping employees satisfied and motivated? Support your answer with solid arguments.
2. Do you agree that the compensation policy of the company required a complete overhauling? Yes or no, why? Give arguments.
3. As a CEO of the company, which of the recommendations made by the committee should be given effect to and why?

Notes

1 See E. E. Lawler, *Strategic Pay* (San Francisco, CA: Jossey-Bass, 1990).
2 J. Schuster and P. Zingheim, *The New Pay* (New York, NY: Lexington Books, 1992).
3 T. P. Flannery, D. A. Hofrichter, and P. E. Platten, *People, Performance and Pay* (New York, NY: Free Press, 1996).
4 R. C. Sharma, *Industrial Relations and Labour Legislation* (Delhi: PHI Learning, 2016), 30.
5 R. C. Sharma and N. Sharma, *Human Resource Management: Theory and Practice* (New Delhi: SAGE Publications, 2018), 322.
6 G. T. Milkovich, J. M. Newman, and C. S. Venkata Ratnam, *Compensation*, 9th ed. (New Delhi: McGraw-Hill, 2011), 6.
7 Ibid., 323.
8 A. Monappa, *Industrial Relations* (New Delhi: McGraw-Hill, 2007), 72.
9 Sharma, *Industrial Relations*, 308.
10 Michael Armstrong and Helen Murlis, *Reward Management* (London: Kogan Page, 2005), 277.
11 Quoted in ibid., 13.
12 See D. Brown and M. Armstrong, *Paying for Contribution* (London: Kogan Page, 1999), ibid., 13.
13 ILO, *International Labour Office Conference*, 31st Session (Geneva: ILO, 1948), 7.
14 T. N. Bhagoliwal, *Economics of Labour and Industrial Relations* (Agra: Sahitya Bhawan, 1985), 503.
15 Sharma, *Industrial Relations*, 319.
16 Ibid.
17 Victor Vroom, *Work and Motivation* (New York, NY: John Wiley and Sons, 1964).
18 Keith Davis, *Human Relations at Work* (New York, NY: McGraw-Hill, 1967), 35.
19 W. G. Scott and T. R. Mitchell, *Organisation Theory* (Homewood, IL: Richard D. Irwin and The Dorsey Press, 1972), 88.
20 Armstrong and Murlis, *Reward Management*, 50.
21 See Milkovich, Newman, and Venkata Ratnam, *Compensation*, 27.
22 Ibid.
23 Michael Porter, 'What Is Strategy', *Harvard Business Review* 74, no. 6 (November–December 1996): 61–78.
24 Milkovich, Newman, and Venkata Ratnam, *Compensation*, 31–39.
25 Ibid., 39–42.
26 Ibid., 53.
27 E. E. Lawler, 'The New Pay: A Strategic Approach', *Compensation & Benefits Review* 27, no. 4 (1995): 14–22.
28 Milkovich, Newman, and Venkata Ratnam, *Compensation*, 17.
29 Denise M. Rousseau, *Psychological Contracts in Organizations: Understanding Written and Unwritten Adjustments* (Thousand Oaks, CA: SAGE Publications, 1995).
30 Michael Armstrong and Helen Murlis, *Handbook of Reward Management* (New Delhi: Crest Publishing House, 2003), 21.
31 Ibid.
32 Ibid.
33 R. Sims, 'Human Resource Management's Role in Clarifying the Psychological Contract', *Human Resource Management* 33, no. 3 (1994): 373–382.
34 Monappa, *Industrial Relations*, 68–69.

2

COMPENSATION MANAGEMENT

LEARNING OBJECTIVES

After studying this chapter, the reader should be able to:

1. Explain the meaning and objectives of compensation management/wage and salary administration (W&S admin).
2. Explain in detail the principles of compensation management and also various methods of wage payment with special reference to various incentive plans.
3. Explain the principles of incentive system of wage payment and also pre-requisites for the successful working of incentive wage plans.
4. Explain the meaning of terms such as 'draws', 'profit-sharing', 'stock option plans' and 'supplementary compensation'.
5. Explain the national wage policy of our country and also the factors that should be kept in view while preparing wage policy at the organizational level.
6. Enlist and explain the functions of compensation management/W&S admin.
7. Explain the designing and monitoring of salary/grade structure and also the guiding principles for grade and pay structures.
8. Enlist and explain the types of grade and pay structures.

DOI: 10.4324/9781032626123-2

Introduction

For the effective functioning of an organization, it is essential to have such strategies and policies that may ensure that employees are compensated and rewarded fairly, equitably and consistently according to their worth to the organization. It is here that compensation management or W&S admin comes into the picture.

Compensation Management

Definition

Compensation management, which is also known as 'reward management', 'wage and salary administration' or 'remuneration management, is mainly the domain for determining employees' appropriate pay and benefits. It uses both financial and non-financial benefits to attract talent, lessen turnover, spur performance and enhance employee engagement.

Compensation management is primarily concerned with the formulation and implementation of such strategies and policies as may compensate the employees in a fair, equitable and consistent manner, keeping in view their value to the organization. Again, it is compensation management that is concerned with the design, implementation and maintenance of compensation processes and practices that ultimately lead to the improvement of performance of the organization.

Of late, technology has started playing a vital role in the arena of compensation management. For example, in order to spot disparities in data and also to ensure that salary rates are competitive, compensation management software has been increasingly relying on machine learning. Besides, to enable platform vendors to make it easier for employers to benchmark pay rates against their competitors, platform vendors have also been adding data analytics tools as well as access to cloud-based anonymized data. However, the basic problem with compensation analysis is that it is primarily based on the past performance of employees rather than on their potential of adding value in the future. While Bamboo HR, UKG, Oracle, ADP, Workday and SAP Success Factors are some of the highest-profile vendors, Talent Comp., Comp Trak, HR Soft, etc., constitute the smaller vendors specializing in compensation management.

Objectives

The aim of compensation management is to develop, implement and maintain an appropriate salary system of policies, processes and procedures because it is only a well-developed salary system that can be instrumental in not only attracting and retaining the desired talent but also controlling the payroll costs of an organization. In order to have an in-depth study of the objectives of compensation management, it will be better if the objectives of compensation management are classified into the following categories:

1. **Organizational objectives:** Every organization has its own targets and goals, and therefore, it is imperative that the objectives of compensation management should synchronize with the objectives of the organization so that its business goals and targets may be achieved. Hence, in this context, the objectives of compensation management are as follows:
    a. To maintain equity and fairness in compensation in similar jobs.
    b. To attract and retain the number and quality of personnel required for the organization.
    c. To determine the salary levels.
    d. To make provisions for incentives.
    e. To boost the morale of the employees.
    f. To increase the productivity.
    g. To ensure that legal obligations are met.
    h. To maintain a satisfactory public-related image.
    i. To promote the desired culture.
    j. To provide rewards for good performance.
    k. To have adequate wage differentials between different levels of jobs as per their relative worth.
    l. To motivate employees towards good performance.
    m. To be cost-effective.
    n. To be simple to understand, explain, operate and control.
    o. To be flexible to accommodate the organizational change.

    In a nutshell, the objectives of compensation management should be in line with the overall objectives of the organization and as such be instrumental in accomplishing the organizational objectives.

2. **Collective objectives:** Compensation management should come up to the expectations of workers, unions and associations that are always keen to secure maximum benefits for their members such as neutralization of the impact of inflation; if not higher, at least, competitive rates of wages; and maintaining internal and external equities. Hence, compensation management should feel the pulse of the workers, unions and associations and try to come up to their expectations. Broadly speaking, collective objectives may include the following:
    a. Matching compensation with market rates.
    b. Giving compensation ahead of inflation.
    c. Eliminating or, at least, minimizing management discretion in the compensation system, especially in awarding increments or promoting people.
    d. Increasing compensation—reflecting the increase in the prosperity of the organization.
    e. Having maximum benefits, both tangible and intangible, for their members.
    f. Keeping the workers, unions and associations satisfied to the extent possible.

g.   Ensuring that consumers' interests are duly protected.

h.   Abiding by legal obligations and government policies.

3. **Individual objectives:** Every individual aspires to be paid in accordance to his worth. He is always in the habit of comparing himself with his counterparts outside the organization as also within the organization and expects to be paid more or, at least, at competitive rates. Hence, compensation management should take care of an individual's expectations while formulating its objectives.

As such, from the point of view of an individual employee, the following should be the objectives of the compensation system:

a.   Securing fair compensation for each employee.

b.   Matching compensation to the worth of each employee.

c.   Objectivity while wage rates are assigned.

d.   Boosting the morale of the employee.

e.   Infusing confidence in each employee.

f.   Maintaining internal and external equities.

Thus, the objectives of compensation management should be correlated with the organizational, collective and individual objectives.

In case we are not interested in classifying compensation objectives, then broadly speaking, the following are the overall objectives of compensation management:

a.   Establishing a fair and equitable compensation.

b.   Compensating or rewarding the employees for the value they create.

c.   Keeping compensation costs in line with the ability to pay.

d.   Ensuring that compensation practices are aligned with the organization's goals, the union's goals and individual employee's goals.

e.   Attracting the desired talent.

f.   Retaining the talent required by the organization.

g.   Rewarding the employees in a manner that sends a clear message as to what is the manner in which the organization expects its employees to behave and what are the outcomes that the organization attaches value to.

h.   Motivating employees by formulating appropriate processes.

i.   Supporting and developing a performance culture.

j.   Developing a psychological contract.

k.   Developing a positive employment relationship.

l.   Developing total compensation processes based on the beliefs and values of the organization.

m.   Improving union-management relationship by taking unions into confidence at different stages.

n.   Complying with legal obligations.

o.   Minimizing favouritism.

p.   Introducing transparency.

q.   Maintaining a good public image.

All said and done, the main objectives of compensation management are as follows:

a. To attract and retain the desired talent.
b. To control payrolls.
c. To motivate employees.
d. To maintain a good public image.
e. To treat every individual fairly and equitably.
f. To match or exceed the reward with the market rates (external equity).
g. To maintain internal equity.

Principles of Compensation Management

Compensation management is a sensitive and crucial aspect because its adequacy or otherwise can affect the competitiveness of the organization either positively or negatively. Hence, it is always advisable that the HR Department of the organization should always follow the principles of compensation management to make it more effective. The main principles of compensation management are as follows:

1. **External relativities:** It is well said that there is no such thing as absolute value. The value of any object is always relative to something else. It is influenced by external economic factors as also by internal relativities. The principle of external relativities acknowledges that factors or variables that are external to an organization impact the levels of compensation in an organization. For example, the ongoing rates of wages in the market demand for and supply of labour and the like have a great bearing on wages. In case such factors or variables are not kept in view while determining wage and salary levels, it may not be possible to attract or retain the desired talent to the required level.

   As a matter of fact, the ongoing rate for a job is its market rate, and usually a job is worth what the market says it is worth. Although internal salary structure may not directly and instantaneously be responsive to market forces at all points of time, it should reflect the changing pressure of the market. The principle of external equity ensures that jobs are fairly compensated in comparison to similar jobs in the labour market.

2. **Internal relativities:** The value of a job within an organization is relative. It is in a sense comparative. Jobs and employees' skills are compared in terms of their relative contributions to the organization's business objectives. Hence, within the organization, pay levels are affected by the real or perceived differences in the value of jobs, and therefore, an ideal salary structure should establish and maintain appropriate differentials based on the objective system of measuring relative internal values. It is the process of job evaluation that is instrumental in finding the relative value of jobs. The compensation system should ensure that more difficult jobs should be paid more. In case, internal

relativities are also taken into account while determining pay levels, it brings satisfaction to all the employees of the organization.

However, both external and internal relativities should be kept in view if an ideal pay structure is to be designed.

3. **Individual worth:** The principle of individual worth states that an employee should be paid as per his performance so that he gets reward according to his contribution to the organization. In other words, this principle aims at ensuring that each individual's pay is fair in comparison to other employees doing the same or similar job in the organization so that 'equal pay for equal work' may be ensured.

4. **Adequacy of wages:** The amount of wages should be enough so as to enable the worker and his family to maintain a reasonable standard of living.

   Flexibility in wage and salary structure: there should be flexibility in the wage and salary structure so as to meet the changing conditions both within and outside the organization.

5. **Regularity in payment:** Payment of wages and arrears, if any, should be affected on due dates and regularly.

6. **Wage committee for revision of wages:** There should exist a wage committee for revision of wages as and when due instead of leaving the matter to an individual judgement.

7. **Compliance with legislation:** Compensation management should never violate any legal provisions and should always comply with it.

8. **Employee participation:** The employees' representatives and/or trade union should be involved in working out the procedures used to establish wage rates and other related issues.

9. **Grievances:** Provision for redressal of wage-related grievances—There should be a well-laid-out procedure for redressal of wage-related grievances within the specified period.

Methods of Wage Payment

Of the two basic methods of wage payment, the first is based on the time period spent on the job, popularly known as the 'time rate method' or time wages. The second method is based on output/result, popularly known as a 'piece rate system' or payment by results. The third method is of 'incentive plan or bonus (premium) scheme'. There are some other methods also though not very popular. The details of the aforesaid methods/systems are as follows:

Time Rate Method/Time Wages

This is perhaps the oldest method of wage payment. As per this method, an employee is paid on the basis of time worked, that is, hourly, daily, weekly or monthly, irrespective of the quantity of work done. Of course, within that time, a certain standard of performance is expected. Payment-by-time rates are quite suitable where the pace of output is machine-determined or where the work done by an employee is difficult to measure such as clerical, supervisory or managerial work. Under this system, wages are calculated on the basis of attendance, that is, wages are computed by multiplying the time units spent by the predetermined time rate.

Merits

The merits of the time rate system are as follows:

1. It is the simplest system, that is, easy to understand and calculate wages.
2. It helps in maintaining the quality of the product, as there is no time limit for the completion of a job.
3. In case production cannot be standardized and, therefore, the productivity of a worker cannot be measured precisely, the time rate system is the best system of wage payment. This system provides a sense of security of income to a worker because, in the case of interruption of production, the worker will get his salary on the basis of time spent on the job.
4. This system is preferred by trade unions also. Hence, no problem of industrial unrest.
5. This system does not create any ill will or jealousy among the workers because all workers doing the same type of work will get the same salary.
6. This system involves less administrative control as the system is easy to operate.
7. There are least damages and depreciation of plant, machinery, tools and so on under this system as the same is handled properly because of no hurry in completing the job.
8. It promotes creativity among workers.

Demerits

However, there are several shortcomings also in the time rate system, which are as follows:

1. Cost of production may be higher as there is no time limit to complete a job.
2. This system does not provide any incentive to an efficient worker. Hence, it decreases the morale of efficient workers.
3. There is relatively less output because the speed of workers gets slow as there is no penalty for less output.
4. It requires close supervision to maintain the output. Hence, supervisory costs may go up.
5. In this system, labour costs keep fluctuating and it is difficult to measure them.

6. Cost of production is likely to go up in this system. Hence, employers do not prefer it.
7. Thus, this system is suitable in circumstances where a worker's output cannot be measured easily or precisely, the quality of output is more important, the nature of job changes quite frequently and interruptions take place frequently.

Piece Rate System/Payment by Results

It is also quite an old method of wage payment. Under this system, wages are paid on the basis of quantum of output of a worker. The worker is paid a fixed rate per unit of output as follows:

$$\text{Wages} = \text{No. of units produced} \times \text{Rate per unit}$$

The rate is determined with the help of time or motion studies or on the basis of analysis of previous performance and establishment of average performance of a particular standard of workmanship.

Merits

The main merits of the piece rate system are as follows:

1. Easy calculation of wages.
2. This system works as an incentive for workers to produce more.
3. It requires less supervision because in order to earn more, workers work on their own.
4. It becomes easier to estimate the cost of production because the piece rate is fixed.
5. Since the breakage of tools or machinery will reduce the output of workers, they handle the same cautiously. Hence, the least damage.
6. The idle time is minimized as the workers know that they will not earn anything during their idle time.
7. More scope for innovation because workers try to invent new methods of producing more.
8. Greater mutual cooperation among team/group members so as to avoid interruptions in work.
9. The cost of product comes down due to bigger output by workers to earn more.
10. This system is more equitable than the time rate system as under this system reward is related to effort.

Demerits

Some of the main disadvantages of this system are as follows:

1. This system may impact the quality adversely as in the urge for more output and resulting more earnings, the workers may not bother for quality.
2. In the urge for more output, the workers may not bother for wastage of material and damage to machinery.
3. It may impact the health of the workers adversely because they may overwork to earn more.
4. If a worker falls ill, he loses his wages for that period.
5. The rate fixed maybe low causing loss to the earnings of workers.
6. The earnings of workers suffer due to interruptions on account of power failure or machine breakdown.
7. The system is frustrating to less efficient workers and may spread feelings of jealously among workers against their fellow workers.
8. There may be a problem of overproduction if the demand for products goes downwards.

For example, the Punjab National Bank (PNB) wants performance to do the wage-hike talking. It has proposed performance-based remuneration (for details, see Exhibit 2.1).

EXHIBIT 2.1 PNB WANTS PERFORMANCE TO DO THE WAGE-HIKE TALKING

Times are changing and we have to change with the times. Now the time has come to recognize performance and it is also to retain talent.

Source: Hindustan Times (9 November 2016).

For decades, remuneration at government-owned banks has been linked to industry-wide negotiations, irrespective of the performance of each employee. In contrast, remuneration at private banks is linked to performance and could vary significantly between two employees of the same rank. Performance-based remuneration was never considered.

The method of wage payment based on results can be any of the following:

1. **Straight piece rate:** In it, the worker gets more or less depending on his actual output. His per unit output is multiplied with the prefixed per unit rate.
2. **Increasing piece rate:** As per this method, as the production increases, the per unit rate also increases. For example, for the first 10 units, the piece rate may be INR 2 per unit; from 11 to 15 units, the rate may be 2.15; and over 15 units, the wage rate per piece may go up to INR 2.25. The efficient workers prefer this system of wage payment.

3. **Decreasing piece rate:** Under this method, the rate of wages per unit goes down as the production increases. For example, for the 10 units, the rate may be INR 2 per unit, for 11 to 15 units, the rate may be INR 1.90 per unit and so on. Employers usually prefer this method of wage payment.

4. **Straight piece rate system with minimum wages:** In this system, a worker is paid minimum wages even if he produces less than the standardized output in a given time, otherwise he is paid on the basis of a straight piece rate.

5. **Balance and debt system of wages:** Under this method, a worker is paid minimum wages even if he produces less than the standardized output in the given time, in the expectation that he will make up for the deficiency of work in the future by doing more work.

Incentive Plans or Bonus (Premium) Schemes

Any system of wage payment that induces a worker to produce more is known as an 'incentive system'. However, the worker is assured of a guaranteed minimum wage. The system correlates earnings to output, thus providing a special financial incentive for increasing effort while guaranteeing the minimum wages. Thus, this system has all the merits minus demerits of the earlier described two systems of wage payment, namely the time rate system and the piece rate system/payment by results. The system offers several incentive plans which can be classified into two categories, namely individual incentive plans and group/collective bonus plans, a brief description of some of the main plans is as follows:

Individual Incentive Plans

The main ones are as follows:

1. **Straight piece work plan:** This plan is just like the straight piece rate system, discussed earlier, but with the only difference that in a straight piece work plan hourly earnings are guaranteed. Hence, this plan resembles the straight piece rate system with minimum wages that has also been described earlier.

2. **Differential piece rate plans:** In such plans, differential piece rates are set for different amounts of outputs. The following are the important plans under this category:
   a. **Taylor's differential piece rate plan:** Initiated by F.W. Taylor, under this plan, there are only two piece rates, namely high rate and a low (or ordinary) rate for each job or task. In other words, if a worker performs the work within or less than the standard time, he is paid a higher piece rate, and if he does not complete work within the standard time, he is given a lower piece rate for low production, that is, he would be able to earn just an ordinary day's pay. This plan can be illustrated as follows:

The following values are given:
Task (standard output) = 20 units
Actual output = 16 units
Rates:High rate = INR 3 per unit
Low rate = INR 2.50 per unit

Calculation of earnings:

In case actual output equals or exceeds standard output:

Earnings = 20 units × INR 3.00 = INR 60.00

In case actual output falls short of standard output (e.g., if actual output is 15) Earnings = 15 units × INR 2.50 = INR 37.50

However, the system is possible in the cases where it is easy to relate effort to production; work is standardized, repetitive and measurable; production methods and machines are standardized; no interruptions in workflow; fixed expenses are more than variable expenses; and production control and supervision are well regulated.

b. **Merrick's multiple piece rate plan:** Instead of dividing the workers into two categories as is the case in F.W. Taylor's differential piece rate plan, D.W. Merrick in his plan introduced three piece rates and made the lowest piece rate equal to the ordinary piece rate which becomes the 'base piece rate'. He introduced the following rates in his plan:

Output (% of Task)	Rate
Less than 83	Basic piece rate
From 83 to 100	110% of basic piece rate
Over 100	120% of basic piece rate

Thus, this plan is a modified form of Taylor's plan and is more suitable for workers.

c. **Gantt's task and bonus plan:** In his plan initiated in 1901, which is a modified form of Taylor's plan, Henry L. Gantt introduced a better feature by mentioning that if a worker's output in a task time is equal to or more than the stipulated task, he is paid a bonus at a certain percentage of guaranteed basic wage. The guaranteed basic wage is always a time rate wage. However, it is necessary that the basic wage rate and the task or the task standards should be determined with caution and care, and further that the tasks set should be reasonable and practical, otherwise, the plan may not be able to accomplish its objectives.

TABLE 2.1 Variation in Bonus According to Nature of Work

S. No.	Nature of Work	Bonus (%)
1.	Work not involving much physical labour combined with close and constant attention, for example, the work of machine attendants	10–15
2.	Work in general machine shop or tool room	35
3.	Work involving constant use of eyes	30–40
4.	Heavy work including skill work	60–70
5.	Work requiring high skill, much physical labour or strain, ability to work under unpleasant conditions and involving acceptance of responsibility	100

Gantt recommended that according to the nature of the work, the bonus might vary from 10 per cent to 100 per cent of the guaranteed wage as shown in Table 2.1.

Table 2.1 makes it clear that more requirements of attention for a job means a progressive increase in earnings. For this reason, Gantt system is also known as the 'progressive rate system'.

Apart from providing financial incentives in his plan, Gantt put much emphasis on improving the efficiency of workers, their training and also on making all possible arrangements so that workers may do their tasks without excessive exertion. Of course, it is not that easy for an employer to make all the arrangements as perfect as suggested in the plan.

3. **Premium or bonus plans or bonus-sharing plans:** A premium or bonus plan or bonus-sharing plan which is a unification of time rate and piece rate systems aims at providing suitable monetary incentives to both employers and employees of the time saved by the worker in completing his task. The main bonus-sharing plans are as follows:

   a. **Halsey plan:** Under this plan, a bonus is shared by the worker and the employer in some definite fixed proportions varying between 25 per cent and 75 per cent, though usually, it is 50 per cent. As per this plan, if the actual hours taken by a worker to complete his task are less than its stipulated standard hours, the total wage for the time saved, calculated on the basis of the guaranteed base ratio of the worker, is shared by the worker and the employer. The worker gets his share of time saved as follows:

   Time wage = Time taken × Time rate + 1/2(Time saved × Time rate)

   Thus, the share of the wages of 'time saved' given to the worker is his premium bonus. Obviously, in addition to this share, he will get the usual guaranteed wage for the time spent by him on his work. An additional feature of this plan is that a premium bonus is also given to foremen or supervisors who affect the increase in the productivity of the workers working under their supervision.

Broadly speaking, 10–40 per cent of the employer's share of bonus is distributed among such foremen or supervisors.

b. **Halsey–Weir plan:** Introduced by G & J Weir Ltd of Glasgow in 1990, this plan is another form of the Halsey premium bonus plan with the difference that as per this plan, a worker gets 30 per cent of the time saved, that is, standard hours minus actual hours, whereas in the Halsey plan, the workers get between 25 per cent and 75 per cent, which is usually 50 per cent. Like the Halsey plan, a minimum wage is guaranteed under this plan also.

c. **Rowan plan:** Keeping in view the guidelines of the Halsey plan, James Rowan of David Rowan and Company Ltd, Glasgow, introduced this plan in 1898. It is a variable bonus-sharing plan. The proportion of the bonus a worker earns varies if the 'time saved' by the worker varies. Thus, the Rowan plan is a 'variable bonus-sharing plan'. Its formula is as follows:

$$\text{Minimum guaranteed wage} = \text{Time taken} \times \text{Time rate}$$

$$\text{Bonus premium incentive} = \frac{\text{Time saved}}{\text{Standard time}} \times \left(\text{Time taken} \times \text{Time rate}\right)$$

Total wages = Minimum guaranteed wage + Bonus premium incentive

For example, suppose the following information is given:

Task time (standard time) = 10 hours
    Actual time taken = 5 hours
Hourly rate = INR 2

In the above case, total earnings (i.e., minimum guaranteed wage + bonus premium incentive) will be calculated as follows:

• Calculation of minimum guaranteed wage:

$$TT \times TR$$

$$\times 5 \times 2 \times 10$$

where TT is the actual time taken and TR is the time rate.

• Calculation of bonus or premium:

$$\frac{TS}{ST} \times TR \times TT$$

where TS is the time saved and ST is the standard time.

Time saved = Standard time – Actual time taken = 10 – 5 = 5

$$\frac{5}{10} \times 2 \times 5$$

$$= \frac{1}{2} \times 10 \times 5$$

Total earnings (Bonus premium incentive + Minimum guaranteed wage)

$$= 10 + 5 = 15$$

• The main advantage of this plan is that in addition to providing good incentives for relatively slow workers and learners, it protects the employer against loose rate setting and also enables the employer to get a share in the benefit of increased output. However, the plan is more complex and expensive than the Halsey plan.

Other premium or bonus plans or bonus-sharing plans are as follows:

   ○ Bedaux Point Premium Plan[1].
   ○ Emerson Efficiency Bonus Plan[2].
   ○ Barth Variable Sharing Plan[3].
   ○ Accelerating Premium Plan[4].
   ○ Baum Differential Plan[5].
   ○ Diemer System[6].

Group/Collective Bonus Plans

Such plans that are useful when an individual worker's output cannot be easily measured aim at ensuring higher productivity, more production and creating a sense of cooperation. Today, several group/collective bonus plans are being practised. Some of the main ones are as follows:

1. **Priestman's production bonus plan:** Adopted by Messrs. Priestman Bros Ltd, Hull, in 1917, this plan provides that the bonus will be payable to that department which gives results higher than the standard output set jointly by a committee representing the management and the workers' union, well in advance every week or every month, as per the following formula:

Percentage of hours = (Increased production / Standard production) × 100

Just to illustrate it, we can take a case where the standard production is 4,000 units and the actual output is 6,000 units, the workers will be given a bonus equivalent to 50 per cent of their wages as follows:

Percentage of bonus = (2000/4000) × 100 = 50%

The plan suits especially to those organizations where the cost of materials is high.

2. **Cost premium plan:** Under this plan, if the actual cost of production comes to less than its standard cost of production, a part of the savings is distributed among the workers as a bonus.
3. **Budgeted expense bonus:** As per this plan, a bonus is based on savings in actual total expenditure compared with the total budgeted expenditure. The percentage of bonus is the predetermined share of savings in budgeted expenditure.
4. **Profit-sharing plan:** This plan provides for sharing of the profits of the enterprise with the workers in a predetermined ratio. The plan aims at motivating the workers to cooperate in increasing the profits of the enterprise.
5. **Towne gainsharing plan:** Introduced by H.R. Towne in the United States in 1896, the plan provides for the calculation of bonuses on the reduction in costs (usually the labour cost) as compared with the predetermined standard. An individual is entitled to one-half of the savings pro rata with wages earned. The supervisory staff too gets a part of this bonus.
6. **Waste reduction plan:** The plan has a provision to provide incentives to workers to reduce wastage. The plan takes the form of a percentage.

Advantages of Group/Collective Bonus Plan(s)

Group bonus plans provide incentives, besides guaranteeing time wages, to work cooperatively with the organization so as to enhance output, reduce wastage and cost of production and so on. Besides, their administrative cost is also less as compared to individual bonus plans. Moreover, they need relatively less inspection and supervision.

Disadvantages of Group/Collective Bonus Plan(s)

Since these plans provide bonuses on a collective basis, efficient workers do not prefer it because they do not get due rewards for their contribution. At times, the amount of bonus is too less to serve the purpose of the plan. Besides, how much amount should be given to which worker is also a problem.

Advantages of Incentive Plans

The main advantages of incentive plans can be studied under the following heads:

1. **Benefits to workers:** Due to incentive plans, the total earnings of workers are likely to go up, leading to improvement in their standard of living. Besides, their working capacity also gets a boost and the morale also goes to a higher level.

2. **Benefits to employers:** It is not only the workers who benefit from incentive plans but also the employers. Since these plans motivate the workers to produce more, reduce the cost of production, avoid wastage of material and so on, the cost of production goes down, output goes up and so is the case with the profits of the organization. Besides, standards are fixed for everything that has to be achieved by workers in case they want to reap the benefits of these plans. The plans also lead to good industrial relations and so on.

Principles of Incentive System of Wage Payment

Incentive system is likely to sustain itself and prove effective if the following principles are adhered to:

1. An incentive plan must be thoroughly worked out, leaving no loopholes.
2. It should be properly conveyed and clarified to all concerned.
3. Bonus should be at least 15–20 per cent higher than the hourly rates.
4. Standards should be based on logic and pragmatism.
5. Job evaluation must be rigorously carried out.
6. Periodic review must be there, and changes may be effected as and when required.
7. Workers' unions should always be taken into confidence while standards are worked out or changes are introduced.

Prerequisites/Essentials for the Successful Working of Incentive Wage Plans

W.H. Spencer has suggested certain basic considerations while planning incentive wage plans. Some of them are as follows:

1. The plan should have support from the top management.
2. It should be easily understandable by the workers.
3. It should have the constant attention of competent supervisory personnel.
4. An increase in the unit labour cost should be a matter of concern.
5. No premium for productivity below what should exist.
6. No increase in pay without a corresponding increase in productivity.

Comparison between Individual and Group Bonus Plans

Group bonus schemes are better than individual premium schemes where it is difficult to measure an individual's output. Group schemes are easier to implement than individual premium schemes. Besides, group schemes develop greater mutual cooperation and team spirit as compared to individual schemes. It is easier to understand a group bonus scheme. It is relatively easier to set targets for a group than an individual.

Linking Pay to Performance

Of late, linking pay to performance is also getting popular. For example, see Exhibit 2.2.

Draws

Draws are usually given to salesmen who work only for commissions. As a matter of fact, a draw is a sort of advance, also known as a predetermined 'draw', given to a salesman, which will be deducted from the commission at the end of each pay period, and whatever is left, goes to the salesman. Thus, a draw gives you money to start with and build. But if you earn less than you draw in a period, you will owe money to your organization which can be paid back later when there is a more profitable pay period. Of course, if one has several bad periods, he/she may soon run into significant debts. Thus, such a salary plan is completely based on the commission earned by an employee. In this, an employee is advanced a set amount of money as a pay cheque at the start of a pay period. At the end of the pay period or sales period, depending on the material agreement, the amount of draw is deducted from the commission earned by the employee.

EXHIBIT 2.2 CAMPUS COMPENSATION: COMPANIES PREFER TO LINK PAY TO PERFORMANCE (VARIABLE PAY, JOINING BONUS, REGISTER INCREASE ACROSS ALL TIERS OF BUSINESS SCHOOLS)

Due to uncertain economic climate, organizations are forced to alter their approach towards campus compensation by reducing the fixed component, and becoming aggressive in pay-for-performance and joining bonus. This is what has been revealed by the latest Aon Hewitt Campus Study.

The objectives are to foster a performance-oriented environment by linking pay with performance and to reduce the year-on-year burden of pay increase linked to the fixed pay component.

Source: The Economic Times (31 March 2017).

Combination Plan

Many organizations could pay their salesmen both salary and commission. This type of combination plan provides some regular income and offers an incentive for better sales.

Profit-Sharing

It is said that the first profit-sharing plan was developed by Albert Gallatin, Secretary of the Treasury, at a glasswork in New Geneva, Pennsylvania, in 1794. In a profit-sharing plan, a fixed percentage of the total profit of an organization is distributed among employees either in the form of 'cash bonus' in which full payment is made to the employees after profits have been worked out quarterly or annually, or through deferred bonus system in which the bonus is credited to the employees' accounts, payable at the time of retirement, severance, death, disability and so on. It is also possible to have a combination of two or more of the above.

Ownership Plans/Stock Options

Stock bonus plans were used originally in the 1920s. Stock options are offered to employees in the form of company stock with the objective of attracting, motivating and retaining them. Such plans are introduced for the same reasons as are offered profit-sharing plans. The logic behind stock options is that after employees become partners in the company, they work harder, sincerely, efficiently and effectively, and the company's interests become their interests. Giving stock options is a common practice in the telecom sector in our country. All leading telecoms such as Bharti Airtel and so on have employee stock option plans.[7] Reliance Jio may also roll out Employee Stock Ownership Plan (ESOP) to reward and retain employees (see Exhibit 2.3). Initially, senior management may only get ESOPs.

EXHIBIT 2.3 RELIANCE JIO PLANS TO REWARD EMPLOYEES WITH STOCK OPTIONS

Mukesh Ambani–owned Reliance Jio Infocomm is planning to roll out stock options for its employees, which could be a reward for the pace at which subscribers are being added as well as a talent retention and attraction strategy of the company.

The stock options programme is currently in the planning stage and could be rolled out later this year.

Reliance Jio, with its 30,000 plus permanent employees, will possibly introduce stock options initially for senior executives. All leading telecoms such as Bharti Airtel, Idea Cellular and Vodafone India have ESOPs.

ESOPs are usually given once a year and can range between 10 per cent and 20 per cent of an employee's salary. These are over and above the compensation and act as a talent retention tool.

Source: The Economic Times (10 January 2017).

Since its official launch in September 2016, Jio with its free voice and data offer has attracted about half a million subscribers a day and is believed to have already added over 65 million customers. Now, the biggest challenge for Reliance Jio would be to ensure that subscribers who have signed up do not migrate to rival telcos, once the free offer ends. And this is where ESOPs will come in handy, especially in retaining key people tasked with customer retention. Jio has seen exits at the senior level, and ESOPs may help in retaining senior-level officers in future. In India, and indeed globally, telecom majors offer ESOPs to senior ranks. This move will help Jio retain employees for a longer period.

Stock appreciation rights are a bonus given to employees, which equals the rise in a company's stock value. Employees do not have to pay the excess price and hence can receive proceeds from stock price increases, without coughing up anything.

Stock plans are in reality employee benefit plans designed to pay their benefits in the form of company stock. In case the value of the stock increases, the stock owners (employees) could, by selling their stock, receive a good return.

Supplementary Compensation

Supplementary compensation (or benefits) is extended to employees over and above their wages, the objective being not only promoting their economic betterment but also providing psychic satisfaction to employees which is instrumental in boosting their morale (for a detailed study of supplementary compensation/benefits, see Chapters 8 and 9).

Essentials of a Satisfactory Wage System

The survival and progress of an organization is dependent on the efficiency and effectiveness of its employees, which in turn depends, to a great extent, on the total earnings the employees get from the organization. An ideal wage system is instrumental in reducing the cost of production, improving the quality of the product/services of the organization, increasing the productivity and profitability of the organization and, above all, providing contentment to the employees. It is, therefore, vital that an organization has a well-planned wage system, and it is also well administered. A wage system can be successful if:

1. It is well-planned.
2. It is simple and easily comprehensible by the employees.
3. It ensures a guaranteed minimum wage for every employee.
4. It is motivating for employees and leads to cost and wastage reduction, and quality improvement.
5. It is productivity-oriented and cost-effective so that it suits the employers also.

6. It is flexible so as to accommodate any change.
7. It maintains internal and external relativities.
8. It is pragmatic.
9. It provides enough incentives for employees to put in their best.
10. It provides contentment to employees.
11. It has wage differentials.
12. It is easy to put into practice.

National Wage Policy in India

Our country is genuinely concerned about the wages of workers, more so because ours is a welfare state and a democratic country. Over a period of time, the following factors have influenced the thinking of the Government of India with regard to its wage policy:

1. Payment of Wages Act (1936).
2. Industrial Truce Resolution (1947).
3. Industrial Policy Resolution (1948).
4. Minimum Wages Act (1948).
5. Constitution of (1951) India.
6. Directive Principles of State Policy (Article 43).
7. 15th Session of Indian Labour Conference (1957).
8. Payment of Bonus Act (1965).
9. First National Commission on Labour (1969).
10. Chakravarty Committee (1974).
11. Equal Remuneration Act (1976).
12. Bhoothalingam Study Group (1978).
13. Five-Year Plans.

The highlights of the contribution of some of the above are as follows:

1. **Industrial Truce Resolution (1947):** Capital and labour to share the product of their common efforts after having paid fair wages to the workers, a fair return on capital to employers, and creating a reasonable reserve for the maintenance and expansion of the organization concerned.
2. **Industrial Policy Resolution (1948):** Fair wage agreement in the organized sector and need-based statutory minimum wage in sweated industries.
3. **Minimum Wages Act (1948):** Fixation of minimum wages and its time-to-time revision after the prescribed period.
4. **Directive Principles of State Policy (Article 43):** Securing living wage for the workforce.
5. **15th Session of Indian Labour Conference:** Wages to be determined on the basis of the basic needs of workers.

6. **First National Commission on Labour (1969):** Recognized the need for a national wage policy.
7. **Chakravarty Committee (1974):** Need for setting up a National Wage Commission and a National Wage Board to evaluate all jobs, work out a grade structure based on skill differentials and fix wages for each grade.
8. **Bhoothalingam Study Group (1978):** Provided appropriate guidelines and principles to help in making corrections and adjustments within the framework of collective bargaining, raising steadily the areas of unduly depressed wages and also reducing disparities to the extent possible. It also made recommendations with regard to the payment of bonus and DA.

Despite different perspectives of the trade unions, employers and the government with regard to wages as also the difference in the observations of different committees, agencies and commissions regarding wages, we cannot and should not escape the responsibility of formulating the national or public wage policy, which should be instrumental in linking reward to effort; sharing gains due to addition in productivity; developing an inbuilt system to control wages, income and prices; promoting skill formulation; and so on.

However, the need to have a national minimum wage still continues to be an idea. Whereas the first National Commission on Labour was not in favour of having a national wage policy, the second National Commission on Labour simply suggested to constitute a high-level committee having representatives of all the stakeholders along with some technical experts, on the issue. It was the Bhoothalingam-headed group on wages, incomes and prices (1977–1978) that came forward with some observations on the national minimum wage though, of course, it should not come in the way of employment generation.

The Ministry of Labour and Employment is keen to have wages of contract labour at par with those of regular workers. There is no doubt that over a period of time because of the relatively better negotiating power of regular workers, their salaries have increased considerably and are not in syn-carbonization with the ongoing market rates. It is despite the fact that contract labour constitutes 55 per cent of the public sector jobs and 45 per cent of the private sector jobs in India, and further that it is likely to cost more than INR 10,000 crore annually[8] in the wage bill of the government if there is parity between the wages of contract labour and regular labour. It was for this reason that through the amendment to the Contract Labour (Regulation and Abolition) Act, 1970, introduced in July 2014, the government had proposed to add new sections in the existing Act so that contract labour is paid the same wages and social security benefits as are paid to the regular workers.

The trade unions too are of the firm opinion that there should be no discrimination in the wages, and benefits should be made available to both the contract workers and the regular workers. The 'trade unions' stand is that how can they expect the contract workers to work at lower rates of wages than the regular workers when commodity prices are touching the roof? Trade unions are critical of the Modi government and label it as pro-corporate, as it has introduced several changes in the archaic labour laws of India in the name of labour reforms. The Indian National Trade Union Congress (INTUC) vice-president has gone to the extent of branding the government as 'pro-capitalists'. There are around 800 lakh contract workers in the country and only 3 lakh are regular workers. The rest do not have any social security benefits.[9]

'Contract labour is preferred by employers because it cost them much less than regular workers. Not only this, the employers can terminate their services as and when they so prefer'.[10]

The passing of the Wage Code Bill, 2019, by the Parliament of India on July 30, 2019, and the Industrial Relations Code Bill, 2020, the Code on Social Security Bill, 2020, and the Code on the Occupational Safety, Health and Working Conditions, 2020, on September 23, 2020, is the new development in the arena of Labour reforms. However, the aforesaid men labour codes, already approved by the President of India on June 2, 2022, are yet to be implemented. All the same, these labour codes, especially the Wage Code, are an indication of the National Wage Policy in India to a great extent.

Wage Policy at the Organizational Level

It is the internal equity, external equity, weightage for merit, control over the cost of production, enhanced productivity, the linkage between pay and performance, ability to attract and retain talent, neutralization of cost of living, keeping workers motivated, increasing 'ability to pay' of the organization and so on that are the main issues that should be kept in view while formulating wage policy at the organization level. A snapshot of some of the main issues, which should be taken into account, is as follows:

1. **External equity:** In order to attract and retain the desired talent in the organization, it is necessary that the pay level and structure should not be less than what are being offered by the competitors to their employees. In case, the issue of external equity is not kept into consideration while formulating wage policy at the organization level, it will not be possible to attract and retain employees.
2. **Internal equity:** Similarly, in order to attract and retain the desired talent, it is equally necessary to ensure that an employee is offered according to his worth and contribution to the organization. Hence, it is necessary that the wage policy of an organization should take wage variations or wage differentials according to the hierarchy and skills required for different jobs in the organization, otherwise there may be frustration among employees, and they may not like to continue in the organization for long.
3. **Seniority and merit:** A wage policy of an organization should attach due weightage to the merit and seniority of the employees. The wage policy of an organization should have pay progression based on merit and seniority, otherwise the employees may leave the organization sooner than later.

4. **Attracting and retaining talent:** The wage policy of an organization should be formulated so as to attract fresh candidates and retain the existing employees, otherwise the efficiency and effectiveness of the organization will be adversely affected.

5. **Cost of living:** Usually, the prices of commodities keep on increasing and going up. The wage policy of an organization should be such that it may neutralize the enhanced wage policy cost of living. It may be done by having a provision in the wage policy to increase DA, which may be linked to consumer price index numbers or the like, that is, it should be ensured that there is a proper balance between the nominal wages and the real wages.

6. **Cost production/productivity:** Since wages usually keep on rising causing an increase in the cost of production, a balance is to be maintained by having a wage policy, which is linked to productivity. It is, therefore, essential that the wage policy should have provisions for incentives, which may be linked to output or contribution by the employee. In other words, there should be a linkage between pay and performance.

7. **Integrity:** In case managerial personnel who have access to and control over resources are not paid well, they can go for compensation practices. Hence, the organizational wage policy should be such that it may keep the managerial personnel content.

8. **Motivation and morale:** In order to motivate employees and keep the level of their morale high, the wage policy of an organization should be such that it may aim at paying the employees 'fair wage' at the competitive level. The employees should feel proud of the level and structure of their pay.

9. **Statutory provisions:** While formulating a wage policy of an organization, due regard should be paid to statutory provisions, otherwise it may give rise to legal problems. However, it may be mentioned that the wage policy of all organizations cannot be uniform because the circumstances and the environment in which they operate differ a great deal.

10. **Wage Code, 2019:** The Wage Policy of an Indian organization should keep into consideration the provisions contained in Labour Codes, especially the Wage Code, 2019, already approved by the President of India in 2022 but to be implemented.

Hence, the factors mentioned above are just a few guidelines in the formulation of wage policy.

Wage Problems in India

India being a poor country with, by and large, a low rate of productivity and abundant supply of labour has not been able to provide appropriate wages to its workforce even in the organized sector, not to speak of the unorganized sector which employs more than 90 per cent of the country's total workforce. Hence, wage rates have always remained a burning issue and also a major irritant in the arena of industrial relations.

Wages are the only source of income for Indian workers. The joint family system is rapidly giving way to the nuclear family way of life. Workers are largely illiterate, ignorant and economically and socially backward. Employers are exploitative, especially in the unorganized sector. The social security system is either at most of the places nonexistent or extremely weak wherever it does exist. There is a lack of standardization of wages. Manpower is being replaced through the process of automation. Under the aforesaid circumstances, the wage problem has always been and continues to attract the attention of the concerned agencies.

Besides, it should not be forgotten that an employee is a human being first and an employee afterwards. As such, he should be paid which may enable him to lead a reasonably comfortable life, and he should feel motivated for self-development and proud of his organization. The Constitution of India too lays emphasis on paying a fair, just and equitable share to the workers of the national domestic product. It is for this reason that the government has to intervene from time to time. That is why statutory steps initiated by the government in this direction, including various wage-related acts passed so far, Wage Boards constituted for different industries, Pay Commissions established, a Committee on Fair Wages, which has discussed the concept of minimum wage, fair wage and living wage, and the recommendations made by a number of committees, commissions and Indian Labour Conference, and so on, have not been able to solve the wage problems in our industries. It is, therefore, essential that all these wage problems should be looked into, and a comprehensive plan should be worked out and properly implemented, otherwise it may have an adverse impact on the psyche of the workers, the output of the organizations and the working of the government.

Components/Functions of Compensation Management/W&S Admin

The compensation management/W&S admin has to perform several functions as follows:

Formulations and Revision of Compensation Policies and Recommending the Same to the Top Management for Its Approval

The formulation of compensation policy is part of the first function of compensation management (for details of compensation policy, see Chapter 1). Once the compensation policy is formulated, it should be approved by the top management. Then depending on the feedback, the compensation policy needs revision from time to time. Revised compensation policy too should be approved by the top management.

Determining Pay/Salary Levels

The next function of compensation management is the determination of pay levels. Hence, it is essential to know what actually the pay level is all about. Pay level is, as a matter of fact, a fundamental unit in the compensation structure of an enterprise. It is used to denote differences in compensation due to the smallest possible change in job specification. Another noteworthy thing about the pay level is that it rises along with the rise in the hierarchy. The pay is determined by the position, responsibility, accountability, level, experience and so on in the company.

A simple compensation structure can be as follows:

Grade	Pay Level	Designation
Grade 3	Pay level 2	Sr marketing manager
Grade 3	Pay level 1	Marketing manager
Grade 2	Pay level 3	Sr sales manager
Grade 2	Pay level 2	Sales manager
Grade 2	Pay level 1	Asst sales manager
Grade 1	Pay level 3	Sr salesman
Grade 1	Pay level 2	Salesman
Grade 1	Pay level 1	Asst salesman

Note: In the above table, salary of Grade 1 and Pay level 1 is the lowest, and salary of Sr marketing manager is the highest.

Salary levels are determined by the process of job evaluation (for details, see Chapter 4). Job evaluation as will be seen in Chapter 4 is a systematic method of appraising the value of each job in relation to other jobs in the enterprise. It is carried out by identifying the key tasks and taking the help of job analysis, thereby arranging them in a grading hierarchy.

However, there is no uniform pattern for determining salary levels or salary scales. Some of the organizations follow the following steps:

Step 1. Assessing the position: It is obvious that before determining the salary levels or salary scales, the value (i.e., the value it provides to the organization) of the position(s) for which the scale is to be determined should be assessed. In this regard, a detailed job description of the job plays an important role.

Step 2. Research wages: Offering a competitive payment is essential. In order to forecast what will be expected by an employee, it is necessary to find out the median pay for a given position through conducting research, which will also indicate whether the organization will be able to sustain the salary intended to be paid to the new hire. It will also indicate how education, qualification and experience influence salary.

Step 3. Deciding a maximum and minimum salary: Having found out the value of a job/position and also the median pay, the organization's baseline and maximum salary can be easily figured out. In between the two, a feasible salary that the organization can comfortably support is worked out. For example, the highest pay that the organization is likely to pay will be determined by working out how the potential hire would put the organization at a disadvantage by working for one of its competitors. In case the organization can find another person for that job for less, the organization may move towards the minimum. Thus, financial parameters play an important role in this regard.

Step 4. Deciding how the organization will pay: An employee may be paid in more than one way. For example, an employee can be compensated outside his salary such as giving certain concessions, stock options, commission, bonuses and club memberships. In such cases, the organization can be closer to the base line.

Step 5. Flexibility and openness to negotiations: It is very desirable that those employees who work very diligently and exceptionally well even during routine work hours or who perform exceptional work, should be sufficiently compensated for their worth. Hence, flexibility, while pay is being negotiated and meeting the new hire halfway, is likely not only to earn the goodwill of the new hire but also to inspire and motivate.

Thus, the organizations following the aforesaid guidelines keep into consideration the applicable knowledge, skills, abilities, experience, market band placement, general market conditions and other things such as budget, internal pay relationships and legal requirements.

Designing and Monitoring Pay/Grade Structures

Grade and pay structures offer a logically designed framework within which an enterprise's pay policies can be executed. Grade and pay structures enable an enterprise to decide where jobs should be placed in a hierarchy. They also define pay levels and the scope for pay progression besides providing the basics upon which relativities can be managed, equal pay can be achieved and also the processes of monitoring and controlling the implementation of pay practices can happen. They also help enterprises in communicating the career and pay opportunities that the enterprise can offer to its employees. Now, it will be in the fitness of things to go through the definitions of grade and pay structures, and the other pay arrangements as follows:

1. **Grade structure:** A grade structure comprises a hierarchy of grades, bands or levels into which groups of jobs that are normally comparable in size are placed. If a grade structure is defined by the pay ranges or grades attached to a 'pay spine', it is called 'pay structure'.
2. **Pay structure:** A pay structure defines the different levels of pay either for jobs or for a group of jobs, keeping in view their relative internal value as by the process of job evaluation. In simple words, a pay structure refers to the process of setting up the pay for a job in an organization. The process deals with internal and external analyses to estimate the compensation package for a job profile. Of course, a grade structure becomes a pay structure as and when pay ranges, brackets or scale is attached to each grade, band or level.

Salary Structure

A salary structure of an organization comprises its salary grades (or ranges) and its salary levels for a single job or group of jobs. A salary structure (or a salary range structure) is a hierarchical group of jobs and salary ranges within an organization. Salary structures are often expressed as pay grades or job grades that reflect the value of a job in the external market and/or the internal value in an organization. It is the job evaluation that plays an important role in designing a salary structure into which all the jobs of an organization can be appropriately graded, based on their relative worth. While designing a salary structure, it is essential to provide for internal equity as well as maintain competitive rates of pay. A salary structure can be either of the following or even a combination of both.

Graded Salary Structure

It has a sequence of salary grades, each having a defined minimum and maximum. A well-designed salary structure should ensure that all the jobs of the organization are allocated into a salary grade within the structure. However, such an allocation should be done on the basis of the assessment of their internal as well as external value to the organization. It should also be ensured that each salary grade consists of a salary range or grade and that no employee holding a job in the grade will cross the maximum of the salary grade till he is promoted. Then, no job should be regraded unless its value has changed. It may happen due to a change in responsibilities and so on. It has also to be ensured that salary grades are wide enough so as to reward employees according to their performance though they are graded at the same level because employees can perform differently. So far as the general increases in the cost of living or in the market rates are concerned, they should be taken care of by the proportionate increase in the minimum and maximum salary levels. It should also be ensured that a differential between the mid-points of each salary grade is maintained so as to provide adequate scope for rewarding increased responsibility or accountability on promotion to the next higher grade. Besides, the mid-point of each grade is the target salary for the grade because it is assumed that the average salary of the employees in the grade will correspond with the target salary. It should also be ensured that all jobs allocated into a salary grade are broadly of the same level and they usually have the same correspondence with the grade boundaries. Besides, since progression within a grade depends on the employee's performance, it is assumed that all fully competent employees in any job in a grade would eventually reach the normal maximum for a grade, even if they are not promoted out of it. However, if it appears that there are no immediate chances for promotion and further that the organization does not want to lose the services of certain employees, some provisions for such exceptional employees should be there so that they may receive more than the grade maximum.

However, how many grades or ranges should be there will depend on a number of factors. For example, it is the number of distinct levels of jobs in the hierarchy that plays an important role in determining the number of grades or ranges. Similarly, the salary levels desirable for the most senior and most junior jobs will also have an impact on the number of grades to be there in an organization. The other factors affecting the number of grades or ranges may be the width of each salary grade or the extent of the overlap, if there is any, between grades and so on.

Since the graded salary structure has a sequence of salary grades, each having an already settled minimum and maximum, there are two options, namely (a) to cover all jobs of the organization by the same structure of salary ranges and (b) to design different structures for different levels or categories of jobs. Each grade includes jobs roughly of the same value and the actual salary earned will depend on the performance or length of the service of an individual. With regard to the advancement through the structure, an individual has two options, that is, either by improving performance or by promotion. In a normal course, employees move steadily from the start of the grade to the maximum limit of the grade unless they move to a better grade. This progression can be, for convenience's sake, classified into the following zones:

1. **Learning zone:** An individual takes his own time, depending on his competence, ability and experience, to familiarize himself with skills, knowledge, attitude and so on needed to become fully conversant and competent for the job. It is known as a learning zone.
2. **Qualified zone:** Having passed through the learning zone, an individual makes efforts to increase his capacity so as to improve his performance and

efficiency. In this zone, in which the starting salary should match the market rates for the job, the mid-point of the grade should be such that it is likely to be achievable by all competent employees. Thus, the mid-point in the grade should be higher than the market rate so that employees do not leave the organization and would continue with it.

3. **Premium zone:** In every organization, there are some employees for whom appropriate promotion opportunities do not exist despite their commendable and exceptional performance. Such outstanding employees are encouraged in this zone by rewarding them appropriately.[11]

Again, it should also be ensured that general increases in the market rates or in the cost of living are taken care of by appropriate increases in the minimum and maximum salary levels. In order to provide adequate scope for rewarding increased responsibility on account of promotion to the next higher grade, a differential should be maintained between the mid-points of each salary grade.

Before moving forward, it is in the fitness of things to study the guiding principles for the grade and pay structures and also the various types of grades and pay structures.

- **Guiding Principles for Grade and Pay Structures:** The main guiding principles of grade and pay structures are as follows:
  - They should synchronize with the characteristics and needs of the organization and employees.
  - They should be appropriate to the culture of the organization.
  - They should be instrumental in accomplishing equity, fairness, consistency and transparency in managing grade and pay.
  - They should facilitate management of relativities.
  - They should facilitate operational flexibility and continuous development.
  - They should be capable of adjusting to pressures emerging from market rate changes and skill shortages.
  - They should be capable of clarifying reward and career opportunities. They should also be capable of clarifying lateral development.
  - They should enable the organization to exercise control over the implementation of pay policies and budget.
  - They should leave adequate scope for rewarding contribution, performance and increase in competence and skills.
  - They should be logical and obvious so that they are easily communicable and understandable by the employees.
- **Types of Grades and Pay Structures:** There are several types of grade and pay structures, the main ones are as follows:
  - **Multi-graded structure:** It is also called a narrow-graded structure. It has narrow pay ranges, for example, 20–40 per cent. It consists of a sequence of job grades (may be 10 or more, see Figure 2.1) into which jobs

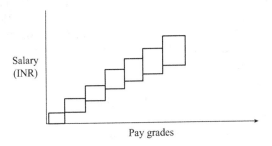

FIGURE 2.1   A Multi-Graded Structure

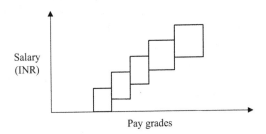

FIGURE 2.2   A Broad-Graded Structure

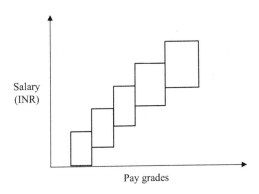

FIGURE 2.3   Broad-Banded Structure

of broadly equivalent value are placed. Grades may be defined by grade definitions or profiles. Progression is usually linked to performance.

○   This multi-graded structure is easily comprehensible and facilitates control. It also clearly indicates pay relativities. At the same time, it creates hierarchical rigidity. It does not suit an organization which is delayered. This structure also encourages 'grade drift', that is, unjustified upgrading, which is not good. It is appropriate for large bureaucratic organizations that have well-defined hierarchies. It is helpful to organizations that have close and rigid control. It also suits where organizations need some scope for pay progression related to performance contribution.

o **Broad-graded structure:** This structure has 6–9 grades (see Figure 2.2) instead of 10 or more grades, which characterizes the multi-grade structure discussed above. It has fairly broad pay ranges, for example, 40–50 per cent. The grades are defined and managed. Progression is linked to contribution.

o However, it may be controlled through thresholds or zones. A broad-graded structure has all the advantages of narrow-graded structures, besides that broader grades can be defined clearly and that better control can be exercised over grade drift. However, the main disadvantages of broad-graded structures are that they may be costly and that despite control mechanisms it may be difficult to manage them. Besides, they have too much scope for pay progression. Broad-graded structures are good in organizations where there exist grade drift problems or where there is more scope to reward contribution.

o **Broad-banded structures:** These structures comprise a multi-graded structure into less number of 'bands', say four or five bands. They have wide pay bands, for example, 50–80 per cent (see Figure 2.3). Progression is linked to competence and contribution. The main advantage is that they are more flexible and fit in new style organizations. They reward lateral development and growth in competence. They suit delayered, process-based, flexible organizations. They are also suitable for organizations where the focus is on continuous improvement and lateral development. They are also appropriate

o where more flexibility in pay determination is required. But these structures cause equal pay problems as also they are difficult to be understood clearly. They also cause unrealistic expectations of scope for pay rises. They also seem to restrict the scope for promotion as subsequently these are extended into zones for individual jobs or groups of jobs, which place restrictions on pay progression (see Figure 2.4).

o **Job family structures:** In a job family structure, there are separate grade and pay structures for a different category of job family containing similar jobs. Job families comprise jobs in occupations or functions such as finance, marketing, information technology (IT) and HR but involve different levels of knowledge, responsibility, accountability, skill or competence. In job family structures, different job families are identified. Thereafter, the successive levels in each family are defined by reference to knowledge, skills or competence required and key activities carried out at a particular level. The main advantage of a job family structure is that it facilitates pay differentiation between market groups. It also defines career paths against clear criteria. However, its main shortcoming is that it may inhibit lateral career development. Besides, it appears to be

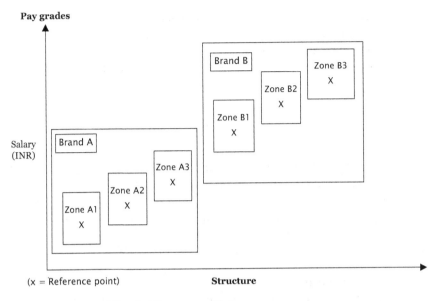

FIGURE 2.4 A Broad-Banded Structure with Zones

divisive. There are also probabilities that such types of structures may find it difficult to maintain internal equity among job families. However, job-family structures are suitable where there are distinct groups of jobs in families and also where there are distinct market groups, which need to be rewarded differently.

○ **Career family structures:** Like job family structures, there are a number of different 'families' in career family structures, but unlike a job family structure, in a career family structure, jobs in the corresponding levels across each of the career families are within the same size range. Not only this, if an analytical job evaluation scheme is used, this is defined by the same range of scores. Besides, the pay ranges in corresponding levels across the career families are the same. Such structures focus on career development and career mapping as part of an integrated approach to HRM.

○ **Pay spines:** Pay spines are a series of incremental 'pay points' covering all jobs. Such pay spine increments vary between 2.5 and 3.0 per cent. Pay spine increments may be standardized from the top to the bottom of the spine. The other possibility is that the increments may vary at different levels, at times widening towards the top. Grades may be superimposed. Pay progression is linked to service.

○ **Spot rates:** When there are no grades at all for any jobs or for certain jobs such as managing director and organizations, use 'spot rates'. A spot rate is the rate for a job or an individual that is not fitted into a job or an individual that is not fitted into a grade or band in a conventional grade structure and does not allow any scope for pay progression. We come across spot rates quite often in retail firms for customer service staff. At times, spot rates may be attached to a person instead of a job. In spot rate, progression is linked to service. Spot rates are easy to manage, and they are not based on managerial judgement, thus leaving no scope for bias. Besides, spot rates are appropriate where it is not possible to measure different levels of performance objectively and consistently. They are also appropriate in voluntary organizations and public sector undertakings where there is a traditional approach and hence fit the culture.

○ **Individual job grades:** Individual job grades are essentially spot rates to which, for providing scope for pay progression, a defined pay range on either side of the rate is attached. Pay progression is based on competence, contribution or performance. Individual job grades are usually restricted to certain jobs, especially at the top management level. They provide a greater amount of flexibility than more conventional structures. The main shortcoming of the individual job grades is that it may become difficult to manage and justify them as they can cause pay inequities.

• **Designing the Salary Structure:** There are several ways to design a salary structure, but a very simple way to do is as follows:

First of all, they should be established by market rate surveys and studies of existing structures, and the differentials of the most senior and most junior jobs to be covered by the structure. In this regard, the survey should be properly designed, market should be properly selected and the pay policy relative to competition should be appropriately in place.

Second, a salary grade structure should be drawn between the upper and lower limits, as already established as per the first step spelled out above, as per policy of differentials, the width of salary grade and the size of overlap between grades.

Third, a job evaluation exercise should be conducted by means of a simple ranking scheme. However, this may be refined by making use of paired comparisons.

Fourth, market data rate should be obtained. Here, it should not be forgotten that there is a possibility of a range of market rates rather than an accurate figure.

Lastly, jobs should be slotted into the grade structure as per the results of both the job evaluations and the market rate surveys. This exercise calls for judicious judgement. Though some decisions on grades will be obvious, the remaining may be quite difficult. In case of any doubt, the borderline cases may be re-evaluated so as to arrive at final marginal decisions. The main benefit of an overlapping structure is that such decisions attract less criticism.

Salary Progression Curves

Salary progression refers to an increase in salary resulting from movement up an incremental scale, pay range or band. Such an upward movement is the outcome of several factors such as seniority, performance appraisal, assessment of skills or competence and success in acquiring formal qualifications. Salary progression curves, also known as maturity curves or career curves, aim at linking an increase in salary over a fairly long period to an increased maturity or experience or the like. They are normally used in the case of professionals or scientific or research or other qualified personnel. It is primarily because the contribution of the aforesaid personnel is almost entirely related to their professional capacity rather than to a fixed set of duties that keep them firmly placed in a rigid hierarchy.

There is also a thinking that there are six major internal factors that are inter-related and can shape the pay structure of an organization. They include the following:

1. Social customs, that is, it is not the economic factors alone that determine wages, but the social environment also affects the determination of the wages. For example, while determining just wages, minimum wages, fair wages, living wages and so on, social factors also play their own role.
2. Economic conditions play an important role. For example, demand for and supply of labour, productivity of labour, and a number of other economic factors affect the determination of pay structure.
3. Organizational factors too play a vital role in determining the pay structure. For example, the type of technology being used by the organization, incentives being offered, work culture and so on also affect the pay structure.
4. Skills and knowledge of the employees, that is, the pay structure is affected by the amount of knowledge and skills possessed by the employees, which make them competent on different positions.
5. Job requirements, that is, jobs requiring greater skills, experience, knowledge and the like than that are required by other jobs. Hence, the former types of jobs are to be paid more than the latter types of jobs. This fact is to be kept into consideration while determining the pay structure.
6. Employee acceptance, that is, employees expect a certain amount which they feel is comparable with their co-workers inside their organization and their counterparts elsewhere. In case the pay structure does not fulfil the expectations of employees, they may not like to continue with the organization and others may not feel attracted towards the organization.

Similarly, there are some external factors which play an important role in determining the pay structure. Such factors include the demand for and supply of labour with various skills and qualifications, demand for specific products of the organization concerned, and finally and more importantly, external competitiveness, which means keeping the operating costs low. While the labour rate relates to the actual amount of pay received by employees for a certain period, for example, INR 50 per hour, the labour costs comprise the total amount received by the employees as also the level of productivity. For example, an organization may have high labour rates but relatively low labour cost in case its productivity levels are high, that is, it is able to take fewer hours to complete the tasks and the quality of its products is better than that of its competitors. In such a case, the organization can choose to have a better pay structure than its competitors.

All said and done, pay must relate to the accomplishment of the goals of the organization concerned and so is the case with accomplishment of the mission and vision of that organization. Besides, the pay system must help the organization to create the desired work culture. It should help to develop the team environment.

Divergent Systems and Institutions for Wage Fixation in India[12]

Thus, it is obvious from the foregoing discussion that compensation management/ W&S admin has to perform a lot of functions starting from formulation and implementation of strategies and policies that may compensate employees in a fair, equitable and consistent manner, keeping their value to the organization.

Due to fast changes happening in the HR environment, workforce priorities are also changing rapidly, and therefore, compensation management will also have to adjust accordingly. There will be greater use of analytical software to meet the diversity, equity and inclusion (DEI) goals of organizations. 'Diversity' relates to all aspects of human differences, social group differences and social identities. Though it includes all these but all the same is not limited only to sex, gender, race, creed, colour, ethnicity, spirituality, age, political perspective, associational references, language, culture, economic status and so on. Equity refers to fair and just practices and policies ensuring that all campus community members can thrive against equality which implies treating everyone as if their experiences are exactly the same. Hence, equal treatment results in equity only if everyone starts with equal access to opportunities. 'Inclusion' relates to a campus community when all its members receive respect, are able to participate, achieve their potential and have a sense of belongingness. Keeping the features of all the aforesaid three, the compensation data will be analysed to accomplish the DEI goals. For example, solutions will have to be found to get rid of current wage disparities; wellness programmes be increasingly focused; financial support for the home office setups of remote and hybrid employees which are also becoming part of compensation management will have to be taken care of; remote work's complexities will have to be entertained as the employees are increasingly located in multiple states and internationally; and so on. In order to solve the aforesaid issues, compensation management software will need the flexibility to handle such issues and also to deal with other new types of benefits and change. Besides, organizations will be increasingly educating their workforce regarding other aspects of their employment like tuition assistance, retirement contributions, discounts, etc. Giving employees continuous updates on their performance, e.g. weekly or monthly—depending on the nature of their job; introducing long-term incentives like ESOP, restricted share units (RSU), performance share units (PSU), etc.; making employees feel a digital reward experience so as to enable them to access their statements and information from any device at any time; continuously keeping employees more engaged; laying more emphasis on building corporate culture and brand; building a culture of ownership among more sections of employees; improving employee engagement with digital platforms; etc., will also have to be taken care of in compensating management in future. Compensating special groups, work-life balance pays, work-life balance flexi-time, compressed work week, strategic compensation management, telecommuting, environmental factors, organizational justice, international remuneration, job sharing, etc., in future compensation management are also likely to attract more attention.

Chapter Review

1. Compensation management/W&S admin helps an organization in accomplishing its goals, through formulating such compensation strategies and policies that may ensure that employees are rewarded fairly, equitably and consistently according to their worth to the organization. Besides, compensation management is also concerned with the design, implementation and maintenance of compensation processes and practices that ultimately lead to the improvement of the performance of the organization.

2. The main aim of compensation management is to develop, implement and maintain an appropriate salary system of processes and procedures. Anyway, the objectives of compensation management can be divided into three categories, namely organizational objectives, collective objectives and individual objectives. So far as the principles of compensation management are concerned, the main ones include external relativities, internal relativities and individual worth.

3. As far as the methods of wage payment, which are decided by the compensation management department, are concerned, they are either time rate method/time wages, or piece rate method/payment by results, or incentive plans/bonus (premium) schemes. All three methods have their own advantages and disadvantages. As far as the third method of wage payment, namely incentive plans, is concerned, it offers several incentive plans which can be categorized under two heads, namely (a) individual incentive plans and (b) group/collective bonus plans. The individual incentive plans have straight piece work plans such as 'straight piece work system' and 'straight piece rate system'; differential piece rate plans such as Taylor's differential piece rate plan, Gantt task and bonus plan, and Merrick multiple piece rate plan; and premium or bonus-sharing plans such as the Halsey plan, the Halsey–Weir plan and the Rowan plan. The group/collective bonus plans have many groups/collective bonus plans such as Priestman's production bonus plan, cost premium plan,

budgeted expense bonus plan, profit-sharing plan, Towne gainsharing plan and waste reduction plan.

4. Incentive plans are beneficial to both workers and employers. Regarding the principles of incentive plans, there are several principles including that bonuses should be at least 15–20 per cent higher than the hourly rates, job evaluation must be rigorously carried out, periodic review must be there and so on. Similarly, there are several prerequisites for the success of incentive wage plans such as they should have support from the top management and should be easily understandable. Besides, of late, linking pay to performance is also getting popular. Then 'draws' are also being given to salesmen by many business organizations.

5. Profit-sharing plans, in which a fixed percentage of the total profit of the organization is distributed among employees either in the form of cash immediately after the profits have been worked out or deferred to be paid later at retirement or death, disability and the like. Stock options are another option of incentive plans in which in order to attract, motivate and retain employees, company shares are allotted to employees. It develops a sense of ownership.

6. The compensation management or W&S admin has to look after supplementary compensation (or benefits) extended to employees over and above their wages. These supplementary benefits not only promote the economic betterment of employees but also provide psychic satisfaction.

7. There are certain essentials of a satisfactory wage system such as it should be well planned, easily understandable, motivating, pragmatic and maintain internal and external relativities. It is always advisable to have a national wage policy to guide the whole country on matters regarding wages. Similarly, there should be a wage policy at the organizational level which should consider factors such as external and internal equities, seniority and merit, cost of living, productivity, motivation and morale. There has always been a wage problem in our country due to the large population with low productivity in both organized and unorganized sectors.

8. There are several components/functions of compensation management/W&S admin such as formulating and revising compensation policies, determining pay/salary levels, and designing and monitoring salary/grade structure. A salary structure can be either a graded salary structure or salary progression curves. A graded salary structure has a sequence of grades, each having a defined minimum and maximum, and ensures that all jobs of the organization are allocated into a grade within the structure. There are many guiding principles for grade and pay structures such as they should be appropriate to the culture of the organization, logical and instrumental in accomplishing equity, fairness, consistency and transparency in managing grade and pay. There are several types of grades and pay structures such as multi-graded structure, broad-graded structure, broad-banded structure, job family structure, career family structure, pay spines, spot rates and individual job grades. Coming to

designing the salary structure, there are several ways to design a salary structure. Coming to salary progression curves, they refer to an increase in salary, which is the outcome of several factors.

9. There are divergent systems and institutions for wage fixation in India (for details, see Chapter 3).

DISCUSSION QUESTIONS

1. Discuss the objectives of compensation management/W&S admin with special reference to organizational objectives.
2. Discuss the various methods of wage payment, especially various incentive plans.
3. Discuss the prerequisites for the successful working of incentive wage plans.
4. Discuss the meaning of terms 'profit-sharing', 'draws', 'supplementary compensation' and 'stock option plan'.
5. Discuss at length the national wage policy of our country.
6. Discuss the factors that should be kept in view while formulating wage policy at the organizational level.
7. Discuss the functions of W&S admin.
8. Discuss the designing and monitoring of salary/grade structure.
9. Discuss the guiding principles for grade and pay structures.
10. Discuss the types of grade and pay structures
11. Discuss what are the four Labour Codes and when these were passed by the 'Parliament of India'.
12. Discuss the future of compensation management in India.

Individual and Group Activities

1. Individually discuss with the HR officials of any big company, as to what are the objectives of their W&S admin.
2. In a group of three, discuss with the HR officials of a manufacturing company the methods of wage payment that are being followed in their organization, and what are the plus and negative points of those methods.
3. Individually pay a visit to a big organization and discuss with the HR manager the factors that the organization keeps in view while formulating its wage policy.
4. Individually discuss with the HR manager of a service organization, the functions being performed by its W&S admin.
5. In a group of three, visit a big organization and discuss with the HR officials there, the various types of grades and pay structures operational in their organization.

APPLICATION CASE

Perception of Equity

Michael, a diploma holder in mechanical engineering, has been working in a bicycle manufacturing company for the last five years. Two of his classmates have also been working in the same industry elsewhere. All three are in regular touch with one another, and they appear to be a lot satisfied as far as their salary is concerned. They are placed in the same grade and drawing almost an equal salary and perks.

One day, both the friends of Michael came to his company on a courtesy call and after taking a round of the company, all three went to have a cup of tea in the company's canteen where every item was available at a concessional rate. They were in a very happy mood and enjoyed their tea and snacks. In the meantime, they noticed that two people were talking to each other while having tea in the same canteen and sitting next to their table. These three friends overheard the two sitting next to their table, who were speaking very proudly about their company located in the same industrial area, producing gears needed in the automotive industry. The three got curious to know more about them and their company. Hence, after having their tea, they got up and moved towards the two who also showed friendly gestures.

The three greeted them and after shaking hands started talking about their factory. During the course of their chatting, the three friends came to know that coincidently the other two were also working as mechanics and that each of them was getting almost 30 per cent more salary than what each of the three friends was getting, along with a fairly good amount of perks. The three friends got upset when they came to know about the higher salary the two mechanics were getting in the gear manufacturing company located in the same area. They started thinking about looking for a job elsewhere.

Questions

1. Do you think that the main reason of the three friends thinking of leaving their present jobs was the disturbance in their perception of external equity? Yes or no, why? Explain in brief.
2. What was the main shortcoming in the job evaluation and fixation of wages in the bicycle manufacturing company?
3. Were you the vice-president, HR, in the bicycle manufacturing company, what steps would you take to overcome such problems in future?

Notes

1 For details, see Sharma, *Industrial Relations*, 342–343.
2 Ibid., 344.
3 Ibid., 344–345.
4 Ibid., 345.
5 Ibid.
6 Ibid., 345–346.
7 *The Economic Times*, 10 January 2017.
8 *The Economic Times*, 12 June 2015, 13.
9 Ibid.
10 Ibid.
11 Sharma and Sharma, *Human Resource Management*, 320.
12 For a detailed account, see Chapter 3.

3

DIVERGENT SYSTEMS AND INSTITUTIONS FOR WAGE DETERMINATION IN PRACTICE IN INDIAN ORGANIZATIONS (WITH SPECIAL REFERENCE TO JOB ANALYSIS AND JOB EVALUATION)

LEARNING OBJECTIVE

After studying this chapter, the reader should be able to:

1. Explain the significance of appropriate fixation of wages.
2. List the divergent systems and institutions of wage fixations presently followed in Indian organizations.
3. Explain the role of job evaluation in designing pay structures.
4. Describe the process and methods of job evaluation.
5. List and describe the techniques/methods of job pricing.
6. Explain methods of pricing managerial jobs.
7. Describe bipartite wage fixation and the role of collective bargaining.
8. Explain the tripartite wage fixation.
9. Discuss statutory wage fixation and also wage fixation through third party.
10. Discuss the 'Code on Wages' 2019.
11. Explain what should be the management's strategy with regard to wage fixation.
12. Point out the recent developments/emerging trends in the field of wages.

Introduction

Having gone through the designing of grade and pay structures in Chapter 2, we can now move on to one of the major issues in the realm of compensating people at work in Indian organizations, namely the determination of wages and

DOI: 10.4324/9781032626123-3

practices being followed by them in this regard. Unfortunately, in our country, there is a great disparity in the income of the people. According to the report titled, 'The Rise of India's Middle Class', authored by Rajesh Shukla, MD and CEO of PRICE (People Research on India's Consumer Economy), the number of 'rich' [of whose annual (2020~2021) household income of more than INR 30 lakh] has increased substantially, consisting of 3 per cent of the total households in the country in 2020~2021. The share of 'middle class' [of whose annual (2020~2021) household income is INR 5–30 lakh] doubled from 14 per cent in 2004~2005 to 30 per cent in 2020~2021. The number of households of 'aspirers' [of whose annual (2020~2021) household income is INR 1.25 lakh ~ INR 5 lakh] and 'destitutes' [of whose annual (2020~2021) household income of less than INR 1.25 lakh] constituted 52 per cent and 15 per cent respectively of the total households in the country in 2020~2021. If we consider the number of households in 'super-rich' [of whose annual (2020~2021) household income is over INR 2 crore (a part of 'rich' class)], it increases from 9800 in 1994~95 to 1.8 million households in 2020~2021.[1] The report further states that by 2047, if the political and economic reforms have their desired effect, the India income pyramid will have a smallish layer at the bottom comprising the 'destitute' and 'aspirer' groups, a huge bulge of the 'middle class' and a big creamy 'rich layer' on top. These revelations suggest that the per household annual income is likely to go up in times to come, but all the same the figures also show that there is a relatively vast disparity in the annual household incomes of different groups. [However, there is also a positive sign that per capita income of the population of India has increased in real terms by 33.4 per cent in eight years since the enactment of the National Food Security Act (NFSA), 2013, taking a large swathe of population out of the vulnerable section of the society.][2] It is therefore, necessary that the vast disparity should be minimized. In case wages are not appropriately fixed, workers are likely to suffer not only in economic terms, but also they get emotionally and psychologically disturbed a great deal—thus affecting their work behaviour (see Exhibit 3.1). Obviously, in such a scenario they cannot contribute their best to the organization, which in turn is likely to cause loss to all the stakeholders in the organization. Hence, wage fixation needs a thoughtful consideration and working out of an appropriate mechanism.

EXHIBIT 3.1 SEVEN IN 10 EMPLOYEES FEEL THEY ARE NOT PAID FAIRLY

Blame manager, HR team for pay disparity, shows a Times Jobs survey of more than 1,600 employees

7 in 10 employees feel they are not paid fairly.	Who is to be blamed for the pay disparity?	Employer's expectations
30% said they felt they were paid fairly. 70% said they were not paid fairly.	40% blamed their managers 30% blamed HR 15% blamed top management 15% blamed themselves, since they need to reskill.	30% said they were clear about their employer's expectations from them and their profile. 70% said they were not clear.
6 in 10 do not see a long-term career in their current organization. 35% said they saw themselves having a long-term career in their current organization. 65% said they did not.		Organizational support for growth and learning 45% said they got support from the company to grow and learn. 55% said they did not.

Source: The Economic Times (6 March 2018).

Divergent Systems and Institutions for Wage Fixation in Practice in India

In our country, a number of systems and institutions for wage fixation are operational; the main ones are as follows:

1. Unilateral wage fixation.
   a. In the organized sector (with special reference to Job analysis and Job evaluation).
   b. In the unorganized sector.
2. Bipartite wage fixation.
3. Tripartite wage fixation.
4. Statutory wage fixation.
5. Third-party wage fixation.
6. Practices in vogue for supplementing base wages.

A detailed discussion of the aforementioned systems is as follows:

Unilateral Wage Fixation

Unilateral wage fixation is common in both the organized and unorganized sectors.

In the Organized Sector

In most organizations in the organized sector, wage fixation is done unilaterally by the employer using the techniques of 'job evaluation' and 'job pricing'. These techniques are used to design pay structures. However, before discussing 'job evaluation' and 'job pricing', it will be desirable to understand 'job analysis' which plays a supporting role in 'job evaluation'.

Job Analysis

Since job analysis spells out the complete anatomy of a job and also the qualifications and other attributes that the job holder should possess, it helps a lot in job evaluation which is one of the main methods of wage determination in the organized sector.

According to Edwin B. Flippo, 'Job analysis is the process of studying and collecting information relating to the operations and responsibilities of a specific job'.[3] Further, according to H.L. Wylie, job analysis is a complete study of a job, embodying every known and determinable factor, including the duties and responsibilities involved in its performance, the conditions under which the performance is carried on, the nature of the task, the qualities required in the worker and such conditions of employment as pay, hours, opportunities and privileges.[4]

Objectives of Job Analysis

i) To prepare a 'job description' for knowing the contents and characteristics of each job in an organization.
ii) To prepare a 'job specification' for knowing the qualifications, expertise, experience and other relevant attributes that the job incumbent should possess.
iii) To provide information gathered for 'job description' and 'job specification' to the organization for its use in human resource planning, recruitment and selection, induction, training and development, wage and salary administration, transfers and promotions, counselling, performance appraisal, job re-engineering, industrial relations and other processes of human resource management.

Areas in Which Job Analysis Provides Information

According to Dale Yoder, job analysis provides information in seven basic areas:

1. Job identification.
2. Distinctive characteristics of the job.
3. What the typical employee does.

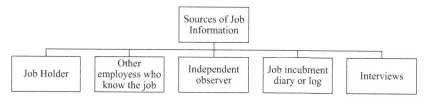

FIGURE 3.1   Sources of Job Information

4. What materials and equipment will be used by the employee.
5. How the job is performed.
6. Required personal KSAO's i.e., knowledge, skills, abilities and other human attributes.
7. Job relationships.
8. Job evaluation.

Sources of Job Information

There are mainly five sources of job information (see Figure 3.1) as follows:

1. Job holder's questionnaires.
2. Other employees who know the job.
3. Independent observer.
4. Job incumbent diary or log.
5. Interviews—Information may also be gathered through interviews of the persons concerned. Some typical questions asked in the interview are shown in Exhibit 3.2.

EXHIBIT 3.2 TYPICAL INTERVIEW QUESTIONS USUALLY ASKED FOR JOB ANALYSIS

- What is the job being performed?
- What are the major duties of your position? What exactly do you do?
- What physical locations do you work in?
- What are the education, experience, skill, and [where applicable] certification and licensing requirements?
- In what activities do you participate?
- What are the job's responsibilities and duties?
- What are the basic accountabilities or performance standards that typify your work?
- What are your responsibilities? What are the environmental and working conditions involved?

- What are the job's physical demands? The emotional and mental demands?
- What are the health and safety conditions?
- Are you exposed to any hazards or usual working conditions?

Quantitative Techniques for Obtaining Information

Though there are many quantitative techniques, the following three techniques are more popular. These include:

1. Functional job analysis (FJA).
2. 'Position' analysis questionnaire.
3. Management position description questionnaire (MPDQ).

Some other quantitative techniques/systems being used include the *Common Metric Questionnaire* (CMQ) and *Occupational Informational Network*.

Process of Job Analysis

Job analysis is a staff function. In order to carry out job analysis we need a trained and highly efficient job analyst. The job analyst can be a member of the HR department provided we have got such an expert in the HR department. If need be, a practician expert can be arranged from outside the organization also. Some big organizations employ a full time trained job analyst. The job analyst should be impartial, trained and well equipped in the modern techniques of job analysis.

The process of job analysis is basically one of data collection. The job analysis process involves a number of steps, as outlined in Figure 3.2, and can be divided into the following parts:

Uses of Job Analysis

The job information provided by job analysis is very vital in almost all important programmes of HR management. In brief, the main uses of job analysis (see Figure 3.3) are as follows:

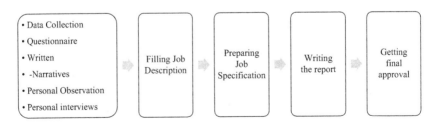

FIGURE 3.2 Process of Job Analysis

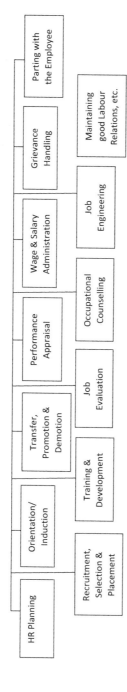

FIGURE 3.3   Uses of Job Analysis

Competency-Based Job Analysis

In a high-performance work environment in which employees are required to seamlessly move from job to job and exercise self-control, job descriptions based on lists of job-specific duties may create roadblocks in the flexible behaviour required by companies. Hence, today entrepreneurs are moving towards new approaches for describing jobs. One such approach is competency-based analysis in which job descriptions are based on competencies instead of job duties. It emphasizes what the employee must be capable of doing, rather than on a list of the duties he must perform. Competencies are observable and measurable behaviours comprising part of a job. As against traditional job analysis which is job focused, competency-based analysis is worker focused and takes into account what he is competent to do.

Scope of Job Analysis

The scope of job analysis comprises of Job description, and Job specification.

Job Description

As the title indicates, job description is a document which is basically descriptive in nature and contains very vital information about the job. A job description is a broad statement of the purpose, scope, duties and responsibilities of a particular job.

According to Edwin B. Flippo, 'A job description is an organised, factual statement of the duties and responsibilities of a specific job'.[5]

In sum, job description should tell what is to be done, how it is to be done and why. It describes the contents of a job.

Contents of Job Description

Following things are described in a job description:

(i)   Job identification.
(ii)   Job summary.
(iii)   Duties performed.
(iv)   Extent of Supervision given and received.
(v)   Machines, tools and equipment used.
(vi)   Working conditions.
(vii)   Relation to other jobs.
(viii) Organizational relationship.
(ix)   Hazards involved.
(x)   Pay.

(xi)   Training and Promotion.
(xii)   Required qualifications of the worker.
(xiii)   Comments.

Using Internet for Writing Job Description

Normally employers write their own job descriptions but, of late, more and more employers are switching over to the Internet (see Exhibit 3.3).

EXHIBIT 3.3 WRITING JOB DESCRIPTION THROUGH INTERNET

Today, writing job descriptions through Internet is getting more popular. The process is simple—search by alphabetical title, keyword, category or industry to find the desired job title. This will take you to a generic job description for that title. Then you can use the wizard to customize the generic description for this position.

Source: Visit www.jobdescription.com.

Characteristics of a Good Job Description

There are primarily two main objectives of preparing job descriptions, to help at the time of recruitment, and to help at the time of job evaluation. A good job description should have the following characteristics:

(i)   Proper title.
(ii)   Comprehensive job summary.
(iii) Completeness.
(iv)   Elasticity.
(v)   Other Characteristics.

A job description having the above characteristic features will prove effective and present the description of the job in a very realistic manner.

Guidelines for Writing a Job Description

(i)   Every sentence should start with a functional verb.
(ii)   It should be written in present tense.
(iii) It should be brief and accurate.
(iv)   It should be written in simple and lucid style.

(v)   It should give a clear, concise and easily understandable picture of the whole job.

(vi)   It should describe in adequate detail each of the main duties and responsibilities.

(vii)   It should give examples of work performed.

(viii)   It should avoid statement of opinions.

(ix)   It should clearly mention the extent of direction received and supervision given.

Advantages of Job Description

Job description is helpful in:

(i)   Recruitment and selection,

(ii)   Working out training and development programmes,

(iii)   Transfers, promotions and demotions, and

(iv)   Giving direction to newly recruited workers,

(v)   Determining wages and allowances,

(vi)   Matching the workers with the job,

(vii)   Reducing frustration among workers to a great extent,

(viii)   Reducing grievances of workers to a considerable extent, etc.

Job Specification

According to Edwin B. Flippo, a job specification is 'a statement of the minimum acceptable human qualities necessary to perform a job properly'.[6] In contrast to the job description, it is a standard of personnel and designates the qualities required for acceptable performance.

Contents of Job Specification

Broadly speaking, besides mentioning job title, department, occupational code, name of the supervisor or boss, wage code, hours, days, shift and job summary, job specification lays special emphasis on the following:

(a) **Physical requirements**

(b) **Mental Requirements**

     (i)   Education.

     (ii)   Language ability.

     (iii)   Special ratings.

     (iv)   Test rating.

Job Analysis in a 'Jobless' World[7]

Today, the concept of a job stands changed significantly because jobs tend to change more varied and loosely defined than what they used to be in the past. The last few decades have made job enrichment, job enlargement and job or position rotation quite common, and, therefore, the concept of job instead of being static has become dynamic. The companies are getting dejobbed. *'Dejobbing'* refers to broadening the responsibilities of the company's jobs and encouraging employees not to limit themselves just to what is on their job description. Again, companies are organizing tasks around teams and processes instead of specialized functions as used to happen hitherto. Self-managed teams which are getting popular today also accept an employee not to be tied down to his job description. Then because of *re-engineering*, an employee's job tends to change more often than not, besides making an employee collectively responsible for overall results rather than just for their own tasks. Today a job has become like a hat which has lost its shape because of it being used by different people. Individual jobs are becoming broader and much less specialized. Hence organizations do not want employees to be limited by a specific set of responsibilities mentioned in a job description and job descriptions have become broad-based rather than static.[7]

Why Managers Are 'De-Jobbing' Their Organizations

Technological change, global competition, deregulation, politsical turmoil, demographic changes, shift to service economy and other challenges being confronted by the companies these days require them to be flexible, responsive and competitive. This, in turn, has weakened the meaning of *job* as a well-defined and clearly delineated set of responsibilities because requiring employees to limit themselves to narrow jobs runs counter to the need to have them willingly switch from task to task as job and team's assignments change. Today, there are a number of organizational factors that contribute to encouraging workers not to limit themselves to narrowly defined job[8] (see Exhibit 3.4).

EXHIBIT 3.4 SAMPLE ORGANIZATIONAL FACTORS ENCOURAGING WORKERS NOT TO LIMIT THEMSELVES TO NARROWLY DEFINED JOBS

- Flatter organizations.
- Self-managing work teams.
- Re-engineering.
- Others.

The Challenge

Today, self-directed teams are getting popularity and efforts are also on how to ensure that employees make best use of skills. In this regard, *competency alignment process* (CAP) can prove of great help in determining the current skill levels of employees in order to identify skill gaps which can be bridged through training, outsourcing, etc. The big challenge is to acquire such job analysts and HR professionals to be able to meet the onslaught of re-engineering processes.[9]

Thus, Job Analysis plays a very significant role as it provides very useful information for various interventions and processes of human resource management including compensation management.

Job Evaluation

An employee is paid according to the worth of work that he does for the organization. However, evaluating the worth of a work or job evaluation is not a simple task. It involves several problems. The technique of job evaluation is used to design appropriate pay structures which obviously influence employee behaviour and help the organization sustain its competitive advantage. Job evaluation involves what to value in the jobs, how to assess that value and how to translate it into a job-related structure.

Job evaluation establishes the relative value of jobs based on their contents, independent of link to the market. It is a tool or technique for evaluation and ranking of jobs to help an organization to evolve a rational and scientific wage structure. Thus, job evaluation is a process of comparing jobs to determine the relative worth of each job with a view to determine what should be the fair wage rate for such a job. According to the ILO, job evaluation is an attempt to determine and compare the demands made by the normal performance of particular jobs on normal workers without taking into account the individual abilities or performance of the workers concerned.[10] According to the Bureau of Labor Statistics, United States, job evaluation is the evaluation or rating of jobs to determine their position in a job hierarchy.[11] However, it should be well understood that job evaluation is the technique for rating the job and not the man, that is, it does not take into account the individual's efforts and abilities. The immediate objective of the job evaluation process is to obtain internal and external consistency.[12]

1. **Single versus multiple plans:** Many employers design different evaluation plans for different types of work because they believe that work content is too diverse to be usefully evaluated by one plan. For instance, production jobs may vary in terms of manipulative skills, knowledge of statistical quality control and working conditions, but these tasks and skills may not be relevant to finance and marketing jobs. Hence, a single universal plan may not suit employees or be useful to managers if the work covered is highly diverse.[13] The number of job evaluation plans used hinges on how detailed an evaluation is required to make pay decisions and how much it will cost. There is no

ready answer to the question of 'one plan versus many'.[14] A good number of organizations use separate plans for major domains of work, whereas some, like Hewlett–Packard, use a single plan.

2. **Process of job evaluation:** The process of job evaluation comprises certain steps which are given as follows:

   a. **Job analysis:** Job analysis is the process of obtaining job facts through the following.

      i. Job description: It mainly describes the duties, responsibilities and nature of the job.

      ii. Job specification: It is a statement of human qualities required to perform the job well.

   b. **Selecting benchmark jobs:** The job evaluators should select benchmark jobs which should be representative of the level and type of jobs to be evaluated.

   c. **Job rating:** It is the use of some method to assign, with the help of job analysis, a relative score to each job.

   d. **Money allocation:** It involves assigning a rate of wages or salary (in terms of money) to each job keeping its rating into consideration.

   e. **Job classifications:** It grades different jobs into certain categories of the pay scale.

3. **Methods of job evaluation:** There are several methods of job evaluation, but for the sake of convenience, these can be grouped under the following two categories:

   a. **Non-analytical or non-quantitative methods:** These methods evaluate jobs as a whole. There are two non-analytical methods which are given as follows:

      i. Job ranking method: This is the oldest and the simplest of all methods of job evaluation. As per this method, each job is evaluated as a whole and is measured in comparison with other jobs in terms of their relative worth to the organization. No specific factors are selected for consideration and job-to-job comparison is made. Thereafter, the total ranking is divided into a certain number of groups, say 6 to 10 or the like. All the jobs falling into one group will receive the same pay. The methodology adopted in this method to establish pay rate may be any of the following: first, the top and bottom jobs are selected as benchmarks for the remainder of the ranking process. The remaining jobs are rated according to their ranks between these two points. As per the second practice, a certain number of key jobs from different departments and of different functions are first rated and then all other jobs are broadly compared with these key jobs to establish a broad rating. Then, there is another technique also which is known as 'paired-comparison technique' in which each job is compared with every other job, one at a time, and thus ranked in order of their merit, and wage rates are fixed accordingly.

Job ranking method is simple, fast, inexpensive, easy to understand and explain to employees, but all the same it is suitable only for smaller organizations where the raters are fully conversant with the jobs which may not be possible in the case of bigger organizations where there are a number of jobs, some of which are of very complex nature. Another shortcoming of this method is that in this method subjective judgement comes into vogue.

ii. Job classification or grading: In this method also, jobs are measured as a whole and a series of classes covers the range of jobs. Class descriptions are labels. A job description is compared to the class descriptions to decide which class is the best fit for that job. Each class is described in such a way that the 'label' captures sufficient work detail, yet is general enough to cause little difficulty in slotting a job description into its appropriate class. The classes may be described further by including titles of benchmark jobs that fall into each class.[15] An example in this direction is as follows:

Job/Grade	Class Description
Unskilled	• No education or training required
	• Works under supervision
	• Little or no responsibility
	• Routine and repetitive task
Semi-skilled	• Some training is required
	• Some experience is desirable
	• Needs a little bit of initiative
	• Needs supervision
Skilled	• Very less or no supervision
	• Trains and guides subordinates
	• Takes initiative
	• Supervision of juniors

The end result is a job structure made up of a series of classes with a number of jobs in each. The jobs within each class are considered to be equal or similar work and are paid equally. Hence, jobs in different classes should be dissimilar and may have different pay rates. Though it is an improvement over ranking method, is inexpensive and easy to understand, but writing class descriptions, which is an art, is not an easy job. Besides, it does not suit an organization which has a large number of jobs of complex nature or the jobs cover a wide range of responsibilities. However, this method can group a wide range of work together in one system, though descriptions may leave too much room for manipulation.

b. **Analytical or quantitative methods:** Under these methods, jobs are assessed and numerical values are assigned under a number of compensable factors such as professional qualifications required, expertise needed, experience required and working conditions under which the job is to be performed. Then by comparing total numerical values, assessors can assign pay rates to different jobs. The main analytical methods are as follows:

i. Point method or manual system: Developed by Merit Lott in 1923, point method is the most widely used job evaluation approach in the United States and Europe and is now quite popular in Indian organizations also. Point methods or point plans have three common features, namely compensable factors, factor degrees numerically scaled and weights reflecting the relative importance of each factor. The following are the main steps involved in this method.

○ *Determining the compensable factors/job factors common to all jobs:* Initially, certain but the most common compensable factors (job factors) are (a) skills, (b) responsibility, (c) effort and (d) working conditions. Having determined the job factors, each of the same is divided into a number of smaller factors given as follows:

Skill	Responsibility	Effort	Working Conditions
Education	Machinery	Physical	Work environment
Professional training	Product	Intellectual	Hazards involved
Experience	Safety and security		
Creativity	Supervision of juniors		

○ *Construction of a scale of values for each job factor:* The next exercise is to construct a scale of values for each factor so as to measure the factors in each job. For doing this, initially we have to decide the total number of points that will be utilized in the entire system. Thereafter, we will have to determine the percentage (of total number of points) to be allocated to each job factor. It can be explained with the help of the following example:

Factor	No. of Points	Percentage
Skill	160	40
Responsibility	120	30
Effort	80	20
Working condition	40	10
Total	**400**	**100**

Having determined the total value of each job factor, scales need to be derived. These scales comprise points and explanations of degrees of each of the factor. To illustrate, let us take the case of 'education' (which is a sub-factor of 'skill') and suppose that it has been assigned 48 points out of 160 points allocated to skill. Now, four degrees of 'education' may be established with an arithmetic progression of 12 points as follows:

12	24	36	48
No Education	Metric	Graduate	Masters and Above

(Scale of value for 'education' sub-factor of 'skill')

○ *Assigning money value to points:* Points scored for sub-factors are added to find out the total value of a job and then its value is translated into terms of money as shown in Figure 3.4.

As per Figure 3.4, we have a line that approximates the going rates for all the jobs in the structure and now wage rates of all other jobs can be interpolated by reading up from the point values to the wage-trend line.

The point method is a very objective method and is therefore acceptable to workers. This method is capable of handling a large number of jobs and has long-lasting stability as the compensable factor remains relevant. Of course, the development and installation of this method involves heavy cost. Besides, it is a very complex and time-consuming process to define job factors and so is the case with determining factors' degrees.

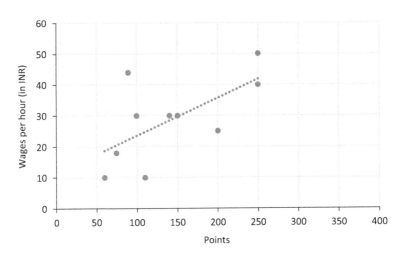

FIGURE 3.4   A Wage-Trend Line

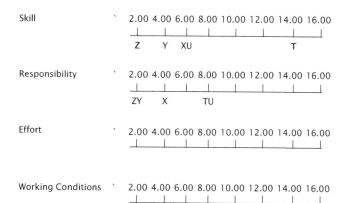

Skill	2.00 4.00 6.00 8.00 10.00 12.00 14.00 16.00
Responsibility	2.00 4.00 6.00 8.00 10.00 12.00 14.00 16.00
Effort	2.00 4.00 6.00 8.00 10.00 12.00 14.00 16.00
Working Conditions	2.00 4.00 6.00 8.00 10.00 12.00 14.00 16.00

Correct Job Rates	Skill	Responsibility	Effort	Working Conditions
T INR24.00	T INR 13.60	U INR 8.00	Z INR 4.80	Y INR 4.00
U INR 22.40	U INR 8.80	T INR 7.20	Y INR 3.60	Z INR 3.60
X INR 17.60	X INR 7.20	X INR 4.80	U INR 3.20	X INR 3.20
Y INR 13.60	Y INR 4.00	Y INR 2.00	X INR 2.40	U INR 2.40
Z INR 11.20	Z INR 1.60	Z INR 1.20	T INR 1.60	T INR 1.60

FIGURE 3.5   Factor Scales of a Factor Comparison System

ii. Factor comparison method: Developed by E.J. Bonge in 1962, this method, which is a sort of combination of the ranking and point systems, is less common these days. Although there may be four to seven factors that are used by the factor comparison system, it is usually the skills, efforts, responsibilities and working condition factors that are usually used.

○ *Process:* The following are the main steps involved in this method:

○ Initially, it is the selection of job factors and their appropriate definitions that need to be done very cautiously. As stated earlier, the factors selected may differ from organization to organization.

○ Second, it is the selection of key jobs which should be fair, stable and relative to other jobs. The pay levels represented by the selected key jobs should be representative of a particular class of jobs.

○ The next step involves determining the correct rates of key jobs as is done in the point system explained earlier.

○ In the fourth step, the key jobs are ranked by one factor at a time. It can be explained by giving the following example in which the rater ranks five key jobs (T, U, X, Y and Z):

Skill	Responsibility	Efforts	Working Conditions
T	U	Z	Y
U	T	Y	Z
X	X	U	X
Y	Y	X	U
Z	Z	T	T

○ In the next step, the correct rate of each key job is allocated among the job factors. For example, suppose the correct rate for job T is INR 24.00, it is divided among skill, responsibility, effort and working conditions (depending on the importance of each of these in job T) as shown in Figure 3.2.

Thus, we have created a series of four scales—each scale consisting of 'key job titles' and 'money'.

○ In the next step, other jobs are evaluated by comparing them with the list of key jobs in each scale. For instance, if new job 'k' is most similar to U in skill (INR 8.80), Z in responsibility (INR 1.20), Y in effort (INR 3.60) and X in working conditions (INR 3.20), then its correct rate is INR 16.80.

○ The final step involves designing, adjusting and operating the wage structure. If it is considered to be slightly different from any of these key jobs, then varying amounts can be allocated and the new job can be placed in the factor scale as a new level of that factor.[16]

Thus, this method is an improvement over the simple ranking method as in this method (factor comparison method) comparisons are made on a job-to-job basis, by factors, rather than as whole jobs. However, this method is a little bit complex and therefore needs a group of specialists to monitor the system. Usually, the whole job can be carried out by a committee constituted for the purpose.

c. **Choosing the best method:** A careful analysis of all the methods of job evaluation clearly reveals that none of the aforesaid methods is flawless, though the point method is the commonly used one. Hence, keeping in view the circumstances prevailing in an organization, different methods may be used for different types of jobs.

Job Pricing

Job pricing is attaching a price tag to each job and creating a wage structure that equitably relates jobs to their calculated values.

1. **Methods or techniques of job pricing:** The following are the main methods of job pricing:

a. **Supply and demand method:** As per this method, the price determination is the function of forces of demand for and supply of a certain type of

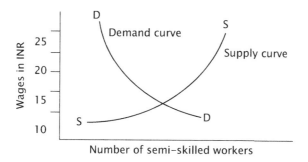

FIGURE 3.6   Job Pricing through Intersection of Demand and Supply Curves

job in the labour market, and therefore, other things remaining the same, the price of a job will be fixed at a point where the demand curve and the supply curve intersect each other as shown in Figure 3.6.

b. **Converting the point values of job into monetary value:** This method requires wage surveys inside and/or outside the organization to find out the going rates for various jobs on the basis of point values assigned to jobs and then to key the entire structure to these rates in the organization. For example, let us take the job of a mechanic, which has been assigned 100 points, the range of average rates for a mechanic's job is INR 10 per hour which means that each point is currently priced at 10 paise per hour.

In order to be more practical, point values are generally compared with the current prices of 10–20 key jobs. This requires, first of all, selecting a sample of organizations in the labour market, getting appropriate wage information from these sample organizations in respect of key jobs selected for the purpose, and then analysing and averaging the data so collected. The rupee value of key jobs is then plotted on the chart as shown in Figure 3.7.

It is clear from Figure 3.7 that price (wage)-trend line which is closest to all points plotted approximates the then going rates for all jobs in the structure. With the help of this, wage rates for all other jobs can be interpolated by reading up from the point values to the price (wage)-line.[17] However, many objections are raised against this system. For example, it is difficult to explain the whole mechanism to rank and file employees.

c. **Establishing labour grades:** In any large organization, individual wage rates for each job calculated from point values could create an undesirable multiplicity of fractional rupee–paise rates. Hence, labour grades are established, each grade representing a range of point values, with one wage rate or range for the entire grade.[18] In other words, instead of treating jobs separately, they are grouped to form a 'job class', and all jobs in a particular class are treated in the same way.

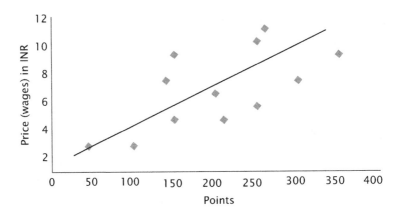

FIGURE 3.7 A Price (Wage)-Trend Line

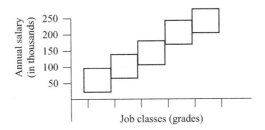

FIGURE 3.8 Job Classes (Grades)

In a point system, job classes are created by dividing the point range into the desired number of classes. To illustrate it, we can say that from 50 to 100 points may constitute one class, 101 to 150 may constitute another class and the like as follows (see Figure 3.8).

An organization has the option either to pay 'flat rates' for each job class (see Figure 3.9) or varying rates within a rate range of each class in which case the per wage structure will be as shown in Figure 3.10.

d. **Red circle rates:** When price tags are attached to job values, some current rates generally show up as distinctly out of line. Some jobs are being paid too much; others may be inadequately compensated. Many out-of-line rates may be due to personal factors such as long services, blood relationship, friendship, personality and so on. Similarly, some may be due to environmental or technological changes. Such 'over' rates are red-circled and are temporarily regarded as personal rates which are to be protected as long as present employees remain in these jobs and are eliminated as soon as the employees concerned leave their jobs.

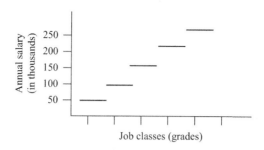

FIGURE 3.9   Flat Rates Wage Structure for Each Job Class

FIGURE 3.10   Varying Rates Wage Structures for Each Job Class

Executive/Manager Compensation (Pricing of Managerial Jobs in the Organized Sector)

Like engineers and scientists, managers are usually regarded as requiring distinctive reward programmes for high-level commitment. Thus, for both staff and line managers, the job evaluation programme is not considered a full-proof solution to problems of equity and holding high-level commitment. It is so because managers should be paid for their capability, that is, for what they can do, rather than for job demands or measured output. Managers reflect a wide range of individual differences in performance and expectations. They may be different in that, as a group, they have more powerful desires for achievement, power and advancement.[19] Hence, great emphasis is placed on incentivization through financial rewards. Managers rely principally on the dangling carrot of greater financial rewards to stimulate superior performance. Present or deferred monetary rewards are assumed to be the principal answer to the question of what makes the manager perform.[20] Hence, most employers, in the case of executive remuneration, supplement the base rate or range established by their job evaluation programme with a wide variety of bonuses, profit-sharing, fringe benefits, employee stock options and so on.

However, Indian executives are relatively paid less as compared to other countries in the Asia Pacific (APAC) region, as has been revealed by the research conducted by leading global advisory working and solutions company Willis Towers Watson.[21] For example, salaries even of the executives at Hindustan Unilever, the country's largest consumer goods maker, fell by a quarter in the fiscal year 2015–2016 (see Exhibit 3.5).

It has been reported that about 129 Hindustan Unilever Limited managers took home more than a crore of rupees in annual salary in the year April 2015 to March 2016, against 169 managers a year ago. More than half of them are less than 40 years of age, equalling all of IT major Infosys' 53 eight-digit salary earners. According to Abneesh Roy, associate director, Edelweiss Securities, 'While the year hasn't been great for HUL, in terms of profitability, the final payout could have been impacted due to variable pay linked to sales, profit or market share. Also payout depends on the company's outlook for next year'.[22] According to Anuj Roy, partner, digital practice at search firm Transearch,

> On an average, HUL salaries are higher by nearly 30% than second tier consumer companies. With part of bonus or employees' shares being vested for 3–4 years in general, many may have exercised the option last year which reflected in a higher number of people earning more than a crore.[23]

EXHIBIT 3.5 HUL'S CRORE-PLUS SALARY CLUB SHRINKS BY A FOURTH

The number of executives at Hindustan Unilever who drew eight-digit salaries fell by a quarter last fiscal as the country's largest consumer goods maker fought slowing sales growth and declining profit in a challenging macroeconomic environment.

Source: The Economic Times (17 June 2016).

According to some critics, the earnings of CEOs have been showing an increasing trend during FY 2018 to FY 2022 (see Exhibits 3.6 and 3.7).

EXHIBIT 3.6 NUMBER OF CEOS EARNING $1MN+ (2018~2022)

Financial Year	Number of CEOs Earning $1mn+
2018	124
2019	146
2020	150
2021	125
2022	171

Source: The Times of India, 05 December 2022.

The total CEO compensation jumped around 55 per cent between 2018 and 2022 (see Exhibit 3.7).

EXHIBIT 3.7 RISE IN TOTAL CEOS COMPENSATION (IN INR CR) BETWEEN 2018 AND 2022

Financial Year	Jump in Total CEOs Compensation (in INR Cr)
2018	2,158
2019	2,457
2020	2,514
2021	2,549
2022	3,957

Source: The Times of India, 05 December 2022

The top ten CEOs' earnings during FY2022 have also gone up considerably if compared to FY 2021 (see Exhibit 3.8). There are nearly five *crorepati* executives per company in the BSE200 group with an average compensation of INR 5.5 crore.[24] The earnings of the ten top CEOs have also gone up considerably in FY 2022 compared to FY 2021 (see Exhibit 3.8).

EXHIBIT 3.8 TOP TEN CEOS' EARNINGS (2021 AND 2022)

S.No	Name of CEO	Name of Organization	Earnings during FY 2021 (in INR Cr)	Earnings during FY 2022 (in INR Cr)
1	Sajjan Jindal	JSW	85	146
2	Shantanu Khosla	Crompton	NA	118
3	Murli Divi	Divi's Lab	81	110
4	Sandeep Kumar Barasia	Delhivery	NA	93
5	Kalanithi Maran	SUN TV	83	88
6	Kavery Kalanithi	SUN TV	88	88
7	Pawan Munjal	Hero MotoCorp.	87	84
8	Thierry Delaporte	WIPRO	64	80
9	Salil Parekh	Infosys	50	71
10	S.N. Subramanyan	L&T	29	61

Source: The Times of India, 05 December 2022

According to some critics, rising pay comes from strong-arming by executives who take more out of the economy than they put back in.[25]

The amount of compensation given to senior executives who receive more than INR 1 crore as salary grew 47 per cent every year between FY15 and FY17, while the profit of the BSE 200 companies rose by 8 per cent. HDFC Bank, India's largest bank by market capitalization, had the largest number of senior executives (105) earning more than INR 1 crore, followed by TCS (91) and Bharti Airtel (82). In FY17, every fourth *crorepati* executive was from the manufacturing sector compared with 1 in 10 about two years ago. There was also a rise in the number of *crorepati* executives at midcap companies, such as Kajaria Ceramics and Bata India. The number of such executives at Kajaria Ceramics increased to nine in FY17 as compared to two in FY15.[26]

1. **The ratio of CEO's salary to average worker's salary:** The compensation of India Inc.'s top 100 senior executives other than promoters holding executive positions has a sharp increase. The average compensation of the sample increased by 12.1 per cent to INR 9.8 crore in FY17.[27] Further, the median salary of the top senior executives is on average 243 times higher than the average salary of employees, according to the data of Capitaline and annual reports.[28]

EXHIBIT 3.9 RBI TO FRAME RULES FOR BANK CEOS' PAY

RBI is working on a set of rules that would link the remuneration of banks' CEOs to parameters like the balance sheet size of a bank, loan delinquency, profits and governance record.

The proposed framework is expected to provide a broad template to the board of directors of banks, while approving increase in salary, performance bonus and stock options to the senior most executive. The regulatory guidance that exists today is a general directive on the remuneration of senior officials in broad functions like 'business', 'control' and 'risk'. What is being considered is one that specifically relates to CEO compensation.

Source: The Economic Times (14 January 2019).

---

2. **RBI to frame rules for bank CEOs' pay:** In order to put some check and link remuneration of bank CEOs to certain parameters, the RBI is working to frame a set of rules (see Exhibit 3.9).

   Even today, RBI clears the remuneration of a bank CEO and has powers to claw back a slice of it in case of non-performance or governance lapses. However, a framework would ensure that the board does not have to shoot in the dark while approving the package for the CEO and referring it to RBI for its clearance. Though such a framework would be significant for private banks, it would also hold relevance for PSU banks which are considering incentives and ESOPs for employees.[29]

Central Bank officials have shared the idea with senior bankers in the course of the conversation. It is understood that the proposal was broadly agreed upon towards the end of Urjit Patel's exit. We tend to believe that RBI would pursue this under the new Governor. Probably, it is also believed that given the turmoil in the banking sector, even a draft guideline on CEO pay giving out the broad contours would send the right signal.[30]

3. **Shares of ESOP in total payout of top executives:** ESOPs are considered to be an effective tool in limiting attrition and improving the engagement of executives since they align the growth of top employees' wealth with that of the company.[31] The shares of ESOPs in the total remuneration of India Inc.'s top executives are on the rise.

The companies make a disclosure about ESOPs in the following two ways:

a. When ESOPs are exercised, they are shown as part of the total compensation of the executive.

b. When ESOPs are granted, the number of shares allotted as ESOPs that can be exercised in future, is disclosed. For example, including the value of ESOPs in total compensation, C.P. Gurnani, CEO at Tech Mahindra, topped the pay charts in FY17. He received ESOPs worth INR 147 crore in FY 2017, taking his total payout to INR 150.7 crore. This was more than the salaries of the boards of IT peers TCS, Wipro and Infosys put together.[32]

Among those who cashed in, Aditya Puri, MD at HDFC Bank, exercised ESOPs worth INR 57 crore in FY17 which had been granted and vested over the previous several years.[33] The pay ratio of the CEO and an average worker's salary in India was the second highest in the world after the United States, according to Bloomberg. The median remuneration of Indian employees was INR 565,748 in FY17, an increase of 8.5 per cent from the year before. The average of global CEO salary is around $3.6 million (INR 23.6 crore), whereas it is $1.5 million (INR 9.76 crore) for Indian CEOs.[34]

The group chairman of India's largest infrastructure company, Larsen & Toubro, was the highest paid key management professional, if employee stock option plans (ESOPs) are excluded, in FY17. He took home INR 78.91 crore in remuneration, an annual gain of 19.3 per cent. Nearly half of his total compensation was due to retirement benefits. His remuneration was 1,102 times the median remuneration of the employees at the engineering giant. The CEO of Dr Lal Path Labs was next on the list with a payout of INR 33.20 crore in FY17, an increase of 12 per cent year-on-year. In his case, perks account for nearly 90 per cent of the total compensation.[35]

4. **Factors affecting the pricing of managerial jobs:** Managerial compensation is influenced mainly by the following factors:

a. Individual's performance: Wipro, India's third-largest software exporter, has overhauled its incentive structure for top executives at the company and completely done away with the previous account-based incentive structure, as part of a broader strategy to regain growth momentum and revive growth. As per the new structure, Wipro is placing an equal amount of importance on both individual performance and the overall company's performance, as it urges top executives and employees to collaborate more closely and work as a cohesive unit.[36]

 As part of the new structure, Wipro is placing an equal amount of importance on both individual performances as well as the overall company's performance, as it urges top executives and employees to collaborate more closely and work as a cohesive unit (see Exhibit 3.10).

 The new structure comes at a time when the broader $160-billion IT industry is taking a fresh look at traditional metrics and benchmarks previously taken into account to reward employees—which has for the better part of the last two decades seen revenue growth directly linked to manpower addition.[37]

EXHIBIT 3.10 WIPRO REWORKS INCENTIVE STRUCTURE FOR TOP EXECUTIVES

Wipro president and chief human resources officer Saurabh Govil in an interview in early June said, 'Our incentive structure has undergone a fundamental shift. We have done away with the previous account-based structure. The new plan which came into effect on April 1, has two parts: 50% of the incentive will depend on the performance of the individual and his team while the balance 50% is linked to the performance of the organization'.

Source: The Economic Times (20 June 2016).

---

b. Organization's performance.
c. Size of the organization, that is, the number of people employed.
d. Nature of industry the managers are employed in.
e. Status of the industry in the economic/industrial structure of the country.
f. Status of the organization concerned in the industry.
g. Manager's span of control, that is, the number of subordinates being supervised/ controlled.
h. Responsibilities assigned.
i. Going rates of pay for subordinates.

5. **Methods of pricing managerial jobs:** Different authors and practitioners have suggested various methods for pricing management jobs. For example, Yoder[38] has suggested the following:

    a. **Comparison data:** Executive and manager salaries are less frequently sampled and reported than those of production and office employees. Some of the largest, most inclusive top salary surveys do not give wide circulation to their findings. However, it should not be forgotten that a policy of full disclosure of salaries may have a net gain, despite the problems it can create. Such a policy might generate powerful pressures for improvements in compensation programmes.[39] Availability of adequate data can help in adopting the same technique(s) for pricing managerial jobs also as is done in the case of other employees for pricing their jobs.

    b. **Incentives for managers:** It is because of the inclusion of formal incentive provisions such as bonuses, profit-sharing, stock options, other special deferred payment fringes and a variety of non-financial payoffs in the salary of managers that complicates salary data in respect of managers. Hence, most organizations include one or more than one of the aforesaid formal incentives in the pay package of their managerial personnel.

    c. **Distinctive fringes:** A number of organizations include tax-exempt services such as company car and driver, club memberships and other fringes in the pay packages of their managers. Some companies grant options to purchase stock and thus develop capital gains which are either non-taxable or taxable at a lower rate, though it is criticized that this encourages giving senior managers an unfair advantage over their juniors.

    d. **Pay package:** In order to maintain wage differentials in executive pay and also to maintain the essentials in the incentive of top managers, the idea of pay package has come into vogue, which comprises a base pay in determining which careful attention is paid to the going rate, some other programmes add a bonus, related to improvement in sales or profits or accomplishment of other stated objectives, to the basic pay. Still some other programmes provide opportunities for deferred benefits and capital gains, in addition to basic pay.

Today, the most common pattern is one that combines some or all of these in a *special package.* Thus, managerial pay packages include both financial and non-financial rewards.

Wage Fixation in Unorganized Sector

In the unorganized sector, it is usually the employers who unilaterally fix the wages of workers. The number of workers engaged in the unorganized sector constitutes around 90 per cent of the total workforce. In a good number of cases, even statutorily prescribed minimum wages are not paid to the workers; the main reason for this sorry state of affairs is the absence of trade unions in the unorganized sector. Even if there are unions anywhere in this sector, these are as good as non-existent. It is, therefore, the unorganized sector which needs immediate attention of the authorities concerned to take care of fixation of wages.

Bipartite Wage Fixation

Of late, collective bargaining which is a bipartite process has come into popularity with regard to settlement of terms and conditions of employment of workers. It is primarily due to trade unions getting stronger and also because of the realization among the employers that they alone cannot work in isolation and that without the cooperation of workers' unions, they will not be able to accomplish the objectives of the organizations. The government is also interested in encouraging the institution of collective bargaining which is perhaps one of the best methods to ensure industrial peace.

In the process of fixing wages through collective bargaining, the trade unions present to the management their demand for a particular pay scale for a particular category of employees or different pay scales for different categories of employees in the organization.

In case the management is not willing to accept the proposal of the trade union in toto, it puts forward a counter-proposal keeping in view the interests of all concerned, to be followed by discussion, arguments, heated exchange of words, haggling, cajoling and what not.

Both the parties present facts and figures from different sources to support their contention. The discussion(s) may lead to different situation(s). For example, both the parties may totally reject each other's viewpoint and there may be deadlock. In such a scenario, efforts are made to resolve the issue through the conciliation machinery or adjudication machinery or even through arbitration.[40] Another scenario may be that the management may not be ready to accept the increase in wages in full as asked for by the union. In such a situation, the two parties can meet again to resolve the issue. In another case, the management may like to do an exercise on its own once again with regard to calculating the cost and other implications likely to be caused if the demand for increased wages is accepted. If this be the case, the negotiations may take place later on. In another case, the management may accept the demand put forth by the workers' union but simultaneously put forth its counter-demand to the union.

In the above process of negotiations, there may be 'haggling bargaining' or 'Boulwarism bargaining' or 'continuous bargaining'. There may also be 'attitudinal structuring', 'intra-organizational bargaining', 'distributive bargaining', 'integrative bargaining' or the like. Any of these approaches or a group of more than one approach may be adopted. Ultimately, both parties, following the 'give and take' approach, may reach an agreement applicable for a particular period of time. For example, in a landmark agreement signed with Pune plant workers on

28 March 2017, Tata Motors, India's largest automobile company by revenues, has initiated a move to bring 15,000–20,000 blue-collar factory workers to a wage structure that is performance-linked.

The company concluded a long-term wage settlement agreement with its Pune workers' union that covers 6,400 workers, after 19 months of negotiations. Tata Motors then worked towards getting workers from Sanand, Lucknow and Jamshedpur factories to sign a similar agreement.[41] It is learnt that about 10 per cent of the Pune plant workers' salary is variable pay and is linked to performance. The wage settlement for Pune plant workers had been signed for a period of three years—1 September 2015 to 31 August 2018. The agreement was implemented with immediate effect.

The total wage package is bifurcated as: a fixed rise of INR 8,600 (in the ratio of 72 per cent, 15 per cent and 13 per cent for a period of three years) and INR 8,700 non-actual, that is, a total of INR 17,300.[42] According to the MD of Tata Motors, 'Here is a clear scheme, as far as performance-based rewards are concerned, just like how it translates for the management or white collar executives, in the same way, the company is introducing performance-linked pay for blue-collar workers'.[43]

In addition to the increment amount, the company has also agreed to pay a gratuity amount to the families of deceased workmen and a wristwatch be given to the spouse of an employee on the completion of 25 years of service. Additionally, various other facilities were agreed upon, including block closure days being increased by six days.[44]

Tripartite Wage Fixation

It was the Royal Commission on Labour, 1931, and the First Five-Year Plan (1951–1956) that had recommended the setting up of wage boards with a tripartite composition in each state and at the Centre to resolve all aspects of wages. Now, let us have a brief description about wage boards.

Wage Boards

A wage board is a tripartite body having the representatives of both employees and employers appointed by the government in consultation with their organizations (unions/associations). The government also appoints an independent economist and an independent consumers' representative who should be a Member of Parliament. The total number of members of a wage board has been varying between seven and nine in the past.[45] Wage boards are constituted with the objectives of working out standardized wage structure for the industry concerned and to protect the interest of consumers/community as well as to promote industrial harmony. Thus, a wage board is expected to follow the principles of fair wage as laid down in the Report of the Committee on Fair Wage and to ensure laying down a wage policy enabling optimum allocation of resources and providing economic progress. These wage boards are set industry-wise and are in great demand by different industries. However, there is a great controversy with regard to giving statutory status to wage boards. It is because of the fact that in some cases the recommendations of wage boards were not given effect appropriately.

The issue has been alive for long. Although the Standing Labour Committee did not approve the idea of making wage boards as statutory bodies, it rather suggested that the parties concerned should implement unanimous decisions of wage boards. In case they do not, only then the government should give a statutory force to such recommendations. However, confronted with the problem of non-implementation of recommendations of some wage boards, the government thought of introducing a Bill in 1961 to give a statutory force to the recommendations of the wage boards but postponed the matter. The matter was again taken up by the Standing Labour Committee in 1967 which constituted a committee to review the wage board system.

With regard to the working of a wage board, the procedure involves issuing an exhaustive questionnaire so as to get the necessary information from the parties concerned, to be followed by assessing the views of the parties and finally making recommendations with regard to wage structure which remains in operation for a period of five years.

A good number of wage boards have already been set up for a large number of industries since 1956. It was in May 1956 that the first wage board was constituted for working journalists, followed by for the cotton textile (March 1957), sugar (December 1957), cement (April 1959), jute industry (August 1960), tea plantations (December 1960), coffee and rubber plantations (July 1961) and so on. Second wage boards were also constituted for certain industries such as cotton textile (August 1964), cement (September 1964) and sugar (November 1965). Even more than two wage boards have also been constituted in certain cases, for example, the third wage board for working journalists was set up in February 1976 and the trend continues.

Wage boards have done a good job, though certain criticism is also there. But the fact remains that no other agency can do more justice than a tripartite body like a wage board because it is the platform where all concerned can put forth their viewpoints, argue and have an opportunity to justify their logic.

Statutory Wage Fixation

Since wages constitute the only economic means of survival for industrial workers, it is essential that full justice should be done in the fixation of their wages. However, this has not been happening in a large number of cases. That is why the Government of India has been interfering from time to time and has undertaken the following measures in this regard.

Legislative Steps/Executive Orders

In order to monitor the wages of the workers, at least, to some extent, the Government of India has undertaken the following steps.

Enactment of the Minimum Wages Act, 1948 and establishing the National Floor Level Minimum Wage, Minimum Wages Act, 1948, empowers the appropriate government to fix minimum rates of wages payable to the persons employed for hire or reward to do any work, skilled or unskilled, manual or clerical and so on, in an employment specified in Part I or Part II of the Schedule appended to the Act and also in an employment added to either Parts of the Schedule subsequently. Under Section 27 of the Act, the appropriate government is empowered to extend the application of the Act to any other employment in respect of which it thinks that the minimum rates of wages should be fixed under the Act. This option is being made use of by several state governments, for example, the Government of Orissa did so in 2002. However, minimum wages were fixed for the first time in 23 employments (by union government [4], Kerala [6], Tamil Nadu [5], Karnataka [5], Maharashtra [2] and Chandigarh [1]). It is the inspecting officers of the Chief Labour Commissioner (Central) usually designated as Central Industrial Relations Machinery.[46]

Adequate steps are also taken to protect minimum wages against inflation. For example, 26 of the states/union territories have made variable DA as a component of minimum wages. The central government too has made provisions for variable DA linked to the consumer price index. Hence, minimum wages in respect of the concerned scheduled employment have been revised from time to time. For example, minimum wages in respect of different categories like unskilled, semi-skilled and skilled in different states/union territories in our country have been revised from October 2022, a few details of the same are as follows (see Table 3.1).

As per the Minimum Wages Act, 1948, both Central and State Governments have dominion over the fixing of wages. So far as the State Governments are concerned, they fix their scheduled employments and further release the minimum wage rates along with the Variable Dearness Allowance (VDA). Hence, the minimum wage rates in scheduled employments differ across states, sectors, skills, occupations and regions due to a lot of differentiating factors. It is, therefore, obvious that there exists no single uniform minimum wage rate across the country and the revision cycle differs from state to state. The basic minimum (Basic) wages per month effective in Delhi w.e.f. October 2022 as per the Delhi Government Notification (October 2022) are as per Table 3.2 below:

In addition to above, Delhi Government has been giving Dearness Allowance (DA) also which is being constantly revised every six months. As such, the Total Minimum Wages (Basic + DA) per month admissible in Delhi w.e.f. October 2022 in case of certain cases are as follows:

The Delhi Government, in October 2022, increased the Dearness Allowance for daily wage workers, resulting in taking up monthly wages for unskilled labourers from INR 16,506 to INR 16,729 per month. Similarly, for semi-skilled labourers wages have been increased from INR 18,187 to INR 18,499 per month. The Dearness Allowance is being constantly revised by the Delhi Government every six months.

TABLE 3.1 Minimum Wages (Category Wise) Revised with Effect from October 2022 in Different States / Union Territories

State	Zone	Unskilled		Semi-Skilled		Skilled	
		Total		Total		Total	
		Per Day	Per Month	Per Day	Per Month	Per day	Per Month
Gujarat	I	363.30	9445.80	371.30	9653.80	380.30	9887.80
	II	355.30	9237.80	363.30	9445.80	371.30	9653.80
Bihar	—	366.00	9516	380.00	9880.00	463.00	12038.00
Madhya Pradesh	—	250.00	6500	271.42	7057.00	324.42	8435.00
Punjab	—	381.06	9907.68	411.06	10687.68	445.56	11584.68
Rajasthan (w.e.f. July 2021)	—	259.00	6734.00	271.00	7046.00	283.00	7358.00
Uttar Pradesh	—	374.73	9743.00	412.19	10717.00	461.73	12005.00
West Bengal (w.e.f. July 2021)	A	355.00	9239.00	391.00	10163.00	473	12297.00
	B	322.00	8380.00	354.00	9216.00	429	11154.00
Delhi	—	—	16792.00	—	18499.00	—	20357.00
Karnataka (w.e.f. April 2022)	I	440.42	11451.00	472.54	12286.00	502.38	13062.00
Maharashtra (w.e.f. July 2021)	II	417.50	10855.00	449.62	11690.00	479.46	12465.00
	III	394.54	10258.00	426.69	11094.00	456.54	11870.00

Source: https://www.simpliance.in/minimum-wages

TABLE 3.2 Basic Minimum Wages per Month in Delhi w.e.f. October 2022

Class of Employment	Class of Workers	Basic Per Month (in INR)
Unskilled	NA	14842.00
Semi-skilled	NA	16341.00
Skilled	NA	17991.00
Clerical and supervisory staff	Non-matriculates	16341.00
Clerical and supervisory staff	Matriculates but not graduates	17991.00
Clerical and supervisory staff	Graduates and above	19572.00

Source: https://www.simpliance.in

TABLE 3.3 The Delhi Minimum Wages Notification (October 2022)

Class of Employment	Class of Workers	Total Per Month (in INR)
Unskilled	NA	16792.00
Semi-skilled	NA	18499.00
Skilled	NA	20357.00
Clerical and supervisory staff	Non-matriculates	18499.00

Source: https://www.simpliance.in

DA Calculation for Central Government Employees

For Central Government employees, the DA amount is calculated as a factor of current rate on employee's basic pay as per the Seventh Pay Commission rules. According to the current percentage rate of 12 per cent, this calculation would be:

$$(\text{Basic Pay} \times 12)/100$$

DA percentage = 12 month Consumer Price Index (CPI) average – 115.76. The result will be divided by 115.76 and then multiplied by 100.

So far as the National 'Floor Level' Minimum Wage (NFLMW), introduced by the Central Government and which is the minimum wage below which no State Government can fix the minimum wage, is concerned, it is INR 178 per day or INR 5,340 per month. Wage rates vary depending on geographical areas and other criteria. While the Indian National Floor Level Minimum Wage remained unchanged at INR 178 per day in 2022 from INR 178 per day in 2021,[47] the same is projected to trend around INR 185 per day in 2023 and INR 190 in 2024. A comparative study of minimum wages with regard to some of the other counties[48] is as follows:

India	178
China	2590
Cambodia	194
Brazil	1212
Egypt	2400
Israel	5400
Myanmar	4800
Vietnam	4680
Russia	15279

Recent Developments

While the gig platforms show to adopt minimum wage policy,[49] organizations like Coal India (CIL) and Singareni Collieries (SCCL) have recently taken concrete steps to increase the wages of their non-executive staff.[50,51] Researchers in recent report have revealed that most of the gig platforms have been reluctant to publicly commit to, and operationalize, a minimum wage policy.[52] On the other hand, Coal India (CIL) and Singareni Collieries have recently agreed to pay a 19 per cent wage hike to nearly 2.8 lakh non-executive employees of these two state-run coal miners. The representatives of the two companies and four trade unions—BMS, HMS, AITUC and CITU—signed an MoU recently on 3 January 2023 envisaging the wage hike, described as 'mutual guaranteed benefit'. A formal pact for the 11th version of the national coal wage agreement, effective from 1 July 2021 for a period of 5 years, is to be finalized after the remaining issues are discussed.[53] Karnataka Government has also hiked the wages of the convicts in jails ranging from 165 per cent to 200 per cent, which will remain valid for three years or until a fresh order, so as to bring it at par with minimum wages fixed by the government. Jail inmates work mainly as carpenters; grow vegetables and fruits; engage in handicrafts and making soaps; etc.[54]

For a long time the minimum wages have been under the purview of the Minimum Wages Act, 1948, but now this will be subject to the provisions of the Code on Wages Act, 2019, which was notified in August 2019. The new Wage Code which replaces four labour legislations, viz. Minimum Wages Act, 1948; Payment of Bonus Act, 1965; and Equal Remuneration Act, 1976, prohibits employers from paying workers less than the stipulated minimum wage. Besides, there is a provision that minimum wages must be revised and reviewed at an interval of not more than five years by both Central and State governments.

One of the main factors responsible for low wages in Indian industries is the low labour productivity (see Exhibit 3.11).

EXHIBIT 3.11 LABOUR PRODUCTIVITY

Labour productivity—defined as the ratio of output (GDP) per employed worker—varies widely in the economies of the APAC. Moreover, it can differ significantly from GDP per person due to the differences in the size of labour force relative to that of the total population.

Labour productivity and output per person in select economies, 2014

Country	Labour Productivity (2011 PPP Dollars)	GDP (2011 PPP per Capita)
Singapore	131,595	78,429
China	22,318	12,552
India	13,091	5,439

Source: The Economic Times (5 May 2016).

The remuneration given under Mahatma Gandhi National Rural Employment Guarantee Scheme (MGNREGS) in Haryana was increased from INR 251 to INR 259 per person per day on 1 April 2016, which was the highest in the country.

Records of job cards, muster roll, employment register, cash book and complaint booklet were initiated under MGNREGS. Of these, over 83,000 had been completed.[55]

Probability of Revision of Wages under National Rural Job Schemes

The government considered revision of wages under the flagship of Mahatma Gandhi National Rural Employment Guarantee Act following a persistent demand for aligning wages under the scheme to minimum wages of individual states closer to the General Election of 2019.

Last time the two wages were aligned in 2009 after which there has been a divergence because several states have arbitrarily increased their minimum wages. Daily wages under MGNREGS for unskilled workers range between INR 168 in Bihar and Jharkhand and INR 281 in Haryana.[56]

However, the minimum wage in Bihar, effective from April 2018, is INR 237, INR 210 in Jharkhand and INR 326 in Haryana. A high-level committee is likely to deliberate on the quantum of hike and its financial implications for the centre. The issue of lower wages came up at the regional conferences NITI Aayog had undertaken for the high-level group set up to lay out a road map for convergence of MGNREGS and agriculture.[57]

In the last few years, the government has set up two committees on MGNREGS wages in 2013 and in 2016. The committee recommended MGNREGS wages to be minimum wage fixed by the respective states or the current wage as per the consumer price index for agriculture labourers (CPI-AL), whichever is higher. However, the Nagesh Singh committee said there was no need for aligning the two wages. The financial implication on the centre on aligning the two wages was estimated at INR 4,500 crore by the Singh Committee, while shifting the index of calculation from CPI-AL to CPI-Rural would put an additional burden of INR 2,500 crore on the union.

Government allocated INR 55,000 crore under the National Rural Employment Guarantee Scheme (NREGS) for 2018–2019. The scheme, launched by the UPA government in 2006, has seen 2,637 crore person days generated and total expense at INR 476,718 crore since inception. The scheme, executed by the rural development ministry under the National Rural Employment Guarantee Act, provides minimum 100 days of employment out of 365 days in a year to every rural household willing to do unskilled manual work.[58]

The Delhi Government was very sincere with regard to implementation of minimum wages.

Hence, it declared a whip in this regard on 5 December 2018 (see Exhibit 3.12).

EXHIBIT 3.12 WHIP ON MINIMUM WAGE VIOLATORS

The Delhi Government will launch a 10-day awareness and enforcement drive to implement minimum wages in the city, Labour Minister Gopal Rai said on Tuesday. As part of the campaign that begins on 10 December, 10 enforcement teams of the labour department will inspect firms and factories to check if owners are paying government minimum wages, the minister said. According to the revised pay scale, workers in the unskilled category will get INR 14,000 per month, semi-skilled INR 15,400 per month and skilled workers INR 16,962 per month.

If anyone is found violating rules, the government will initiate action in accordance with the Minimum Wages (Amendment) Act, 2017, the minister said. The government has issued a helpline number 011-155214 on which complaints can be lodged. The minister said employers found not paying minimum wages may be fined INR 50,000 or a jail term extending to six months or more according to the law.

Source: Hindustan Times (5 December 2018).

Present Scenario of Rural/Agricultural Wages

The latest available data suggests that the nominal rural wage growth (for men) has fallen to its lowest level since November 2014. The value would be negative if one were to adjust for inflation. This means wages have fallen in real terms. A slightly long-term perspective shows a different picture. Rural wages rose sharply under the UPA government until 2011. This was followed by an equally sharp fall. While the downslide was arrested under the NDA, the quarterly wage growth has been stagnant.[59] Slow rural growth makes sense when seen in the context of poor agricultural growth. Also, wages have not risen appropriately despite most of the Centre's rural spending schemes meeting their targets. This shows that headwinds to rural wages, most of which are generated in the unorganized sector, due to policies such as demonetization and GST, have overpowered the tailwinds that government spending must have generated.

Statistics show that caste is an important determinant in deciding whether a person employs agricultural labourers in rural areas or gets employed as one. Most of the upper caste and dominant Other Backward Class population belong to the former category, whereas an overwhelming majority of the Scheduled Caste and rural poor belong to the latter. If a low growth in rural wages were accompanied by a high growth in agriculture, the former would have gained in a big way. Because this has not happened, neither of the groups is likely to have benefited. This could trigger rural discontent across the class and caste divide.[60]

Now that the oil cycle has been reversed, financial status is likely to change. If the government takes a haircut in its petroleum taxes to reduce prices, its ability to spend more in rural areas will decrease. This can put more downward pressure on rural wages. If it does not, growing fuel prices are bound to lead to an inflationary upsurge, to which rural labourers are among the most vulnerable.[61]

Coming to thinking about companies in any country is complicated, but entrepreneurs essentially create two kinds of companies: a baby or a dwarf. Both are small, but the baby will grow, whereas the dwarf will stay small. India is a nation of enterprise dwarfs; we have 63 million enterprises of which 12 million do not have an address, 12 million work from home, only 6.4 million paid indirect taxes till GST, only 1.2 million pay social security and only 18,500 companies have a paid-up capital of more than INR 10 crore. Formality and size matter greatly for productivity; when you can rank manufacturing enterprises by size there is a 22 times difference in productivity between somebody at the 90th and 10th percentile. With a 22 times difference in productivity, you will never pay the wage premium, but if you do not pay the wage premium, you will never be productive.[62]

Our low national productivity—it took 71 years for the GDP of 1.2 billion Indians to cross the GDP of 66 million Britishers—is a child of the Avadi Resolution of 1955 that unleashed the License Raj and ensured that firms did not have clients but hostages. Implementation of GST in 2017 is an important disruption; we added 4.7 million new enterprises in the last one year.

Not every enterprise will become a large employer, but this huge addition of enterprises substantially increases the odds of formal employment and India producing more babies.

Thinking about wages needs acknowledging three fault lines: gross versus net, nominal versus real and government versus market. The gross versus net transmission losses of 40 per cent are highlighted by job seekers responding to salary numbers with the question '*Haath waali salary ya chitthi waali salary?*', that is, the salary in the letter or in my hand. Nobody argues that gross should equal net, but the current levels of confiscation for poor value-for-money schemes breed informality. The nominal versus real divergence is summarized through an incident whereby a kid in Gwalior said 'Give me INR 4,000 per month in Gwalior, 6,000 in Gurgaon, 9,000 in Delhi and 18,000 in Mumbai; my bags are packed and tell me where you want me to go'.[63]

Bridging the Wage Gap between Genders

Is regulation the key to gender pay parity? The question was put to a panel of expertise at the *ET Women's Forum*. In a session on 'Gender and Pay: Towards Greater Parity', Shanmugh Natarajan, MD, Adobe India; Rostow Ravanan, CEO and MD, Mindtree; Sonal Agarwal, Managing Partner, Accor India; and Archana Vadala, Head of Staffing, Facebook India, thrashed out the issue and suggested possible solutions; when it comes to closing the gender pay gap, regulation alone is not enough. 'The drive to effect change should come from leadership'. Adobe announced in January 2018 that it had achieved pay parity in India, closing the wage gap between male and female employees.[64]

A few things can be better from the regulation perspective; for instance, a law in some states in the United States bars employers from asking job applicants their prior salaries. The objective is to narrow the gender wage gap. Closing the pay gap requires concerted efforts. For their part, companies can also decide to assign pay by roles. Plus a woman can ask about median pay, while talking to a potential employer and even from her current one, Ravanan suggested, adding this would steer the conversation in the required direction. There is no denying that foresting gender diversity is a business imperative. 'In corporate board rooms, having a very diverse view may make it difficult to reach a decision'.

Recent 'Labour Reforms' and Wages

In his tweet on the passing of the Labour Reforms Bill on 23 September 2022, PM Narendra Modi said, 'The new Labour Codes universalize minimum wages and timely payment of wages'.[65] For this purpose, the Central Government has amalgamated four Labour Laws in the Wage Code, 2019, which will ensure that all the workers of organized and unorganized sectors across the country will have the Right to Minimum Wages.

Benefits Available in Labour Code (Wage Code), 2019

As per the Labour Code (Wage Code), 2019, the following benefits will be available to the workers of both organized and the unorganized sectors throughout the country:

1. The guarantee of minimum wages is available to 50 crore workers of organized and unorganized sectors.
2. Review of minimum wages in every 5 years.
3. Guarantee of timely payment of wages to all workers.
4. Equal remuneration to male and female workers.
5. For the first time, around 40 crore workers of the unorganized sector in the country have got this right. To remove regional disparity in minimum wages the provision of floor wage has been introduced. The determination of minimum wages has been made easy. It will be based on criteria such as skill level and geographical area.
6. From 28.08.2017 Payment of Wages Act has increased the wage ceiling from INR 18000 to INR 24000.[66]

Pay Commissions

It is for fixing/revising the salaries of central government employees that Pay Commissions are constituted. So far, seven Pay Commissions have been constituted and their recommendations with necessary modifications, wherever the government thought it essential, have already been implemented. For example, the recommendations of the Seventh Pay Commission (see Exhibit 3.13) have come into force with effect from 1 January 2016. The state governments and some other agencies also usually adopt these recommendations—again with modifications if they so prefer. The minimum wage fixed by the Third Pay Commission was a need-based minimum wage based on dietary recommendations of the Indian Council of Medical Research Expert Group in 1968. This group had calculated dietary requirements for a family of three units as 7,600 calories.

However, it has also been pointed out that at times the recommendations of Pay Commissions tell heavily on the profits of concerned undertakings. For example, as per the *Economic Times* reporters, the recommendations of the Seventh Pay Commission were viewed by Public Sector undertakings as a costly proposition (see Exhibit 3.14).[67]

EXHIBIT 3.13 RECOMMENDATIONS OF THE SEVENTH PAY COMMISSION

The Commission report submitted in November 2015 recommended an overall 23.55 per cent increase in salaries, allowances and pensions of which salaries could rise by 16 per cent and allowances and pensions by 63 per cent and 24 per cent, respectively. The Commission also recommended a health insurance scheme for staff and pensions and doubled the gratuity ceiling to INR 20 lakh but retained the annual increment at 3 per cent.

Source: Hindustan Times (6 July 2016).

EXHIBIT 3.14 PAY PANEL SUGGESTIONS MAY DENT PSUS' PROFIT

The Seventh Pay Commission recommendations may dent profit growth of PSUs who have limited ability to pass on their increased employee cost to customers. These include BHEL, BEL, BEML, SAIL, MOIL, NALCO, GAIL, HPCL, BPCL and IOC. Regulated return entities such as NTPC and Power Grid Corporation of India Limited (PGCIL) will have no effect as wage increase is a pass-through.

Source: Hindustan Times (6 July 2016)

As a matter of fact, employee cost constituted on an average 60 per cent of the total gross profit (revenue minus raw material) in FY 2016 for the sample. This ratio hovers in the range of 11 per cent (for BPCL) and 154 per cent (BEML), according to data compiled by the ET Intelligence Group from Capitaline.

The impact was more pronounced for companies such as BHEL, SAIL and BEML, where employee cost as a proportion of gross profit was more than 80 per cent, and they were likely to feel the pinch more. For example, BHEL had a high percentage of slow-moving orders in the backlog that kept FY 2017 execution and margin under pressure; this meant an increase in employee cost would affect the company's margin even more. Analysts believed that BHEL had been using aggressive pricing to win orders and put its capacity to use. This together with the wage increase impacted profitability.

It may also be mentioned that the condition of public sector banks (PSBs) was not very encouraging either: the salary increase came at a time when their profits had been under pressure for the past few quarters due to higher proportion of non-performing assets and related provisions.

In FY 2010, when the Sixth Pay Commission–related wages were implemented, the cost–income ratio based on the aggregate financials of 12 leading PSBs had risen by nearly 460 basis points to 53.6 per cent. This was the biggest increase in the ratio of the PSBs in the last eight fiscals. In contrast, for a sample of five prominent private sector banks, excluding Kotak Mahindra Bank, the measure had improved by 480 basis points in FY 2010 to 61.3 per cent.[68]

Third-Party Wage Fixation

The third-party wage fixation method involves the role of the third party which usually is either 'adjudication' or 'arbitration'.

1. **Adjudication:** In case a problem related to wages is not resolved mutually between the employer and the workers' union or the collective bargaining fails to yield the desired results, the wage dispute may be referred to adjudication machinery comprising labour courts, industrial tribunals or national tribunal, the judgement of which is binding on both the parties, that is, the employers and the workers. However, adjudication is not preferred as it is a time-consuming process and its judgements leave a bitter taste in the mouth of the losing party which continues, and at times even aggravates its efforts, to show down the winning party at an appropriate time—thus disturbing industrial harmony.

2. **Arbitration:** It has also been observed that when the workers and the employers fail to resolve their differences on wage issues, both may agree to refer the issue to an arbitration whose decision is binding on both the parties. When both parties at their own agree for referring the wage issue to an arbitrator, it is known as voluntary arbitration. However, if the government on its own refers to the issue for arbitration, even if both the parties or either of the two parties do/does not agree to it, then it is known as compulsory arbitration. In such a case also, the mandate of the arbitration is a binding on both the parties to comply with. Of course, compulsory arbitration is usually frowned upon.

Practices of Supplementary Pay

In addition to the above practices of wage fixation operational in Indian organizations, base pay fixed through job evaluation and so on is also supplemented by many organizations through contingency pay comprising performance-related pay (PRP), competence-related pay, skill-based pay (SBP), shop-floor incentive and bonus schemes, salesforce incentive schemes, executive incentive and bonus schemes, employee and executive share schemes, team rewards, gainsharing, profit-sharing, then profit-related pay and beyond, other cash payments and so on (all of which have been given fairly good treatment in Chapters 5 and 6).

All the aforesaid methods/systems of wage fixation have their own plus and negative points. There is always a scope for improvement, and therefore, the concerned parties should continue to overcome the flaws involved in the aforesaid methods.

Management Strategy

Wage fixation is a highly sensitive issue for both the management and the workers. It is because wages are the only source of income in the case of workers who, by and large, are poor as well. For employers also, wage fixation is very crucial because wages alone constitute a big chunk of the total cost of production, and therefore, their profits go down if the wages are fixed at a higher side. Hence, it will be highly desirable for the management to formulate an appropriate wage strategy.

In this regard, the management should conduct job evaluation and job pricing on scientific lines so as to lay down a sound basis for wage fixation and then through collective bargaining fix the wages. In case the job evaluation and job pricing have been carried out justifiably, the workers' union will also appreciate the logic of the management in fixing wages in a particular fashion. It will be desirable if the management takes workers' union into confidence while conducting the process of job evaluation and job pricing. In case the organization concerned comes under the purview of the wage board, the management should prepare itself with as an exhaustive information and documentation as possible so that it may convince the other parties to see reason in its contention and stand taken by it during the course of proceedings of the wage board. In case the organization constitutes a part of the unorganized sector, then also the wage strategy of the management should be such that it may protect the interest of both its own-self and of workers also because it is the workers whose role is the deciding factor in making an organization a success or a failure.

Chapter Review

1. It is desirable to have an idea about the current practices with regard to wage fixation in Indian organizations. In case wages are not fixed appropriately, workers are likely to suffer not only economically but also emotionally, socially and psychologically. Hence, wage fixation deserves great attention. In our country, there are divergent systems and institutions for the fixation of wages, such as unilateral wage fixation, bipartite wage fixation, tripartite wage fixation, statutory wage fixation and third-party wage fixation.

2. So far as the wage fixation in the 'organized sector' is concerned, it is usually done *unilaterally*, usually by employers, through the process of job evaluation and job pricing. The methods of job evaluation are classified into two categories, namely non-analytical methods (job ranking method and job classification method) and analytical methods (point method and factor comparison method). All these methods have their own plus and negative aspects. After the relative worth of jobs is determined and their hierarchy is determined through job evaluation, a price tag is attached to every job by following the process of job pricing. However, for pricing managerial jobs, job evaluation and job pricing are not the right answers. Hence, their

jobs are priced through comparing data collected from different sources, determining their incentives and distinctive fringes, and deciding their pay packages.

3. Wage fixation in the 'unorganized sector' is done *unilaterally* by the employer which is usually on the lower side as there are neither the trade unions in this sector nor the process of collective bargaining is effective.

4. *Bipartite wage fixation* is common in a good number of organizations/industries through the process of 'collective bargaining'. *Tripartite wage fixation* is prevalent in industries for which 'wage boards' are constituted. Though wage boards' recommendations are not mandatory, in most of the cases, they are accepted by the parties concerned. A good number of wage boards have been constituted, and in some cases more than two/three wage boards have been constituted for certain industries.

5. *Statutory wage fixation* is another method wherein the government fixes wages, through 'legislative steps' and constituting 'Pay Commissions'. The Labour Code (Wage Code), 2019, will also play its own role.

6. *Third-party wage fixation* involves the role of 'adjudication' and 'arbitration' machinery as per the provisions of the Industrial Disputes Act, 1947.

7. The base pay fixed through job evaluation and so on is also supplemented by many organizations through contingency pay, that is, paying for performance, competence, skills and so on.

8. Keeping in view the sensitive nature of wage fixation, the management should formulate such a strategy in this regard as it may protect not only its own interest but also of the workers and the community.

DISCUSSION QUESTIONS

1. Discuss why wage fixation is very important to both the workers and the employers.

2. Discuss what methods of wage fixation are prevalent in Indian industries.

3. Discuss how wages are usually fixed in the organized sector.

4. Discuss the methods of job evaluation and job pricing and point out which methods are more popular in Indian industries.

5. Discuss how managerial compensation is fixed in our country and how it is that job evaluation does not have any significant role in this regard.

6. Discuss how wages are fixed in the unorganized sector.

7. Discuss the bipartite wage fixation in Indian industries. Also, discuss how far collective bargaining has been able to play its role in this direction.

8. Discuss how far the wage boards have proved their worth in the fixation of wages in Indian industries. Will it be desirable to give statutory force to the recommendations of the wage boards.

9. Discuss how far statutory wage fixation has been effective in our country.
10. Discuss the Labour Code (Wages Code), 2019.
11. Discuss whether the adjudication machinery and arbitration should be used for fixation of wages or not. What are the advantages and disadvantages of these mechanisms?

Individual and Group Activities

1. In a group of two members, visit some big organizations in the private sector and discuss with the HR officials there how they fix wages of their employees. Do they go for job evaluation and job pricing or not and why? Prepare a brief report after the discussion is over.
2. Individually talk to the senior HR officials of a big manufacturing organization and find out how their company fixes managerial compensation.
3. In a group of two members, visit a medium-scale organization where the wage board has fixed wages for its employees. Find out the reaction of trade union officials there with regard to the appropriateness of the wage board recommendations.
4. Individually discuss with the HR officials of a company where collective bargaining has played an important role in the fixation of wages of its employees. Find out from them how it has all been possible and what has been the role of workers' representations in this regard.
5. In a group of three members, visit a few big organizations and discuss the issue of wage fixation with both the HR officials and trade union leaders of each organization. Prepare a management's strategy which can be used, of course with some modifications, in most cases.

APPLICATION CASE

Incentive System of Wage Payment

Harry has been working as an operative staff in a company where wages were paid as per time rate system. Accordingly, he was being paid on a monthly basis like other operative staff. The company where he was employed has not been progressing well, and two years back the company suffered a substantial amount of loss. Having analysed the factors responsible for poor performance and also making a comparative study with some other companies in the same trade, it was revealed that in Harry's company labour cost per unit of output was considerably higher as compared to other companies.

The manager of the company convened a meeting of the concerned departmental heads as also the head of the HR department to take a fresh look at the wage system and find out a better alternative so that labour cost per unit of output may be reduced. All sorts of suggestions were put forward and deliberated upon. After a marathon session of the meeting, the general consensus of opinion emerged that in order to motivate individuals to produce more individually, an incentive system of wage payment may be introduced wherein each worker will receive a guaranteed minimum wage whether he is able to produce standard output within the standard time or not. Further, those who produce more than the standard output will be entitled to payment per piece of their output at a pre-decided rate.

After a week when necessary preparations for the introduction of the new method of wage payment had been made, the new system of wage payment was introduced. To a great satisfaction of the top management, the output per member of operative staff went up and the labour cost per unit of output came down by 30 per cent, and the workers, especially those who were more efficient, were found extremely happy as their total earnings went up considerably. Even marginal workers had nothing to complain about as everyone was assured of minimum guaranteed wage.

Questions

1. Identify the main cause of reduction in the labour cost per unit of output after the incentive system of wage payment was introduced.
2. What is the difference between the time rate system of wage payment and the incentive system of wage payment?

Notes

1 Quoted in *The Times of India*, 2 November 2022.
2 *The Times of India*, 12 November 2022.
3 Edwin B. Flippo, *Personnel Management* (Tokyo: McGraw-Hill Kogakusha Ltd., 1976), 110.
4 See H.L. Wylie, *Office Organisation and Management* (New Delhi: Prentice Hall of India Pvt Ltd., 1961), 254.
5 Flippo, *Principle of Personal Management*, 110.
6 Ibid., 111.
7 See R.C. Sharma and N. Sharma, *Human Resource Management* (New Delhi: Sage Publications, 2017), 132.
8 Ibid.
9 Ibid., 133.
10 ILO, *Job Evaluation, Studies and Reports*, New Series, no. 56 (Geneva: ILO, 1960), 8.

11 United States Department of Labour, Bureau of Labour Statistics, *Glossary of Currently Used Wage Terms*, Bulletin 983 (Wellington: U.S. Government Printing Offices, 1950).

12 Edwin B. Flippo, *Principles of Personal Management* (Tokyo: McGraw-Hill Kogakusha, 1976), 291–292.

13 Milkovich, Newman, and Venkata Ratnam, *Compensation*, 106–107.

14 Ibid.

15 Ibid.

16 E.B. Flippo, *Personnel Management*, 6th ed. (New Delhi: McGraw-Hill International Editions, 1984), 303.

17 See Flippo, *Principles of Personal Management*, 309; Dale Yoder, *Personnel Management and Industrial Relations*, 6th ed. (New Delhi: Prentice Hall of India, 1976), 644.

18 See Yoder, *Personnel Management and Industrial Relations*, 643.

19 See T.A. Mahoney, 'Compensation Preference for Managers', *Industrial Relations* 3, no. 3 (May 1964): 135–144.

20 Yoder, *Personnel Management and Industrial Relations*, 644.

21 *The Economic Times*, 27 December 2016.

22 *The Economic Times*, 17 June 2016.

23 Ibid.

24 *The Economic Times*, 23 March 2018.

25 *The Economic Times*, 14 March 2017.

26 *The Economic Times*, 19 March 2018.

27 Ibid.

28 Ibid.

29 *The Economic Times*, 14 January 2019.

30 Ibid.

31 *The Economic Times*, 20 March 2018.

32 Ibid.

33 Ibid.

34 Ibid.

35 Ibid.

36 *The Economic Times*, 20 June 2016.

37 Ibid.

38 Yoder, *Personnel Management and Industrial Relations*, 645–648.

39 See E. E. Lawler, 'Secrecy about Management Compensation: Are There Hidden Costs', *Organizational Behavior and Human Performance* 2, no. 2 (May 1967): 182–189.

40 For details, see Sharma, *Industrial Relations*, 102–149.

41 *The Economic Times*, 30 March 2017.

42 Ibid.

43 Ibid.

44 Ibid.

45 See Ministry of Labour & Employment, *Report of the National Commission on Labour* (New Delhi: Ministry of Labour & Employment, Government of India, 1969).

46 For a detailed study, see Sharma, *Industrial Relations*, 631–648.

47 https://tradingeconomics.com.

48 Ibid.

49 *The Times of India*, 28 December 2022.

50 *The Times of India*, 5 January 2023.

51 *The Times of India*, 28 December 2022.

52 Quoted in *The Times of India*, 28 December 2022.

53 *The Times of India*, 5 January 2022.

54 *The Times of India*, 29 November 2022.
55 *Hindustan Times*, 30 March 2017.
56 *The Economic Times*, 23 April 2018.
57 Ibid.
58 Ibid.
59 *Hindustan Times*, 25 May 2018.
60 Ibid.
61 Ibid.
62 *Hindustan Times*, 5 September 2018.
63 Ibid.
64 Ibid.
65 *New Labour Code for New India*, Ministry of Information and Broadcasting, Government of India, New Delhi, 2021, p. 0.
66 Ibid., 10–11.
67 *Hindustan Times*, 13 September 2016.
68 *Hindustan Times*, 6 July 2016.

4

CONTINGENT PAY

Pay for Performance, Competence, Skill—I

LEARNING OBJECTIVES

After studying this chapter, the reader should be able to:

1. Explain what is contingent pay as also its various types.
2. Explain what is performance-related pay (PRP) and what are its objectives.
3. Explain why PRP is criticized or what are its shortcomings.
4. Explain whether to introduce PRP or not.
5. Explain the prerequisites necessary for the introduction and success of PRP in an organization.
6. Explain how to develop a PRP programme/scheme.
7. Describe how to operate PRP and how to evaluate it periodically.
8. Define the term 'performance appraisal' and point out the objectives and importance of performance appraisal.
9. Differentiate between 'performance appraisal' and 'performance management'.
10. Enlist and describe the main methods of performance appraisal.
11. Describe the process of performance appraisal and problems involved in appraising performance.
12. Describe the concept of potential appraisal and also explain the methods of potential appraisal.

DOI: 10.4324/9781032626123-4

Contingent Pay

Introduction and Definition

Contingent pay aims at covering the additional financial rewards in addition to the base rate. According to Armstrong and Murlis,[1] contingent pay consists of payments related to individual performance, contribution, competence or skill or team or organizational performance.

Types of Contingent Pay

There are various types of contingent pay, but the main types of contingent pay as identified by Armstrong and Murlis[2] are as follows:

1. Individual PRP.
2. Competence-related pay.
3. SBP.
4. Shop-floor incentive and bonus schemes.
5. Sales force incentive schemes.
6. Executive incentive and bonus schemes.
7. Employee and executive share scheme.
8. Learn rewards.
9. Gainsharing.
10. Profit-sharing.
11. Profit-related pay.
12. Other cash payments.

The reasons for justification of or rationale for contingent pay are not far to seek. First, it is always fair that an employee should be paid as per his performance, contribution, competence or skill. This logic is based on the principle of 'equity'. Second, contingent pay is justified because it 'motivates' employees to work hard and produce more as they will be paid as per their performance, competence or skill. Next, PRP sends a clear message across the organization that the organization attaches great importance to performance, competence and skills, and further that certain aspects of performance, such as quality, teamwork and customer service, and certain values and work behaviours are of utmost significance for the organization.

While this chapter takes care of the first type of contingent pay, namely individual PRP and some of its relevant issues such as performance appraisal and potential appraisal, the next chapter deals, in brief, with the remaining types of contingent pay.

Performance-Related Pay

Despite negative reports from many research projects and opposition from many trade unions, performance pay is quite popular and continues to be a traditional constituent of the pay packet of (a) most sales personnel who get it in the form of commission based on their performance, (b) shop-floor employees who get it based on the quantum of their output, and (c) executives who get it normally in the form of bonus/profit-related pay/gainsharing/profit-sharing.

PRP links pay progression to a performance rating, which is usually conducted during a performance review though some organizations conduct it at a different time exclusively for PRP purposes.

Performance is usually applicable in the case of individuals though attention is also being paid to performance criteria related to teamwork.

Objectives

The objectives are as follows:

1. To motivate every employee to perform better and put his heart and soul into his job.
2. To attract and retain high-quality employees who are hard-working.
3. To make employees result and performance-oriented and change the work culture accordingly.
4. To reduce supervision.
5. To focus on the key performance issues.
6. To reduce the cost of production.
7. To help in raising the standard of living of employees.
8. To encourage teamwork, innovation and so on.
9. To reward employees according to their contribution.
10. To make obvious to the employees that the organization is genuinely concerned with output/performance.

Growth of PRP

Although PRP has not found favour with a good number of organizations, it is popular because PRP schemes impact the behaviour of high performers favourably. Besides, money is considered to be a powerful motivator and affects the work behaviour positively. In addition to this, paying people according to their contribution is considered to be fair play.

Why Is PRP Criticized?

1. It has often been observed that financial incentives are short lived and lose their momentum in the long run.

2. Since the additional payments as per PRP schemes are not very significant, they do not attract quite a good number of employees, especially those who are not hard-working or who are less confident.
3. In the urge to earn more, some employees work beyond their capacity, which may affect their health adversely.
4. Similarly, in order to earn more, employees care only for the quantum of their output and do not pay adequate attention to the quality of their product.
5. In the same way, some employees pay less attention towards reducing wastage and damage to the plant, machinery and equipment because their priority is to increase output.
6. It may also affect teamwork adversely.
7. In a good number of cases, it is not possible to measure individual performance objectively and accurately.

Despite limited impact of financial incentives, the fact remains that 'the achievement of a reward is a tangible means of recognition and can, therefore, provide for less direct but possibly longer-term motivation'.[3]

Whether to Introduce PRP or Not?

Keeping in view the pros and cons of PRP, its introduction everywhere cannot be recommended point-blank. There are many ifs and buts. Much depends on the objectives of the organization, cultural orientation of the organization, working environment of the organization and so on.

However, PRP may be deemed necessary in certain organizations because of market compulsions so as to secure an edge over their competitors. The very belief in the soundness of the contention that employees should be paid according to their contribution goes in favour of introducing PRP. It is a different story whether their belief proves true or not. However, the very introduction of PRP in an organization gives an obvious message to the employees that the organization attaches great importance to performance and, therefore, the employees are supposed to focus on their output.

Prerequisites Necessary for the Introduction
and Success of PRP in an Organization

The first requirement is that it should be ensured that PRP should not only fit the culture of the organization but also support it. It should also be able to act as a lever to change the culture as and when needed. Second, the top management should be firmly committed to PRP and be able to work with the processes of PRP. Besides, not only the line managers should be staunch supporters willing to own PRP, but the employees too should have a feeling that they will benefit if PRP is introduced. All the departments, especially the HR department, and management must have the confidence that they will make PRP work.

Third, the organization should be in a position to evolve methods of measuring performance fairly and consistently. The management, especially the HR department, should have a clear understanding of the language of behavioural competencies. Fourth, there should be a possibility of making the process of PRP an integral part of business planning. PRP should also have the support of the communication system of the organization. There should also be an efficient and effective process of performance management enabling the measurement and assessment of performance against the targets and standards prescribed. Possibilities for evolving effective guidelines on how pay should increase within the pay structure, already operational, should also be there. Above all, there should be adequate chances of having desired control over PRP so that it works within reasonable costs.

Fifth, the management should not only be capable of planning objectives appropriately in full agreement but also assessing levels of competence of personnel of the organization. The management should also be capable of measuring as well as rating the performance of the employees of the organization.

It is also necessary that the HR department of the organization should be competent enough to extend the guidance required and to provide necessary support besides making the desired resources available. The managers should be able to manage PRP in their departments on their own and should not depend much on the support of others, especially the HR department. It is equally important that managers should be effective in 'using the PRP as part of a total performance management process which will involve joint assessments and agreements of performance and individual development needs'.[4] It has also to be assessed that costs incurred on introducing PRP are just and capable of generating the desired returns in terms of increased output. It has also to be found out whether PRP will be instrumental in accelerating the overall performance of the organization concerned.

Armstrong and Murlis[5] have suggested the following factors to be taken into account when introducing PRP in an organization:

1. Matching the culture (i.e., successful PRP schemes need to match the culture and core values of the organization).
2. Linking PRP to the performance management process.
3. Balancing performance measures (i.e., a balanced mixture of both input and process factors [skills and competences] and output factors [performance and contribution]).
4. Flexibility (in the criteria of reward and the method of payment).
5. Teamwork (i.e., the significance of teamwork should be recognized in structuring the scheme, and also in designing critical success factors and performance indicators).
6. Avoiding short-termism (i.e., not to pay attention only to short-term results at the expense of more important long-term objectives).
7. Involvement in the design process (of the PRP schemes).
8. Getting the message across.

Thus, we see that there should be full scope for cost-effectiveness, Besides, the reward accruing should synchronize with the expectations of the employee concerned. It is also to be ensured that there exists a fair and effective mechanism for measuring performance and contribution made by the employees, and there is a link between performance and contribution of employees and subsequent reward to the employees.

Developing a PRP Scheme/Programme

PRP is not a magic wand that will resolve all the motivational and performance problems of an organization. Hence, no PRP programme should be introduced in haste as it is a very sensitive matter. The top management should be made fully aware of what PRP is capable of doing and what it is not. The key considerations explained in the foregoing paragraphs should be taken due care of before venturing into the launching of a PRP programme.

Although it is difficult to work out a rigid sequence of steps to be undertaken while developing a PRP programme, the sequence of activities being spelt out in the subsequent lines may prove quite useful and effective. First, the objectives of introducing a PRP development programme should be clearly spelt out, that is, why do we want to introduce a PRP programme? What is it that we are looking for out of such a programme? Second, we should find out whether the organization is ready for introducing a PRP programme. To answer this problem, we have to assess whether the culture of the organization is appropriate for introducing the PRP and in the same way whether PRP is appropriate to the culture of the organization. We should go ahead only if the answer to both questions is affirmative. The other questions to be answered in this respect may include: Are the attitudes of the employees and the management conducive for the initiation of the PRP programme, and further that whether there exist performance management and other relevant processes required for the effective working of PRP? It has also to be assessed whether the employees possess the required skills and resources. Again, it has also to be ascertained whether the costs involved in developing and operating the PRP programme will be able to generate enough additional performance.

The third step may involve taking a decision on whether to introduce PRP or not. For this, we will have to take into consideration all the issues discussed earlier under the head, 'whether to introduce PRP or not'. In case the answers to all such issues are conducive, we should move towards the fourth step, that is, identifying the objectives of PRP. A discussion in this regard has already been undertaken in the earlier paragraphs. The fifth step in the direction of developing PRP, which is vital for the success of the PRP programme, is involving the employees of the organization. They should be briefed about the intentions of the management and what the management intends to get out of such a programme. The suggestions put forward by the employees should be taken due care of. Then comes the sixth and a very important step, that is, designing the programme. This involves choosing the criteria for determining PRP onwards. In this regard, Armstrong and Murlis[6] have suggested the consideration of the use of an appropriate mixture of the following:

1. Input criteria.
2. Process criteria.
3. Output performance indicators.

Designing the PRP programme involves consideration of a lot of issues such as the availability of performance measures, which form of rating system to be used, how to ensure the fairness and consistency of ratings, whether PRP reviews should be separated in time from performance reviews, how the costs are going to be controlled, use of performance metrics, maintaining PRP, evaluation of the effectiveness of the PRP programme, policies on the rate of progression, limits to progression within the existing pay ranges and finalizing the PRP programme.

The seventh step involves briefing and training the line managers on the PRP programme. It involves making the line managers understand the programme, how it will function, what benefits are likely to accrue to them and the like.

The eighth step is concerned with the implementation of the PRP programme. In this direction, PRP should be started with a pilot scheme so that it may enable the management to understand the principles, advantages and problems. Only thereafter when necessary precautions have been taken, the PRP programme should be launched. In the initial stages, the PRP programme should be properly monitored so that the probable problems can be visualized and solutions worked out.

Ninth and the final step in developing a PRP scheme programme is the evaluation of the scheme, that is, whatever was intended of the PRP scheme could be achieved or not. Whether the scheme could be monitored consistently well? Were the persons entrusted with the implementation of the programme able to perform their job well? Who will be responsible for overcoming the problems and taking corrective steps? A detailed discussion in this direction is contained in the subsequent pages.

Operating PRP

As stated earlier, the most typical PRP system usually uses valuable progression within a pay range. The main operational features of the aforesaid system, according to Armstrong and Murlis,[7] may involve the following:

1. Basis characteristics.
2. Rating arrangements.
3. Size of increase.
4. Progression rates and limits.
5. Progression guidelines.
6. Use of performance metrics.
7. Control.

Evaluating PRP

At the end of the stipulated period, the PRP programme should be evaluated to know whether the desired outcomes could be obtained or not and then take corrective steps.

This can be achieved by finding out the extent to which the desired objectives of the PRP programme have been achieved. How many costs were incurred on the implementation of the PRP and what advantages could be obtained, that is, how much PRP could be effective in improving the performance of individuals, teams and organization as a whole. How do the organization personnel feel about the programme?

Whether the employees concerned feel that their expectations with regard to the quantum of reward have been met? Whether the rewards are linked to key and measurable areas of performance? Whether any modifications in the existing RPP programme are required? Whether the existing PRP programme should be allowed to continue as such or its alternatives should be identified? Such queries will go a long way in sustaining and improving the RPP programme developed and making it effective.

Performance Appraisal

Since in PRP, an individual or a team is paid as per his/its performance, contribution, competence or skill, it becomes essential to appraise the performance of the individual/team concerned so as to ensure that payments being made are justified. It is for this reason that performance appraisal comes into the picture at this juncture.

It is perhaps again for this reason that Edwin B. Flippo has rightly remarked,

> No firm has a choice as to whether or not it should appraise its personnel and their performance. Just as training must and does take place after hiring, it is inevitable that the performance of the hired personnel will be evaluated by someone at some time. The choice is one of the methods.[8]

The performance appraisal is also very important, for other reasons, to ensure that employees are being paid as per their actual contribution. Therefore, an employee's performance appraisal is essential on a continuing basis during the working life of an employee. Hence, here we are concerned with the periodic and systematic evaluation of employees' performance, which is usually carried out by the management in the case of its employees at all levels.

Meaning and Definition of Performance Appraisal

Appraisal is the evaluation of the worth and quality of merit. It is the evaluation of an employee's current and/or past performance and future capabilities. It is the evaluation or appraisal of the relative worth to the company of an employee's services on his job.

As a matter of fact, performance appraisal is a systematic, periodic and, so far as humanly possible, impartial rating of an employee's excellence in matters pertaining to his present job and to his potential for a better job.

Performance appraisal is a continuous activity. The management should plan it in a systematic and orderly manner. It must be conducted by trained and experienced experts. If organized and operated carefully, it eliminates the chances of personal prejudices and subjectivity in the appraisal. Systematic appraisals are instrumental in boosting the morale of the employees and also enabling them to know where they stand and whether they are being paid according to their contribution to the organization.

Performance Appraisal versus Performance Management

While 'performance management' is a process that consolidates goal settings, performance appraisal and development into a single, common system so as to ensure that the employee's performance is supporting the aims of the organization, 'performance appraisal' is just a part of performance management, which is a process of evaluating an employee's current and/or past performance vis-à-vis his performance standards.

Why Appraise Performance?

Dessler and Varkkey[9] have suggested four reasons in favour of appraising subordinates' performance: (a) most employers still base their pay and promotional decisions on the employees' appraisal, (b) performance appraisal plays an integral role in the employer's performance management, (c) performance appraisal lets the boss and the subordinate develop a plan for correcting any deficiency and (d) appraisal serves a useful career planning purpose.

Objectives of Performance Appraisal

Broadly speaking, there are twin objectives of performance appraisal, namely 'judgemental', that is, to judge or evaluate what the worker has done and what are his potentialities, and 'developmental', that is, keeping his performance and potentialities in view, formulate the plans for the development of the worker (see Figure 4.1).

However, broadly speaking, the objectives of performance appraisal are as follows:

1.   To measure the job performance of an employee, and thus help in the determination of PRP.
2.   To make the compensation plans more scientific and rational.

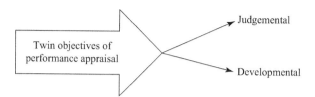

FIGURE 4.1   Objectives of Performance Appraisal

3. To identify an employee's potential for other work.
4. To identify the need and areas for further training and development of the employees so as to improve their performance.

Process of Performance Appraisal

Dessler and Varkkey[10] include three steps in the performance appraisal, namely (a) defining the job, (b) appraising performance and (c) providing feedback.

Establishing Evaluation Criteria

The dimensions of performance upon which an employee is evaluated are called the criteria of evaluation.[11] According to Ivancevich, an effective criterion of evaluation should possess the characteristics such as reliability, relevance, sensitivity and practicality.[12] Only then and then alone, the appraisal can be meaningful.

Appraisal Interview

In appraisal interviews, the supervisor and subordinates review the appraisal and chalk out plans to overcome deficiencies and reinforce strengths. The following types of appraisal interviews are more popular:

1. **Unsatisfactory–uncorrectable:** If the performance of the employee is unsatisfactory and the situation is uncorrectable, there is no point in formulating a future plan for him. Either his services can be terminated or tolerated for the time being.
2. **Unsatisfactory–correctable:** In such a case, a plan can be formulated for correcting the unsatisfactory performance.
3. **Satisfactory–not promotable:** In such a case, steps such as enlargement of job, appreciation and a few incentives can be undertaken so that the employee maintains his performance.
4. **Satisfactory–promotable:** In such a case, a specific action plan for the professional development of the employee concerned should be formulated keeping in view, of course, the career plans of the employee.

While conducting appraisal interviews, an all-out effort should be made to let the employee speak the most. He should be encouraged to tell more about himself. Open-ended questions by the interviewer can be of great use in this direction. Queries and conversations should be direct and specific, and not beating about the bush, for example, productivity records. The interviewer should also ensure that he does not get personal. For example, instead of comparing the employee's performance to that of other employees, it should be compared to the standards laid for the purpose. All the same, it should be ensured that at the end, the interviewee (appraisee) understands where he has gone wrong and how things will be better and within which time framework.

Appraisal Methods/Evaluation Techniques

When it comes to appraising the performance, there are two basic issues: (a) what to measure—usually speaking, it is the quantity, quality and timeliness of work. But all the same, it is also desirable to measure performance with respect to developing one's competence or accomplishing the targets, and (b) how to measure—there are several ways to evaluate employees' performance/methodologies. For convenience sake, these may be divided into three categories as shown in Figure 4.2.

Casual, Unsystematic and Often Haphazard Appraisal

It is an old and very common approach, but of late, it is being replaced by the 'systematic' and 'management by objective' approaches.

The casual appraisal is more common among small organizations. A casual appraisal does not evaluate all performances of the employees in the same manner, utilizing the same approach. As a result, ratings obtained of separate personnel are not comparable. This approach lays more emphasis on the evaluation of the employee's worth as a person. In this approach, there is always a scope for human bias and prejudice. Besides, in this system, appraisal is not made regularly after a fixed period.

Traditional and Highly Systematic Appraisal

Various studies have revealed that an increasing number of firms are opting for some formal types of appraisals. When formal programmes of appraisals are utilized, most organizations use one of the many traditional and systematic methods of appraisal. In a systematic appraisal, performance of all the employees of a particular category is evaluated in the same manner, utilizing the same approach so that the ratings obtained of separate personnel are comparable. The systematic appraisals are made at regular periodical intervals according to a predetermined

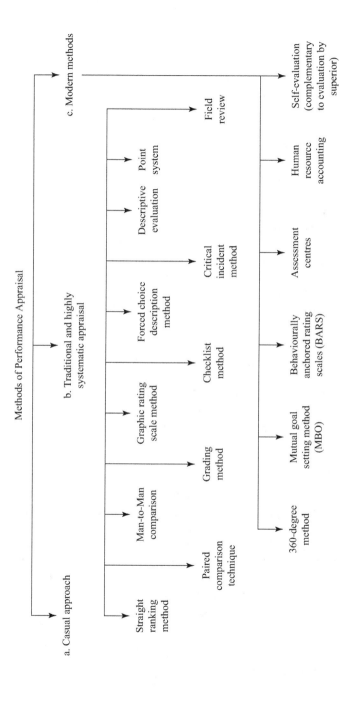

FIGURE 4.2   Methods of Performance Appraisal

plan. In a systematic appraisal, evaluation is made of 'what the person does' rather than 'what he is'.

Systematic performance appraisal is of great value as it provides very useful and well-in-time information needed for making decisions at the time of promotions, transfers, pay increases and so on. Besides, it also provides the information in a form that permits the making of comparisons because all personnel have been appraised in the same manner, utilizing the same approach.

There are various traditional performance appraisal systems used by different organizations.

The important ones are as follows:

Straight Ranking Method[13]

This is the simplest and oldest method of performance appraisal. Here, an employee is not treated separately from his job. One person is compared with all others for the purpose of placing them in simple rank order of their worth. In this way, all the employees are placed in order of their relative worth. Thus, this method separates the efficient from the inefficient. However, this method suffers from a number of inherent defects. First, it does not appear to be desirable to compare one person with another because different persons have different traits and qualities.

Second, this method simply tells us who is better than the other, but it does not indicate how much better he is than the other. Third, this method may be used only in the case of small organizations. If a company employs a large number of employees, it may not be possible to rank all of them in order of their worth. Fourth, this system is based on snap judgement and does not have any systematic procedure to determine the relative worth of an employee. Hence, in order to overcome the defects of this system, the paired comparison method has been developed.

Paired Comparison Technique

As per this method, each employee is compared with all other employees of the organization, one at a time. Suppose there are six employees in a particular firm. First, A's performance is compared with B's and a decision is taken as to whose performance is better. Then A is compared with C, D, E and F in order. Then, the next employee B will be compared with all other employees individually, and in the same way C, D, E and F will also be compared one by one with all other employees. Thus, in all, 15 decisions would be taken, involving only two employees in each decision. The number of decisions is determined by the following formula[14]

$$\text{Number of comparisons} = \frac{N(N-1)}{2}$$

where N equals the number of personnel to be compared. The result of these comparisons can be tabulated and in this way a rank can be created from the number of times each employee is found better.

This method of performance appraisal is also not practical in the case of big organizations where a large number of employees are engaged because in such cases, the number of judgements to be made becomes too large.

Man-to-Man Comparison

In this method, for appraisal, more variables are ascertained such as leadership, qualifications and faithfulness. After this, for each variable, a master scale is prepared in which for execution of each job, strata are maintained according to qualities. For that work, the most efficient person and the least efficient person are selected. These persons are the two ends of the scale. After that, at a medium point, an average person is selected. Later on, the two points are marked below and above the average. In this way, five points are ascertained. Comparing these points, a person's qualities are known. Thus, in this method, instead of comparing 'whole people' to 'whole people', personnel are compared to 'key persons', one factor at a time.

In performance appraisal, although this method is used to know the qualified person by the comparison of variables, the preparation of the master scale is a difficult problem.

Grading Method

In this method, everybody is grouped serially from the most to the least efficient for their every quality and is grouped as extraordinary, best, good, average, bad and worst (see Exhibit 4.1). These groups are also explained. These groups could be increased or decreased. Dr Kimball has put this in the following way in his book, *Principles of Industrial Organisation*.

Graphic Rating Scales Method

It is the simplest and most popular method for appraising performance. As per this technique, the rater is presented with a set of traits such as job knowledge, quantity, quality and initiative and is asked to rate employees on each of these traits. The number of traits rated may vary from a few to many. The rating can be in a series of boxes (as shown in Exhibit 4.2) or they can also be on a continuous scale of 0–9 or the like, and in the case of using a continuous scale, the rater places a check above descriptive words ranging from none to maximum. These ratings are then assigned points such as 'outstanding' may be assigned a score of 5 and 'unsatisfactory' a score of 0. The total score is then computed.

EXHIBIT 4.1 GRADING METHOD REPORT

Name of employee ....   Job Division ....
          Name of the evaluator ....

Merit	Extraordinary	Best	Good	Average	Below Average	Worst
1. Quantity of jobs						
2. Kind of job						
3. Problem-solving power						
4. Industry						
5. Cleverness						
6. Faithfulness						
7. Cooperation						
8. Leadership						
9. Health						

EXHIBIT 4.2 TYPICAL GRAPHIC RATING SCALE

Name of employee ....   Department ....

Date	Outstanding	Above Average	Average	Below Average	Unsatisfactory
Job knowledge: Clarity about the factors relevant to the job comments.	☐	☐	☐	☐	☐
Output: Quality of acceptable work under named conditions.	☐	☐	☐	☐	☐
Cooperation Willingness and ability to work with subordinates, peers and superiors' comments.	☐	☐	☐	☐	☐

Later on, in order to make the scale more effective, two modifications have been designed, namely (a) mixed standard scale in which the rater instead of just rating a trait such as 'job knowledge' is to tick mark one of the three statements given to describe that trait and (b) adding operational and benchmark statements to describe different levels of performance.[15]

Checklist Method

This is also known as the questionnaire method. In this method, a checklist is prepared in which several questions related to the performance of a particular job such as 'is equipment maintained by him (rate) in good condition?' 'Is he respectful to his superiors?' 'Does he listen sincerely to his subordinates?' and so on are included. The rater is simply to mark 'tick' against the column of 'yes' or 'no'. In other words, the rater simply reports the behaviour, and the evaluation of the 'reported behaviour' may be done by the HR department. This system has the possibility of partiality as the rater does the work by himself. Second, each department or work needs separate checklists as nature, character and responsibilities of different jobs have vast differences. Hence, it involves more work.

Forced Choice Description Method

This method reduces the chances of rater bias because the rater has to make a choice between the two descriptive statements seemingly of equal worth. Out of each pair, the rater has to select one statement which according to him is the most characteristic of the employee who is being rated. For example, the rater will have to make a choice out of the following two statements:

1. Can he be relied upon to any extent?
2. Maintains good relations with his subordinates.

Only one statement in each pair is correct in identifying the better performance, and this scoring key is kept secret, unknown to the rater. After the rater completes his assessment, he sends it to the HR department where it is compiled and the result is ready.

This is a simple method and is an improvement over the grading procedure. There is no partiality, but this method is not able to cast directions on the future development of the worker. At times, the evaluator has to take such decisions, which he does not prefer.

Selection of Critical Incident Method

This method is based on the assumption that there are certain key acts of behaviour which are responsible for the success of a job.

The supervisor–rater keeps on recording such acts/events that take place in the performance of the ratee's job. These acts/events are critical incidents. For example, the sales officer may keep on noting whether the salesman has been courteous to the customers or whether the salesman attends to telephone calls effectively and so on. All these acts may be considered critical incidents. Thereafter, all the collected critical incidents may be ranked in order of their importance or frequency or both. In this way, numerical weights can be obtained, thereby providing the basis for a rating score for the evaluation of the performance of the ratee. Thus, we find that in this method, the supervisor–rater has to be very vigilant, and very pertinent critical incidents have to be identified.

Descriptive Evaluation

In this method, the evaluator prepares a written report in relation to the execution of the job by the employee, containing details about the personality, merits, quantity and quality of work, and so on. The clarity and extensiveness of the report (description) play an important role in the effectiveness of evaluation.

Point System

In this method, for every unit of every work some points are specified. A manual or a scale is used in which all units' description points for evaluation and evaluation procedure are given. Generally, some units are determined as cleverness, responsibility, effort (mental or bodily) and job conditions. Each person's each merit is given the points from the maximum determined points. Afterwards, all the points are totalled, and it is the evaluation of that person.

Field Review Method

Under this method, the evaluator asks the supervisor questions about the workers working under him and gets his opinion and records it. These are signed by the supervisor and kept for future reference as a context.

Modern Methods of Performance Appraisal

Some of the modern methods of performance appraisal are as follows:

The 360-Degree Techniques

Meaning and process: The process of 360-degree feedback was originally developed by NASA to evaluate their space programmes. Now most 'Fortune 500' companies use 360-degree feedback with considerable success. Consultant, Peter Ward, introduced this technique at Tesco (UK). Some other major companies using this process in the United Kingdom include W. H. Smith, Forward Trust and so on, while in the United States of America, companies such as General

Motors, Mobil and Motorola fall in this category. In India, we can mention the names of some companies such as Reliance Industries Ltd, Godrej Soaps, Infosys and Wipro.

All this goes to illustrate that with its origins in the 1960s and the 1970s, this approach has a growing number of exponents and fans.

'Multi-rater feedback', 'all-round feedback', 'peer appraisal', 'upward appraisal', '180-degree appraisal', '360-degree appraisal', '400-degree appraisal', '540-degree appraisal' and so on are the names by which 360-degree feedback has been labelled, the reason being that all these terms represent different ways of describing the same thing. The variation in the numbers indicates the variation in the rater groups used. For example, while 180-degree feedback describes top–down and bottom–up feedback, 360-degree feedback includes feedback not only from the boss and the subordinates but also from peers and so on. The 540-degree feedback comprises feedback from almost all stakeholders even if they are from outside the organization. Thus, it is a process of systematic collection and feedback of performance data on an individual or group, derived from a number of stakeholders, in their performance. While the traditional performance appraisal involves only bosses assessing their staff, the 360-degree feedback is based on the concept that people other than bosses, who actually work with us, for example, subordinates, peers, customers, suppliers and so on, may also provide for more vital, accurate and useful insights into our strengths, weaknesses and scope for development.

It involves collecting responses through structured questionnaires about a manager from his bosses, peers and subordinates. The techniques span over several parameters: performance as well as behaviour, how effectively a manager handles his boss and his juniors, how clearly he communicates, how deftly he delegates and how abrasively he administers. Values, ethics, fairness, balance and courtesy, nothing is excluded from the ambit of appraisal, and neither crucially is the question of how inspired a manager's leadership is.

The questions are formulated so as to elicit one of the five responses to the subject's rating on a parameter: significant strength, strength, meets requirements, developments required and cannot rate. Normally, questions relating to behaviour are more effective than performance-related queries. The latter requires judgement, which can not only be difficult but also biased. By contrast, the former elicits reportage, which is simpler and more reliable.

Each manager is assessed by a minimum of 15 colleagues, at least two of them being his bosses, four of them peers and six of their subordinates. While immediate supervisors are best placed to evaluate performance parameters, peer judgement provides comparative and even competitive perspectives. And including juniors is crucial: many an apple of the boss's eye metamorphose into a brutal bully with subordinates, often hoarding responsibility rather than delegating it. The best 360-degree system polls customers too.

Crunched and graphed by a computer, the responses are presented collectively to the subject of the appraisal with specific comments being presented later. Bar chart for each parameter indicates what percentage of respondents in each category—boss, peer or subordinate—rated the subject. Then interpretations of what the findings are actually telling their subject follow. And finally, counselling sessions tackle ways to solve the specific problems and weaknesses identified by the 360-degree assessment.

In 360-degree feedback, the role of evaluation is shared, shifting the responsibilities from one individual to many, reducing the severity of any one person's shortcomings as an evaluator, including errors of leniency, personal bias, subjectivity and so on.

The 360-degree feedback reflects many directions from which information is provided on a set of pre-defined competencies. Feedback comes from many sources, and it provides a more balanced evaluation that is usually more acceptable as fair and objective. Peers and subordinates are regarded as credible feedback sources because they have a greater opportunity to observe the manager's behaviour than supervisors do. This hot new form of assessment, known as 360-degree feedback, involves having a manager rated by everyone above, alongside and below him.

Every organization wants to know everything about a man. That is why the 360-degree method should be on the top of the CEO's wish list and that is why the companies referred to above and some others are using this technique to find out home truths about their managers. Although deployed mostly as a fact-finding and self-correction technique, 360-degree feedback is also beginning to be used to design promotion and reward. It involves collecting responses through structured questionnaires about a manager from his bosses, peers and subordinates.

How does 360-degree feedback score over other forms of appraisals? Normal performance appraisal systems judge the outcome of a manager's efforts but ignore the road taken. They focus on achievements rather than the intrinsic qualities that a manager must have in order to lead. But these qualities are what the appraisal reveals. Remember, it will not tell your managers whether they have met their hard targets but will praise or warn them about their styles. 'It is like having a close look at yourself in the mirror'. How will your managers benefit?

They will learn which of their techniques hurt more than help, learn that his subordinates thought he was insecure and, therefore, did not delegate. For example, Godrej Group's CEO Adi Godrej was amazed to realize that his managers wanted him to curb his authoritarianism.

Communicated to your managers, their ratings will push the onus for changing directly on each of them. Says Adi Godrej, Managing Director, Godrej Soaps, the first manager in the company to take a 360-degree appraisal: 'It is a powerful tool for self-development, especially at the senior level, which is where one tends to get insulated'.

Naturally, your organization will gain from the improvements that heightened self-awareness generated among your employees, among the other benefits that will flow.

Now, the question arises: whom should you subject to a 360-degree assessment? Although applicable across functions and anywhere in the hierarchy, the tool is most effective when used from the top–down. The fact that the CEO and the top managers have been administered the test convinces everyone else to go through it too.

Of course, do not be surprised if the results are uneven. Individual reactions can vary, and not every manager in your company will accept and benefit from the findings. According to R.R. Likhite, group senior vice-president (HR department), Mafatlal Industries, 'such assessment may be applicable to some managers, but not all'.

Then the next question is that should your managers' pay cheques reflect their appraisals? Used to complement performance assessments, the feedback can be a useful compass for pointing out directions to compensation. But do not deploy it as the sole arbiter of reward. After all, performance in terms of meeting targets must be fundamental to evaluation. Manab Bose, Director (HR and corporate affairs, India region), General Electric, remarks, 'You cannot deduct five per cent of someone's increment because he trampled over two people to achieve his goals'. Alright, but how can you ignore, when determining increments, the leadership ratings the 360-degree test gives to your managers? To resolve the contradiction, Amex uses a target-based performance appraisal to award a performance bonus at the year's end and the leadership rating of the 360-degree assessment is linked to promotions and increments.

Thus, managers have to make the numbers for a one-off reward and earn high grades on the 360-degree test for permanent gains. Approves Mr. Bose of General Electric: 'The high performer who shoots past targets but is low on leadership skill will be forced to change.... Do not replace your current system with 360-degree assessment but do add it to your appraisal arsenal'.

Merits: 360-degree method is preferred because of the following:

1. It unfolds strengths and weaknesses in the managing style of the assessee.
2. It forces inflexible managers to initiate self-change.
3. It helps create a team spirit.
4. It reveals truths about organizational culture and ambience.
5. It promotes a democratic climate in the organization and thus makes it more open and transparent.
6. It focuses on customers and suppliers also.
7. It suits flatter structures.
8. It is useful because direct line managers may not know all the aspects of an individual's work.
9. The predictive ability of the 360-degree feedback approach highlights long-term success.

Demerits: The following are the demerits of the 360-degree method:

1. Colleagues' responses may be biased.
2. Ignores performance in the term of reaching goals.
3. Assesses usually deny the truth of negative feedback and, at times, feel threatened.

In order to make the whole exercise meaningful, individual employees and functional groups should be encouraged to take charge of getting feedback from their constituents on a regular basis. This ensures an organization-wide performance management system that is ongoing and decentralized.

Besides, traditional appraisal systems are organizational requirements. They establish role clarity, enable one to plan performance, establish abilities and facilitate performance monitoring, assessment and rewards. The 360-degree feedback, on the other hand, is an awareness-building, impact-assessing, reflective and developmental tool. Interest and enthusiasm are very critical for success. 360-degree feedback offers promise for the development of managers. The essential prerequisite is how the individuals react to the feedback and a desire to profit from it. One has to look at oneself critically with a desire to accept shortcomings and try to overcome them. It is like having a close look at yourself in the mirror.

Management by Objectives (MBO) Method

The second approach, namely MBO, has emerged as a reaction to the traditional management practices.

In the famous phrase of McGregor, traditional measurement asks the supervisor 'play God' and sit in judgement upon his fellowmen.[16] As against this, in the MBO programme, there is a special provision for mutual goal setting and appraisal of progress by both the appraiser and the appraisee(s). The philosophy of MBO is based on the behavioural value of fundamental trust in the goodness, capability and responsibility of human beings.[17]

Behaviourally Anchored Rating Scales (BARS)

This method combines elements of the traditional rating scales and critical incident methods. Using BARS, job behaviours from critical incidents—effective and ineffective behaviours—are described more objectively. In this method, services and expertise of those individuals are used who are familiar with a particular job to identify its major components so that they may rank and validate specific behaviours for each of the components.

Process for constructing BARS: The following are the main steps involved in constructing BARS:

1. Collect critical incidents.
2. Identify performance dimensions.
3. Reclassify incidents.
4. Assign scale values to the incidents.
5. Produce the final instrument.

Assessment Centres

It was the German Army that applied this method for the first time in 1930. It is a system where the assessment of several employees is done by various experts using various techniques discussed in this chapter and also other techniques such as travelling allowance (TA), role playing, case studies, in basket and simulation exercises.

In this approach, employees from different departments are brought together to spend two to three days and assigned the task which they would be expected to handle if promoted. The observers then rank the performances of every partici-pant in the order of merit.

HR Accounting

In it, we work out the cost and contribution of an employee. The cost of the employee is worked out based on money spent on him in terms of manpower planning, recruitment, selection, induction, placement, training and development, wages, benefits and so on. Employee's contribution is the monetary value of an employee's services. If the percentage of surplus contribution to the cost of the employee is more, it is considered positive.

Optimism Index (Oi 1.1)

As the test, 'Oi 1.1', recently developed by Padmakali Banerjee, is a measure of present performance also; it can be used as a tool in the process of performance appraisal.

Self-Evaluation as a Complement to Evaluation by Superiors

Performance appraisal by superiors has been the basis for promotion, training and development for long. However, subordinates are critical of the assessment done by their supervisors when they feel that the superiors do the following:

1. Judge them in terms of their own self-images; appraise low-level role perfor-mance by comparing it with their own high-level role performance.
2. Adopt different criteria of assessment in different cases.
3. Do not give them an opportunity to explain the causes of their failures or unsatisfactory performance.
4. Keep their assessment confidential so that it may not be challenged.
5. Evaluate them on the basis of certain incidents or happenings which may not be a regular feature of their behaviour or work situation.
6. Rely too much on past records and remarks by their predecessors.

Self-assessment by employees may be complementary to evaluation by the superiors. McGregor's theory is based on three important postulates: self-direction, self-control and self-appraisal. The average human being, according to him, learns under proper conditions not only to accept but also to seek responsibility. The capacity to exercise a relatively high degree of imagination, ingenuity and creativity in the solutions to organizational problems is widely distributed in the population. People should be given a degree of freedom to direct their own activities to achieve the goals that are set in consultation with them. This will satisfy their egoistic and self-fulfilment needs and will make them less dependent on their superiors and assume more responsibility. Thus, the philosophy of self-assessment is based on the theory of human behaviour. Self-assessment is successful when it ensures that the subordinates rate themselves in an objective manner without the fear of being victimized.

The proforma for self-assessment should be designed in such a manner that the employee may have the opportunity to tell about his performance on the job both in qualitative and quantitative terms, his interest and aptitude, his relations with superiors, colleagues and subordinates and so on. If the assessment is done in a free atmosphere, he will not hesitate in pointing out his weak points as well as his expectations from the bosses to guide him in improving his performance and potentialities.

Self-assessment may result in subordinates doing the following:

1. Accepting the organization's goals and working activity for the same.
2. Cooperating with superiors in implementing plans and policies.
3. Maintaining discipline, giving due respect to superiors and working in harmony with colleagues.
4. Improving product's efficiency by reducing waste.
5. Improving employee morale.

Some Practices of Performance Appraisal in Indian Industries/Feedback about Performance Reviews

So far as performance appraisal practices in Indian industries are concerned, there is no uniformity and different methods are being followed by different organizations. Some organizations have been shifting from one method of appraisal to another. For example, recently three top IT firms—Wipro, TCS and Infosys—have abandoned 'bell curve' appraisal and adopted a new one. The central idea behind this shift is that not only do these companies want individuals and their teams to win, but their victories should contribute to the success of the organization. To use a cricketing analogy, a century makes sense only if it helps the team win. For example, at Wipro, the new structure is different from the previous one, as the emphasis on the performances of individual client accounts has been placed on employees working closely as a team (see Exhibit 4.3). The new structure will further underscore the importance of collaborative behaviour and bring teams together to work towards a common goal. Simply put, the company is not looking for individual heroes; they want a team of champions. The new structure will be applicable to CEO, Abidali Neemuchwala, his direct reports and a level below them across verticals and horizontals.[18]

EXHIBIT 4.3 ABANDONING 'BELL CURVE' APPRAISAL SYSTEM

Under the previous incentive structure, Wipro rewarded employees and executives based on the performance of a particular client account and not that of a particular business vertical or horizontal.

Source: The Economic Times (20 June 2016).

EXHIBIT 4.4 TCS PLANS TO STRAIGHTEN OUT THE BELL CURVE WITH NEW APPRAISAL SYSTEM

There will be separate appraisal systems for IT and BPO employees and the company is even looking at how senior executives should be appraised. This is all being tested out now. Nothing firm has been decided...TCS is looking to adopt a system of *continuous feedback*, a goal that may be hard to achieve, given the number of employees.

Source: The Economic Times (25 November 2016).

As the Indian IT sector moves away from the relative ranking of its 30 lakh employees, most companies are bringing in new models. TCS is rebuilding its appraisal system from the ground up. To begin with, some employees will be assessed after a project is completed instead of half yearly (see Exhibit 4.4).

Another IT firm, namely TCS, is also rethinking how it appraises its employees. It plans to straighten out the 'bell curve' with a new appraisal system (see Exhibit 4.4).

Indian IT services companies and large firms across the world will keenly watch how TCS manages its appraisals, given the scales of the exercise. KPMG, Microsoft, Accenture and Deloitte have abandoned the bell curve, a performance rating system that requires managers to rank employees against each other.

It was reported earlier also that TCS was building a technology platform to manage the process of regular feedback. The TCS executive said that the company will modify an existing platform for IT appraisals, while for BPO employees it would be more of a social media system. Like the internal Knome platform TCS uses, the system for BPO employees would be more based on social media. The change in the performance review process has started for some TCS employees. Earlier in November 2016, a subset of employees received an email detailing the modifications. 'This is with reference to certain changes being introduced in the Performance Management System. Stage-wise timeline for appraisal process were discontinued last year to encourage continuous feedback', the email said. TCS is now moving towards having one appraisal cycle for the entire year applicable for all employees.[19]

EXHIBIT 4.5 INTRODUCTION OF NEW STRUCTURE CALLED ICOUNT AS PART OF INFOSYS PERFORMANCE APPRAISAL SYSTEM

As part of iCount, employees will be offered feedback and subjected to reviews throughout the year rather than just an annual appraisal. An Infosys spokeswoman said the company had leveraged 'design thinking' to enable the changes as part of Chief Executive Vishal Sikka's broader 'new and renew' strategy.

Source: The Economic Times (8 February 2016).

Instead of half-yearly appraisals, targeted employees would move to a project-end appraisal cycle—and the project could last anywhere from two months to one year. These appraisal cycle changes are in beta mode and will get rolled out to other employees over time. TCS is not the only IT company building new platforms, HCL Technologies has one called iSuccess and Wipro's is called Performance Next. Infosys launched its iCount platform this year and is building a mobile application to record real-time feedback.[20]

Infosys has put in place a new incentive structure called iCount as part of its performance appraisal system for employees that seeks to disproportionately reward individual performers based on specific targets, an overall that comes months after India's second-largest software exporters gave up the so-called bell curve assessment tool (see Exhibit 4.5).

Infosys had in September 2015 bid adieu to the bell curve method that fits categories of performers into a certain bracket depending on whether they have met their targets. Infosys has changed the way performance management is done, with a higher focus on individual performance rather than relative performance. It has moved away from the forced ranking curve and has given managers more flexibility and empowerment, while still retaining focus on maintaining a high-performance culture.[21]

IBM recently adopted the Checkpoint model, in which employees are put through four reviews in a year, instead of one annual appraisal.[22] Another global tech firm, Accenture has also ditched annual appraisals and bell curve system.[23] HCL Technologies is also in the process of overhauling existing appraisal systems.[24] Microsoft, GEC and HCL Technologies have also moved away from forced rating in some form or the other.

As progressive organizations move towards creating the future workplace, there is a decisive case for companies to give up the punitive system of forced ratings. One's accomplishments should stand for what one actually does, and not against what someone else does.

The removal of rating, however, does not mean that differentiation in recognition and reward will not happen. Organizations know that they need to differentiate and ensure higher rewards for performers. In a globally competitive environment, it is all about impact. Teams that make an impact deserve to be rewarded. Otherwise, organizations will be left with low-performing, complacent teams.

Some Recent Innovations in Appraisals: Setting the Standards

Some of the recent innovations in performance appraisal[25] are as follows:

Axis Bank

Axis has introduced the Enhancement Program. This is a 'second chance' where employees can volunteer to take on stretch targets to get a retrospective upgrade in their rating. With this, the bank has managed to do away with employees' negative perceptions around lower performance ratings while keeping the meritocracy intact.

Deloitte India

Deloitte India launched 'Reinventing Performance Management' (RPM)—a system that has no once-a-year review or 360-degree feedback tools. Instead, it is hallmarked by speed, agility, engagement and a one-size-fits-one approach. It also offers the staff real-time performance feedback from the team leader. RPM also gives instant feedback to professionals, 80 per cent of whom are millennials.

Godrej Industries

Godrej focuses not only on the achievement of specific goals (the 'what') but also how they are achieved with reference to Godrej capability factors, a set of key capabilities unique to the organization ('the how'). Technology is used to analyse the performance of each team member and enable managers to cascade their expectations to the team.

Sun Pharma

PRIDE was designed as the new global performance management process for Sun Pharma, enabling an employee to perform, reflect, invest, develop and excel. This process is tech-enabled and includes long-term professional development objectives, backed by a formal mid-year process.

Accenture

Accenture has shifted from an annual performance management process to perform achievement. The company has eliminated performance reviews, ratings and rankings. The focus is on setting priorities, growing strengths and creating rewarding career opportunities for the people to help them be more successful. This means the leaders spend more time coaching and talking with employees.

EXHIBIT 4.6 FOR WHOM THE BELL TOLLS

'You are rated "3: Meets expectations" this year.' With this one sentence, the world of a performer comes crashing down. She does not hear the rest of the feedback where the manager is telling her how diligent she is or how the organization values her work ethics. Emotions are on the boil.

At that moment, she is antagonized that her manager, super manager and the organization have all failed to acknowledge her hard work with: 'You have done well, but then ratings are a function of the bell curve. Others have done better than you.' That, in a nutshell, is the performance appraisal experience that 65 per cent of the employees go through at 75 per cent of the companies in corporate India—65 per cent because forced rating would usually put about 35 per cent employees above the rating of '3' or whatever similar system an organization has put in place.

Source: The Economic Times (2 May 2016).

EXHIBIT 4.7 REASONS FOR DISSATISFACTION ABOUT PERFORMANCE REVIEWS

- 8 per cent of the respondents said there was a mismatch in self-appraisal and manager's review.
- 45 per cent of the respondents said poor informal feedback.
- 22 per cent of the respondents said rating was bias.
- 25 per cent of the respondents said hypocrisy.

Source: The Economic Times (1 December 2015).

Performance appraisal in Indian industries leaves much to be desired. For example, in the bell curve system, a large number of employees get antagonized that their managers, super managers and the organization have all failed to acknowledge their hard work (see Exhibit 4.6).

As per Times Jobs survey performance reviews of over 1,000 employees, reported in the *Economic Times* on 1 December 2015, nearly 60 per cent of India Inc. employees are unhappy with their performance reviews. Poor informal feedback and hypocrisy are reasons for dissatisfaction with performance reviews (see Exhibit 4.7).

Most of the respondents held their immediate reporting manager responsible for performance review dissatisfaction (see Exhibit 4.8).

EXHIBIT 4.8 PERSONS PRIMARILY RESPONSIBLE FOR PERFORMANCE REVIEW DISSATISFACTION

- 12 per cent of the respondents held HR responsible for performance review dissatisfaction.
- 86 per cent of the respondents held immediate/reporting manager responsible for performance review dissatisfaction.
- 2 per cent of the respondents held the CEO responsible for performance review dissatisfaction.

Source: The Economic Times (1 December 2015).

EXHIBIT 4.9 EFFECTS OF BAD PERFORMANCE REVIEW ON PRODUCTIVITY AT WORK

- 40 per cent of the respondents said it kills the motivation to work.
- 33 per cent of the respondents said it has a distracting effect.
- 20 per cent of the respondents said it hampers productivity but is temporary.
- 7 per cent of the respondents said it did not hamper productivity.

Source: The Economic Times (1 December 2015).

The survey referred to above also revealed bad performance review on productivity at work (see Exhibit 4.9).

So far as satisfaction on performance reviews is concerned, the survey under discussion revealed that while 42 per cent of the respondents were happy, 58 per cent were not happy with the way they were reviewed (for more details, see Exhibit 4.10).

As far as qualities of an ideal performance review process are concerned, the survey revealed that 34 per cent of the respondents cited fairness and transparency as the most important qualities of an ideal performance review (for more details, see Exhibit 4.11).

PwC dropped the bell curve evaluation for its 12,000 employees[26] in India earlier in 2015. At Persistent, performance is assessed objectively with the help of clear goals and measurable key result areas.

A forced relative ranking like bell curve is yesterday's approach. It's antiquated and small thinking. If the goals are measureable and aligned with the organisation's goals then it is good for us if talent meets the 'Goals' because that means the organisation meets its 'Goals'.[27]

EXHIBIT 4.10 SATISFACTION ON PERFORMANCE REVIEWS

- 42 per cent of the respondents said they were happy with the way they were reviewed.
- 58 per cent of the respondents said they were not happy with the way they were reviewed.
- 90 per cent of the staff in IT/telecom and internet/dotcom cos said they were not happy.
- 85 per cent of the employees in manufacturing said they were not happy.
- 90 per cent of the employees in automobile and retail said they were happy.
- 74 per cent of the employees in metros said they were not satisfied.
- 58 per cent of the employees from tier I and II locations said they were not satisfied.

Source: The Economic Times (1 December 2015).

EXHIBIT 4.11 QUALITIES OF AN IDEAL PERFORMANCE REVIEW PROCESS

- 34 per cent of the respondents cited fairness and transparency.
- 32 per cent of the respondents said a lack of bias.
- 20 per cent of the respondents said feedback was shared regularly to update on performance hiccups.
- 20 per cent of the respondents said a bottom-up approach to appraisals.

Source: The Economic Times (1 December 2015).

EXHIBIT 4.12 SURPRISE APPRAISALS: IT COULD HAPPEN TO YOU ANYTIME ...

Working hard just ahead of the appraisal season may not be enough. Be prepared for *surprise appraisals* throughout the year. Many companies such as *KPMG, RPG Enterprises* and *BookMyShow*, and technology giants such as *HCL Infosystems* and *IBM* have begun a system of instant appraisals.

Source: For more details, see *Hindustan Times* (15 August 2016).

Surprise Appraisals

Today, many organizations such as BookMyShow, KPMG, RPG Enterprises, IBM and HCL Infosystems have initiated a system of instant appraisals (see Exhibit 4.12).

The new assessment styles have also turned informal. While some companies have turned to quick, app-based appraisals, some of them do it over a cup of coffee. For example, KPMG India now allows managers to catch up with employees and have a chat on their performance as and when required. 'The benefit is immediate feedback and guidance, rather than delayed post-mortem'. It may be recalled that in appraisals, activities that one can recall from the last few months often tend to take precedence. The appraiser may not be able to attribute certain accomplishments to the defined metrics, thus throwing a different result.[28]

There are also some other examples of instant appraisals. For example, HCL Infosystems has introduced a weekly evaluation programme that uses a mobile-enabled platform to assess employees. The idea is to fill the binary responses to a set of short and crisp questions in the app; there is no appraisal form. The focus is on self-assessment for employees and course correction, wherever required, on a weekly basis. Everything is now instant, then why wait for a year to fix loopholes. Another example is BookMyShow which has a system of weekly appraisals, every Friday. Managers get a reminder SMS that their team needs to be rated.

IBM too uses a mobile app to assess employees. The app, ACE, is used for instant feedback on employees. However, headhunters confess that annual performance sessions still have relevance. According to KPMG, changes are taking place.

Of course, success is heavily dependent on the maturity of the organization. A wrong sense could lead to the entire people's strategy going astray.[29]

Introducing an Executive Performance Appraisal Programme

Performance appraisal programme has evolved as a valuable tool of HR management because it offers a number of advantages to the employees as well as to the management. But caution is essential in the use and introduction of this technique.

The following care or prerequisites should be observed before introducing an effective performance appraisal programme:

1. **Analysis of jobs and responsibilities:** The first step of performance appraisal is the assessment of a person's jobs and responsibilities. For reaching the extracts of rights and responsibilities, one should go through the details of jobs first.
2. **Ascertainment of the standard of job execution:** While ascertaining the standard, employees and supervisors should be consulted. Besides, one should study the evaluation programmes of other industries concerned also, taking into consideration special facts and features of those programmes.
3. **To look on job execution:** Evaluators must be fully trained for this purpose. Then alone, he can rightly evaluate the person.
4. **Guess of ability:** After preparing different statements of job descriptions and so on, necessary information should be obtained about the persons so that their measure of ability by any one method may be done and their future progress may be estimated.
5. **Labour management discussions:** After this, there may be discussions with employees and supervisors, and clarification on the evaluation strata may be given. On the basis of filled reports on occasions, a supervisor guides and trains the personnel.

EXHIBIT 4.13 ROLE OF TECHNOLOGY IN PERFORMANCE APPRAISAL

The most common cliché is 'performance appraisal is dead'. What it means is that the annual performance appraisal is dead and most organizations today are adopting regular, real-time, anecdotal and casual feedback. Just as young people do not write emails any more but use WhatsApp, similarly we do not have to write a long performance appraisal at the end of the year.

Source: The Economic Times (3 February 2017).

---

6. **Formulation of scheme of the development of employees:** Supervisor prepares the evaluation report of work of a subordinate employee. Supervisor submits this report to the report committee, and the committee reviews and accepts it. Supervisor or higher official on the basis of that evaluation talks to the employee in private. Afterwards, both higher officials and supervisors jointly plan the scheme for job amendments of the employee, if needed.

7. **Review of the progress:** At times, progress is subject to review and evaluation. Employees should be reviewed necessarily for the job execution and also for the objectives he is supposed to accomplish.
8. **Technologies in the service of performance appraisal:** Today, technology plays the most crucial role in providing the platform to have fast and quick informal communication needed for performance appraisal, and the organizations are no longer required to write a long performance appraisal at the end of the year (see Exhibit 4.13).

As a matter of fact, a great appraisal requires not only consistent performance round the year but also playing with your strengths and avoiding some pitfalls. Varuni Khosla finds out the following five ways to work towards a stellar performance appraisal:

1. Focus on outcomes.
2. Be data-driven.
3. Ownership of outcomes.
4. Regular feedback.
5. Be a team player.

Today more and more companies are moving to real-time performance appraisal and that is why in their system everything is shareable and real time. And technology plays the most crucial role in providing the platform to have fast, quick and informal communication.

Shedding the Tag of Poor Performance

Nobody wants to be seen as a poor performer. There is always a reason why you are being perceived that way, and it is your job to find out the reason. There are five ways to shed the tag of poor performer (see Exhibit 4.14).

EXHIBIT 4.14 SHED TAG OF POOR PERFORMER

1. Find the root cause.
2. Seek feedback.
3. Take initiative and deliver.
4. Work with high performers.
5. Take small steps.

Source: The Economic Times (16 December 2016).

With regard to the first step, namely 'find the root cause', Swapnil Kamat, founder, Work Better Training, says that the first step towards shedding the tag is to dig deep to find out where the poor performance stems from. Is it a lack of skill to do the job or is it a lack of motivation to perform? Once you know and accept why you are underperforming, it becomes relatively easy to take corrective action.

So far as 'seek feedback' is concerned, according to Vikramjit Singh, president, Lemon Tree Hotels, it involves seeking constant 360-degree feedback to understand your shortcomings and work on them. Analyzing feedback in a positive manner will help you grow professionally and personally. Take criticism constructively and learn from past mistakes.

Regarding 'take initiative and deliver', Kamat says that if it is the lack of ability or skill, you must take the initiative to train yourself on the particular skill you lack. Have an honest conversation with your manager and let her/him know that you need training to improve your skills if that is what you are lacking. When an employee is proactive, managers are more than happy to help. Once you have been trained, apply your learning to the task at hand. Delivering consistently helps you come out of the shadow of being a poor performer.

As far as 'work with high performance' is concerned, Vikramjit Singh says that while working in teams or on group projects, seek to work with high-performing team members or those whose work has been responded to positively in the past. This will help you learn from their experiences as well as showcase your work in a positive light.

Coming finally to 'take small steps', Kamat says that the label of a poor performer comes when you have not been delivering over a period of time. It is not easy to get rid of it. However, the quickest way of doing so is to perform well at smaller tasks that are more short term in nature. A number of such small wins will help you be known as a good performer. When you become consistent, it leads to a change in how people see you.[30]

Advantages or Utility of Performance Appraisal

Performance appraisal programme is an important instrument of HRM. Its main advantages are as follows:

1. Helpful in determining PRP.
2. Helpful in making compensation plan more scientific and rational.
3. In the development of personnel.
4. In making mutual comparison.
5. In maintaining high morale.
6. Helpful to supervisor.
7. Helpful in proper placement.

8. Useful for management.
9. Other advantages.

Constraints of Appraisal Systems

Performance appraisals, although very widely used, have well-recognized short-comings and limitations. Even when the process emphasizes appraisal rather than counselling, it is far from universally satisfactory.

There are certain barriers which work against the effectiveness of the appraisal system. The identification of these barriers is necessary to minimize their impact on the appraisal programmes. These barriers are as follows:

1. **Faulty assumptions:** Because of the faulty assumptions of the parties concerned, the superior and his subordinates in the appraisal system, it does not work properly or effectively. These assumptions work against an appraisal system in the following manner:
    a. The assumption that managers naturally wish to make fair and accurate appraisals of subordinates is untenable. It is found that both supervisors and subordinates show tendencies to avoid formal appraisal processes.
    b. Another faulty assumption is that managers take a particular appraisal system as perfect and feel that once they have launched a programme, then it would continue forever. They expect too much from it and rely too much on it. It should be recognized that no system can provide perfect, absolutely defensible appraisals devoid of subjectivity.
    c. Managers sometimes assume that personal opinion is better than appraisal, and they find little use of systematic appraisal and review procedures. However, this 'management by instinct' assumption is not valid and leads to bias, subjectivity and distorted decisions based on partial or inaccurate evidence.
    d. Managers' assumptions that employees want to know frankly where they stand and what their superiors think about them are not valid. In fact, subordinates resist being appraised, and their reaction against appraisal has often been intense.
2. **Psychological blocks:** The value of any tool, including performance appraisal, lies largely on the skills of the user. Therefore, the utility of performance appraisal depends on the psychological characteristics of managers, no matter what method is used. There are several psychological blocks that work against the effectiveness of an appraisal system. These are manager's feeling of insecurity, appraisal as an extra burden, being excessively modest to treat their subordinates' failure as their deficiency, disliking of resentment by subordinates, disliking of communicating poor performance to subordinates and so on. Because of these psychological barriers, managers do not tend to become

impartial or objective in evaluating their subordinates, thereby defeating the basic purpose of appraisal.

3. **In avoiding technical pitfalls:** The design of performance appraisal forms has received detailed attention from psychologists, but the problem of adequate criteria still exists. At best, appraisal methods are subjective and do not measure performance in any but in the most general sense. The main technical difficulties in appraisal fall into two categories: the criterion problem and distortions that reduce the validity of results.

   a. **Criterion problem:** A criterion is the standard of performance the manager desires of his subordinates and against which he compares their actual performance. This is the weakest point in the appraisal procedure. Criteria are hard to be defined in measurable or even objective terms. Ambiguity, vagueness and generality of criteria are difficult hurdles for any process to overcome. Traits too present ambiguity. A particular trait is hard to be defined and variations of interpretation easily occur among different managers using them.

   b. **Distortions:** Distortions occur in the form of biases and errors in making the evaluation. Such distortions may be introduced by the evaluator consciously or unconsciously. An appraisal system has the following possible distortions:

      i. **Halo effect:** This distortion exists where the rater is influenced by the ratee's one or two outstandingly good or bad performances and he evaluates the entire performance accordingly. Another type of halo effect occurs where the rater's judgement is influenced by the team or informal group with which a subordinate has associated himself. If the group is not well-liked by the rater, his attitude may affect the rating of the individuals, apart from the actual performance.

      ii. **Central tendency:** This error occurs when the rater marks all or almost all his personnel as average. He fails to discriminate between superior and inferior persons. This may arise from the rater's lack of knowledge of the individuals he is rating, or from haste, indifference or carelessness.

      iii. **Constant errors:** There are easy raters and tough raters in all phases of life. Some raters habitually rate everyone high; others tend to rate low. Some rate on potential rather than on recently observed performance. In such a situation, the results of the two raters are hardly comparable.

      iv. **Rater's liking and disliking:** Managers, being human, have a strong liking for people, particularly close associates. The rating is influenced by personal factors and emotions, and raters may weigh personality traits more heavily than they realize. Raters tend to give high ratings to persons whom they like and low ratings to whom they dislike.

Overcoming the Obstacles

Systematic performance appraisal is a measurement process and as such must be reliable which means that it must be accurate and consistent. Two main obstacles that come in the way of a reliable appraisal system are technical characteristics of the system itself and the abilities of the appraiser to exercise objective judgement and apply the tools provided. Taking appropriate actions in this direction may reduce the impact of these obstacles if not altogether eliminate them. The following measures may be taken:

1. The reliability of a rating system can be obtained by comparing the rating of two individuals for the same person. It can also be obtained by comparing the supervisor's present rating to another rating in future.
2. The appraisal system can be designed to help in minimizing undesirable effects. The system should focus on objective analysis of performance in terms of specific events, accomplishments or failures. The raters may be required to give their ratings through as much continuous and close personal observation as possible.
3. The rating must be made by the immediate superiors. However, a staff department can assume the responsibility of monitoring the system. Though the staff department cannot change any ratings, it can point out inconsistencies to the rater such as harshness, leniency and general tendency.
4. The rating should be reviewed with the ratee. It helps him to know where he stands, what he is expected to do, what are his strengths and weaknesses, and what further actions he should take. This not only puts subordinates in a position to improve performance; it also minimizes their resistance to appraisal if a proper atmosphere has been created.
5. The most important factor in an effective appraisal system is the supportive management philosophy. Without an appropriate basic philosophy to generate the continuous support of all the managers, the appraisal system cannot succeed. According to Myers, a goal-oriented climate in the organization proves to be more favourable for effective performance appraisal.

How to Give Negative Feedback to Employees?

Feedback at work is important for an individual's development. However, some people are oversensitive to negative feedback, which makes it crucial for managers and leaders to understand how to convey it. Exhibit 4.15 shows some ways to convey it.

EXHIBIT 4.15 WAYS TO CONVEY NEGATIVE FEEDBACK

Following are some of the ways to convey negative feedback:

1. Be objective.
2. Combine negative and positive.
3. Importance of feedback.
4. Choose words carefully.
5. Give feedback in private.

Source: The Economic Times (9 December 2016).

So far as 'be objective' is concerned, it is necessary to ensure that the person receiving the feedback knows that the feedback is not a personal vendetta. According to Sudhir Dhar, director HR, Motilal Oswal Financial Services, this kind of fundamental attribution error has the employee linking the negative feedback to the person giving it. So, if you ask someone reporting to you the reason for being late, she/he might interpret that you are a control freak. Sadly, nearly all the time, the attribution strains the relationship between the two parties.

Coming to 'combine negative and positive', according to Swapnil Kamat, founder of Work

Better Training, the ideal way of giving feedback to someone who is extremely emotional is to go for the sandwich method. Here, you sandwich the negative feedback between two layers of positive feedback. This helps in softening the impact of the negative feedback. By starting and ending in positive words, you ensure that the negative feedback has the right impact.

Regarding 'importance of feedback', according to Kamat, one should begin by highlighting the importance of feedback—both positive and negative—in a professional's life. You could then follow that up with an example of how constructive feedback has helped you or someone you know or the said employee knows, positively and made that person a better professional. While doing this, always make sure that your tone is calm and composed, and like that of a mentor, rather than a rude, condescending or angry one.

Coming to 'choose words carefully', Kamat is of the opinion that rather than telling someone outright that they are bad at something, it is better when you word it in a less harsh manner, and also provide suggestions and solutions to help them get better at what they are currently bad at. According to Sudhir Dhar, sometimes, the most innocuous of sentences is perceived in a way which makes it seem threatening and derogatory. The key is to make the employee feel safe. Only when she/he feels safe, would they be in a state of mind to understand and appreciate what you are saying.[31]

Getting over the Fear of Negative Feedback

According to the product development manager, Work Better Training, when it comes to preparing oneself for mid-year, annual or quarterly feedback, receptivity generally varies. However, instead of worrying, you should learn to get over your fears, and only you can help yourself (for details, see Exhibit 4.16).

EXHIBIT 4.16 GETTING OVER THE FEAR OF NEGATIVE FEEDBACK

1. Think of it as an opportunity.
2. Trust the person giving you feedback.
3. Eliminate negative thoughts.
4. Acknowledge and admit where you went wrong.
5. Make following-up a habit.

Source: Hindustan Times (27 December 2016).

While preparing for the mid-year/annual/quarterly feedback, receptivity generally varies. For example, some get cold feet, sweaty palms and creases on their forehead, thanks to stress and fear, while others look forward to it. If you fall in the former, then it is apparent that your fear stems from the fear of being criticized and corrected. But then it is important to understand that regardless of whether it is positive or negative feedback, it helps you grow. You will learn from your mistakes and be guided to perform better. Worrying has not done anyone any good. You need to learn to get over your fears (see Exhibit 4.16), and only you can help yourself.

As far as 'thinking of negative feedback as an opportunity' is concerned, you should stop thinking of review sessions as a personal attack on your potential. It will only hurt you if you are unwilling to hear it or are reluctant to grow. Instead, look at it as an opportunity to get your acts together. If you have made a mistake, learn from it instead of brooding over it and assuming that the world is plotting a plan against you to stop you from succeeding. Coming to 'trust the person giving you feedback', you should know that whether it is the first time or the tenth time, you are being reviewed, you have to trust the reviewer and the feedback being given to you. Should you have any concerns, raise them. Reframe their statements to make sure you have got exactly what they mean. Regarding 'eliminating negative thoughts', why should you waste time dwelling on thoughts of being shamed during the meeting? Why imagine? Why presume? Why fear? You know the amount of hard work you have put in and that if you have done it right, you will be praised for it, and if not, then you probably do deserve an appropriate response. Again, coming to 'acknowledge and admit where you went wrong', it may be pointed out that when discussing work-related scenarios where you have erred, own up to where you went wrong and seek advice on what you can do to avoid a similar situation in the future. So far as 'making following-up a habit' is concerned, once you have received feedback, work on ways to improve your action points and ask your manager's opinion on how you are faring.[32] Thus, negative feedback is an opportunity to get your acts together.

As a matter of fact, an average performer needs to know what exactly went wrong and the strengths which he could capitalize on. We are so focused on dishing out programmes for star performers that we need to have suitable interventions in place to take care of average performers who are in a true sense the backbone of the system. They should receive regular feedback all through the year to help them take corrective steps in time. This increases their motivation levels to push themselves.

It is also important to let the individual do a self-evaluation and introspect. Tools like 360-degree feedback help the individual understand how he is perceived from different perspectives—his managers, peers, subordinates and even customers.[33]

Many times people may not be even aware that their performance is not at par and when the year-end performance review happens, this comes to them as a surprise. That is why it is very important to give timely feedback to employees on their performance. At Persistent, there is a continuous performance feedback process where the focus is on frequent interactions between line managers and their troops to discuss goals and performance. This helps employees in getting feedback in real time. Employees are offered opportunities to learn new skills so they remain fresh and challenged.[34]

Organizations that trust each employee definitely stand to gain. It has been often seen that an average talent improves its performance considerably after appraisals. Transparency, meritocracy and clarity of role are the three most important factors that can boost the employee's performance. Identifying the gaps in employee performance, addressing these by providing the right learning platforms, and undertaking coaching and mentoring sessions to sustain their performance are also critical.

It is important that organizations keep communicating with their people. There should be transparency regarding employee role, their career growth, organizational performance and how he or she performs.[35]

Should Appraisals Be Done Away With?

Though lots of things have been said about the ineffectiveness of appraisal and many research studies also corroborate this contention, the fact remains that it is not practical to do away with appraisals. You cannot drive everybody with the same rod (see Exhibit 4.17).

It is no surprise that companies such as IBM and Microsoft have decided to round-file the practice as ineffective in some countries.

A report by researchers from the London School of Economics and Political Science, the University of Toulouse and the Warwick Business School says that most evaluators were unaware of the real policies they used to write evaluations. When asked to rank the factors they used to evaluate employees, 'their answers were at variance with their actual judgments' the research said. Other studies have found that negative reviews do not necessarily encourage performance improvement as much as they generate ill will and make workers less likely to strive to be better and more likely to leave the organization.[36]

Surprisingly, a substantial majority of appraisees feel that bosses are not serious enough regarding the process and that performance appraisal does not reflect their work truly (see Exhibit 4.18).

EXHIBIT 4.17 PERFORMANCE REVIEWS ARE NOT LIKED MUCH

It is no secret that the annual employee evaluation drill is dreaded and disliked, depending more on the evaluator than the employee being assessed.

It is not just employees who wish there are no reviews. Most assessment administrators, who give feedback throughout the year, also rue the time that formal appraisals take. And there is not much evidence that formal performance reviews actually improve the performance.

Source: For more details, see *Hindustan Times* (15 March 2016).

EXHIBIT 4.18 PERFORMANCE APPRAISAL DO NOT IMPACT EMPLOYEE PRODUCTIVITY: SURVEY

In a survey of nearly 1,050 working professionals by TimesJobs on performance appraisals, 70 per cent of the respondents said that their bosses are not serious enough regarding the process and 65 per cent feel it is not a true reflection of their work.

Source: The Economic Times (11 April 2017).

Not only this, but they also revealed that 90 per cent of the respondents feel that performance appraisal does not have any impact on employee productivity. Five per cent said that it lowers productivity. Regarding the impact of performance appraisal on employee engagement and retention, 80 per cent said that employee engagement and retention are affected by performance appraisal.[37]

Besides, employees want and need feedback regarding how they are doing and appraisal provides an opportunity to give them that feedback. What is really needed is a fair and just appraisal system, which can be effective and yield results in today's quality-oriented and team-oriented scenario. In this regard, the total quality management (TQM) approach can play an important role.

Potential Appraisal

Meaning, Need and Importance of Potential Appraisal

Of late, in addition to performance appraisal, more and more companies are moving towards conducting potential appraisal and keeping it also into consideration while working out their pay. Some of the renowned organizations that have started stressing on potential appraisal include GlaxoSmithKline, Philips India, Cadbury India, Mafatlal Industries, Pfizer, Procter & Gamble, Sandoz, National Organic Chemical Industries and so on. Measurement of potential is a highly challenging job because people are like icebergs. What we see above the surface (i.e., performance) is only a small part. A large part of the attributes (i.e., potential) needed to perform excellently in a future job is not immediately visible. It is hidden below the surface.

One has to exert a lot to uncover the iceberg, but that is a must if the organization is to survive because people have to be prepared to take up higher responsibility.

According to Dr Moorthy K. Uppaluri, managing director and CEO, Randstad India, performance and potential are typically the two most critical factors that are considered to differentiate employees. However, what differentiates an average employee from a talented one is the extent to which the latter is high on potential as well as on performance compared to the former.[38]

Usually, the various parameters that are considered by organizations while identifying talent with potential are commitment, drive, ability to influence people, competency levels, willingness to learn and be a strong team player, and aspiration to take on higher responsibilities. These are usually unique characteristics that are considered to be game-changers for the organization.[39]

According to Sameer Bendre, Chief People Officer, as a policy at Persistent Systems, talent is defined not just based on past performance but along with the potential that the talent can contribute towards the organization's overall growth.[40]

It is perhaps because of the increasing importance of potential appraisal that a large number of companies have redesigned or are in the process of redesigning their systems, that is, to shift from simple performance-oriented appraisal to a potential-cum-performance-based appraisal system.

Methods of Potential Appraisal

Some of the popular methods/models of potential appraisal being used by big organizations are as follows:

Philips Hi-Lo Matrix

In it, a 2 x 2 matrix is used to evaluate performance and potential in a single process as depicted in Figure 4.3

It is evident from Figure 4.3 that the low potential–low performance employees are considered question marks. If they fail to bring about the desired improvements in their performance, the organization moves towards a planned separation of such employees. In the next quadrant of high potential–low performance come the problem children. Such employees require close monitoring and need a new scenario for work as a strategy so as to tap their full potential. The third quadrant of high potential–high performance pertains to 'star performers' who need to be engaged with complex assignments and groomed for top positions in the organization. The fourth quadrant of low potential–high performance relates to employees called 'solid citizens'. Such employees have high skills but low potential to go beyond their current jobs.

Philips NV Holland Model

This system includes a 5-point scale ranging from excellent to insufficient and provides for evaluation of employees on the following four qualities:

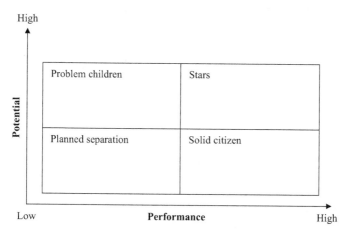

FIGURE 4.3   The Philips Model

1. Conceptual effectiveness.
2. Operational effectiveness.
3. Interpersonal effectiveness.
4. Achievement motivation.

The employee is also assessed by the management development team. Efforts are also made to identify star track career development indicating the highest level they can reach and then forecasts are made for 5–10 years or even beyond that.

Psychometric Tests

Through such tests, which have been developed mostly abroad, the organizations try to capture the abilities of the employees on several fronts such as aptitude, logic, deduction and inference. These tests, for example, are conducted at GlaxoSmithKline where potential appraisal is a prerequisite to succession planning. At GlaxoSmithKline, there is also a provision in the performance appraisal form for assessment of an individual's potential vis-à-vis attributes such as initiative, attitude, commitment, accountability, ethics, leadership, judgement and drive by the superior of the employees. In addition to above, some other exercises are also carried out to identify the true potential of the employees.

Review Appraisal

Through such appraisal, which is carried out by the immediate supervisors and departmental heads, insights are obtained into the potential of the employee. This method, for example, has been used at Cadbury since 1993. The review process evaluates the potential for growth and determines the action plans for career development. Then, efforts are made to rate the employee on six generic competencies, namely job knowledge, thinking clarity, goal setting and planning, relationships, leadership and innovation. These competencies are rated on a 5-point scale.

There are also some other methods of potential appraisal, which are generally modified by the user companies to suit their requirements.

Best Practices of Potential Appraisal

The following are the best practices of potential appraisal being used by some organizations:

1. Ensuring to distinguish reward for potential from reward for past performance.
2. Incorporating the appraisal and reward of potential in the assessment system.
3. Communicating potential appraisal to all the employees regularly.
4. Explaining to all employees the attributes used for evaluating potential.

Thus, we find that potential appraisal, if used scientifically, can serve a very useful purpose in developing employees for their future assignments. The organization too gets benefitted from the efforts of developed employees.

Chapter Review

1. Contingent pay aims at covering the additional financial rewards in addition to the base pay. It may include individual PRP, competence-related pay, skill-based pay, shop-floor incentive and bonus schemes, sales force incentive schemes, executive incentive and bonus schemes, employee and executive share schemes, team rewards, gainsharing, profit-sharing, profit-related pay and other cash payments. The rationale for contingent pay is based on the considerations of equity, motivation and sending a strong message across the organization that it attaches great importance to performance. In the present chapter, only PRP and related issues have been dealt with.
2. Whether to introduce PRP or not is based on the objectives of the organization, cultural orientation of the organization, working environment of the organization and so on.
3. The prerequisites essential for the introduction of PRP include: PRP should fit the culture of the organization; top management's commitment to PRP; organization's ability to evolve methods of measuring performance; organization's capability of assessing the levels of competencies of personnel of the organization; organization's HR department's capability of extending necessary guidelines and support to PRP; organization's ability to balance performance measures and output factors and so on.
4. In order to develop a PRP programme, the steps to be taken involve: clearly spelling out the objectives of PRP programme; readiness of the organization for introducing PRP; decision-making for the introduction of PRP programme; developing PRP; designing the programme; briefing and training the line managers on the PRP programme; implementation of the PRP programme; and finally, the evaluation of PRP programme.
5. For the successful operation of the PRP programme, certain requirements should be fulfilled such as basic characteristics, rating arguments, progression rates and limits, and programme guidelines. Even the PRP programme should be evaluated from time to time and remedial steps should be taken.
6. Performance appraisal is a systematic, periodic and as far as humanly possible, impartial rating of an employee's excellence in matters pertaining to his present job and to his potential for a better job. While in 'merit rating', an employee's internal merits and qualities, such as his nature, bodily and mental merits, are studied, in 'performance appraisal', evaluation is made of quantitative factors based on production quantity, quality and strata of work.
7. Performance appraisal is essential because (a) most employers still base their pay and promotional decisions on the employer's appraisal, (b) performance

appraisal plays an integral role in the employer's performance management, (c) performance appraisal lets the boss and the subordinate develop a plan for correcting any deficiency and (d) appraisal serves a useful career planning purpose.

8. Performance appraisal is important because it provides systematic and timely information about an employee's performance and his potential, which can be used in different processes of HR management. Broadly speaking, there are twin objectives of performance approval—judgmental and developmental.

9. Defining the job, appraising performance and providing feedback are the three main steps in the process of performance appraisal. An organization should, therefore, establish evaluation criteria that should be reliable, relevant, sensitive and practical.

10. Unsatisfactory–uncorrectable, unsatisfactory–correctable, satisfactory–not promotable and satisfactory–promotable are the four main types of appraisal interviews.

11. The appraisal methods/evaluation techniques can be grouped under three heads, namely:
    (a) casual, unsystematic and often haphazard appraisal, (b) traditional and highly systematic appraisal (straight ranking method, paired comparison technique, man-to-man comparison, grading method, graphic rating scale, checklist method, forced choice description method, selection of critical incidents method, descriptive evaluation, point systems, field review method) and (c) MBO method. Self-evaluation should be taken as complement to evaluation by superiors.

12. An effective appraisal programme is one that includes analysis of jobs and responsibilities, ascertainment of the standard of job evaluation, looking on job execution, labour management discussions, formulation of scheme of the development of employees, review of the progress and so on.

13. The main barriers in the way of appraisal systems are faulty assumptions, psychological blocks and technical pitfalls, which should be overcome by taking appropriate measures. However, with all its constraints, performance appraisal cannot be done away with.

14. A potential appraisal is very important because people are like icebergs. What we see above the surface (i.e., performance) is only a small part. A large part of the attributes (i.e., potential) needed to perform excellently in a future job is not immediately visible. It is hidden below the surface—it has to be uncovered and traced.

15. There are four main methods of potential appraisal, namely Philips Hi-Lo Matrix, Philips NV Holland Model, psychometric tests and review appraisal.

DISCUSSION QUESTIONS

1. Discuss the meaning and types of contingent pay.
2. Discuss what PRP is.
3. Discuss the prerequisites essential for the introduction and success of a PRP programme.
4. Discuss how to develop a PRP programme, and also how to operate and evaluate it.
5. Discuss the concept of 'performance appraisal' and how it differs from 'performance management'.
6. Discuss the steps involved in the process of performance appraisal and also the evaluation criteria, especially the performance interview.
7. Discuss what should be done to introduce an effective performance appraisal programme.
8. Discuss the main constraints that come in the way of performance appraisal and how to overcome the same.
9. Discuss the concept of potential appraisal.
10. Discuss the methods available for potential appraisal.

Individual and Group Activities

1. In a group of three members, visit some organizations and find out what types of contingent pay are being paid to different categories of employees.
2. In a group of two members, talk to the HR officials of some big organizations and discuss all relevant issues related to PRP.
3. Individually, visit a big service organization, contact HR officials there and find out the method(s) of performance appraisal their organization follows.
4. In a group of three members, contact the union officials in a big organization and discuss with them if the employees are, by and large, satisfied with the appraisals conducted in their organization. In case they have any suggestions to make in this direction, take a note of the same.
5. In a group of two members, visit some organizations of a large size. Discuss with the HR officials if they conduct potential appraisal of their employees. If yes, which method do they follow?

APPLICATION CASE

Non-Recognition of Potential

Krishnamurthy is a fellow of IIM, Ahmedabad, and has a Bachelor of Technology (Mechanical Engineering) from IIT, Kharagpur. He has 10 years of rich experience to his credit.

He joined a renowned company as its CEO and performed well in the first two years. He was successful not only in reducing overhead expenses but also in increasing the company's share in the market.

However, in the third year as CEO, he could not perform well and the company suffered loss for the first time in the history of the company. Though there were many reasons for the adverse results, for example, the number of competitors of the company had increased substantially during the last two years, resulting in an increase in the supply of the product the company and its competitors were producing and thus, causing fall in its price; there was erratic supply of power throughout the year affecting both the quality and output of the product of the company; due to heavy demand for raw material in some new industries, its prices also went upward, and the like. However, the main reason was that Krishnamurthy could not concentrate on his job as much as he was capable of and perhaps could have faced the storm well. It was due to the sudden and serious illness of his mother to whom he was greatly attached. Nobody in the company was aware of it.

In the Annual General Body Meeting of the shareholders of the company, the issue of financial loss incurred by the company was the first item on the agenda of the meeting. The issue was deliberated upon with all sorts of arguments. While a few members present in the meeting defended Krishnamurthy, the general consensus of the opinion was that Krishnamurthy was mainly responsible for the poor performance of the company during the year under review. Krishnamurthy, a man of self-respect, never brought the fact of the illness of his mother to the notice of the general body. Consequently, the next day he resigned from his position and the same was readily accepted, and Krishnamurthy was relieved of his duties.

Questions

1. Was it appropriate on the part of shareholders to blame exclusively Krishnamurthy for the poor performance of the company, ignoring his qualifications, rich potential, long experience, his good performance in the company in the previous two years and adverse external factors? Yes or no, why? Give arguments.
2. Was it desirable on the part of Krishnamurthy not to bring the fact of sudden and serious illness of his mother to the notice of top authorities, and abruptly resign?
3. Were you a shareholder holding a large number of shares of the company, what would have been your reaction in the general body meeting?

Notes

1 Armstrong and Murlis, *Handbook of Reward Management*, 273.
2 Ibid., 272–273.
3 Ibid., 283.
4 Ibid., 291.
5 Ibid., 292–293.
6 For details, see ibid., 295–296.
7 For details, see ibid., 285–290.
8 Flippo, *Principles of Personal Management*, 263.
9 Gary Dessler and Biju Varkkey, *Human Resource Management*, 11th ed. (New Delhi: Pearson Prentice Hall, 2008), 342.
10 Ibid., 343.
11 J.M. Ivancevich, *Human Resource Management* (New Delhi: McGraw-Hill, 2008), 256.
12 For details, see ibid.
13 For details of technical features of the ranking method, see Ghiselli and Brown, *Personnel and Industrial Psychology* (New York, NY: McGraw-Hill, 1948).
14 Flippo, *Principles of Personal Management*, 265.
15 For details, see Ivancevich, *Human Resource Management*, 264–265.
16 Douglas McGregor, 'An Uneasy Look at Performance Appraisal', *Harvard Business Review* 35, no. 3 (May–June 1957): 88–94.
17 Flippo, *Principles of Personal Management*, 263.
18 See *The Economic Times*, 20 June 2016.
19 See *The Economic Times*, 25 November 2016.
20 Ibid.
21 Ibid.
22 *The Economic Times*, 8 February 2016.
23 Ibid.
24 Ibid.
25 *The Economic Times*, 7 April 2017.
26 *The Economic Times*, 27 December 2016.
27 *Hindustan Times*, 24 May 2016.
28 For more details, see *Hindustan Times*, 15 August 2016.
29 Ibid.
30 For more details, see *The Economic Times*, 16 December 2016.
31 See *The Economic Times*, 9 December 2016.
32 See *The Economic Times*, 27 December 2016.
33 *Hindustan Times*, 24 May 2016.
34 Ibid.
35 Ibid.
36 For more details, see *Hindustan Times*, 15 March 2016.
37 For more details, see *The Economic Times*, 11 April 2017.
38 *Hindustan Times*, 24 May 2016.
39 Ibid.
40 Ibid.

5

CONTINGENT PAY

Pay for Performance, Competence, Skill—II

LEARNING OBJECTIVES

After studying this chapter, the reader should be able to:

1. Explain the meaning and definition of competency and also linkage between compensation and competency.
2. Explain the meaning of competency-based pay (CBP), its rationale/merits and when to introduce competency-based pay.
3. Explain the meaning of skill-based pay (SBP) and the purpose of the skill-based structure and enlist the main features and working of SBP.
4. Enlist different types of SBP structures and explain each of them and also how to establish and implement SBP systems.
5. Explain the meaning and purpose of team-based pay (TBP)/rewards and explain its merits and demerits and its acceptance in the corporate sector.
6. Enlist the main approaches, processes and factors affecting team-based pay/rewards.
7. Explain the meaning and definition of gainsharing and also its primary components, design and benefits and demerits.
8. Explain the concept, characteristics, objectives and types of profit-sharing.
9. Explain the meaning, definition, objectives, approaches and merits and demerits of profit-related pay.

DOI: 10.4324/9781032626123-5

10. Explain the concept of other cash payments and allowances such as payments in response to market pressures, payments as reward for special circumstances, attendance bonuses, shift pay, pay for person, pay for excellence, management compensation and rewards, and sales force incentive programmes.

Competency-Based Pay

Introduction

It is an undoubted fact that the success of an organization depends on its competent workforce. Hence, the concept of 'paying for competence' is getting more and more acceptance, especially in the corporate sector. By implementing this concept, the organizations are, as a matter of fact, looking forward, not back, which is the case with 'performance-related pay' (PRP). Competency-related pay appears to be fair because as per this method of wage payment, an employee is paid on the basis of what he is capable of doing and not for results. In the latter case, one may not get the due reward for his performance as results depend not only on the performance but also on several other factors over which the employees may have no control.

Competency-based pay refers to a salary structure where an employee is paid or compensated by his organization, based on his knowledge, skills and abilities, rather than his job title or position in the organization. As such, a competency-based pay plan is instrumental in improving an employee's abilities and efforts so as to achieve pay according to his knowledge, skills, abilities and market relevance. It takes inspiration from flat organizations.

Meaning and Definition of Competency

Competency has different meanings and remains one of the most diffuse terms in the management development sector. Before moving forward, it will be in the fitness of things to distinguish between the words 'competence' and 'competency' which though appear to be the same, and further that the dictionary definitions of both the words are very similar, they have an odd relationship.

The two terms 'competence' and 'competency' have a common etymology as both these two words come from the French word 'competence' meaning a skill, talent or capability. The French word 'competence' comes from the Latin word *competentia* meaning an agreement, conjunction and possible expertise. It appears that the two words, that is, 'competence' and 'competency', split from each other sometime in the Middle English period and had different meanings. However, presently, though these two words have different technical meanings, they are used interchangeably.

So far as the term 'competence' is concerned, it refers to the ability of an individual to do a job efficiently or successfully. In case we go to the roots of the term 'competence', it appeared as a concept for performance motivation in R.W. White's article published in 1959. The term further got momentum through the writings of David McClelland (1973), T.F. Gilbert (1978) and some others. Competence refers to the adequacy of knowledge and skills that enable an employee to act in a wide variety of situations. It is a combination of knowledge, abilities, skills and commitment that makes an employee act effectively in a job or situation. Broadly speaking, competence relates to the state of being able to do something, that is, if an employee has competence, he is able to do a certain task. Thus, competence is the ability of a person to do a job properly. Since each level of responsibility has its own requirements, competence can occur in any period of an employee's life. It can also occur at any stage of his career.

Competence is skill-based and standard is attained. It is measured also. Competence is related to technical knowledge, functional knowledge and functional information. It includes both interpersonal and communication skills. Time management skills, team-building skills and leadership skills are the other features of competence.

Job-related knowledge is a part of it. So is the case with decision-making skills and business knowledge, which are also constituents of competence. Capacity to learn quickly, self-confidence, team player, handling ambiguity well, taking initiative, focusing on client success, integrity, motive, trait, aspects of one's social image, social role, a body of knowledge and so on are some of the main characteristics of an employee that reflect competence which can result in effective and/or superior performance in a job/role. According to Armstrong,[1] there are 'hard' or work-based competences which are expectations of work performance and the standards and outputs people carrying out a role should attain. Soft competences are personal characteristics which employees bring to their roles.

So far as the term 'competency' is concerned, it was Boyatzis who brought it into the public arena in the United States in the early 1980s. The term 'competency' refers to a set of defined behaviours that offer a structural guide helping in the identification, evaluation and development of the behaviours in an individual, though in routine, 'competency' refers to the general description of qualities required in employees for accomplishing the objectives of the organizations. It is an underlying characteristic of an individual which is causally related to effective or superior performance. It may also be mentioned here that irrespective of training, competency is likely to grow through experience and the ability of an employee to learn and adapt. Competency is behaviour based and it is a manner of behaviour. Self-motivation, self-confidence, honesty and integrity are some of the main characteristics including learning from mistakes, perseverance, being result-oriented, enterprising, winning and positive attitude, and strong determination. Thus, while 'competence' is a label for the ability to perform, 'competency' describes behaviour needed to perform a role with competence.

Difference between Competency-Based Pay and Performance-Related Pay

The term 'competency-based pay' refers to a pay system that pays employees for *using* their skills rather than for the *results* they produce, which is the case with regard to 'performance-related pay'. Competency-based pay is a pay structure that compensates an employee based on his skill set, knowledge, experience, and market relevance whereas performance-related pay is a pay structure that compensates an employee based on his performance or contribution towards accomplishment of company goals.

Rationale for/Merits of Competency-Based Pay

It is on the basis of knowledge, skills and experience that organizations using competency-based pay structures compensate their employees rather than on the basis of their job title or position. The reason for their doing so is not far to seek. The basic objective is to motivate employees, to make them aspirational, to develop their skills and to make use of these at their workplace. Since the employees are rewarded for something, they feel they deserve it, they get loyal to the organization. Besides, though competency-based pay is simple to structure, it can be difficult to alter the salary structure during times of economic hardship. Then it utilizes readily accessible salary tables.

Even subordinates can also earn more as compared to seniors based on their competency level. Competency-based pay is justified because it helps in pushing employees beyond their comfort zone because they feel that they can earn more based on their competencies.

Armstrong[2] says that if the scheme is introduced in the right way and for the right causes, the competency-based pay can promote the need for greater competence and facilitate lateral career development. It helps in integrating role and generic competencies with organizational competences and encourages employees to take responsibility for their own career development.

Similarly, some other benefits have been suggested by some other writers. For example, competency-based pay, if introduced appropriately, boosts cooperation and teamwork. Not only this, the scheme provides a framework for salary progression, especially when promotion opportunities are inadequate. The scheme focuses on the totality of the job instead of what is accomplished. The scheme is instrumental in increasing employee satisfaction through the provision of development opportunities. Besides, the scheme enables a link between the reward strategy and overall corporate objectives.

The competency-based pay scheme is more effective in improving employee motivation, especially in service-based organizations. An employee feels motivated to acquire more knowledge and improve his skills and abilities as he knows that pay is based on his above-mentioned qualities. It is also in the interest of the company as it becomes a company of employees who are actively seeking to improve their skills and thus help in improving the profitability of the company. It encourages employees to continue their self-development and training. The scheme is also helpful in reducing the rate of turnover. A substantial percentage of employers feel that the scheme encourages better performance and increases flexibility among the employees. It also brings about the desired change in the behaviour of employees and enables them to have access to job progression.

The scheme also helps in introducing multi-skilling and provides greater objectivity in pay determination.

Not only this, the competency-based pay scheme is a more holistic approach and avoids many pitfalls associated with individual performance-related pay schemes. For example, the scheme avoids difficulties that we come across while establishing measurable performance targets for qualitative factors like team-building. It also avoids the difficulties involved in taking into account factors outside the individual's control in accomplishing targets. It avoids adverse impacts on team-building objectives and puts checks on the manipulation of the system by employees to receive high levels of performance pay. It also avoids to a great extent the difficulties in converting variable performance against a range of targets into a single assessment rating.

The scheme considers the person's overall performance as in the case of customer services. It is an absolute measure of performance, meaning that employees can always improve unlike in ranking systems. Besides, more options are offered by the competency-based pay scheme than by other schemes in that the scheme can be used to determine the progress of a pay band and movement within or between bands.

Though the competency-based pay scheme has many points to its credit, there is a lack of concrete evidence to establish that the introduction of the scheme will improve performance. However, it is an integrative approach as much as it has the advantage of linking recruitment and selection, performance appraisal and development.

Extent of Use of Competency-Based Pay

Competency-based role profiles have been used to help determine pay in the UK Passport Agency since 1998. In a survey conducted by an industrial society in 1998, cited by Homan,[3] it was found that a third of employers had a competency-based pay system or had plans to introduce it within the next one year. Anyway, most employees use competencies for personnel processes in recruitment and selection, and training and development, rather than reward/pay.

What Is Competency-Based Pay?

It is difficult to define exactly what the competency-based pay is. It is because there are a variety of different pay arrangements, some of which are indistinguishable from SBP. Some of them involve payment for the acquisition of knowledge or skills which are necessary for the effective delivery of a job role. There are some other pay arrangements that are basically performance-related pay known by other names, in which competency is measured and rewarded in terms of the performance that competency produces. As such, rewarding the 'use' of competency and rewarding the 'acquisition' of competency make a difference.

Theoretically, there is an obvious difference between competency-based pay and individual performance-related pay. However, the two distinguishing features of competency-based pay are: (a) it is based on an agreed framework of competencies and (b) it is not based on the achievement of specific results, like targets achieved or projects completed. Of course, it is concerned with the attainment of agreed standards of performance. In case an employee is compensated as per his type or level of obtained skills that are applied in the workplace, it is known as competency-based pay. Armstrong[4] is of the view that competency-based pay involves paying for the development and application of essential skills, behaviours and actions which support high levels of individual, team or organizational performance. Thus, it is not just behaviours but also skills and actions that have been focused.

Why Competency-Based Pay Not to Be Used?

It is not all roses for competency-based pay. There are several cons too. For example, it is also possible that in certain cases, it can lead to favouritism towards a particular employee. Again, it is also possible that due to competition within the organization, a disjoint in a team may occur, which affects the overall output.

It was pointed out in *Competency Emotional Intelligence Quarterly*[5] that there are several reasons for employers not to link pay to competencies. The employers felt that the competency-based pay is likely to impact other competency initiatives and that it is likely to face employees' reactions. Besides, they had doubts in general about linking competencies to pay. It was pointed out in the above survey that one organization, which was one of the first companies to introduce competency-based pay, was now rethinking the whole basis for its involvement with competency-based pay.

The competency-based pay system is time-consuming and costly to implement. Time, cost and resources required for the implementation of the scheme are some of the general problems associated with the competency-based pay system. Again, the managers find the objective measurement of competencies difficult. Besides, in case the competency is linked with other means of determining reward, the link with pay is likely to be unclear and reduce the motivational impact of the system.

There is also a possibility of inaccurate measurement of company needs. It is also not easy to determine which skills are important to a company or to identify which skills translate to productivity.

Then, in order to implement the system effectively, the system makes considerable demands on online managers in terms of additional training and support which involves a lot of cost. 'There is also a possibility that if the system is not monitored and controlled properly, there is a risk of pay drift with performance improvement, especially when there is a "soft" grading approach'. In an inadequately controlled implementation, there is a likelihood of additional resource burdens on the company. It has also been observed that with the passage of time, raters get more lenient. Then there is a possibility of manipulation in appraisal scores if it suits both the appraiser and the appraisee.

Gender and ethnic bias are also a possibility. For example, it has been observed that generally female employees are consistently rated lower as compared to male employees so far as leadership abilities are concerned. The line managers at times are not fair while granting pay rises to female employees.

Besides, the scheme is a little bit expensive as it involves more administrative work because, in this model, the company is required to track individual assessments, lesson results, wages and salaries, to evaluate pay.

Prerequisites for Competency-Based Pay

In case an organization intends to introduce a competency-based pay scheme, it has to ensure the following:

- First, it has to ensure that a well-established competency framework has been working in the organization effectively for other HR processes for quite some time. A competency framework should combine both core competencies applicable to jobs all across the organization and competencies that are specific to particular jobs. Then competency frameworks are developed via a process of internal research and consultation whether external expert assistance is sought or not.
- Second, there should have been in existence a credible, tried and tested system of assessment of competencies for reward purposes.

In case the aforesaid two requisites are in place, steps can be taken to introduce the competency-based pay system. In this regard, Armstrong[6] has suggested the following steps:

Initially, the purposes and potential benefits of the competency-based pay should be well communicated to all concerned and the views of all the stakeholders should be obtained. This done, the broad approach to be used should be defined and decisions be taken as to what is to be done to develop it. Such a decision may include issues such as revised or a new job evaluation scheme, how competency assessment will be linked to reward, introduction of a broad-banded pay structure and how the scheme will be maintained and controlled.

When to Introduce Competency-Based Pay?

When is it appropriate to introduce competency-based pay? In this regard, Armstrong[7] suggests that competency-based pay may be introduced when there is a well-established competency framework already in use in the organization for recruitment and development and when there exists a well-established criterion for the measurement of competencies. It can also be appropriate when the organization has a specific objective of increasing the level of competence of employees and has a plan to move to a broad-banded pay structure or such a pay structure is already in place and it further intends to move to a flatter structure. In organizations, the competency-based pay structure becomes appropriate when there is an overemphasis on outputs, results are as important as your job and a fit with performance appraisal is required. It is also appropriate when an organization needs cultural change towards greater flexibility and also when a new value system is to be introduced.

However, in practice, competency-based pay systems are rarely used in a pure form as the only means of determining reward. Instead, a good number of companies combine two or more systems.

Linking Compensation and Competency

Linkage between compensation and competency is usually attempted (a) when competencies are used in designing the grading structure, (b) competencies are used to determine pay rises or pay cuts, (c) when competencies are used to determine promotions and (d) when competencies are used to determine how an overall pay rise should be divided into pay shares.

Linking competency and compensation also takes place when in a job-focused process, competencies are used wholly or partially as a way to evaluate jobs, and/or in a people-focused process, an individual's pay is linked to his level of competence. However, in a good number of organizations, the link between competency and compensation (pay) is loose.

Skill-Based Pay (SBP)

SBP is one of the most talked about, widely implemented, poorly understood and under- researched HR practices of today. Why is it so? It is due to the fact that SBP is not a single system.

It is rather a family of loosely related systems having different origins, suitability to different types of organizations and distinct traditions. Not only this, opinions about SBP apply to one form, without taking into consideration the other forms that may be equally or even better suited for a given organization.

Broadly speaking, a skill is a learned ability that improves with practice over a period of time. However, with regard to SBP, the skills learnt should be relevant to the job.

SBP is also known as knowledge-based pay. However, the two terms are used interchangeably, knowledge implying the understanding of how to do certain tasks.

SBP is a compensation system that rewards people with additional pay in exchange for formal certification of an employee's knowledge, mastery of skills and/or competencies. Armstrong has rightly remarked that SBP provides employees with a direct link between their pay progression and the skills they have acquired and can use effectively.[8]

While skill is acquired and is observable expertise in performing tasks, knowledge is acquired information used in performing tasks. As against these two, competencies are more general skills or traits required to perform tasks, usually in multiple jobs or roles. However, in SBP systems, people get additional pay only after they display skills, knowledge and/or competencies that are rewarded by the system. While in more common job-based pay systems, pay is based on the job, which the people are entitled to irrespective of their proficiency reflected in their position, the SBP system is an employee-based system since instead of a job, it is based on the characteristics of the person.

Armstrong and Murlis have also remarked that SBP focuses on what skills the business wants to pay for and what employees must do to demonstrate them.[9] Thus, competency-based pay is a people-based rather than job-based approach to pay the employees as it is not linked simply with the scope of a defined job or a stated set of tasks.

According to Milkovich et al.,[10] skill-based structures link pays to the depth or breadth of the skills, abilities and knowledge a person acquires that are relevant to the work. Structures based on skill pay individuals for all the skills for which they have been certified regardless of whether the work they are doing requires all or just a few of those specific skills. Unlike a job-based plan in which employees are paid for the job assigned to them regardless of the skills they possess, in skill-based structures wages are attached to the person. As per skill-based structure, two employees with the same designation may receive different pay rates for doing essentially the same job. It may be due to the varying qualifications and length of experience these two employees possess, the presumption being that the employees with more knowledge are more effective and more flexible, hence able to take up more responsibilities. Thus, the depth of knowledge is reflected in higher qualifications, specialization, experience and so on. Coming to the breadth of knowledge, it is based on several things. It is like a generalist having knowledge of all phases of operations. In a multi-skill-based system, an employee earns pay increases by acquiring new or additional knowledge.

However, such knowledge should be specific to a range of related jobs. In such a system, pay increases do not come with job assignments. They come with certification of new skills as such employees can be assigned to any of the jobs for which they have been certified.

Purpose of the Skill-Based Structure

Milkovich et al.[11] have identified four main purposes in this direction given as follows:

1. It supports the strategy and objectives.
2. It supports the workflow.
3. It is fair to the employees.
4. It motivates behaviour towards organization objectives.

Who to Be Involved in SBP Plans?

Since employees and managers are the source of required information, they need to be involved in formulating SBP plans. It is they who can be helpful in defining the skills, bundling them into skill blocks, arranging them into a hierarchy and verifying whether an employee actually possesses the skills he claims to possess.

Main Features and Working of SBP

In this regard, Armstrong and Murlis[12] have pointed out the following:

1. Skill blocks are defined. These include individual skills or clusters of skills that employees are required to use and for which the organization rewards by extra pay when they have been acquired and the ability to use them effectively has been clearly demonstrated.
2. The skill blocks are arranged in a hierarchy with natural break points between clearly definable different levels of skills.
3. Methods are properly established to verify that employees have acquired skills at defined levels and that they can use them effectively.
4. On successful completion of a skill module, an employee will receive an increment in pay as per the procedure laid down for the award of extra skills.
5. Arrangements are made for 'cross-training'. These may comprise learning modules and training programmes for each skill module.

Application

Initially, SBP was applied mainly to operatives in manufacturing organizations and was later extended to technicians and other employees in the retailing, distribution and other service industries.

There is a clear similarity between skill-related pay and competence-related pay as both are concerned with rewarding the person as well as the job. However, the two can be differentiated by the way in which they are applied. The competence-related pay, which relates to expected behaviour as well as to knowledge and skill requirements, is broadly similar to SBP for managerial, professional and administrative staff as well as knowledge workers.

However, it should not be forgotten that SBP plans are expensive to implement and maintain as this demands a substantial investment not only in skill analysis but also in training and testing. Theoretically speaking, as per SBP an employee is paid only for necessary skills, but in practice employees may not be making use of those skills at the same time and the same may be used rarely. Hence, payroll costs are likely to go up, although the suppliers of SBPs claim that their plans are self-financing because they result in increased productivity and operational efficiency. But there is not much evidence to support this claim. That is why skill-based schemes have not been very popular and have therefore, been abandoned by many organizations.

Types of SBP Systems

While comparing different SBP types, Gerald E. Ledford, Jr and Herbert G. Henemam III[13] describe the type of skill emphasized, the goals and the organizational conditions that best fit each type. In Types A, B and C, the type of skill emphasized includes depth (in Type A), breadth, depth and/or self-management skills (Type B) and depth-oriented bonuses (Type C). In respect of goals, Type A includes deeper employee expertise, Type B includes greater employee capability and flexibility, broader perspective, increased self-direction, new and/or deeper skills, and Type C includes managing rapid changes in talent availability and skill needs, and attraction and retention of critical skills.

With regard to conditions that best fit each type, Type A includes competitive demand for specialized expertise, multi-year training cycles for key skills and making employee retention highly desirable; Type B includes high involvement and lean organizations that require high employee versatility and capability, organizations requiring new or deeper skills of managers and professionals; and Type C includes rapidly changing demand for specialized skills.

They have also explained different types of SBP structures given as follows:

1. **Depth-oriented base pay systems:** Depth-oriented plans are old and familiar in the United States and elsewhere also. They reward employees for acquiring greater expertise or existing skills. In such systems, employees build skills over a period of time, getting only one or two promotions during their careers. The analogous white-collar system rewards deeper levels of expertise rather than through the management hierarchy because the goals of these systems are building critical specialized skills and attracting and retaining talented

employees over the long period, for example, in the areas of pharmaceuticals, high technology, aerospace and so on. However, the main shortcoming of these systems is that they create overly specialized employees who instead of identifying with the mission of the organization identify more with their profession.

2. **Breadth-oriented base pay structure:** It is most often recognized as 'SBP'. In it, those employees are rewarded who acquire the ability to do different jobs in the organization. This type of system is often found in manufacturing organizations and also in some other types of organizations that need high employee skill and employee involvement like call centres. The origin of this pay system can be traced to Procter & Gamble where it was introduced in the 1960s in its greenfield high-involvement plants. Employees of Procter & Gamble learned technical, managerial and social skills required to manage complex technical systems without managerial support or with little managerial support. In other words, the system is likely to be more effective in organizations employing knowledge workers. SBP is often used to motivate employees to acquire skills needed in cost-reduction efforts, adapting to changes in market demand for different products, teamwork, cross-training, self-inspection and so on. Competency-based pay is being used for a long period in the case of managers and professionals. It helps in building distinctive competencies that meet organizational requirements. SBP has been common in the area of education also. As per a survey of Fortune 1000 firms by the Center for Effective Organizations in 2002, it was revealed that 56 per cent used SBP (broadly defined), though a substantial majority of users covered less than half of their workforce with SBP. Again, it was revealed in a study by American and Japanese researchers that 'knowledge and skill' is one of the three roughly co-equal factors in determining pay. The popularity of this type of system is also evident from the fact that available studies focus on what has to be described hitherto as Type B.

3. **Bonus systems:** This is applicable in the armed forces of the United States. This is shown as System C and has not been academically researched. The main objective of this system is to attract and retain occupational specialists. In case the services find it difficult to attract and retain the desired number of qualified personnel, a temporary enlistment and or reenlistment bonus is offered. In the US armed forces, bonuses are used for both officers and enlisted personnel like Special Forces. However, the amount of bonuses and the specialties for which bonuses are paid keep on changing frequently. Of course, bonuses in principle could be used to reward any type of skill development.

The types of skills have also been classified as[14]:

i) **Horizontal skills**—i.e., the skills which involve a broadening of skills in terms of range of tasks,

ii) **Vertical skills**—i.e., the skills involving acquiring of skills of a higher level, and

iii) **Depth skills**—i.e., the skills involving a high level of skills in a specialized area relating to the same job.

Advantages of Skill-Based Pay[15]

The advantages of skill-based pay may be enumerated as follows:

i)   It increases productivity and quality.
ii) It contributes to job enlargement by breaking down arrow job classifications.
iii) It enables job rotation.
iv) It reduces staff turnover because of continuous training, higher pay level and job enlargement through the broadening of skills.
v)   It is a sort of incentive for self-development.
vi) It leads to less competition among individuals as the rewards flow from the application of skill without reducing opportunities for others to similarly increase their skills and earnings.

It reduces the role of subjectivity as the pay increases on account of skills and is linked to measurement standards.

Establishing SBP

In order to establish SBP in an organization, the following steps can be initiated:

1. First of all, it is necessary to identify potential SBP jobs in which development of skill depth and/or breadth is possible as well as desirable.
2. Identify the specific skills, both depth and breadth, sought for each job level.
3. Work out the potential costs and benefits of the SBP plan and go ahead only if benefits far exceed the potential costs.
4. Develop proper techniques to assess new skills, knowledge and competencies acquired and/ or developed.
5. Work out certification standards and processes for employees to establish their successful acquisition of the skill(s) concerned.
6. Work out the rupee amount of SBP for the acquired skill.

Implementation of SBP Systems

Implementation factors include developing specific implementation plans, involving all concerned, communicating to all the stakeholders and then carrying through on the implementation plan.

Though increases in pay and well laid-out career paths under SBP make these plans attractive to employees, many employees like senior employees who are likely to retire shortly or employees with low growth needs or with low ability to learn new skills do not like SBP plans. Limited training and certification opportunities, the high costs involved in acquiring new skills and administering these plans are some of the other obstacles in the way of implementation of SBP systems.

In order to implement the SBP plan, the first thing to be ensured is management's commitment to developing a design that has a positive ROI. Then comes communicating the goals and mechanism of the plan to the employees concerned, taking care of inevitable problems that emerge and updating the plan from time to time.

What is more important is that the executives fully understand the costs and benefits of SBP in the context of their situation, and also how SBP is going to yield ROI. Besides, the appropriateness of SBP should be properly diagnosed. Here, the help of the task team can also be taken. Workforce characteristics, how well the organization has identified and documented the skills needed in the work process, training capability, change in technology and work processes should also be identified and assessed. Only those design options of the plan should be accepted which may maximize benefits and minimize costs. It should be clearly understood as to which categories of employees should be covered under the plan and so on. Implementation challenges should be visualized. These may include convincing the employees that SBP is in their interest or how time will be managed for training or how to reach an agreement on key design choices, developing a comprehensive communication plan and so on. Finally, develop a risk management of the situation.

Team-Based Reward

The concept of team-based corporate structure came into play in the United States in the 1980s and 1990s, prompted by success stories of successful Japanese companies, and since then the use of team-based pay has ticked up war. For example, in 1990 around 59% of the Fortune 1000 companies surveyed were following a team-based compensation system. The figure had risen to 80% by 1999.

Of late, there has been a trend in some organizations to shift from individual performance-related pay, which has not been very successful in delivering the results in terms of incentivization expected of it, to team-based pay and other methods of rewarding teams. However, team rewards are more talked about than done which is evident from the fact that as per a survey,[16] only 6 per cent of respondents had team-based pay.

According to Armstrong and Murlis,[17] team-based rewards are payments or other forms of non-financial rewards provided to members of a defined team, which are linked to the performance of that team.

Purpose of Team-Based Rewards

The main purposes of team-based rewards are as follows:

1. They convey a message that the organization recognizes effective teamwork.
2. Team-based rewards make it clear what teams are expected to accomplish because rewards are related to the attainment of agreed targets and standards of performance and behaviours.
3. Team-based rewards are meant to encourage group effort and mutual cooperation as they provide incentives and recognize team achievements.

Benefits and Acceptance of Team-Based Rewards

With the increasing emphasis on team-based work in organizations, research suggests that there is a growing acceptance and interest in team-based rewards.

The organizations are now accepting 'the conventional wisdom that team-based pay is the best way to encourage cooperation'.[18] According to Bamberger and Lavi,[19] team-based rewards:

1. Enhance team members' pro-social behaviours.
2. Boost members' capabilities.
3. Boost members' responsiveness.
4. Increase flexibility.
5. Increase productivity.

Haines and Tagger[20] have pointed out the following benefits of team-based rewards:

1. They can foster collaboration and teamwork.
2. They allow team goals to be clearly integrated with organizational objectives.
3. They provide incentives for the whole team to improve.

Team-based pay has several points in its favour. Research has revealed that over half of the organizations with team-based pay are confident that it is contributing to the improvement of team performance. For example:

1. It encourages teamwork.
2. It clarifies team goals.
3. It provides for the integration of organizational and team objectives.
4. It encourages cooperative behaviour.
5. It enhances the incentive for the group collectively to increase performance.
6. It encourages fewer effective employees to improve their performance to come to the team standards.
7. It is helpful in developing self-managed multi-skilling.

8. It enhances flexible working.
9. It acts as a lever for cultural change.

Demerits of Team-Based Pay

Despite an explosion of interest in teams and team compensation, many of the reports from the front line are not encouraging.[21] As per reports from companies, they are generally not satisfied with the way their team compensation systems work. There are several factors responsible for slow or no progress in the functioning of team-based pay which are as follows:

1. It is not possible to prescribe a standard mode or approach to develop pay because there are many different varieties of teams and many different types of schemes. There are full-time teams like work groups organized as a team. There are part-time teams like teams having experts from different departments pulled together for doing a specific job. Then there are full-time temporary teams in which cross-functional teams are pulled together to solve a specific problem or to complete a project and so on. Having so many varieties, it is difficult to have one consistent type of compensation plan or to have a uniform team-based pay plan.
2. The success of team-based pay depends on the existence of well-defined teams which are rare.
3. The conditions required for the effective introduction of team-based pay are tough, and many companies may not be able to meet them.
4. It may not work effectively if the team comprises members who keep their interests above the interests of the team.
5. The success of team-based pay depends more on the culture, working environment of the organization and management style than on the mechanics of the scheme.
6. Team-based pay may not seem appropriate to those individuals whose feelings of self-worth get diminished in the team.
7. It is not easy to develop performance measures and methods of rating teams.
8. High performers in low-performing teams may get frustrated.
9. Pressure from peers compelling individuals to conform to group norms may be at times undesirable.
10. Problems of uncooperative behaviour may be shifted from individuals to teams.
11. There is also a feeling that the team is either inadequate or inappropriate for improving its performance.
12. Some people, including team members, are hostile to any pay system that does not reward individual contributions.
13. 'Level problem' is another constraint because if we define teams at a very broad level, for example, the whole organization may be called a team, a lot of motivational impact of the team-based pay can be missed. In a large-size team, say of 2,000 employees, an individual worker may not be convinced

that his extra effort will significantly affect his team's overall performance. Then why should he exert too much? If teams are of very small size, there are other problems to be confronted with.

14. Another disadvantage of team-based pay is that often teams do not allow star performers to be transferred to other teams even if they are needed for the greater good of the organization.

15. Not only the above, more often than not, teams are found reluctant to accept a new employee as their team member for the fear that time will have to be spent to train him, though the additions in the team are necessary in the longer duration.

16. It is not uncommon to come across bickering when awards are given. Since teams have different performance objectives, it is not easy to equalize differences in different performance objectives. Inevitably complaints may arise.

17. Some team-based pay plans are simply too complex to be taken care of.

18. Controlling a team-based pay plan is another problem. There are a good number of factors which may be uncontrollable in the case of a particular team. Should the consequences of such uncontrollable factors affect team-based pay or not so that the same may not appear unfair to other teams? Without fairness, employees seem to have less sense of responsibility for the team's outcomes.[22]

19. Another problem is that of communication which affects the performance of the team. It has been observed that team-based pay plans are not well communicated. More time and attention are paid to designing the plan rather than how to explain it.

Though there is a lot of pessimism about team-based pay, many companies are rewarding groups of employees for their interdependent work efforts. Companies using team-based compensation typically set team performance standards in terms of customer satisfaction, productivity improvements, quality of goods produced, services rendered, financial performance, and paying their employees accordingly. Research studies are ongoing and perhaps some solution to the problems highlighted above may be found.

Approaches to Team-Based Rewards

The following are the main approaches to team-based rewards:

1. The first approach is to create an incentive and also a clear definition of performance. It can be done by identifying targets in advance and setting out a sum of money for accomplishing them.

2. The second approach suggests to reward teams retrospectively for good work done under agreed criterion, that is, recognizing the contribution.

3. The next approach relates to rewarding individuals for their contribution to team results or their demonstration of teamwork competencies. It helps in reinforcing an emphasis on teamwork.

In order to create and manage team rewards appropriately and also to decide which of the aforesaid approaches is more suitable, it is necessary to understand the factors affecting team-based pay/rewards and the basics of a team, namely nature and type of teams and how they work. A brief account of factors affecting team-based pay/rewards is as follows:

Factors Affecting Team-Based Pay/Rewards

Nature and Types of Teams

It is a matter of common knowledge that teams outperform individuals acting alone or in large organizational groupings, especially when performance needs multiple skills, judgements and experiences.

In a team, there are a small number of employees having complementary skills and are committed to a common goal and approach for which they are mutually accountable.

There are several types of teams, but they can be broadly divided into four types which are as follows:

1. **Process or work teams:** These are the ones in which members work together to carry out a process. These are usually full-time and permanent teams.
2. **Parallel teams:** These are part-time teams, often cross-functional, and are constituted to resolve a particular problem. Once the problem is solved, they are dissolved or meet from time to time to deal with issues.
3. **Project or time-based teams:** These are full-time, time-bound teams that aim at completing a project within a given period of time.
4. **Hybrid teams:** Such teams comprise both full-time and part-time in changing numbers.

Depending on the type of team and the environment in which it is functioning, a suitable reward approach can be decided, that is, whether the approach should be incentive-based or bonus-based and so on.

Characteristics of an Effective Team

The main features of an effective team include the following:

1. It is purpose-oriented and serves the desired purpose.
2. All the members of the team are dedicated and committed both collectively and individually to the desired purpose.

3. All the members are supportive of each other in pursuing the team's purpose, though their individual agendas may differ.

An effective team sets its priorities and roles of its members, sets out its processes and establishes members' interpersonal relationships.

Team Reward Processes

It can be discussed under the following heads:

1. **Justification for team rewards:** Team rewards are developed to encourage group behaviour and desired cooperation. Through team-based pay, the organization conveys the message that it attaches a lot of importance to teamwork and values high-performing teams, innovation, quality and customer service.
2. **Basics for team rewards:** While introducing team-based pay, we should decide whether the team is to be rewarded financially, non-financially or in both ways and further that it is the extrinsic rewards as distinguished from intrinsic rewards on which the organization can rely and to which extent. It is not that the team rewards should be financial ones; these can be non-financial ones also. They should be rather motivating and satisfying. Research has revealed that at times non-financial rewards are more effective, though nothing can be said with certainty.
3. **Methods of providing team-based pay/bonus:** A team can be rewarded in more than one way. For example, managerial, technical, professional and office staff can be distributed a bonus in cash, related to team performance. So far as shop-floor employees are concerned, there are various bonus/premium-related schemes in which bonus is linked to the output of a team.

Bonus can be determined based on performance related to defined criteria (as at Lloyds Bank) or it can be based on achievement of predetermined organizational and team objectives (as at Bank of Xerox).

Bonus can be distributed in several ways. For example, it can be distributed in the form of a lump sum to each team member usually based on a scale of payments. It can also be paid as a percentage of base salary—this method is very common as well as popular. It appears to be more reasonable as the base salary indicates the value of an individual's contribution to the team.

Introducing Team-Based Pay

In order to introduce team-based pay in an organization, it is desirable to follow the following steps:

First, the existing situation be properly analyzed and so is the case with requirements. Second, the teams to be rewarded with team-based pay should be identified because it may not be necessary to cover the whole organization under team-based pay.

Next, the appropriate form of team-based pay should be identified for each team. The objectives of team-based pay should also be worked out. Another step in introducing team-based properly designed, bonus formulas should be prepared, and the methods of measurement and distribution should be properly worked out and then the scheme should be introduced. The team and team leaders should be properly trained. Communication should be properly channelized, and the scheme should be appropriately monitored and evaluated.

Requirements for Team-Based Pay

According to Armstrong and Murlis,[23] team-based pay can be more effective if the team:

1. Stands alone as a performing unit.
2. Has clear targets and standards that can be agreed upon.
3. Has a considerable degree of autonomy.
4. Is composed of people whose work is interdependent.
5. Is stable.
6. Its members are used to working with one another, know what is expected of them by fellow team members and also know where they stand in comparison to those members.
7. Is mature.
8. Is composed of individuals who are multi-skilled, flexible and good team players and are still able to express a different point of view and carry that point forward if it is in the interest of the team.

Thus, there are several organizations which have a culture of good teamwork and consider it an important element that will make team-based pay an attractive proposition. There is no doubt that team-based pay can be useful in the right circumstances. However, it is not easy to design and manage team-based pay. Also, there is no one team-based pay scheme which may suit every organization. There are many organizations which are satisfied with their existing individual performance-related scheme and, therefore, may not like to go to team-based pay.

Gainsharing

Meaning and Definition

Broadly speaking, gainsharing is a system of management used by an organization to increase profitability by motivating its employees to boost their performance through involvement and participation. According to Armstrong and

Murlis,[24] gainsharing can be best defined as 'a commitment to employee involvement that ties additional pay to improvements in workforce performance'. With the performance improvement, employees share financially in the gain, that is, in the improvement.

Gainsharing is also known as 'gainshare' and 'saving sharing'. In it, the organization shares with its employees the savings from improved performance. The gainsharing system comprises two parts, namely (a) bonus calculation and (b) structured system for employee involvement, and it is because of this that gainsharing is viewed as an 'organizational development'. As such gainsharing is not just a bonus or incentive plan.

As a matter of fact, gainsharing is 'an involvement system with teeth in it'.[25]

Primary Components of Gainsharing

According to Armstrong and Murlis,[26] the primary components of a successful gainsharing plan include:

1. A formula to keep track of gains,
2. A link between the formula and process improvement initiatives and
3. Effective communication of how employees-generated improvements are improving gains.

Today, organizations use gainsharing to both measure performance and reward employees when it improves. Organizations use a predeterminable formula to share the savings with their employees. The goals of an organization's gainsharing plan depend on its cost structure and a long-term competitive strategy and are tailored to fit the industry. The organization shares information regarding the measures, formula and gains with its employees on an open and regular basis. Gainsharing develops among its employees a sense of ownership towards their work and the company because of the monetary gains shared by the organization with its employees. Gainsharing relates its payouts much more specifically to productivity and performance improvement which is directly under the control of employees.[27]

Gainsharing History

The history of gainsharing goes back to the 1930s when Joe Scanlon, an MIT lecturer and a labour leader, emphasized that a 'worker' can offer more than a 'pair of hands', that is, manual effort. Scanlon was of the opinion that the best and simplest solution to a problem lies with the worker closest to the problem. Accordingly, when Scanlon was in the process of helping a troubled company, he and the company owner asked the employees for their ideas and suggestions for reducing waste and cost. Consequent upon the implementation of ideas and suggestions of the employees, many improvements were effected and the company became more successful. Thereafter, Scanlon was asked to help to save some other companies also. He went on to develop a system for organizational development and gainsharing which ultimately came to be known as the Scanlon plan. The plan developed a method to measure and calculate gains. The monetary gains were then shared with all the employees of the organization. Based on the principle of equity, the concept asserts that since everyone in a company makes a contribution to the success of the organization, it is fair to share the gains with all concerned and not limit it to a few selected ones. Sharing the gains with all sends a message to the workforce, 'We all contribute. The contribution is respected. Let us share in the financial gains'.

Goals of Gainsharing

The basic objective of gainsharing is to bring about improvement in organizational performance by creating a motivated and committed workforce. The main goals of gainsharing are as follows:

1. To be instrumental as a change agent, especially when cultural change is needed.
2. To stimulate productivity and improve quality, especially when there is much of competition.
3. To reduce cost of production.
4. To overcome disillusionment with traditional incentive, bonus and premium schemes.

Besides, the gainsharing scheme may aim at seeking the help of all employees in coming forward with new ideas and support to improve performance, empower employees, attract the attention of all employees towards the key issues affecting performance, create a win-win environment wherein everyone is benefitted as productivity goes up, encourage better teamwork, increase cooperation at all levels, improve communication, share gains accrued due to improvement in performance on account of increased productivity, promote trust between the management and the employees and so on.

Fundamental Principles of Gainsharing

Ownership, involvement and communication are the three master strokes in gainsharing.

Gainsharing cannot be successful and effective until and unless a feeling of ownership is created among the employees of an organization. The organization should involve the employees in the gainsharing plan so that they identify themselves with the organization and become committed to the organization and core supporters of the organization. In case the employees are involved while the plan is being designed, they will own the plan and ensure its grand success. Coming to involvement, as stated earlier, the increased involvement is the major source of gainsharing. Involvement is the opportunity offered by management, and the responsibility which only employees can accept, to affect the work and processes in employees' areas of competence. Hence, for the successful working of gainsharing, the involvement of the employees concerned in the designing of the scheme is a must. Finally, comes communication. There should be a free and effective flow of communication—management furnishing performance information to the employees and the employees forwarding their ideas for performance improvement back to the management. Employees should know how their work behaviour influences the performance of the organization and the organization should be committed to providing timely all relevant information on the performance of the workers and how it affects organization's gains and gainsharing.

Formulae

The Scanlon plan, the Rucker plan and Improshare are the three plans that demonstrate the roots of gainsharing. The Scanlon plan is viewed as the first to connect employee involvement and employee-generated gains with pay. In it a standard ratio of employment cost/sales, say 35 per cent, is determined, and if labour costs go below this proportion, the savings are shared between the company and the employees based on a predetermined sharing formula.

The Rucker plan too is based on employment costs. This plan determines a constant share of whatever added value is created by the joint efforts of employees and management. Improshare is based on an established standard that spells out the expected hours needed to produce an acceptable level of output. Any savings emerging from an increase in output in fewer than expected hours are shared between the employees and the organizations as per a predetermined formula. Both the Rucker plan and Improshare are only a formula for tracking gains and pay no attention to an improvement means to generate gains or offer a link to employee involvement respectively. Besides the aforesaid three plans, there is also a value-added gainsharing plan whereby increases in value-added are shared between the company and the employees.

Usually, the employees' share varies between 25 and 35 per cent in the early years of a plan and can exceed even 50 per cent in the later years, say 5 to 10 years. Such a plan has a provision for an incentive to be paid as gains increase beyond a reference point and vice versa if the gains fall below the reference point.

Developing a Gainsharing Formula

While developing a gainsharing formula, Armstrong and Murlis[28] have pointed out a few key points to be kept into consideration. This first key consideration is how should value-added be calculated? What reference points or thresholds should be used to trigger payments? What happens if value-added falls below the reference points? How can subjective factors such as quality or customer service be incorporated into the plan? How should gains be shared between employees and the company? What should be the performance period for the plan? What level of incentive can be achieved? And what should be the basis of the distribution of gains to employees?

However, it should not be forgotten that there is no standard gainsharing formula that can be applied uniformly in all organizations. There will always be a choice and the organization will have to decide which formula will suit the best.

Introducing Gainsharing

In case an organization has to introduce gainsharing, it should initiate in a systematic manner by taking the following steps:

1. First, the justification should be made, that is, why the new culture should be introduced and also spell out its objectives.
2. Second, the organization's culture, processes, structure, technology and strategy for growth should be reviewed. It will be desirable if inputs on business focus, team independence, empowerment, willingness and ability to change and HR programmes are gathered because these five are the enablers of gainsharing success.
3. Take the views of workers' unions, line managers and other employees as to what is their attitude towards gainsharing.
4. Prepare the design of the scheme in full consultation with the employees and line managers and involve all concerned in the exercise because gainsharing is about involvement. A project team may be set up having representatives of both the employees and the management. The employees should be told about the philosophy of the programme, and the basis upon which the formula will operate and be revised. They should also be told how they will be involved and how they are going to be benefitted from the programme. The programme be reviewed after a desirable gap of time and necessary changes be effected whenever necessary.

Gainsharing and Work Culture

In a gainsharing plan, a comparison of an organization's current performance is made with its historic performance, that is, baseline period. Since the savings above the baseline period determine the gains, employees and the company together should improve in order to make a gain. Performance thresholds should be corrected periodically. As people like money, gainsharing can be a very powerful tool to motivate employees. Gainsharing encourages the need to improve continuously in case a proper culture is created.

Keys to Successful Gainsharing Implementation/When Does Gainsharing Work Best?

Gainsharing works best when the performance levels of the organization can be easily quantified, the work environment is based on openness and trust, employees understand the plans clearly, and there exists a supportive system of employees.

The two main keys to successful implementation are simplicity, that is, the employees must understand the plan clearly, and involvement, that is, the more the number of people involved in a plan's design, the more ownership they will take in it.

Gainsharing Implementation

A 'design team' should be constituted to make policy decisions on matters such as employee eligibility, plan measures, frequency of payouts and methods of communication. Such a design committee should be approved by the top management. Having got approved, the design committee becomes responsible for conducting meetings with all employees and passing on the details of the plan to them. Follow-up training should also take place.

Key Elements in Designing a Gainsharing Plan

Milkovich et al.[29] have suggested seven key elements in designing a gainsharing plan which are as follows:

1. Strength of reinforcement, that is, what role should base pay to assume relative to incentive pay?
2. Productivity standards—to be set keeping in view some baseline year.
3. Sharing the gains split between management and the employees.
4. Scope of the formula.
5. Perceived fairness of the formula among the employees.
6. Ease of administration.
7. Production in variability.

Thus, gainsharing is a vital component in an organization's compensation strategy. It cannot work in isolation. Therefore, it must be developed and maintained as part of an integrated process of business communication, employee involvement, reward management and process improvement. It is a participative process. It offers opportunities for the involvement of workers enabling them to establish clear links between their performance and rewards which is essential for the success of any pay-for-performance plan. In a gainsharing plan, gains and resulting payouts are self-funded depending on the savings generated by improved performance. Although the plan usually applies to a single plant, site or stand-alone organization, organizations can have levels of sharing across multiple locations or corporation-wide. Payouts are made either monthly or quarterly. Performance is measured across departments, units or functions. Measures are typically based on operational measures such as productivity, quality and customer service. Employees are frequently involved in the designing process of the plan. Bonus is paid as an equal percentage of compensation rather than on the basis of individual performance. All employees are eligible for plan payments. Plans are reviewed periodically, usually once a year, and remedial steps are taken.

As a matter of fact, a gainsharing plan relates to awards that share economic benefits accruing because of improved productivity, quality or other measurable results. It focuses on group, plant, department or division results. It is designed in a fashion to capitalize on the untapped knowledge of employees. In it, there are clear performance-rewards links. It leads to productivity and quality improvements. It fosters teamwork and cooperation. It leads to an increase in the employees' business knowledge. However, it can be administratively complicated and can also result in unintended effects like a decline of quality. Then pay-outs can occur even if the organization's financial performance is poor. However, there is no doubt that it supports a major productivity/ quality initiative like TQM. It also leads to a teamwork environment and aims at rewarding employees for improvements in activities that they control.

Profit-Sharing

Englishman Theodore Cooke Taylor, one of the earliest pioneers of profit-sharing, introduced the practice of profit-sharing in his woollen mills during the late 1800s.[30]

A profit-sharing plan is also known as a deferred profit-sharing plan (DPSP). Under this plan, employees are given a share in the profits of a company. As per this plan, an employee receives a percentage of a company's profit which may be based on its quarterly or annual earnings. This practice gives the employees of a company a sense of ownership in the company. According to Armstrong and Murlis,[31] profit-sharing is a plan under which an employer pays to eligible employees, in addition to their normal remuneration, additional sums in the form of cash or shares in the company related to the profits of the business. The amount so shared is determined either entirely at the discretion of the employer or as per an established formula. Usually, profit-sharing schemes are applicable to all the employees of the company. In the United States, a profit-sharing plan can be set up where all or a part of the employee's profit-sharing amount can be contributed to a retirement plan. The share of profits paid to the management, or the board of directors, is also called the *tantieme*, a French term which is usually applied in describing the business and finance practices of certain European countries such as France, Germany and Sweden. It is paid in addition to the manager's or the director's fixed salary and bonuses. Of course, laws vary from country to country.

Characteristics

The main characteristics of a profit-sharing plan are as follows:

1. The share in profit is paid to the employees in addition to their normal wages.
2. The payment is made based either on seniority or wages calculation of the employees.
3. The payment is effected from net profits which implies that it is not a part of cost of production or a charge against the profit and loss account.
4. Employees are paid a part of profits exceeding a certain limit.

Objectives of Profit-Sharing

A substantial number of companies operating profit-sharing scheme have one or more of the following objectives:

1. To recognize the right of employees for sharing the prosperity of the organization.
2. To encourage employees to identify themselves more closely with the company by developing a common concern for its progress and by creating a sense of ownership.
3. To maintain good industrial relations.
4. To encourage better cooperation between employees and management.
5. To supplement workers to feel themselves as members of the organization rather than only as employees.
6. To earn goodwill of the employees.
7. To reward success in businesses where profitability is cyclical.

Types of Profit-Sharing Plans

Basic types of sharing plans can be categorized under the following heads:

1. **Cash plans:** A proportion of profits is paid directly to employees in the form of cash, cheques or stock. In some countries, it is tax-free, whereas in most others, it is taxed as ordinary income when distributed. The main features of typical cash schemes are as follows:
    a. Eligibility and formula for calculating profit share: All employees are eligible subject to completion of one year (or so) before a share in profits becomes due to an employee. The amount to be paid to an employee is in relation to the pay earned by him. So far as calculation of profit share is concerned, one option is to use a predetermined and well-publicized formula for distributing a fixed percentage of profit. Thus, there is a clear relationship between company profits and the amount distributed among

eligible employees. This practice helps in maintaining good industrial relations. The demerit of this practice is that there is no flexibility
because the percentage of profits to be distributed is predetermined and,
therefore, the amount paid to the employees keeps on fluctuating with the
changes in the amount of profits of the company.

b. The second option is that the board may decide unilaterally the amount
of profit share without the use of any predetermined formula. The board
uses its own discretion keeping in view the circumstances under which
the company is functioning. Thus, this practice allows the board some
flexibility in deciding the amount of profit share. However, workers'
unions do not approve of this practice because it may be misused by the
management. The third option is a combination of the first two methods.
Under this practice, a profit threshold is set below which no profits will be
shared. A maximum limit is also set on the proportion of profits that may
be shared.

c. So far as the methods of distributing profit shares are concerned, there
are several methods in this regard. For example, a fixed sum irrespective of earnings of employees may be distributed. But the method is not
appreciated because this does not produce an equal motivational impact
on the employees. Another method is to distribute profits in proportion to
salary and some measure of individual performance.

d. This practice involves difficulty in measuring the relationship between
profits and performance. Another method of distributing profit shares is
to distribute profits as a percentage of basic pay. This is also a very common and popular method because profit shares should be related to the
individual contribution of the employee which is reflected by his basic
pay. Another method of distributing profit shares is to determine it as a
percentage of earnings with payments related to length of service. This
method promotes among employees loyalty towards the organization. As
far as timings of distribution of profit-sharing are concerned, it is usually
distributed once a year though some companies do so even two to four
times a year. The amount to be distributed as profit shares depends on the
sole discretion of the board, but most organizations provide some limit,
say between 5 and 20 per cent of profits.

2. **Deferred plans:** Under these plans, profit-sharing contributions are not paid
out immediately. They are rather deferred to individual accounts set up for
each employee. The amount so credited along with any investment earning
on this amount is paid at the time of retirement or death or disability of the
employee, whichever is earlier.

3. **Combination plans:** Under these plans, an employee has the discretion of
deferring all or a part of the profit-sharing amount which is to be credited to
his amount and is treated as per the deferred plan mentioned above.

Benefits of Profit-Sharing

There is a correlation between profit-sharing and profitability, and further that profit-sharing scheme is good both for employers and employees. Some of the main benefits of profit-sharing scheme are as follows:

1. **Increase in productivity:** Since employees know that high productivity means high profits and vice versa, they work hard and sincerely in order to get higher amounts as their share of profits.
2. **Cordial industrial relations:** As employees and employers both know that strikes and lockouts lead to reduction in profits and, therefore, they will get less amount as their share in profits; both try to avoid strikes and lockouts and maintain good industrial relations. Industrial peace means good industrial relations.
3. **Additional income to employees:** Profit shares are in addition to their routine wages and salaries. Hence, their profit shares increase their total income which leads to higher standard of living.
4. **Reduced supervision:** Since the interest of employees lies in increased profits, they work hard and sincerely and do not need much supervision.
5. **Social justice:** Under the profit-sharing scheme, the entire profits do not go to the pockets of employers. The same is shared between the employers and the employees. It leads to equal distribution of income and social justice.
6. **Reduction in labour turnover:** It has been observed that employees do not want to leave those organizations where the profit-sharing scheme is in operation. This leads to a reduced rate of labour turnover.
7. **Team spirit:** Since team spirit is beneficial for increasing output and subsequent high profit, employees develop team spirit so that output of the company may go up and employees may get higher share due to increased profit because of increased output.

Thus, profit-sharing offers an opportunity to employees to have a share in their organization's success. As the level of success of an organization is directly related to profits which often define the amount of profit-sharing allocation, employees develop a sense of involvement and ownership and put in their best to increase the amount of output, reduce wastage and improve quality of the product produced which is in the interest of all the stakeholders. There are several types of profit-sharing schemes such as cash plans, deferred plans and combined plans. As profit-sharing has several benefits, it is likely to grow further.

Profit-Related Pay and Beyond

Meaning and Definition

Profit-related pay is a form of profit-sharing scheme used in the United Kingdom. It is a situation in which pay is related to the profit made by the organization. This was a widely used scheme that gave employees significant income tax benefits in the United Kingdom. Under this scheme, wages would vary according to the organization's profitability.

Purpose and Objectives

The purpose and objectives of the profit-related pay are primarily threefold and are given as follows:

1. **To increase motivation:** It improves the motivation of employees because they know that the higher the amount of profit, the higher will be their pay.
2. **To develop commitment:** Under this plan, the employees get committed to the cause of the company because they know well that their commitment will increase the profit and, therefore, they will also get increased pay.
3. **To promote efforts by the employees:** Profit-related pay creates among the employees a positive stake in the commercial success of the organization as a result of which employees work hard on their own.

Approaches

Profit-related rewards are usually offered either:

1. To allocate an amount from the surplus generated by the company, and thus to share it among the employees, and in order to secure maximum equality, this will be given as a percentage increase in the salary of all the employees, or
2. To offer shares in the organization.

Merits and Demerits

Normally, wages tend to remain unchanged even when an organization's profitability declines that puts the employer at a great loss. But if profit-related pay is in place, it comes to the rescue of the employer. Hence, employers also support it. Similarly, in the absence of profit-related pay, wages continue to be the same even when the organization's profitability increases, thus depriving the employees of sharing the increased profitability of the organization. But if a profit-related pay system is in operation, employees' salary also goes up with the increase in the organization's profitability. Hence, employees also prefer this system.

Supporters of this scheme hold the view that this scheme helps in reducing unemployment by making wages more variable. According to them, unemployment happens because the price of labour is stuck at too high a level, and they argue that profit-related income can build flexibility into labour markets. They further state that profit-related schemes enable some flexibility in labour markets because of the automatic profit-related cushion. Employers will be slower in laying off employees during a recession and quicker to employ more workers when conditions are favourable.

Besides, profit-related hires are more motivated than wage earners, and they improve productivity of their organization since their own interest is involved due to profit-related pay.

However, the biggest danger happens when profits of a company are wiped out by an industry 'price war' or due to reduced demand in times of recession or due to any external mishap. In such circumstances, employees have to pay a heavy price for no fault of theirs.

Other Cash Payments and Allowances

In order to meet market competition and also to maintain a balanced set of remuneration policies, companies have to make additional payments. Such payments have been divided by Armstrong and Murlis[32] into the following two categories:

1. Payments in response to market pressure—the need to attract and retain talent.
2. Payments to reward special circumstances or working practices.

1. **Payments in response to market pressures:** Such payments are widely used in the United Kingdom both in the public sector and the private sector and have now been getting popular in other countries as well. These are lump sum payments or continuing allowances used to secure competitive advantages, especially when labour market is tight. These may be used to attract and retain talent without disturbing the organization's normal salary structure. Such payments may include:

    a. **Golden hellos:** Often called recruitment bonuses, these payments are made to tempt sought-after individuals or specialists to join the company at particular positions. The amount can be paid either as a lump sum or in instalments spread over a period of one to two years. In some cases, the company may enter into an agreement laying down that such payments made to the employees will be returnable to the company in case the employee leaves before the stipulated period of stay. The amount of payment can vary depending on the urgency and need of the company for the specialist concerned. There is no uniform pattern for determining the amount of such payment which may vary between one year's salary and a few thousand rupees depending on the worth and need of the specialist for the company. Some companies offer 'upfront' market premium payments like a luxury company car that is normally provided to others holding almost the same rank.

        Some other such payments may include relocation allowance or housing assistance. At times, this may have a demoralizing effect on the current employees who were recruited earlier when the market pressure was not as much as it is when the new hire is recruited. In such circumstances, some adjustment to their compensation package may also be considered to make the team work together and enthusiastically.

b. **Golden handcuffs:** These payments are made to retain people in the organization. These payments are also being used in the United Kingdom in both the public and the private sectors and now in other countries too. The payments are also called 'retention payments'. Such payments are made in the form of phased lump sum payments or in the form of guaranteed bonuses. These payments, typically deferred payments, are provided by an employer to discourage an employee from leaving a company. For example, sometimes it is said that 'his five years golden handcuffs are released next year'. In other words, employers offer deferred incentives to certain employees to encourage a longer employment term, usually offered to senior managerial employees or employees with specialized skills, or high-performing employees. These payments can be tied to delivery or performance criteria, especially when some major organizational change is taking place, as retention bonuses. Sometimes these payments are made to retain employees until a plant or site is closed down. In the case of senior executives, such payments are made in the form of shares to make them more committed as they start having a feeling of ownership.

c. **Large-city allowances:** Since in big cities housing is a costly proposition, some allowance as a proportion of basic salary is paid to the employees so that they may not think of leaving the organization.

2. **Payments to reward for special circumstances:**

   Golden handshakes: These are essentially termination payments. These have become very popular all over the world. In India too, the practice is becoming common, especially in the public sector organizations for cutting down the extra flab. A golden handshake may be one of the terms and conditions in an executive employment contract providing the executive with a significant severance package if the executive loses his job through restructuring, fining or even scheduled retirement. It was in the mid-1960s that the term, 'golden handshake', originated in Britain. The term was coined by the city editor of the *Daily Express*, Fredrick Ellis, getting currency later on in New Zealand in the late 1990s on account of the controversial departures of various state sector executives. Golden handshakes are paid usually to top executives of companies in order to ensure that they leave with a financial cushion and also without making any fuss. According to Armstrong and Murlis,[33] they are commonly negotiated as part of the 'compromise agreements' used to enable senior executives who may 'no longer fit' to depart with dignity, pursue 'other interests' or even 'spend more time with their family'. However, of late, the scheme has been introduced to non-executive employees also, though certain terms and conditions apply. The amount of golden handshake is usually the salary for the unexpired period of the employment contract, if there exists one. In case there is no employment contract, the amount may be tied to the time the individual is likely to find a new job. Anyway, there is no uniform pattern for determining the amount of golden handshake, and it often gives rise to litigations. All the same, there is also a growing public grievance against 'rewards for failure'. It is, therefore, in the interest of all concerned that there exists a negotiated agreement for separation payment. Some of the companies extend out placement counselling to the employees offered golden handshakes and thus help them to decide what to do next.

Golden handshakes are given mostly to high-ranking executives by major corporations just to offset the risk inherent in taking the new job. It is so because high-ranking executives have a high likelihood of being fired. But some people have concern against handshake practice because it has also been observed that while under their stewardship, their companies lost millions of dollars and hundreds of employees were laid off, these to be separated (to be done away with) executives cashed their stock options.

In our country, many employers use the term 'voluntary retirement scheme' (VRS) for 'golden handshake', whereas trade unions call it 'voluntary retrenchment scheme', and for the government it is 'unstated exit policy'. VRS is a legal way to downsize the organization. Introduced in the early 1980s in central public sector undertakings (PSUs) to reduce the extra workforce, VRS is the latest mantra of many corporate and public sector units. It has now become the golden route to cut the excess flab of an organization. VRS is a scheme whereby the employee is offered to voluntarily retire from his services before his retirement date. Today, especially in India, VRS is the most common HR technique to retrench the employees in the country. It is the golden handshake for the employees and the only option for the companies to reduce organizations' staff.

As the name suggests, VRS is strictly voluntary, that is, one can neither compel the workers to accept it nor apply it selectively to certain individuals. However, an employer can choose the levels, units and age groups among whom one wants to offer VRS. The company can always accept or reject the application for VRS.

Since the VRS is a legal way to downsize, it involves certain technicalities. For example, in our country, the VRS candidates must have worked for the organization for at least 10 years and also the age of the worker must be minimum 40 years. Employees not complying with these conditions still can apply for the early separation, but it would not be counted as VRS legally. Such employees, therefore, will not be able to avail the benefit of tax exemption. The eligible employees receiving VRS can get the tax exemption for the amount of INR 5 lakh lump sum. Anyone receiving more than INR 5 lakh would be charged under the Income Tax Act.

Besides, an employee leaving under VRS gets his provident fund, encashment of accumulated leave, gratuity, salary for the notice period and cost of transfer to the hometown.

These techniques that are suggested give the humane touch to the downsizing.

This is very necessary because it is not only the post that is downsized, but also there is a human being involved in this process. The organization must convince the employees that the posts in the organization have become redundant and not the person and the organization still values the person. As emotions and feelings are involved in this process, every care must be taken by the management that the process is carried out in such a fashion that it keeps the dignity of the employees intact. However, at the same time it should achieve the objectives of the scheme in a tactful manner.

Trade unions play a crucial role in the introduction of VRS in any organized sector firm. The scheme cannot be implemented without, at least, the tacit approval of the representative union. Sometimes without the consent of the trade unions, workers legalize VRS by accepting it in mass. Recently, the entire workforce of Sri Ram Mills (1,400 workers) has accepted VRS, whereas the major union opposed the scheme tooth and nail. Other companies such as Ind Auto, SKF Bearing and Novartis have also been able to successfully reduce their workforce by introducing VRS. When the workers are convinced that the scheme is sufficiently attractive monetarily and/or the company is in deep crisis, the employees opt for the scheme.

Overtime Payments

Overtime pay is the amount paid to each employee in a pay period. In case an employee works more than a specified number of hours in a week, the additional hours are called overtime. Usually, pay for any hours worked as overtime is paid at a higher rate than regular hours, say one to two times of the rate of regular hours. Such arrangement may cover any specific category of employees of the organization or may be extended to all categories of employees of the organization. However, managers and professionals are excluded from the entitlement of overtime payments.

As stated earlier, overtime payments are typically made as and when standard working week is exceeded on a regular basis. The rate of payment of overtime pay may also vary depending on whether the work is done at weekends or on weekdays or on national holidays and so on. For example, in European countries, the rate of overtime pay, if worked on Christmas Day, goes as high as up to four times the rate of regular hours. Usually, it is calculated as follows:

$$\text{Hourly pay rate} \times O \times \text{Overtime hours worked}$$

$$\text{Where } O = \text{Overtime pay rate.}$$

In certain countries, salaried employees are typically exempted from overtime in case their income is more than a specific amount.

In many countries, overtime payments are regulated statutorily. For example, in the United States, it is the Wage and Hour Division of the US Department of Labour that regulates overtime pay provisions. In our country, Industrial

Employment (Standing Orders) Act, 1946, and Payment of Wages Act, 1936, contain some provisions related to overtime pay.

Attendance Bonuses

Attendance bonuses, according to Armstrong and Murlis, are generally paid to categories of staff where absenteeism is a problem and the organization wishes to encourage more constant attendance.[34] Thus, attendance bonuses are given to employees who have maintained perfect attendance for a period of time, usually a year or full quarter. It is normally paid in the form of a flat cash amount, additional paid time off or gift awards after completion of the period of perfect attendance. Attendance bonuses are usually paid where the work itself or the work environment is unpleasant, and it is beyond the power of the employer to improve it. Many employers reject this concept because it is payment over and above what has already been negotiated at the time of entering into an employment contract.

Shift Pay

Shift pay is a way of paying a premium to employees who work the less desirable hours a business must operate. The premium so paid, also called a shift differential, compensates those employees who are scheduled for a second or third shift, that is, shift pay is given where the pattern of working hours differs from the typical working day. It is usually paid where 24-hour cover for services is essential, such as production employees, various medical staff and broadcasting employees. It should be ensured that work practices should be sensible and competitive. Some organizations pay a shift differential for working holidays, split shifts or weekends.

Shift pay comprises a base rate plus the premium. Base rate pay means the employee receives for working only daytime hours Monday through Friday.

In some organizations, employees work under the terms of collective bargaining agreements that include provisions for shift pay. There are mainly two methods to work out the premium amount which is added to the base rate: either may use the employer a flat rate formula under which a specified amount is added to the base rate or a percentage method under which the employee's base rate is multiplied by a percentage.

According to Culpepper Compensation Surveys and Services, shift pay is paid by 59 per cent of customer support businesses and 83 per cent of manufacturing firms. However, shift pay is usually paid to hourly workers.

Clothing Allowances

According to Armstrong and Murlis,[35] clothing allowances are paid to staff who need to buy special clothing for work when the company does not provide uniforms. Some companies also pay dry-cleaning charges as per their policy. Clothing allowances may be paid either as an initial clothing allowance whereby it is paid to enlist members upon initial enlistment or upon other special qualification or entitlement. Initial issue may be either an in-kind or a combination of in-kind issue and cash payment. The other option is cash clothing replacement under which allowances are paid to enlisted members on the occasion of the anniversary month, each successive year. Cash clothing replacement is meant for replacement of required uniform items. The third option is known as extra clothing allowances which are over and above initial and replacement allowances and do not reduce, replace or otherwise affect them. These allowances are paid for unusual circumstances like when an enlisted member may require civilian clothes to discharge his assigned duties or when an enlisted member may require additional uniform items.

Christmas Bonuses and 13-Month Payments

It is because of tradition in some organizations that Christmas bonuses are paid, which are relatively small except in certain exceptional cases. The primary objective of these bonuses is generally to reward loyalty and meet the extra costs of the season. Thirteen- or even 14-month payments came to the United Kingdom from Europe. These payments are given as 'double month' salaries paid either at Christmas or in the summer or sometimes divided between the two.[36]

Honoraria

These lump sum payments are made to recognize specific contributions or expertise. These are psychologically more satisfying.

Payments for Qualifications

In order to recognize their added value to the organization, some organizations make these payments upon achieving some degrees such as PhD, MBA and BTech and some other technical or professional ones. It is usually the lump sum payment that is given to the achievers of the aforesaid qualifications. Some organizations also grant one to four annual increments for achieving additional qualifications.

Pay for Person

Pay for the person is attached to the person. Structures based on skills pay individuals for all the skills they provide irrespective of the fact whether the work they do requires all or just a few of those particular skills.

Pay for person or person-focused pay or knowledge-based pay or SBA or competency-based pay structures link pay to the depth or breadth of the skills, competencies, abilities and knowledge a person acquires and applies to the work.

Pay for person attaches weightage to the demonstrable characteristics of a person including skills, competency, behaviours and knowledge that enable performance. It takes into account the market demand of a person's unique skills, expertise and experience, having identified pay market premium for competencies and/or skills in short supply in the market.

Pay for Excellence

Most of the people talk about pay for performance all the time. It is usually observed that everyone likes to be paid for performance when there are great years—higher sales, higher profits and so on, especially when targets have been achieved or goals have been overachieved. Employees are excited about pay for performance. But when there is a tough year—when business is down or goals have not been achieved despite hard work of employees, nobody talks about pay for performance. Then employees talk about their hard work and efforts and not about performance. They think they should be paid for their hard work and effort.

But employees cannot have it both ways. It is not desirable that when employees perform well, they should be compensated for it and when they perform poorly, they should be compensated for that performance and not for their effort. If the performance of employees is down from the previous year, their compensation should also be less than that of the previous year because they have produced lesser results. Because in such a case, the organization may not be able to pay its bills. New profits and programmes cannot be funded through good intentions and hard work alone. There are both upsides and downsides in every business. But employees cannot choose to be healthy with the upside only and not to taste the consequences of the downside. Accountability is blind to that.

Employees want to be better compensated. But it is in the hands of employees to be better compensated. If the employees meet or overachieve their targets, their compensation will increase when that occurs. It should not be forgotten that an increase in your pay will become effective when you also become effective. They have to be excellent.

Managerial Compensation and Rewards

In order for the compensation to be motivational, it needs to be variable and, therefore, proportional to the result or goals already settled. Such a payment is known as incentives. Managers can be rewarded accordingly.

Compensation and rewards can also be designed based on the profile of managers and the nature of work. However, rewards should be significant and meaningful to the recipients.

There can also be an option to choose from a range of rewards as it makes the recipients feel the reward is personalized to them.

Though most organizations prefer pay for performance, these organizations use time-bound compensation plus cost of living as an indicator for salary increment. But, of late, they have been recently shifting from annual increment to performance increment (for more details, see Chapter 4).

Sales Force Incentive Programmes

Sales force incentive programmes can serve a good purpose in motivating sales personnel. Such incentives can be either in the form of cash, merchandise, tips or gifts depending on how much the organization can afford. However, it is essential to consult sales personnel and get input from them while developing the incentive programme. This will make the incentive more motivating.

In a top-seller programme, the salesperson making the highest sales within a stipulated period is rewarded and thus generates a friendly competitive environment among the salespersons. As against this, in the case of a large sales force, it can be divided into teams which can compete against each other causing team competition, though members of a team work together. At the end of the stipulated period, teams can be rewarded depending on their rank in making sales.

It is also possible that the entire sales force can work together as one unit to achieve a common sales target. It facilitates including new salespersons who can learn how to work as one unit. The senior and highly experienced salespersons can act as mentors and prizes can be awarded if the goal is achieved.

Point system is another method of rewarding salespersons. Incentives programmes can be based on a point system. In this programme, for each sale made, the salesperson will be awarded certain points depending upon the size of the sales, and thus salesperson scoring higher points can be rewarded.

Another method can be *quota system* under which each salesperson is assigned a quota based on his geographical territory. In case territories are not used, every salesperson is allotted the same quota. Awards can be given for meeting the quota or exceeding the quota (for more details, see Chapter 4).

Chapter Review

1. The success of an organization depends, to a great extent, on its competent workforce. Hence, the concept of 'paying for competence'. The term 'competence' refers to the ability of an individual to do a job efficiently and effectively. It is, therefore, skill-based and standard-based. On the other hand, the term 'competency' refers to a set of defined behaviours that offer a structural guide

helping in the identification, evaluation and development of the behaviours in an individual, though in routine, 'competency' refers to general description of the requirements of employees in organizations. It is behaviour-based and is a manner of behaviours.

2. In case an employee is compensated on the basis of his type or level of obtained skills that are applied in the workplace, it is known as competency-based pay. Since in the competency-based structures, an employee is compensated on the basis of his knowledge, skills, experience and so on, it motivates employees to develop their skills, knowledge, behaviour in teamwork, lateral career development, hard work, sincerity and so on. It is quantitative in nature and reflects greater objectivity. Competency-based pay system is time-consuming and expensive to implement. Besides, objective measurement of competencies is difficult and managers involved in competency-based systemsf have to be trained and they have to put in extra effort. The gender and ethnic bias are also a possibility.

3. Before introducing a competency-based pay system, it should be ensured that a well-established competency framework has already been working in the organization effectively for other HR processes and that there has already been in existence a credible, tried and tested system of assessment of competencies for reward purpose. The purpose and potential benefits of the competency-based pay should be well communicated to all concerned. The broad approach to be used should be defined and decision be taken as to what is to be done to develop it. The linkage between compensation and competency be ensured.

4. SBA is a compensation system that rewards employees with additional pay in exchange for formal certification of an employee's knowledge, mastery of skills and other competencies. SBA is also known as knowledge-based pay, though the underlying idea behind the knowledge-based pay is that it implies the understanding of how to do certain tasks. The purpose of the skill-based structure is to support the strategy, objectives and workflow, motivate the employees towards organization objectives and also to be fair to employees.

5. All concerned should be involved in the formulation of SBP plans. There are three types of SBP structures, namely depth-oriented base pay systems, breadth-oriented base pay structures and bonus systems. In order to establish SBP in an organization, certain steps have to be taken, like identifying potential skill-based jobs, identifying the specific skills required for each job level, working out costs and benefits of the SBP plans, developing proper techniques to assess new skills, working out certification standards and also working out the rupee amount of SBP for the required skill. In order to implement such plans, there should be management commitment, proper communication of goals and mechanism of the plan(s), taking care of inevitable problems, understanding the appropriateness of the plan to be implemented, identifying

the appropriate design, identifying the skills required, which category of employees to be covered, developing a risk management plan and so on.

6. Team-based pay/rewards are payments or other forms of non-financial rewards provided to members of a defined team, which are linked to the performance of that team, implying that organization recognizes teamwork, makes the team effective and encourages group effort by providing incentives and recognizing team achievements. Team-based rewards enhance the pro-social behaviour, boost members' capabilities and productivity, increase flexibility and so on. The main demerits of the team-based pay include: rarity of well-defined teams, difficulty in establishing standards, selfishness of some of the team members, unfavourable work environment, uncooperative behaviour of team members, opposition of the plan by some team members, frustration of high performers in low performing teams and so on. Among several approaches to team-based rewards are: recognizing contribution, clarifying incentives and definition of performance, demonstrating teamwork competencies and so on.

7. There are several factors affecting team-based pay/rewards such as nature and type of team (like process or work teams, parallel teams, project or time teams) and characteristics of the team. So far as team reward processes are concerned, they can be discussed under the heads such as justification for team rewards, basics for team rewards and methods of providing team-based pay/bonus. However, it is not easy to design and manage team-based pay.

8. Gainsharing is a commitment to employee involvement that ties additional pay to improvements in workforce performance. The main goals of gainsharing include stimulating productivity and quality, reducing cost of production, motivating workers and working as a change agent. There are several principles of gainsharing, the main being involving the employees in such a fashion that they identify themselves with the organization. The key elements in designing a gainsharing plan are strength of reinforcement, productivity standards, splitting the gains, ease of administration and production in variability.

9. Profit-sharing, also known as DPSP, involves sharing a part of profits of the company with the employees as per predetermined formula, the main objective being to provide motivation to employees to work vigorously and also win their goodwill. The types of profit-sharing include cash plans, deferred plans and continuation plans. Such plans lead to higher output, reduced supervision, extra income to workers, team spirit and so on. Profit-related pay is a form of profit-sharing in which pay is based on profits earned by the organization, its objectives being to increase motivation, create commitment and promote efforts by the employees.

10. Other cash payments and allowance include: payments in response to market premises such as golden hellos, golden handcuffs and large-city allowances, payments to reward special circumstances like golden handshakes, overtime

payments, attendance bonuses, shift pay, clothing allowance, Christmas bonus, honoraria, payment for qualifications, pay for person, pay for excellence, management compensation and awards, sales force incentives programmes and so on.

DISCUSSION QUESTIONS

1. Discuss the meaning and definition of competency. Also, discuss why competency-based pay is justified.
2. Discuss the prerequisites for introducing competency-based pay.
3. What are the purpose and features of SBP structure? Also, discuss how to establish and implement SBP systems.
4. Discuss the meaning and purpose of team-based pay/rewards and why it should or should not be introduced in an organization.
5. Discuss the main processes and factors affecting team-based pay systems.
6. What is gainsharing? Also, discuss the primary components, designing, merits and demerits of team-based pay systems.
7. Discuss the concept, meaning, characteristics, objectives and types of profit-sharing.
8. What is the concept of profit-related pay? Also, discuss its objectives, approaches, merits and demerits.
9. Discuss the implications of 'golden hellos', 'golden handcuffs' and 'golden handshakes'.
10. Discuss the terms, 'attendance allowance', 'shift pay', '13-month payments', 'pay for person' and 'pay for excellence'.

Individual and Group Activities

1. Individually visit a large-scale organization where competency-based pay systems are in operation. Find out from the HR personnel there whether the systems are functioning alright. If not, what are the problems involved?
2. In a group of three, visit an organization where SBP systems are being followed. Discuss with the HR head if the systems are yielding the desired results. Or they need some changes. If yes, what?
3. Discuss in a group of two with the trade union leaders of an organization where the team-based pay systems are in vogue and find out whether the members of their union are satisfied with its functioning. Yes or no, why? Prepare a detailed report.
4. Individually visit some organizations of high repute and find out the difference between 'gainsharing' and 'profit-sharing' schemes as also their merits and demerits.

5. In a group of three, visit some big organizations and find out from the HR personnel there what other cash payments and allowances, over and above their pay rates, are being paid to the employees. Collect all relevant details and prepare a detailed report.
6. Individually visit a large-scale organization where competency-based pay systems are in operation. Find out from the HR personnel there whether the systems are functioning alright. If not, what are the problems involved?
7. In a group of three, visit an organization where SBP systems are being followed. Discuss with the HR head if the systems are yielding the desired results. Or they need some changes. If yes, what?
8. Discuss in a group of two with the trade union leaders of an organization where the team-based pay systems are in vogue and find out whether the members of their union are satisfied with its functioning. Yes or no, why? Prepare a detailed report.
9. Individually visit some organizations of high repute and find out the difference between 'gainsharing' and 'profit-sharing' schemes as also their merits and demerits.
10. In a group of three, visit some big organizations and find out from the HR personnel there what other cash payments and allowances, over and above their pay rates, are being paid to the employees. Collect all relevant details and prepare a detailed report.

APPLICATION CASE

Henry has a master's degree in Business Administration from one of the top institutes in the country. Wherever he had been earlier as a senior executive, he always proved his credentials and therefore used to be suitably rewarded for his efforts and calibre. However, in his last assignment in a paint manufacturing organization, he felt that his contribution was not duly recognized as much as it should have been. He continued in that organization for some time, and one day he resigned from his job and joined another organization as its chief operating officer (COO).

Henry got very confused when he found that though the organization had been sustaining itself, most of its highly competent employees and executives were not happy. Henry, therefore, convened a meeting and invited all the departmental heads, but in the case of the HR department, he invited all the executives who had been with the organization for more than five years. Without wasting any time, he came to the main issue. He told all the members present in the meeting that he has been with this organization for the last few months but based on his observation he feels that while employees, by and large, appear to be happy, the most competent people do not appear to be so. The company, therefore, will have to pay the price for it sooner than later.

Hence, the problem demands an immediate solution. He invited suggestions from all concerned. The meeting was called off. In about a month, whatever suggestions were received, they were looked into and whichever appeared to be sound and implementable were executed, but nothing came out of it.

One day when Henry was handed over the cheque for his monthly salary, all of a sudden he felt as if he had got the solution to the problem. He immediately called Mr Franklin, the vice-president of the company, and also the HR head. He asked them that they should go through all the HR processes, especially with regard to salary thoroughly and brief him within a couple of days. He asked them, in particular, the changes effected in any process during the last two years because he had the feedback that earlier the highly competitive executives, who appear to be disheartened now, were quite happy.

During the next couple of days, Mr Franklin and the HR head had three sittings. Having examined all the documents related to HR processes in operation now and also consulting other staff of the HR department, the duo came to the conclusion that no major changes have taken place during the last two years except in the case of determining pay. Earlier, salary was competency-based, but for the last one year the basis was changed from competency-based to team-based. Consequently, the now aggrieved highly competitive executives who were earlier paid on the basis of their competence are presently being paid on the basis of the performance of their teams as a result of which their pay has been slightly adversely affected. The duo prepared a detailed report. Besides other things, they also worked out the total pay paid to the aggrieved executives individually year-wise during the last two years. On comparing the pay received by each of these aggrieved executives during the last year, when each of them was paid on the basis of performance of their respective teams, with the pay received by each of them during the year earlier, when each of them was paid on that basis of their competences, it was found that all of them got 2–3 per cent less pay in the last year.

After receiving the detailed report, Mr Henry convened a meeting inviting Mr Franklin and the HR head to join him in the meeting. They discussed the whole issue and Mr Henry asked them to think over the matter, find out a solution and report back to him.

Questions

1. Identify the main cause of the present grievance of the highly competitive executives.
2. Visualize the factors that might have been responsible for the company to change the mode of determining pay from competency-based to team-based. What precautions should have been taken before switching over to team-based mode?
3. What will be your stand if you are asked to resolve the problem now?

Notes

1 M. Armstrong, *Employee Reward*, 2nd ed. (Hyderabad: Orient BlackSwan/University Press, 1999), Chapter 21, 293–309.
2 Ibid.
3 G. Homan, 'Skills and Competency-Based Pay', in *Strategic Rewards Systems*, eds. R. Thorpe and G. Homan (Upper Saddle River, NJ: Prentice Hall, 2000), 288–301.
4 Armstrong, *Employee Reward*.
5 K. Adams, 'Employers' Practice in Using Competencies for Pay, Progression and Grading', *Competency & Intelligence Quarterly* 7, no. 1 (1999): 16–27; K. Adams, 'Performance, Development and Reward at the Registers of Scotland', *Competency & Emotional Intelligence Quarterly* 6, no. 3 (1999): 10–15.
6 Armstrong, *Employee Reward*.
7 Ibid.
8 Armstrong and Murlis, *Reward Management*, 297.
9 Ibid.
10 Milkovich, Newman, and Venkata Ratnam, *Compensation*, 132.
11 Ibid., 135.
12 Armstrong and Murlis, *Reward Management*, 299.
13 Gerald E. Ledford, Jr. and Herbert G. Heneman III, 'Skill-Based Pay' (prepared for the Society for Industrial & Organisational Psychology, Inc. SIOP Science Series, published by the Society for Human Resource Management [SHRM], June 2011).
14 For more details, visit https:/www.whatishumanresource.com.
15 Ibid.
16 CIPD, *Reward Management 2004*. A Survey of Policy and Practice (London: CIPD).
17 Armstrong and Murlis, *Reward Management*, 24.
18 K. Merriman, 'Low Trust Teams Prefer Individualized Pay', *Harvard Business Review* 86, no. 11 (2008): 32.
19 P. A. Bamberger and R. Levi, 'Team-Based Reward Allocation Structures and the Helping Behaviours of Outcome-Interdependent Team Members', *Journal of Management Psychology* 24, no. 4 (2009): 301.
20 V. Haines and S. Tagger, 'Antecedents of Team Reward Attitude', *Group Dynamics: Theory, Research and Practice* 10, no. 3 (2006): 194–205.
21 American Management Association, 'Team-Based Pay: Approaches Vary, but Produce No Magic Formulas', *Compflash* (April 1994): 4.
22 Ibid.
23 Armstrong and Murlis, *Reward Management*, 349–350.
24 Ibid., 354.
25 R. Masternak and T. Ross, 'Gainsharing: A Bonus Plan or Employee Involvement?' *Compensation and Benefits Review* 24 (January–February 1992): 46–54.
26 Armstrong and Murlis, *Reward Management*, 25.
27 Ibid.
28 Ibid., 359–360.
29 Milkovich, Newman, and Venkata Ratnam, *Compensation*, 269–270.
30 Jumpup, 'Obituary—Mr Theodore Taylor, a Pioneer of Profit Sharing', *The Times*, 21 October 1952.
31 Armstrong and Murlis, *Reward Management*, 364.
32 Ibid., 406.
33 Ibid., 408.
34 Ibid., 409.
35 Ibid.
36 Ibid., 410.

6

ADMINISTERING AND CONTROLLING SALARY COSTS AND SALARY REVIEW

LEARNING OBJECTIVES

After studying this chapter, the reader should be able to:

1. Explain the meaning and definition of 'salary costs', and also enlist and explain the various categories of employment costs.
2. Explain the term 'salary planning' and what is it that is decided in the process of salary planning.
3. Explain what is meant by 'salary budget' and how it differs from salary planning, especially in the context of their purposes.
4. Explain the term 'salary control' and also the process of salary control.
5. Explain the term 'salary reviews' and also guidelines for the salary review process.
6. Explain how to respond to negative salary review.
7. Enlist and explain the steps involved in the process of wage and salary fixation.

Introduction

The success of an organization depends, to a very large extent, on how well it administers and controls its salary costs and conducts salary reviews. That is why financial planning is integral to managing compensation. The cost implications of pay structures, increasing

DOI: 10.4324/9781032626123-6

merit pay, instituting various benefit schemes, implementing gainsharing or providing incentives are critical for making sound decisions. Budgets account for all such costs. Hence, a clear idea of salary costs, proper financial planning and budgeting is important for the success of an organization. Here, we start with salary costs first.

Salary Costs

The word 'salary' originated from the Latin word *salarium*. Roman soldiers were given some quota of salt in addition to their pay. When it was found highly inconvenient to preserve and transport a huge bulk of salt, the soldiers were compensated in terms of cash in place of salt. The money so paid was referred to as *salarium* or salt money which was later called 'salary' in modern English. It is not surprising that a good number of employees may not have an idea of how much exactly they cost to their organization, thinking that their salary and benefits are the only costs that the organization might be incurring on them. It is a well-known fact that salaries and wages alone constitute a significant percentage of an organization's employee compensation expenses. For example, according to the US Bureau of Labor Statistics (BLS), salaries and wages alone account for 69.6 per cent of an organization's compensation expenses. Most organizations' total compensation makes up to at least 50 per cent of operating expenses.[1] Whereas some costs are controllable, some are not. For example, salary-related costs beyond base salary can be controlled to a great extent, but not the base salary costs. It is, therefore, essential to know the various heads under which labour costs are usually incurred, which are as follows:

First comes the 'hiring costs. All employees cost something to the organization before they were even hired. For example, recruiting costs start from getting a job advertisement inserted. in newspapers, periodicals, journals and so on or getting them advertised on TV and other media forums, and creating websites, portals and so on. Again, conducting tests and interviews involves a lot of expenditure. Travelling expenses must be paid to the candidates invited for their interviews and to the outside experts invited to conduct tests and interviews. Their fees are also to be paid. In some cases, consulting and outsourcing firms are also involved in the recruitment process, which is also to be paid their heavy fees. For example, in many cases, the consulting firms' fees come to about 20 to 35 per cent of the candidate's first-year salary, especially in the case of senior positions.

Besides, in addition to basic pay paid to the employees, some taxes have also to be paid by the organization to the government. Then, most organizations incur costs on providing fringe benefits to their employees, which may be in many forms like paid time off, including vacations, holidays and all types of paid leaves, including maternity leave. For all these paid time offs, no tangible work is done by the employees to offset the cost. Medical allowance or medical expenses reimbursement, accident injury/disablement/death compensation, retirement plans and other benefits extended to the workers—all cost the organization. The working space and related equipment are to be provided to the employees. The space that an employee is provided occupies a percentage of the rent the organization pays for the facility (or of the cost of creating that facility in case space is not taken on rent by the organization). The organization also provides space for common facilities such as washrooms, hallways, kitchens and so on for the employees. The costs incurred on the above are also salary-related costs. Then office equipment provided to the employees such as desks, chairs and cabinets, electronic equipment in the form of personal computers, software and printer, cell phones, office phones, internet access and various technological devices and their maintenance costs are included in salary-related costs. In almost all situations, equipment costs are substantial and are to be borne by the organization.

Based on the above, employment costs fall into the following several broad categories:

1. Recruiting expenses.
2. Basic salary.
3. Employment taxes.
4. Benefits.
5. Space.
6. Equipment.
7. Others.

There are many factors that affect labour costs. It can be explained with the help of the following equation:

$$\text{Labour cost} = \text{Employment} \times (\text{Average cash compensation} + \text{Average benefit costs})^2$$

As per the equation, the three main factors that need controlling in order to manage labour costs are employment (e.g. the number of employees and the hours they work), average cash compensation (such as wages/salaries and bonuses) and average benefit costs. Hence, the above-mentioned three factors require attention if labour costs are to be managed well.

There is also another approach to calculating salary costs.

When it is difficult to calculate salary costs incurred over and above base salary, the same can simply be estimated on general observation and considered. For example, in some businesses, employees are billed for projects on a time and material basis. In such cases, their base salary can be multiplied by say 1.25 to cover employment taxes and benefits. That number then can be multiplied by 1.75 to cover rent, equipment and so on. In this way, an estimated figure can be worked out.

Salary Planning

Salary planning is an integral part of the budgetary process of an organization, and it is through the salary planning process that a company examines the labour market and compares the results of the examination with the current pay being paid within the company. Salary planning is an annual feature. The planning process takes care of how much of the company's resources will go into salaries and details the salary rate for each employee of the company. Salary planning is a good exercise in case the company is interested in optimizing its expenditure on employees.

Salary increase is a highly scrutinized activity and is an unending problem. Salary increases have not only a cumulative effect but also a year-after-year effect on an organization's cash flow and determine the well-being of an organization. It is therefore, obvious that if the managers of an organization do not pay adequate attention to determining the appropriate method of salary increases, they must face the music later as this may lead to serious consequences including uncontrolled expenses and aggrieved employees.

It is in the salary planning process that it is decided what is it that the organization wants to do and how it is going to get it done. Formal salary planning processes are an essential part of salary administration. What to do and how to do depend to a very great extent on a couple of things. First is the external environment which may make the accomplishment of goals either more or less tough. Therefore, the salary planning manager or his team must have knowledge and information about the current employment environment. Second, the salary planning manager or his team should be able to estimate whether the actions taken by the organization, that is, 'the how', will in fact create the desired state, that is, 'the what'.

Now the question arises of how to start the process of salary planning. First, the data related to jobs, and the wage and salary structure is to be collected and compared with the present salaries to be followed by a competitive analysis. This helps the organization in determining the increases to be made to salaries as well as to structure, and finally, this is presented in a budgetary format to be used for control purposes.

Salary Budget

A budget is a statement in quantitative, and ordinarily, financial terms. Similarly, a salary budget is a statement in quantitative/financial terms of the planned allocation and use of resources to meet the operational requirements of the organization. A salary budget involves forecasting the levels of activity, indicating the number of different categories of employees that are required for the period of the budget. The annual salary budget is primarily a product of the number of employees to be engaged and the rates at which they will be paid. The salary budget, therefore, must consider the financial resources available to the company as per salary planning. This will influence the ability to pay for performance management and threshold increases and/or the number of people to be employed. A salary budget helps in controlling as it enables the organization to compare budgeted costs with actual costs and take corrective action and finding out whether salary policies and guidelines have been properly implemented.

Salary Control

Controlling of Employment (Number of People to Be Employed)

Salary costs depend mainly on the number of people employed. Hence, in order to reduce their number to the minimum, we should collect such information about competitors and try to have a competitive number of employees. Some companies, especially in the industrially advanced countries of the West, divide their workforce into two groups, namely core employees and contingent employees. The companies maintain long-term relationships with core employees with whom a long-term relationship is desired. The employment agreements of contingent employees cover only short, specific time periods. For achieving flexibility and control labour costs, many employers expand or contract this contingent workforce. Some companies keep fewer core employees and more contingent employees as the number of the latter ones can be easily increased or decreased and labour costs can be controlled effectively.

Today, in many companies, rather than defining employment as the number of employees, hours of work are often used. For example, if a company engages a smaller number of employees and pays them overtime, and if they are put on duty for more than 40 hours per week, it will have to incur 50 per cent more expense for overtime work as the overtime rate is one and a half times more than that of regular wages. Hence, in order to control labour costs, the company can think of whether hiring more regular workers who will have to be paid overtime pay, which is usually one and a half times more, will be useful or not. But this proposition must be compared with the average cash compensation which comprises average salary level plus variable compensation payments such as gainsharing, bonuses or profit-sharing and needs to be effectively controlled. According to Milkovich et al.,[3] adjustments to the average salary level can be made (a) 'top-down', in which top management determines the amount of money to be spent on pay and allocate it 'down' to each sub-unit for the plan year, and (b) 'bottom up', in which individual employee's pay for the plan year is forecasted and summed to create an organization-wide salary budget.

Controlling Salary Level: Top-Down

Top-down budgeting starts with an estimate from the top management of the pay increase budget for the whole organization. After the total budget is worked out, it is then allocated to each manager. He then plans how to distribute it among his subordinates. Among the many approaches in top-down budgeting, one typical approach—also known as planned pay level rise—is the percentage increase in the average pay for the unit that is planned. Of course, there are several factors that affect the decision on how much to increase the average pay level for the next period: how much the average level was increased this period, ability to pay, competitive market pressure, turnover effects and cost of living.[4] Current year's rise is the percentage by which the average wage changed in the past year. It can be reflected as under:

$$\text{Percentage level rise} = 100 \times \frac{\text{Average pay at year end} - \text{Average pay at year beginning}}{\text{Average pay at the beginning of the year}}$$

Then comes the 'ability to pay' of the organization. It is in part a function of the company's financial circumstances to take a decision with regard to increasing the average pay level. While well-off organizations may like to maintain their competitive positions in the labour market and share their financial success through profit-sharing and bonuses, troubled employers may not be able to maintain their competitive market position. The traditional approach is to reduce employment.

However, potential cost savings can be exercised by analysing pay and staffing at each level. The other way out can be to reduce the rate of increase in average pay which can be effected by controlling adjustments in base or valuable pay or both. Reducing benefits can be another option. Then, competitive market pressures are also to be dealt with. The going market rate changes each year depending on the turnover effect, cost of living and so on. This also needs to be investigated.

Controlling Salary Level: Bottom-Up

Bottom-up budgeting starts with managers' pay increase recommendations for the upcoming plan year leading to a budget for the upcoming plan year for each organization's unit and also an estimated pay treatment for each employee. The top management can modify to a very limited extent such recommendations and control salary level to some extent.

Embedded Controls

In addition to a formal budgeting process for controlling managers' pay decisions, there are controls that are inherent in the design of the techniques such as job analysis, job evaluation, skill-based Pay (SBP), competence-based pay, performance evaluation and gainsharing. These techniques are also instrumental in regulating managers' pay decisions by guiding what managers are able to do and what they cannot do. As a matter of fact, controls are built into these techniques which direct managers towards the objectives of the pay system. Such controls may include: ranging maximums and minimums, variable pay, compa-ratios, analysing costs, analysing value added and so on.[5]

Thus, in order to have effective salary control, salary administration procedures should have the following features:

1. Ranges with minimum and maximum to which all jobs are allocated based on their value should be clearly defined. All employees of the organization should be paid within the ranges for the jobs performed.
2. Methods of progress within the range based on specific criteria should be well-defined and explained.
3. There should be a detailed salary budget which should be based on the number of employees required to carry out the desired volume of work.
4. Forecasts of salary levels keeping in view the effects of general and incremental increases.
5. Forecasts of the probable effect on salary costs of changes in the numbers employed and of differences between the salary levels of those joining or leaving.
6. Forecasts of promoters and promotional increases and the number of people joining and leaving the organization.
7. Specified authority at each management level who is empowered to award or to confirm increments, effecting changes in salary and check their consistency with policy.
8. Clarity in salary review guidelines. It should clearly specify the limit to which the payroll costs of each department can increase due to merit awards and the number of maximum awards that can be granted and how the awards will be distributed based on performance and salary grades.
9. Clear procedures for auditing increases and salary levels to ensure that the same is in line with the salary policy laid down for the purpose and to ensure that the same does not exceed the budgeted costs.

Salary Reviews

In the gone years review of salary was not practised by organizations, but of late most organizations have started conducting pay reviews; the objective is to enable organizations to award their best-performing employees, keeping them motivated so that they may give their best to the organization. Besides, there is a logic for increasing salaries in line with the length of service and increased responsibility as the organization intends to reward or retain talent. Salary reviews are also desirable if the economy of the organization or the country is recovering or going downward, or job opportunities are expanding or shrinking so as to initiate necessary steps in the interest of the organization. Otherwise, also, it is always good to conduct a salary review to protect the interest of all concerned and also let the employee concerned know where he stands and what he should do. Excessive wage increases or cuts may damage both workers and the organization in the long run if salary reviews are not conducted and necessary remedial measures are not taken. A word of caution here. Salary negotiations can be difficult and, if not handled effectively, can cause an employee to be demotivated. It is therefore essential for any organization to decide on a consistent approach to salary reviews and also to train their managers to deliver this process in all cases.

While some organizations prefer to define a clear matrix of criteria to warrant an increase with a regular review cycle, for example, annually, others instead may prefer the flexibility to react as and when requests arise. It is a matter of convenience for the organization.

In the context of salary reviews, it must be realized by the managers that the value of the role that an employee performs is different from their value as an individual. Employees may have a very high potential value, but if their role is such that it does not enable them to perform to their fullest extent, then their reward level may have to be reduced. Thus, if the limit of the value that can be placed on a particular role has simply been reached, the decline in the salary increase is not a reflection of an individual's value to the organization. In such cases, the managers should find or develop a role which needs a higher value, and therefore salary. This can be done by agreeing and assigning wider responsibilities and targets for employees whereby they can contribute more to the organization.

Salary reviews can be either 'general salary' reviews which are conducted when a salary increase is desired in all or most salaries as a result of, say, a spurt in the cost of living or ongoing rates in the market, or 'individual salary reviews' the purpose of which is to decide increments that should be given to individuals based on the merit of each individual because there is certainly not a blanket case of 'better for all' in every annual salary review.

The salary review process should have a mechanism to control expectations and determine where an increase is due. It is always good if this process is discussed with the employee.

Guidelines for Salary Review Process

There is no salary review process which can be uniformly applied in all cases. However, the following guidelines may be helpful in achieving the desired objectives of salary review:

1. **Review the budget:** It will be in the fitness of things if, first, the salary budget is investigated as the provisions made in it will make it easy to make decisions during the review.
2. **Identify the objectives of the salary review:** The next and very important step is to identify the objectives of the salary review. For example, one objective may be to motivate the employees to work hard and produce more to take advantage of the high increase in the demand for the organization's product(s) in the market. Another objective can be to reduce wage bills because of low demand for the organization's product(s) in the market or severe competition

questioning the very sustainability of the organization. The objectives may differ from organization to organization depending on the environment in which they are functioning. It will be good if the employees or their trade unions are also consulted while identifying the objectives of the salary review. They should be told the reasons for the pay review and the whole criteria to discourage the expectations of non-deserving employees to the extent possible.

3. **Reaching out to the market and analysing market pay data:** Having gone through the data maintained by the organization internally, reach out to the market for analysis and make sure that changes, if any, have been effected in the pay scales or promotions have been taken care of when the data has been compiled internally. In order to ensure the reliability of the data, the organization should not go for free data. The sources of collection of data should be genuine and reliable.

4. **Issues to be considered during the review:** During salary review, factors such as accountability of the employees, their competency, working environment, their behaviour at work, ability to deal with other employees, extra efforts put in by them and the like must be kept into consideration while deciding pay rises. It should be ensured that the latest changes in rules, regulations and the system have been duly taken care of and that the system appears to be transparent and objective. Employees should be provided with clarifications as and when they seek on any issue.

5. **Getting the self-evaluation form filled in:** Next step can be to get the self-evaluation forms filled in by the employees. In many cases, the salary expectations of the employees may be surprising. However, through these self-evaluation forms, it may be learned what unpleasant things occurred last year which can be compared to the present ones. The filled self-evaluation forms may reveal the good performance given by certain employees and now the managers come to know about their achievements which might have been forgotten by them and may save them from the embarrassment of not knowing the good work done by employees. It will also help the managers to decide whether those employees deserve higher salaries or not, depending on their performance.

6. **Review of the employee job description:** The next step involves reviewing job description of employees which may help in knowing the shortcomings of employees. It will also spell out the responsibilities and the competencies they are supposed to have. It will also give an idea about what expectations they have met and where they have gone wrong. In case the employees are not competent in getting increases in their salary, they should not be given surprises during the review. Rather the same should have been discussed with them earlier because no employee welcomes negative feedback at the time of salary review.

7. **Reviewing the principles for rewarding employees:** It is also important to review the principles for rewarding employees. For example, see if the criteria

for who will be promoted or rewarded have been set. Also, check if there is consistency or not and so on.

8. **Establishing the proper rating system:** The employees must be rated as to where each employee stands and what will be the amount of pay rise as per their rating. The employees can be rated as unsatisfactory, satisfactory, very satisfactory or exceptional. The employees should be informed of the amount of their pay rise. The aforesaid rating should be well defined, and employees be informed of the same so that no employee has any grievance in this regard.

9. **Proper planning and ensuring rules:** Appropriate planning can be instrumental in keeping the employees satisfied. In case the planning is done well, it is likely to be appreciated by one and all, and things will move smoothly and swiftly. The leaders of the organization must be clear about everybody's rating and should be able to satisfy all concerned. Due weightage should be given to factors such as positive attitude, confidence, ability to adapt to changes and learning attitude.

10. **Communicate and be timely:** Everything that needs to be communicated to the employees should be communicated clearly and timely. It should not appear that the organization is hiding anything from the employees. Nothing should be ambiguous. It should be duly communicated and published timely.

11. **Involving line managers:** Line managers should also be involved in the pay review process because it is usually they who have a lot of relevant information with them. Training may also be provided to them regarding pay review.

12. **Fine-tune and give final touch:** When the whole exercise is completed review it and give final touches so that it becomes refined and presentable. It should be ensured that there is no discrimination, and everything is transparent.

13. **Explain the final decisions to employees:** All employees should be informed about the outcome of the pay process, maybe the result ends up affecting the employee adversely. Line managers may be asked to explain this to the employees in case any employee needs any clarification. At the end of the review, every employee should have a feeling that he has been treated fairly.

14. **Reviewing the salary review system:** In case during salary review any confusion or problem has arisen, the salary review system should be critically examined, and remedial steps taken so that any confusion or problem experienced this time may not be confronted in the future.

Some Other Guidelines

1. In case an employee will not be getting a pay rise during salary review due to his marginal or unsatisfactory performance, letter to this effect justifying the nature of performance deficiencies should be submitted to the office concerned and may be kept in his file.

2. If an employee's performance warrants it, his merit increase can be deferred.

3. The authorities concerned have also the option of giving a one-time lump sum to the employee instead of adding it to his base salary.

4. The authorities concerned should have already scheduled the time when the employees would receive their performance feedback and a written performance review which may include a career development plan as well as performance goals.

5. The whole process of salary review should be planned appropriately and well in time and documented in a proper format.

6. It should be ensured that all the managers assigned the job of salary review are competent and properly trained for the job.

7. From time to time, feedback should be obtained from the employees about the objectivity and transparency of decisions of the review committee. In this regard, some benchmark criteria can also be established to ensure that employees are treated properly and fairly. Such benchmarks should be clearly understandable by both the managers and the employees.

8. The rating system chosen for the purpose must be fair and free of prejudice or biases. All ratings should be explained in detail spelling out clearly what and how much is expected by a particular rating.

9. Ensure that pay review is as per procedure laid out for the purpose and that every employee gets a pay rise according to what he deserves.

Responding to Negative Salary Review

It is not an uncommon experience that an employee receives a negative salary review, and therefore, equally dispiriting salary adjustments. Not only this, but an employee may also experience a disastrous review and no salary adjustment at all. Under such a scenario, how should an employee react?

First, he should not allow his emotions to run wild. There is no doubt that receiving bad news about your earning capacity is never enjoyable. But all the same, one should not get agitated also. The affected employee should try to absorb the news and remain composed. It is advisable that he should take some time to evaluate the situation and may request a meeting with the reviewer or reviewing committee later. This will give time to the aggrieved employee to compose himself in between and address the issue in a calm and quiet manner.

Quite possible the reason for a paltry pay rise despite your good performance might be genuine from the point of view of the organization. For example, though convinced with the employee's good performance, the organization may not find it possible to grant the employee a reasonable pay rise due to the difficult financial period the organization may be going through. Such circumstances should be explained to the employee concerned and he should also take it in the right spirit.

In case a low salary adjustment is due to poor performance of the employee himself, unit or organization, the employee should take a close look at why this happened. He should be honest and fair to understand it. If the reviewer feels that the employee is underperforming, there would certainly be a reason for him to feel so. It may be the case that the employee may not be putting forth the efforts, though he may be capable of doing so. Such things do not happen in a vacuum. Hence, the employee should review the situation objectively, though it may not be that simple.

In case the employee feels that his pay rise is not reflective of his performance, he should ask the reviewer for re-evaluation after a gap of time, say three months or so. This will reflect the employee's willingness to demonstrate his commitment to his work.

There is also a possibility that the boss of the employee does not see the value the employee brings to the organization or that the organization pays its staff less than the market value of the employees. In such a scenario, it is time for the employee to start looking for a job elsewhere because the fastest way to get a big raise is to change jobs and find a better one. To say this does not mean that this would happen every time. This should happen only when an employee feels that he can be better paid elsewhere.

Thus, in case salary review is conducted appropriately, it proves to be a motivation booster and works as a pump that motivates employees to work harder and to perfection—resulting in the interest of both the employer and the employee.

Five Key Steps: Manager's Guide to Annual Salary Review

The following are five key steps that may help managers use their limited pay budgets to make meaningful base pay recommendations. Hence, these should be taken into consideration during salary review.

1. **Job's worth:** The most important factor which should be kept into consideration while reviewing pay is the value of each position. To begin with, the compa-ratio should be looked at, that is, the salary being paid to employees compared to the market mid-point for similar positions at other organizations. Although comprehending this alignment gives clear insight, to a great extent, into the value of each job, that alone is not enough to make merit pay decisions. Hence, in addition to knowing the value of the job for their organization, the managers should also fall in line with the compensation philosophy of their organization. They should have a vivid picture of how important the job for their organization is and how critical the job is for the effectiveness of the organization. What are the skills involved in a particular job and what is the position of availability of these skills in the market? Is the company in a position and willing to pay more for that type of job? Once the managers have answers to these questions, they can do better justice while determining merit increases.

2. **Performance of the employee:** Employee performance is the base for determining the merit increase. Hence, the managers will have to find out if the employee is meeting the expectations of the job requirements, and further

at what level the employee is demonstrating skills, that is, below or above the expected ones. Is the employee competent to do the job or not? If not, is he expected to reach the desired competence level with or without training? Is there any need for grooming the employee? The managers should have answers to the aforesaid questions also if they want to do justice in determining merit increase and also to assess how it aligns or does not align with the job requirements at present and in the future.

3. **Comparing the job to similar jobs:** It is difficult to judge the performance of an employee in isolation until and unless his job is compared with other similar jobs in the same grade. If there is a gap, it is desirable that the past and current performance, experience in the job, career path and so on of the employee are kept into consideration. A separate plan to close the gap identified after making the comparative study can also be established for the employee if need be.

4. **Current and future expectations from the employee:** Current performance of an employee gives a reasonably good idea about the potential of the employee of what he can do in the future. Where does a manager see the employee's role in the next 2–3 years and how to correlate this with pay? Should managers take aggressive steps now for training, development or determining pay? Are employees close to their promotion? Managers should have answers to all such questions. Only then and then alone can they do justice in pay reviews. Keeping the above questions into consideration, managers can take steps in the direction of establishing development and career development programmes and establishing a compensation plan.

5. **How it all stacks up:** In case the manager can have an idea about the employee's performance and career path, it becomes easier to design it with compensation. Whether the employee is meeting or not meeting or exceeding expectations? Now the manager is in a better position to decide where base pay should be if it is positioned appropriately in the ranges around the midpoint. Of course, employees' skills, performance and experience must be kept in view. The aforesaid guideline can be instrumental in enabling managers to make appropriate adjustments to base pay. In case, the employees are displaying higher level skills and promotions are not in sight due to non-availability of position or for any other reason, the employee should be considered for giving even more pay increase to get him closer to the pay grade of the next higher job. It is an established fact that differential pay increases send a clear-cut message to the employees that their performance has a meaningful impact when pay increases are determined.

Fixing of Salary

Setting salaries for employees has always been one of the trickiest things to do for managers, making it harder if the manager has never done it earlier. It is so because on one side, you want to attract the best talent and on the other side, you have financial constraints. The organization does not want to overpay.

However, one need not get panicky. Since the objective is to attract and retain the required talent, which is possible only when the organization is willing to pay fairly to the candidate(s), and the organization would never like to pay more than the job(s) is/are worth to the organization; otherwise, it will become a costly proposition and in the long run it will be difficult for the organization to sustain itself. The first thing, therefore, to be done by the manager is to determine the highest amount he can afford to pay.

Determining the Upper Limit

It depends on how much more valuable a particular candidate will make the organization. However, it is easier said than done. Anyway, it may not be that difficult to determine how much value a person will add to the organization and then determine the upper limit to which the candidate can be paid, in the case of certain types of jobs. For example, in the case of a salesperson, it is not difficult to answer the said question. It is so because a salesperson brings in revenue to the organization by generating sales, and therefore the manager can decide if that can cover his salary. For example, if the new salesperson can bring in 400,000 in profits, then he can be paid (including his commission) maximum to that, of course, leaving an adequate margin of profit to the organization.

However, to determine how much value will be added to the organization by a new candidate is a difficult task in the case of administrative and support staff as they do not bring money but all the same the organization cannot do without them. Their worth depends on how much money they save for the organization instead of how much money they bring to the organization. What can the manager do in such cases? The answer to the question is to determine what it would cost not to have them in the organization. Therein lies the answer to the question to justify their salary. For example, if the organization does not have a computer operator, how much effort, time and money would cost the organization to get the same work done otherwise? That gives an idea of how much maximum can be offered to the computer operator if appointed through some other factors like earning adequate profit for the company must be kept into consideration while fixing the salary. There might also be a case where the new candidate is the best person in his profession and asking for a certain amount of pay but his services for the company may not be up to that level. Under such circumstances, he can be ignored. Appointing him at his expected salary will not be a good proposition as he is too expensive, though he is an expert in his field.

There is also a possibility that while hiring candidates for a particular position, you find that everyone is asking more than what the organization is willing to pay and therefore disqualify everyone. It implies that the organization has not rated the job properly, that is, the job has been undervalued. The organization should therefore revalue that job.

Determining the Lowest Limit

Having determined the upper limit of pay that the organization may offer to a new candidate (or even promotion, if an old employee), the next step is to work out the least the organization would pay. Where in between the upper limit and the lower limit the pay will be determined is where the market forces come into the picture. Market rates affect candidates' expectations also. It is because of market forces' interplay that at times even very good candidates do not get what they really deserve and vice versa. Besides, the minimum expectation of candidates is, at least, what market rates are unless they are compensated otherwise. It is therefore essential for the managers to know the market scenario, that is, what are prevailing market rates for various jobs in your geographical territory so that you may get an idea about candidates' expectation as they also have some information with them in this regard.

It is also advisable for managers to remain in touch with their counterparts in other organizations of their industry as also with other industries to have information readily at their hands, which may be possible by becoming members of various associations, chambers and clubs. They should share the relevant information with other members of the associations or business networking groups. In order to collect data for administrative and staff jobs, local staffing agencies can be contacted and information regarding salary data can be collected and compiled. In the case of high-profile jobs, consultants, headhunters and recruiters are another important source to collect information. They may favour the managers in the expectation of receiving some call of service they can render to the managers.

Method of Paying Salary

Once you have got the desired information, that is, what the job is worth, what is your own capacity to pay, what are the expectations of the candidates and what is the market scenario, managers will have to decide how they will pay, that is, fixed salary per month or hourly pay. In this regard, again managers will have to take into consideration the current practices being followed in their neighbourhood organizations. However, it has been noticed that usually white-collar jobs and managers are paid a fixed salary per month, whereas assembly line workers may be paid on an hourly basis as productivity is directly related to hours on the line.

In our country, wages and salaries are usually paid to most employees on a monthly basis at fixed rates. (Anyway, the managers will have to look to their own convenience, market practices and so on.)

It is so because in most jobs, it is not convenient to measure in terms of hours the contribution made by employees. It may be his imagination, creativity and expertise that may be involved in one's job and it may not be that simple to measure them in terms of hours, for example, scientists, researchers, consultants, artists and managers. Whatever they do depends on insight and results, not the hours they work. Not only this, but it is also a matter of common knowledge that salaried employees work for longer hours but usually do not get any overtime payment, especially in the case of managerial personnel. That also prompts organizations to pay fixed salaries per month.

Paying commission is another option for salary payment. It is usually in the case of salespersons who are paid a commission depending on the revenue they generate for the organizations. In this case, the base salary is very low, and the upside is decided by what they sell or generate revenue for the organization.

They are paid commissions based directly on the revenue generated by them for the organization. Paying through commission motivates the employees to perform better, like salespersons increasing the volume of their sales. This is a very common and popular method across the country, especially regarding sales jobs. So far as fixing the percentage of commission is concerned, it varies from organization to organization and industry to industry.

The bad part of this method is that some organizations do away with the services of some salespersons who earn too much by way of commission. So senior managers get jealous and prejudiced and discontinue the services of salespersons. It is not fair. After all, they are making a lot of money for the organization also.

Paying in the form of a bonus also is another option. Bonuses may be tied to specific project results. They may also be tied to the overall organization performance. If an organization fairs well, a part of the profit is distributed as a bonus to employees due to whose labour it could be possible to make money by the organization. Bonus can be given to only those employees who have done excellent jobs. However, the amount of bonus gets increased or decreased depending on the performance of the organization.

Flexibility

Some sort of flexibility in how the organization would pay, especially in the case of executive and senior managers, becomes a problem due to a lack of proper guidelines. Some organizations pay the upper echelons of their business staff a mix of salary, stock and bonuses. ESOP encourages employees and develops a sense of ownership among the recipients of stocks that further boosts the performance of the company. Now the question arises: how much should be offered? It depends on the worth of the stock today and what it will be worth someday.

However, liberty is taken, and rules may be flouted if the organization is hiring somebody who is a specialist and is a must for the organization, and further that his substitutes are not easily available. But this should be an exception, not a rule. In such cases, everything depends on negotiations and the managers will have to be flexible while fixing their salaries. One option is that in such an exceptional case, there can be short-term salary, long-term bonus or stock and performance-based targets.

There is another option whereby the organization may offer non-financial rewards that may hook people and draw them in. There are several such things that may play the trick. For example, telecommuting, impressive titles, flexible hours, more time off and a host of other facilities can be offered to the new candidates (or promoters) in lieu of cash. Facilities for self and professional development, training facilities and so on are some of the other temptations. Here, the creativity of managers in fixing the pay will play a key role. They should have all the relevant information and fix everything—cash payments and non-financial rewards.

Thus, in a nutshell, the managers should determine the upper limit of the salary, determine the bottom of the scale, that is, know the market to determine the least the organization would pay, know the worth of the job to the organization, use the bonus for adjusting, customize the deal in the case of expert's upper managers and fix the salary.

Process of Wage and Salary Fixation

There are several steps to be undertaken in the process of wage and salary fixation which are as follows:

1. **Job analysis:** It is a statement of duties, nature of work, responsibilities, working conditions and interrelationships between the job as it is and the other jobs with which it is associated. In the designing of pay systems, job description, which is one of the two parts of job analysis, plays a significant role. Job specification which is the other part of job analysis, and which identifies the qualifications, experiences, expertise, physical requirements and so on, too plays a vital role in the designing of pay systems. This is so because these two help in defining, determining and weighing compensation factors such as skills, experiences, effort and writing environment, for which the company pays to the employees. As a matter of fact, it is after job analysis that the actual process of grading, rating and evaluating starts. Rating of a job involves determining its value in relation to other jobs in the company which are also to be evaluated. The next step is to attach a price tag to each job which involves translating the job classes into rate ranges.

2. **Salary Survey:** Conducting a salary survey is the next step in pricing the job, which may be formal or informal, though a formal survey is better than the two. The informal survey is usually conducted when the number of jobs is relatively small and there is a shortage of time or resources. For example, the company needs an auditor urgently and therefore, an advertisement is to be inserted in the newspaper(s). Advertise it in the newspaper, and in the meantime, the company can find out telephonically from some other companies the pay they are offering to an auditor. As against these, in formal

surveys, companies conduct their own surveys with the help of question-naires, personal interviews with the managers of other companies and with the personnel agencies. Companies can also use the results of packaged sur-veys conducted earlier by labour bureaus, employee associations and other well-recognized bodies. A lot of relevant information about differences in wage levels for kinds of occupations and so on can be collected through these surveys. The surveys can be used in different ways. For example, some jobs, say around 20 per cent or so, are priced directly in the marketplace as to what competitive companies are paying for comparable jobs; or survey data can be used to price benchmark jobs around which the other jobs are slotted, based on their relative worth to the company; and survey data on sick leave, insur-ance, vacations and other benefits can be used while decisions on extending certain benefits to candidates are decided.

3. **Grouping similar jobs into pay grades:** The next step involves assigning pay rates to each job. However, it requires first-group jobs to pay grades. A pay grade refers to a group of jobs of almost equal difficulty or importance as determined through the job evaluation process. Pay grading helps because it facilitates the pay fixing committee to deal with only limited types of jobs, say eight to ten or so.

   Pricing each pay grade: Having completed grouping similar jobs into pay grades, the next step is assigning pay rates to pay grades which is done with a wage curve. A wage curve shows graphically the pay rates presently being paid for jobs in each pay grade. It is relative to the points of ranking assigned to each job or grade through the process of job evaluation. A price curve aims to show the relationship between the value of the job and the cur-rent average pay rates for the grades. Thus, pricing jobs with a wage curve involves: finding out the average pay for each grade, plotting the pay rates for each pay grade, fitting a wage line through the points just plotted and finally pricing the jobs.

4. **Fine-tune pay rates:** It involves correcting out-of-line rates and developing rate ranges.

5. **Wage administration rules:** Finally comes the development of rules of wage administration. It is in the interest of all the stakeholders that information regarding average salaries and ranges in the salaries of the group should be communicated to all concerned to maintain transparency. Therefore, the employee should be appraised, and the wage fixed for the grade he is found appropriate.

Chapter Review

1. The success of an organization depends, to a large extent, on how well it administers and controls its salary costs and conducts salary reviews. That is why financial planning is an integral part of salary reviews.

2. Salary costs alone constitute a significant percentage of an organization's employee compensation expenses, say, somewhere between 50 and 70 per cent. While it is difficult to control base pay, salary costs beyond base pay are controllable to a great extent. Labour costs include in addition to base pay, hiring costs which include advertisement expenses, costs incurred on conducting tests and interviews, employment taxes, fringe benefits, working and other space charges, expenses incurred on providing common facilities and office equipment provided to employees and so on.

3. In view of the heavy costs incurred on salary and benefits and so on it is necessary to go for salary planning because it is in the salary planning process that it is decided what is it that the organization wants to do and how it is going to get it done. That is why salary planning is an integral part of the budgetary process of the organization and it is through the salary planning process that the organization examines the labour market and compares the results of examination with the current pay being paid within the organization.

4. Hence, a salary budget is to be prepared, which is a statement in quantitative/financial terms of the planned location and use of resources, to meet the operational requirements of the organization. A salary budget involves the levels of activity indicating the number of different categories of employees that are required for the period of the budget.

5. Since salary costs are heavy, they need salary controls. Salary controls are exercised in many ways. For example, controlling the number of people to be employed because salary costs depend mainly on the number of people employed, some of whom are core employees, and the rest are contingent employees. While contingent employees can be reduced without much hype or fuss, it is difficult to touch the core employees. Hence, the organization must plan in this regard. Today, many organizations instead of defining employment as a number of employees express it in the number of hours.

6. In order to control salary costs, the organization can follow any of the many approaches. For example, in the top-down approach salary budgeting starts with an estimate (of pay increases) from top management. Out of the total amount, so earmarked, further allocation is made for each manager for his doing the needful. In the bottom-up approach, the managers make pay increase recommendations for upcoming plan years which are modified or accepted as such by the top management. Then, there are embedded controls which are inherent in the design of techniques such as job analysis and job evaluation. These techniques are also instrumental in regulating managers' pay decisions.

7. There are many other things which in order to have effective salary control, the wage and salary administration should keep into consideration, for example, clarity in salary review guidelines, and clarity in procedures for auditing increases and salary levels.

8. In order to enable organizations to award their best-performing employees and keep employees motivated so that they may give their best to their

organization, most organizations have started conducting pay reviews. Salary reviews can be either 'general' salary reviews which are conducted when a salary increase is desired in all or in most cases due to a spurt in the cost of living or in ongoing rates in the market and so on or 'individual' salary reviews, the purpose of which is to decide increments that should be given to individuals based on their merit.

9. There are several guidelines for conducting a salary review process such as reviewing the budget, identifying the objectives of salary review, reaching out to the market and analysing market pay data, keeping in view the issues to be considered during the pay review, getting self-evaluation form filled in, reviewing job description of the employee, reviewing the principles for rewarding employees, establishing the proper rating system, proper planning and ensuring rules, communicating and keeping to the schedule, involving line managers, fine-tuning and giving final touch, explaining the final decision to employees and reviewing the salary review system. There are some other guidelines also in addition to the aforesaid ones.

10. How should an employee react to a negative salary review? It is an important issue as it has emotional dimensions also. First, the employee should not allow his emotions to run wild. If he feels justified, he can ask for re-evaluation after a gap of time, say three months or so. If still not satisfied, he should start looking elsewhere if he can be better paid elsewhere.

11. There are five key steps that can help managers use their limited pay budgets to make meaningful recommendations. These key steps are finding out the job's worth, assessing the performance of the employee, comparing the job to similar jobs, working out current and future expectations from the employee and how it all stacks up.

12. Another important aspect is fixing the salary. It involves determining the upper limit, determining the lowest of scale, the method of paying salary and flexibility.

13. So far as the process of wage and salary administration is concerned, it involves job analysis, salary survey, grouping similar jobs into pay grades, pricing each pay grade, fine-tuning pay rates and developing wage administration rules.

DISCUSSION QUESTIONS

1. Discuss what salary costs are. Also, discuss what they consist of.
2. Discuss what is done in the salary planning process.
3. Discuss the purpose of the salary budget.
4. Discuss how salary costs can be controlled and what are the bottom-up and top-down approaches in this context.
5. Discuss the objectives of salary reviews and the difference between general salary reviews and individual salary reviews.

6. Discuss the guidelines for a salary review process.
7. Discuss how an employee should react to a negative salary review.
8. Discuss the five key steps in the context of manager's guide to annual salary review.
9. Discuss what does the exercise of salary fixation involve.
10. Discuss the process of wage and salary fixation.

Individual and Group Activities

1. In a group of two, visit any large-scale organization. Discuss with the HR and accounts officials there what they include under salary costs and also how they calculate it.
2. As an individual, pay a visit to some big organization and discuss with the officials of its finance department how they prepare the salary budget of the organization.
3. In a group of two, discuss with the concerned officials of a big organization, located in the close vicinity of your place, how they control salary costs. Also, find out from them what are the features of their salary and administration procedures which help to have effective salary control.
4. As an individual, discuss with the HR head of an organization employing around 3,000 people, how is salary review conducted in his organization and what sort of guidelines are followed in the organization.
5. In a group of two, visit some big organization and find out from the concerned officials there what process of wage and salary administration fixation is being followed in their organizations.

APPLICATION CASE

Mr Vishwanathan, CA, having experience working with big organizations of high repute for over two decades, was invited by a home appliance manufacturing company to join it as senior vice-president (finance) at a handsome salary. The aforesaid organization has been using state-of-the-art technology for manufacturing home appliances. It has captured a good percentage of market share, especially because of its quality products. The company has also been exporting its products for quite some time. Despite all this, the company has not been earning adequate profits. It was a matter of great concern for the board and all the senior officials of the company. In view of the above situation, the company had constituted a high power committee which had the company's CEO, all the vice-presidents and four senior officials of the HR department.

After having a couple of meetings, the committee came to the conclusion that the company is spending a huge amount on the salary and benefits given to the employees. The committee, therefore, recommended to appoint an experienced finance expert to look into the problem and control salary costs. It was because of this recommendation that Mr Vishwanathan was appointed as senior vice-president (finance) of the company.

Immediately after reporting for his duty, Mr Vishwanathan was assigned the job of salary control. Mr Vishwanathan appeared to be quite confident in resolving the problem. After a week of his joining the position of senior vice-president, he desired to have the two senior most officials of the HR department to assist him. This group of three senior officials, headed by Mr Vishwanathan, examined all records thoroughly and was convinced that salary costs were relatively higher. The group decided to conduct a salary survey to know what is being paid by their competitors to different categories of employees and what are the market rates. The group also worked out hiring costs including expenditure incurred on advertisement for recruitment, conducting tests and interviews, TA/DA and consulting fees paid to experts, and also to candidates invited to attend interviews. The group also got the expenses incurred on benefits extended to the employees.

In a nutshell, the amount being spent on total compensation paid to the employees was worked out and compared with the amount being spent by their competitors and they came to the conclusion that the company was spending around 25 per cent more on total compensation as compared to its average such competitors.

Mr Vishwanathan formulated a plan to control salary costs, especially that part of the labour costs which is controllable. A salary budget was also prepared. As there was little hope of applying any cut in the base pay, the remaining constituents of total compensation/reward were considered for cutting expenditure on them. The group revisited the number of employees engaged in different activities in the organization and applied a cut wherever it was possible. It also applied the top-down approach in preparing the salary budget. The group also took advantage of embedded controls that are inherent in the design of techniques such as job analysis, job evaluation, SBP, performance evaluation, gainsharing and so on.

Not only the above, but the group also got salary reviews conducted so that salary increases may be just and fair. Appropriate guidelines were also issued to managers who were supposed to conduct salary reviews. In some cases, salaries were also appropriately fixed.

The exercises undertaken by the group yielded concrete results and salary costs came down, though not to the extent the group expected. However, it was a good beginning.

Questions

1. What was the major factor responsible for the company not earning adequate profit?
2. What efforts were made by the group to control salary costs?
3. Do you approve of the steps taken by the group to control salary costs? Would you suggest some more efforts? If yes, what?

Notes

1 Milkovich, Newman, and Venkata Ratnam, *Compensation*, 553.
2 Ibid.
3 Ibid., 557.
4 Ibid.
5 Ibid., 565.

7

DESIGNING AND OPERATING FRINGE BENEFITS AND SERVICES, AND INTERNAL AUDIT OF COMPENSATION AND BENEFITS (I)

LEARNING OBJECTIVES

After studying this chapter, the reader should be able to:

1. Explain the importance of benefits in total compensation.
2. Explain the concept, philosophy and definition of fringe benefits as also its objectives and significance.
3. Explain the various types of fringe benefits.
4. Explain the origin of the concept of social security and highlight its objectives and need.
5. Point out the forms of social security and describe its scope.
6. List and describe the various Acts related to social security passed in our country.
7. Understand and explain the recent biggest 'Labour Reforms' initiated by the Government of India through Labour Reforms Bill, 2022.
8. Explain the Social Security measures initiated through the Labour Reforms Bill, 2022.

Introduction

Despite the fact that employee benefits and services constitute a significant part of total compensation, there is yet no clear answer to the following questions:

DOI: 10.4324/9781032626123-7

1. Do employee benefits and services facilitate an organization's performance?
2. Does a sound employee benefits programme impact favourably an organization's ability to attract and retain its employees?
3. Do employee benefits and services motivate employees to give their best to their organization?

Although no research study has yet been able to provide conclusive proof of answering the above questions in the affirmative, the fact remains that benefits and services extended to workers have always been in vogue, though in different forms and under a variety of titles such as 'non-wage benefits', 'employee benefits', 'wage supplements', 'perquisites other than wages', 'fringe benefits', 'social charges' and 'supplements'. However, the basic concept in the use of all these terms is the same.

The findings of a research study[1] also revealed that non-wage benefits cost 22.24 per cent of the total labour cost. Almost a similar trend was found in a survey of comparison of wage and benefit costs (private versus state and local governments) conducted in 2005 wherein fringe benefits constituted 22.2 per cent of total compensation in the private sector and 32.1 per cent in the state and local governments.[2] The significance of benefits and services is further corroborated by the findings of the survey wherein it was revealed that 89 per cent of executives feel that employee benefits play a vital role in attracting as well as retaining good employees.[3] As a matter of fact, an extension of fringe benefits is a great source of contentment to the workers as these benefits supplement their income, make their lives comfortable and improve their status and standard of living. Since a contended worker is an asset to an organization, he is instrumental in the overall progress of an organization. That is why today a substantial majority of organizations provide fringe benefits to their workers, though their type, quantum and timings differ a great deal. A large majority of employees today prefer new benefits, like health insurance or paid time off, over a pay raise (see Exhibit 7.1).

EXHIBIT 7.1 PERKS

Perks and benefits are among the top things employees consider when deciding whether to accept a job. Almost 80 per cent of employees say that they would prefer new benefits, like health insurance or paid time off, over a pay raise.

Source: The Economic Times (20 June 2016).

Before going ahead, it will be in the fitness of things to understand the concept, philosophy, definition and other relevant issues of fringe benefits.

Fringe Benefits

Concept, Philosophy[4] and Definition of Fringe Benefits

The term 'fringe benefits' is of recent origin and did not come into use till 1950,[5] though such benefits to workers, in some form or the other, have been in vogue for quite a long time. Although labour economists[6] have realized the potentialities of fringe benefits in the execution of production plans, they have not been unanimous in giving a uniform definition of fringe benefits. Of course, they all agree that the main purpose of fringe benefits is to supplement money wages of workers, and thus narrowing the gap left between the money wages and the cost of living.[7] Fringe benefits are usually the extra benefits provided to the workers in addition to the compensation paid in the form of wages or salary.

We come across different definitions of the term 'fringe benefits'. For example, Cockmar says that fringe benefits are 'those benefits which are provided by an employer to or for the benefit of an employee and are not in the form of wages, salaries and time-related payments'.[8] Belcher defines these benefits as 'any wage cost not directly connected with the employee's productive effort, performance, service or sacrifice'.[9] Thus, the benefits provided to the workforce apart from the negotiated wages are nowadays termed as either fringe benefits or supplementary benefits or non-wage benefits. However, the substance of all these terms is the same.

As a matter of fact, a fringe benefit is primarily a means in the direction of ensuring, maintaining and increasing the income of the worker or employee. It is a benefit which supplements a worker's ordinary wages and which is of value to him and his family in so far as it materially increases his comfort.

According to ILO, wages are often augmented by special cash benefits, by the provision of medical and other services or by payments in kind, that form part of the wage for expenditure on goods and services. In addition, workers commonly receive such benefits as holidays with pay, low-cost meals, low-rent housing, etc. Such addition to wages is sometimes referred to as fringe benefits. Benefits that have no relation to employment or wages should not be regarded as fringe benefits though they may constitute a significant part of the worker's total income.[10]

It is also worth noting that fringe benefits usually act as maintenance factors rather than as motivators.[11] One of the major factors responsible for a variety of definitions of fringe benefits is that some employers and employees interpret the meaning of fringe benefits in their own way, that is, as it suits them. In view of the differences in opinions of different authorities, and in order to have a proper understanding of its connotation and implementation in the Indian industrial structure, it may be desirable to refer to Section 2(vi) of the Payment of Wages Act, 1936; Section 2(b) of the Minimum Wages Act, 1948; Section 2(22) of the ESI Act, 1948; and some provisions made under the Employees' Provident Funds and Miscellaneous Provisions Act, 1952, and the Payment of Bonus Act, 1965. However, some clarifications with regard to fringe benefits are also found in the Industrial Disputes Act, 1947, and in certain rulings and judgments of different High Courts and the Supreme Court of India.

Objectives of Fringe Benefits

Broadly speaking, fringe benefits are instrumental in accomplishing certain social, human relations and macroeconomic goals. The main objectives of fringe benefits may be as follows:

1. To meet the needs of employees and safeguard them against certain hazards of life, particularly the ones which an individual, especially of small means, cannot himself provide for.
2. To attract and retain employees.
3. To earn the gratitude and loyalty of the employees.[12]
4. To remain competitive in the market with regard to the provisions of fringe benefits.[13]
5. To boost the image of the organization.
6. To seek meaningful cooperation of employees in the production process.
7. To infuse confidence, motivate and boost the morale of the employees.
8. To reduce the rate of absenteeism and labour turnover.
9. To reduce the influence of trade unions.
10. To reduce statutory interference.
11. To improve human and industrial relations.
12. To promote employee welfare and provide a qualitative work environment.
13. To provide a tax-efficient method of remuneration which reduces tax liabilities compared with those related to equivalent cash payments.[14]
14. To improve the quality of life of workers and promote their well-being.

Significance of Fringe Benefits

Fringe benefits benefit all the stakeholders in an industry in the following manner:

1. *Benefits to workers*
   a. Reduce gap between nominal wages and real wages of the workers.
   b. Provide contentment to workers.
   c. Improve their standard of living.
   d. Maintain their self-respect.
   e. Make workers more responsible.
   f. Help in their growth and development.
   g. Improve their productivity.

2. ***Benefits to employers***
    a. Present attractive areas of negotiation when large wages and salary increases are not practical.
    b. Help in attracting and retaining employees.
    c. Reduce the influence of trade unions on workers.
    d. Help in reducing the cost of production.
    e. Help in reducing wastage and depreciation.
    f. Help in increasing productivity.
    g. Help in increasing profits.
    h. Help in increasing output.
    i. Help in improving quality.
    j. Boost the image of the organization.
    k. Help in reducing the rate of absenteeism.
    l. Help in reducing supervisory expenses.
    m. Improve human and industrial relations.
3. ***Benefits to society***
    a. Availability of goods and services at reasonable prices.
    b. Increase in gross national production.
    c. Educational upliftment.
    d. Promote peace and harmony.
    e. Improvement in standard of living.
    f. Elimination of social evils.
    g. Reduction in social costs.

Intangible Benefits

The power of intangible benefits is no less than that of tangible benefits. Rather, at times, intangible benefits prove more powerful and effective. Even at the time of applying for a job, an applicant weighs up both the tangible and intangible benefits offered by different employers. Some of the intangible benefits that may attract the attention of an applicant during the process of making a decision whether to apply/ join or not a particular organization may include praise/recognition for achievements, power/authority, opportunities for growth, working environment, work-life balance, flexi timings, the structure of the organization, opportunities for career progression, dignity of labour and the like.

Factors Responsible for the Need and Growth of Benefits

The beginning of the need for fringe benefits can be traced back to wage and price controls initiated by certain countries during the Second World War. Consequently, the employees felt the pinch of inadequate rise in their wages, and therefore, their trade unions started putting forward their demands for the introduction and enforcement of new benefits in their then-existing benefits. Besides, the cost-effectiveness of benefits also encouraged the demand for benefits because most of these were not taxable and some of them, such as accident insurance, life insurance and health insurance, can be obtained at concessional rates if asked for on a group basis.

In addition to the above, statutory requirements also made it obligatory on the part of employers to extend certain benefits. For example, in our country, the Employees' Compensation Act, 1923; the Employees' State Insurance Act, 1948; the Factories Act, 1948; the Payment of Bonus Act, 1965; the Employees Provident Fund and Miscellaneous Provisions Act, 1952; the Payment of Gratuity Act, 1972; and so on have made it mandatory on the part of the employers to make benefits and facilities available to the employees. Employers also started extending certain benefits voluntarily so as to attract competent employees as also to create a good image of themselves. *Humanistic* considerations that a worker is a human being first also prompted employers to extend certain benefits. *Paternalistic* considerations on the part of the employers to take care of their workers in case of illness, employment injury, unemployment, poverty and so on were also instrumental in the extension of employee benefits. *Keen competition* among employers so as to acquire and retain competent employees also encouraged the extension of employee benefits. The recent 'labour reforms' being introduced are going to play an important role in the promotion of benefits.

Benefit Policies and Practices

In order to control benefits costs and to accomplish the desired objectives, an organization should formulate its benefit policy which should clearly specify the range of benefits, for example, holidays, leaves and so on, that is, what benefits would be available to all the employees and what will be the additional benefits among which an employee can exercise his choice, for example, transport facilities, housing facilities and the like. Similarly, the policy should also mention the size of each benefit and be made available to the employees taking into consideration its perceived value to the employees as also its cost to the company. Again, the percentage of each benefit to total compensation should be specified, though it will depend a great deal on the range and size of benefits made available to the employees. Then comes the issue of options given to the employees to choose a package of benefits according to their requirements. Not every hat fits on the head of every person. Similarly, a number of packages of benefits should be worked out, from which an employee may choose any one according to his personal requirements. The exercise of choice will be guided by an individual's typical needs depending on the size of his family, age group and so on. While formulating policies, harmonization should also be taken into consideration, that is, there should be no distinction at any level in the hierarchy between the benefits provided. However, they may differ depending on the length of service and so on. In the same way, *government policies*, especially those that have tax implications with regard to benefits, should also be kept in view while formulating benefit policy. *Competition packages* of benefits being offered by the competitors of the company also affect a company's benefits policy in determining what is necessary to enable the company to sustain itself in the market. The status of the trade union operating in the company has also to be taken care of while formulating the organization's benefits policy. It is always desirable to keep the trade union in confidence while formulating a benefit policy, otherwise, there may be problems later. Trade unions may help in the selection of typical benefits and how they should be administered.

However, when it comes to the practice of providing benefits to employees, it differs from industry to industry and organization to organization. For example, there is a great variation in this regard in private and public sector organizations, and so is the case in organizations where labour costs constitute a small part of total costs and where such costs constitute a substantial part of total costs. Similarly, the practices of providing benefits differ depending on the employer's view or intention with which the benefits are being extended and so on.

Anyway, it is always desirable to adopt a balanced approach so that while following the best practices, the benefit costs do not rise beyond a desirable level.

A detailed discussion on factors affecting fringe benefits and the coverage and types of fringe benefits available in Indian organizations are given below.

Planning, Designing and Administration of Benefits

The planning and designing of benefits depend a great deal on the compensation objective. Only those benefits should be introduced which meet the compensation objectives. For example, if the compensation objective is to put a check on high rate of turnover, then there can be several options to achieve this objective such as increasing wages and introducing incentives. Having tried these objectives if you find that the objective of reducing the turnover rate is not being achieved, another option can be to introduce an employee stock option, that is, if an employee continues his job for three years, he will be entitled to company shares to the tune of 10 per cent or so of his salary if he continues for five years, then he will be getting the shares to the extent of 15 per cent or so and if he continues for 10 years, he will be getting the shares to the tune of 20 per cent and the like of his salary. Similarly, typical benefits can be planned and designed if female employees have to be attracted. In such a case, women-oriented benefits such as transport and crèche facilities, flexible working hours, work from home, etc., can be thought of.

In the same way, an external survey with regard to benefits offered by your competitors can be conducted so that your benefits are at least equivalent to those of the competitors or if not, then some justification can be put forth for the same. Cost-effectiveness and affordability of the organization are other issues to be taken care of while administering the benefits programme. There should be full justification for increasing a particular amount of expenditure on a specific benefit. Case benefit analysis in this direction can play an important role. Another issue that needs to be taken care of during the administration of benefits programme is who should be covered under a benefits programme, that is, whether all employees—males and females—or only permanent employees or both permanent and temporary employees or even probationers can be included or even retired employees can also be covered, for example, medical treatment even after retirement and so on. Such decisions have wide implications for the administration of benefits.

The next administrative issue can be choosing a suitable benefits package. It must be decided if only a standard benefits package, which is uniformly applicable to all employees, is to be introduced or if it must be or not be supplemented by a cafeteria-style package. In the latter case, an employee can choose any of the benefit packages which meet his/her requirements the most. Cafeteria-style packages are in the interest of both the employees and the employer.

The third issue related to the administration of employee benefits is whether the cost of benefit is to be borne extensively by the employer (non-contributory) or both by the employer and the employee (contributory), and if so, in what proportion. However, it is always advisable to make benefit options contributory so that the beneficiary does not misuse it or waste it.

In case there is any legal requirement from the side of the government, then that also needs to be complied with. In case any benefit is not tax exempted, legal requirements should be taken care of.

Current Approaches

There are three main current approaches in the arena of fringe benefits which are given as follows:[15]

1. **Innovative approach:** Under the innovative approach, new dimensions are being added to certain benefits. Also, new benefits are being added to minimize the impact of the tax. Benefits are tailor-made to meet the needs of individual employees. Aligning benefits of blue- and white-collar employees is also part of innovation in the design and administration of fringe benefits.[16]

2. **Flexibility:** 'Flexible benefits' is a blanket term for employers giving employees more control over their reward packages without increasing extra costs.[17] Today, organizations have become sensitive to tailor-make the benefits to suit the requirements of individual employees instead of offering common standard packages. In our country, this is more applicable in the case of managerial employees and the staff and workers are yet to taste it. The flexible approach responds to an employee's needs, helps recruitment and retention, makes the employer look flexible and forward-looking, highlights the aggregate value of the package, makes employees more loyal and so on.

   Some examples of existing flexible benefits include private medical insurance, insurance benefits, company cars, pensions, holidays and so on.

Following are the four main plan architectures[18] of flexible benefits:

a. Individual plans operating independently.
b. Umbrella plan.
c. Flex fund plan.
d. Voluntary ('affinity') benefits.

   While designing and implementing a flexible benefits project, it is advisable to associate employees concerned, and realistic deadlines must be fixed for its implementation and whenever required to liaise with interested third parties. Of course, in the implementation of a benefit project, certain barriers like communication of a benefit project and administrative problems are likely to be confronted.

3. **Harmonization:** Harmonization seeks to bring in a measure of equity and fair play and is supposed to contribute to improvements in employee attitudes and performance and the signification of payroll procedures and fringe benefits administration.[19] Under harmonization, an attempt is made to have a single statute for the entire workforce of an organization. However, it is especially in the case of deduction for coming late on duty, marking attendance, working hours, distinction of pay and so on that the harmonization process is involved, though it can be extended to all conditions of services and work practices.

Factors Influencing Choice of Benefits Package

There are a number of factors that influence benefit choice. For example, from an employee's point of view, his age, sex, marital status, size of the family and so on will be the determining factors, when choosing a benefit package.

Reviewing and Modifying the Benefits Package

Reviewing the effectiveness of a benefits package from time to time, that is, whether the extension of a particular benefits package could serve the desired purpose, is also very important because only then it may be decided whether a particular benefit should be allowed to be continued or discontinued, or its quantum needs to be reduced or enlarged and so on. However, measuring the impact and effectiveness of a particular benefit(s) is not an easy task. Of course, there are certain indicators which may provide a clue in this direction, e.g., the enthusiasm of employees towards overtaking a particular benefits package, expression of a sense of satisfaction of employees.

   Regarding a particular benefits package, demand from the employee for more choice in the benefit packages made available to them, change in the policy of taxation by the several towards certain benefits and so on.

   Keeping in view the feedback received at the time of the review of benefits packages as well as the latest happenings, one may ask for rendering the benefits packages. It is, therefore, desirable to redesign them. However, while redesigning a benefits package, in addition to taking into consideration the feedback received from reviewing of existing benefits package, it is also essential to give due weight-age to the new trends and best practices with regard to benefits packages, especially the ones being adopted by your competitors, as well as to the new aspirations of the employees, the demands being put forward by trade unions, taxation policy of the government related to benefits package, current stations of employee value proportion and so on.

Informing the Employees about Benefits Package

Simply having good benefits packages designed and making them available is not enough. What is equally important is to make the employees aware about them as also about their value to the employees and that how much it will cost the organization per employee. It should also be communicated to the employees as to with what intention the benefits package has been introduced. This can be taken care of by mutual discussion, various publications of the organization, display of attractive charts and so on.

Factors Affecting Fringe Benefits and Services

The extension and availability of fringe benefits are affected by a number of factors such as organization's financial health, the trade union's bargaining power, employers' philosophy with regard to fringe benefits, employers' consciousness of their social responsibility, the cost of fringe benefits, employees' needs, taxation policy of the government with regard to fringe benefits, statutory requirements regarding fringe benefits and utility of a particular item of fringe benefits to workers.

Coverage, Classification and Types of Fringe Benefits

Based on the study of relevant Acts, rulings and judgements of various courts, the following types of payments fall in the category of fringe benefits:

1. They should be computable in terms of money,
2. They should not be part of any contract, indicating when the sum is payable, and
3. The amount of such payment is not predetermined.

While Cockmar classifies fringe benefits into two categories, namely (a) those which are offered on the basis of status such as car, foreign travel, telephones, secretarial services and company scholarships, and (b) those which are key benefits such as retirement benefits and house purchase schemes. The US Chamber of Commerce divides fringe benefits under five heads, namely (a) payments to be made under any specific legislation (i.e., statutory benefits), (b) pensions and other payments as agreed, (c) paid rest period, lunch breaks, wash up time, to get ready time, travel time and so on, (d) payment for time not worked at all such as holiday pay and lay-off pay, and (e) other items such as bonus and profit-sharing.

Again, while Hodge[20] has classified the fringe benefits into two categories, namely (a) extra pay for time worked such as incentive bonus, old-age insurance, unemployment compensation and shift subsidy, and (b) payment for time not worked such as paid rest, lunch breaks, travel time and vacation pay, Dale Yoder and Paul D. Standohar have classified fringe benefits into four categories, namely (a) for employment security such as unemployment insurance, overtime pay, maternity leave with pay and lay-off pay, (b) for health protection such as health insurance, medical care and hospitalization, (c) for old age and retirement such as pension and gratuity, and (d) for personnel identification, participation and stimulation such as attendance bonus, housing, canteen and stress counselling.

According to another classification, fringe benefits may be for (a) payment for time not worked such as paid holidays and paid vacation, (b) employee security such as lay-off compensation and retrenchment compensation, (c) safety and health such as safety measures and health benefits, (d) welfare and recreational facilities such as housing, canteen, counselling, holiday homes, educational facilities, picnics and transportation facilities, and (e) old age and retirement benefits such as pension, provident fund, gratuity and post-retirement medical benefits.

Benefits have also been divided into (a) direct benefits (which help the employees directly, e.g., medical facilities), and (b) indirect benefits (which help the employees indirectly, e.g., providing free furniture to the canteen contractor). Benefits have also been categorized as (a) statutory benefits, and (b) voluntary benefits.

Fringe Benefits and Current Practices (I)

The three main categories of fringe benefits are (a) social security benefits, (b) labour welfare facilities, and (c) bonuses. While a brief discussion about social security is as follows, the discussion on labour welfare activities and bonus is contained in Chapter 8.

Social Security

In the modern industrial set-up, workers are exposed to various contingencies of life including employment injury, occupational diseases, illness, old age, death and so on. With almost no or very less savings with the workers, it is difficult for them to sustain themselves during such contingencies. Hence, there should be some mechanism that may enable them to face such contingencies when their earning capacity is lost either temporarily or permanently. It is here that social security comes into picture because it takes care of employees from womb to tomb. The provision of social security measures in an organization makes workers feel more confident, more loyal and dedicated to their jobs and give their best to their organization.

The Concept and Definition of Social Security

Although the concept of providing social security to workers has always been there in one form or the other, it has always been less than required. The modern concept of social security became popular when the Beveridge Plan, prepared by Sir William Beveridge, was presented to the Parliament of the United Kingdom in December 1942. The Plan provides for a unified system of income maintenance to cover needs arising from a variety of causes. However, the origin of the concept of social security can be traced to the general feeling that a worker in distress should be helped by capable members of the community, or the employer, or the State or by all of them together. But such a distress should have been caused by the contingencies of life such as industrial accidents, occupational diseases, illness, unemployment, old age and death. Although the desired funds to provide social security to the workers should come from their employers or State or the community, either individually or jointly, it will be appropriate if the workers are also made a part of this joint fund, though in a very modest way. It is perhaps for this reason that an ILO publication defines social security as the security that society furnishes, through appropriate organization, against certain risks to which its members are exposed. These risks are essentially contingencies of life which the individual of small means cannot effectively provide for by his own ability alone or even in private combination with his fellows.[21]

Objectives of Social Security

The objectives of social security are usually categorized under three heads, namely (a) to compensate (i.e., income security during the period of calamity) (b) to restore the earning capacity (i.e., restoration of earning capacity through re-employment or rehabilitation as well as medical treatment of the diseased or invalid worker), and (c) to prevent the contingencies (taking steps to avoid the loss of productive capacity caused due to illness, unemployment or employment injury or occupational disease(s)).

Need and Significance of Social Security in Indian Industries

Workers in lower-middle-income countries like India are more exposed to the various contingencies of life. Besides, workers in such countries are poor and physically weak. Hence, the need for social security measures is greater in such countries than for the workers of industrially advanced countries. The reasons that call for the need for social security for industrial workers in our country may be summarized as follows:

1. Indian industrial workers are more exposed to various contingencies of life and fall victim to such contingencies more frequently for a variety of reasons.
2. Because of their low wages, their capacity to save is either nil or extremely low.
3. In a good number of cases, Indian workers are indebted. It is said that Indian workers are born in debt, live in debt and die in debt.
4. The old joint family system is giving way to the nuclear family system—thus leaving no dependable source to rely on at the time of contingency.
5. Social security maintains the self-respect and dignity of workers as they get social security benefits as a matter of right.
6. Social security restores the lost working capacity of the affected workers at the earliest possible.

Forms of Social Security

'Social insurance' and 'social assistance' are the two main forms of social security, a brief description of which is as follows:

1. **Social insurance:** It aims at the maintenance of the minimum standard of living of the employee during the period of contingency of life. It is obligatory for all employees to become its members once it is introduced in any organization, industry or state. Its funds are drawn from employers, the state and the employees, though the contributions made by the employees are nominal. It maintains the self-respect of the employees as benefits under it are granted to members as a matter of right and without any means test.
2. **Social assistance:** It is a purely government affair and therefore, financed exclusively by the government and benefits are granted on fulfilling prescribed conditions, though benefits are claimed as a matter of right. The overall objective is to help people when they fall victim to certain contingencies of life.

Scope of Social Security

While 'social insurance' is the main form of social security and therefore, falls under the scope of social security, 'social assistance' is considered to be within the scope of social security. However, whether 'commercial insurance' is a constituent of the scope of social security is a little bit controversial issue because, first, it is voluntary in nature. Then its aim is not the maintenance of a minimum standard of living, and finally, the help available depends on the amount of premium paid by the beneficiary.

Social Security in India

Social security used to be provided in the past also to people, in general, and to workers, in particular, which is evident from our ancient scripts such as Manusmriti, Kautilya's *Arthashastra* and *Naradasmriti*. However, it used to be the joint families, orphanages, trusts, panchayats, other local bodies, philanthropists, widow homes and so on that were the main institutions for providing social security to people in distress. But due to the industrial revolution and gradual social changes happening over a period, these institutions failed to provide social security either at all or inadequately. Hence, the state had to intervene but not much could be done till very recently. Anyway, the Report of the Royal Commission on Labour in India, the publication of the Beveridge Report in the United Kingdom, the adoption of the ILO convention No. 102, Social Security (Minimum Standards), 1952, and the Directive Principles of State Policy enshrined in the Constitution of India provided the much-desired fillip to strengthen the institution of social security and the role of the government to be played in this direction.

Present Status of Social Security in Indian Industries

If compared with the industrially advanced countries, it will not be an exaggeration to say that in India we have just made a beginning both quantity-wise and quality-wise so far as social security for industrial workers is concerned, though it is a good beginning and a promising one. While voluntary social security (through trade unions) is as good as missing, employers have done only a little bit in this direction. It is the statutory social security that is ruling the roost, though even in this respect there remains much to achieve. The Government of India has passed certain Acts to make provisions for employment injury, occupational diseases, health insurance, maternity benefits, provident fund, pension schemes, retrenchment and lay-off compensation and so on. A brief description of various Acts passed in this regard is as follows:

The 'Employees'[22] Compensation Act, 1923[23]

The Act aims at paying some amount of compensation at the time of invalidity or death caused by employment injury or occupational diseases as laid down in the Act. In case of 'temporary disablement', the amount of compensation payable to the eligible employee is a half-month payment of the sum equivalent to 25 per cent of the monthly wages of the employee in accordance with the provisions of the Act. However, such half-monthly payments can continue for a maximum period of five years. The half-monthly payment is payable to the employee on the 16th day from the date of disablement if it continues for a period of 28 days or more and thereafter half-monthly during the disablement or during a period of 5 years, whichever period is shorter. In case such disablement lasts for a period of less than 28 days, the injured employee will be paid after the expiration of a waiting period of 3 days from the date of disablement. If the injury results in his death, the employer is required to deposit an additional sum of not less than five thousand with the Commissioner which will be payable to the eldest surviving dependent of the employee as funeral expenses. In the case of 'permanent partial disablement', the amount of compensation payable to the eligible employee is calculated according to the percentage loss of earning capacity caused by injury, as laid down in Schedule I of the Act. If the employee is 'permanently totally disabled', the amount of compensation shall be 60 per cent of the monthly wages of the disabled worker multiplied by the relevant factor indicated in Schedule IV of the Act or an amount of INR 140,000,[24] whichever is more, subject to a maximum of INR 5.48 lakh. However, in case of the death of an employee, the amount of compensation is equal to 50 per cent of the monthly wages of the deceased employee multiplied by the relevant factor indicated in Schedule IV of the Act (linked to age) or an amount of INR 120,000,[25] whichever is more, subject to a maximum of INR 4.56 lakh. The Act ceases to be applicable in those establishments where the ESI Act, 1948 is applicable. The wage ceiling limitation for eligibility has been increased to INR 8,000 per month effective from 18 January 2010. The affected employee is entitled to reimbursement of the actual medical expenditure incurred by him for treatment of injuries caused during employment. There is no ceiling on it. Thus, the Act is quite meaningful, though many scrupulous employers, especially in the small sector, play with the provision of the Act to avoid payment of disability compensation to the affected worker.

The Maternity Benefit Act, 1961[26]

This Act has provisions for granting 12 weeks (now revised to 26 weeks) maternity leave with average daily wages plus the medical bonus of 25 per cent (now revised to 3,500 from 19 December 2011)[27] if prenatal confinement and postnatal care are not provided free of charge. This leave can be further extended under certain conditions as laid down in the Act. The Act also entitles the mothers to avail of two nursing breaks, over and above the initial normal rest, of prescribed duration for nursing the child until the child becomes 15 months old. Thus, the Act provides great help to expecting female workers both financially and physically, though certain improvements are still required. As per the latest amendment of the Act in 2017, with effect from 10 April 2017, the period of maternity leave has been increased to 26 weeks and the female employee will be deemed to be in continuous service for this period.[28] Besides, earlier in the year 2018, the High Court of Uttarakhand struck down as unconstitutional a state rule that denied maternity leave to a woman upon her third pregnancy. The High Court held that the rule violated the provisions of the Maternity Benefit Act, which did not authorize discrimination of this kind. However, the High Court also observed that the rule contravened the spirit of Article 42 of the Constitution, which mandates the State to provide for 'securing just and human conditions of work and for maternity relief'.

The Act has been made applicable to adopting or 'commissioning' mothers also from the date the child is handed over to the adopting mother. A commissioning mother refers to a biological mother who uses her egg to create an embryo implanted in any other woman. Employers are required to provide a mandatory crèche facility (within the prescribed distance from the establishment), either separately or along with other common facilities. At present there is no wage limit for coverage under the Act.

There have been several instances of retrenchment of female employees or clamping down on women employment by firms afraid of a bloating salary bill after the government extended the period of maternity leave to 26 weeks from the earlier 12 weeks.

According to the Indian Staffing Federation (ISF), the Employees' Provident Fund Organisation (EPFO) contribution criteria should be limited to three months and the government should consider reimbursing paid leave for 14 weeks instead of 7 weeks for a period of one year. This will help companies ease into the change in policy, where eventually the government can reduce the compensation percentage over a period of three years, ISF suggested. Under the Maternity Benefit (Amendment) Act, 2017, the government extended maternity leave from 12 weeks to 26 weeks with effect from 1 April 2017. Following this, there have been several instances brought to the notice of the ministry wherein employers have either retrenched female employees on flimsy grounds or are not hiring too many female workers fearing it will inflate their wage bill,[29] and that these female employees may not join back after availing six months of paid leave.[30] Trade unions welcome the move saying it will ease the burden of employers and bring in some formalization to the country's workforce, they share ISF views threshold is not legitimate.[31]

The ESI Act, 1948[32]

The ESI Act is an integrated Act taking care of many contingencies and is considered a very bold attempt in providing social security to industrial workers. The Act applies to factories using power and employing 10 or more persons.[33] ESI Scheme will also be applicable to establishment preparing sweets with the aid of LPG [*Employees' State Insurance Corporation V. Premlal*, 2009. LLR (Kar HC)]. An advertising agency is a "Sharp" [(*Kuriacone V. ESI Corp.* (1988) 2 CLR 301 (Ker.). Employees of factories drawing monthly wages up to INR 15,000 per month and INR 25,000 per month for persons with disabilities are covered under the scheme.[34] The limit of wages for coverage of an employee under the Act is subject to change as and when the Central Government so decides, following the set procedure. The scheme is financed by contributions from the employees at the rate of 1.75 per cent and from employers at the rate of 4.75 per cent of the wages of the employees. The state government's share of expenditure on the provision of medical care is to the extent of 12.5 per cent (1/8th within the per capita ceiling).[35] The ESI scheme is now operated in 815 centres scheduled in 31 states/union territories. Under the 'sickness benefit', the affected employee is entitled to a cash payment at the standard benefit rate, corresponding to his daily average wages for a maximum period of 91 days in two consecutive benefit periods, extendable to 120 days in certain cases. 'Maternity benefit' is payable at double the standard benefit for 12 weeks (now revised to 26 weeks) as per conditions laid down for the purpose. The benefit is available in case of confinement, miscarriage or sickness arising out of pregnancy, premature birth of a child and so on. The 'disablement benefit' is paid in cash and in instalments to the insured person for the temporary, permanent (both total or partial disablement) disablement arising out of employment as per conditions laid down for the purpose. 'Dependent benefit' comprises cash payments to the dependents of an insured person who dies as a result of occupational diseases or employment injury, as per the schedule and conditions laid down for the purpose. 'Medical benefit' includes treatment of the insured person and the members of his family, covering primary health care to super specialist facilities, outdoor and indoor treatment, domiciliary visits, provision for drugs and dressings, supply of artificial limbs, dentures, spectacles and hearing aids free of cost when these are necessitated by employment injury. The 'Employees' State Insurance Corporation runs 36 hospitals (as on 31 October 2014) including 50 district centre hospitals in various States.[36]

There are some other benefits also which are available to an insured person. 'Other benefits' include funeral expenses, rehabilitation benefits and so on.

The Employees' Provident Fund and Miscellaneous Provisions Act, 1952[37]

The Act aims at providing social security and timely monetary assistance to industrial employees and their families when they are in distress and/or unable to meet family and social obligations and to protect them in their old age, disablement, or early death of the breadwinner and in some other contingencies. The Act is applicable to establishments employing 20 or more persons, as well as to undertakings owned by the central or state governments or by a local authority. Only those employees come under the purview of the Act whose wages do not exceed INR 6,500 (revised to INR 15,000 with effect from 1 September 2014) per month, likely to be increased further. The Central Government is empowered to revise the wage limit for coverage of the employees. There are 1,183,905 establishments covered under this Act with 220,513,525 employees.

There are provisions for the following in this Act:

1. **Employees' Provident Fund Scheme:** Under this scheme, both employees and employers have to contribute mandatorily at the rate of 12 per cent of the monthly wages (in case of general establishments) and 10 per cent of the wages (in case of notified establishments) of the subscriber. The employee at the time of retirement or leaving the organization is entitled to withdraw the amount (with interest) lying in his account, subject to certain conditions.

2. **Employees' Family Pension Scheme, 1971:** It was introduced in 1971 but ceased to operate in 1995.

3. **Employees' Pension Scheme (EPS),**[38] **1995:** Members attaining the age of 58 and having rendered a minimum of 10 years' contributory service (including the membership period with the ceased Employees' Family Pension Scheme, 1971) shall qualify for superannuation pension. The other members will get the withdrawal benefit or as the rules permit. The scheme of 1995 provides several benefits to the members and their families such as monthly member pension, disablement pension, widow/widower pension, children pension, orphan pension, disabled children/orphan pension, nominee pension, pension to dependent parents and withdrawal benefit. The scheme is financed by transferring 8.33 per cent of the provident fund contributions from employers' share and by contributions at the rate of 1.16 per cent of the basic wages of employees by the central government. The pensioners who were drawing benefits under the erstwhile family pension scheme of 1971 will continue to draw family pension under the EPS, 1995.[39]

4. **Employees' Deposit Linked Insurance Scheme, 1976:** This scheme is applicable to all factories/establishments with effect from August 1976. All members of the Employees' Provident Fund Scheme are required to become members of this scheme. Under this scheme, employers are required to contribute towards the insurance fund at the rate of 0.5 per cent of pay. The benefit under para 22 of this scheme on the death of an employee has been further increased by 20 per cent in addition to the benefits already provided therein. During the year 2013–2014, 28,441 employees' deposit linked insurance claims were settled, and at the end of the year (2013–2014), the EPFO had cumulative investments of 13,711 crore under this Scheme.[40]

Recent Developments

As per report in the *Economic Times*, of 18 February 2019, the Central Board of Trustees (CBT) of the EPFO was to meet on 21 February 2019 to consider the increase in the minimum pension for subscribers. The doubling of the minimum pension under the EPS of the EPFO will benefit nearly five million subscribers. The sub-committee on pension has reviewed the proposals of the high-empowered committee to double the minimum pension to INR 2,000 from INR 1,000, restrict its withdrawal before retirement and introduce some amount of contribution from the beneficiaries during their work life. Employees are automatically enrolled in the EPS if they are EPFO members. Subscribers pay 12 per cent of their salary every month into the EPF account. Out of the matching contribution of 12 per cent by employers, 8.33 per cent goes to the EPS, subject to a maximum of INR 1,250 a month, 0.5 per cent to the Employee's Deposit Linked Insurance Scheme and the rest to the provident fund. The central government contributes 1.16 per cent of the basic salary plus daily allowance to the EPS account. The hike in minimum pension will benefit five million EPS subscribers and will cost the government around the annual outgo of INR 9,000 crore per annum on the pension scheme. The EPFO covers 190 industries (mentioned in Schedule 1 of the EPFA Act) with over two million accounts in over 1.13 million establishments.

Proposal to Increase the Pension Limit under the Atal Pension Yojana (APY)

The government investigated the proposal to double the pension limit under APY. It was under active examination as there was a need to increase the value of pension under APY. The proposal was sent to the finance ministry with the aim to increase the subscriber base of APY, which stood at 10.2 million. Currently, there are five slabs of pension from INR 1,000 to INR 5,000 per month. There has been a lot of feedback from the market asking for higher pension amounts because many people feel that INR 5,000 at the age of 60 years, 20–30 years from now will not be sufficient. Pension Fund Regulatory and Development Authority (PFRDA) has sent two more proposals to the ministry—auto-enrolment for APY and increasing the maximum age bar to enter the scheme to 50 years. At present, the age limit for enrolling for APY is 18–40 years. Increasing it to 18–50 years will help in expanding the subscriber base. About five million new subscribers were added under the scheme in 2017–2018 and it was hoped to add another six to seven million in the next financial year.[41]

Payment of Gratuity Act, 1972[42]

The Act is applicable to employees engaged in factories, mines, oil fields, plantations, ports, railway companies, shops and other establishments or for matters connected therewith or incidental thereto, employing 10 or more persons.[43] All the employees (including managers and supervisors) engaged in the aforesaid establishments are legally entitled to gratuity at the rate of 15 days wages multiplied by the number of completed years of service, subject to fulfilment of certain conditions laid down under the Act. The ceiling of the amount of gratuity has been increased from INR 3.5 lakh to INR 10 lakh with effect from 24 May 2010.[44]

With the passage of the Payment of Gratuity (Amendment) Bill, 2018, with a voice vote by the Rajya Sabha in March 2018[45] and subsequent signing into law by the presidents, the tax-free gratuity for public and private sector employees got raised to INR 20 lakh from INR 10 lakh. The Seventh Pay Commission had already raised it to INR 20 lakh for government employees. The amendment has now ensured harmony among employees in the private and public sectors as well as autonomous organizations that are not covered under the Central Civil Services (Pension) Rules. The act is applicable to employees who have completed at least five years of continuous service.[46]

EXHIBIT 7.2 WITHDRAWAL LIMIT RAISED TO INR 20 LAKH

The gratuity withdrawal limit has been raised to INR 20 lakh from the current ceiling of INR 10 lakh. The tax exemption limit on gratuity is also set to increase to INR 20 lakh. Mint cited a labour ministry spokesperson as saying on 23 February 2016 that all stakeholders—states, the Centre, unions and industry representatives—agreed to this.

Now the gratuity withdrawal limit has been raised to INR 20 lakh from the earlier ceiling of INR 10 lakh (for more details, see Exhibit 7.2).

Retrenchment Compensation

1. 'Lay off' and 'retrenchment' are two of the most serious problems employees are confronted with as they face a lot of economic problems while they remain laid off. The ongoing disturbances in the global economy and the danger of economic recession which is looming large, are compelling many employers to lay off or terminate or retrench their employees on a large scale (see Exhibits 7.3 to 7.8).

EXHIBIT 7.3 JOB CUT BY COMPUTER MANUFACTURER

HP said it expects to cut up to 6,000 jobs by the end of fiscal 2025, or about 12% of its global workforce, at a time when sales of personal computers and laptops are sliding as shoppers are tightening the budgets.

Source: The Times of India (24 November 2022).

EXHIBIT 7.4 AIRLINES PUSH FOR LONE PILOT FLIGHTS TO CUT COSTS DESPITE SAFETY FEARS

Airlines and regulators are pushing to have just one pilot in the cockpit of passenger jets instead of two. It would lower costs and ease pressure from crew shortages, but placing such responsibility on a single person at the control is unsettling for some.

Source: The Economic Times (24 November 2022).

EXHIBIT 7.5 GOOGLE'S PARENT CO ALPHABET MAY LAY OFF UPTO 10K

Alphabet Google's parent company is reportedly gearing up to lay off about 10,000 'poor performing employees'. These form around 6% of its workforce. The move comes amid the Big Tech Layoff season kicked off by Meta, Amazon, Twitter, Salesforce and more due to rough global conditions.

Source: The Economic Times (23 November 2022).

EXHIBIT 7.6 META CUTS 11K JOBS IN 1ST BIG LAYOFF IN CO'S HISTORY

Meta (which runs Facebook, Instagram and WhatsApp) CEO Mark Zuckerberg said the company will cut more than 11,000 jobs in the first major round of layoffs in the social media giant's history. Meta is taking steps to pare costs following several quarters of disappointing earnings and a slide in revenue. The reduction is equal to about 13% of the workforce. The company will also extend its hiring freeze through the first quarter.

Source: The Times of India (10 November 2022).

EXHIBIT 7.7 JUST A DOZEN STAFF LEFT IN TWITTER INDIA

Meta (which runs Facebook, Instagram and WhatsApp) CEO Mark Zuckerberg said the company will cut more than 11,000 jobs in the first major round of layoffs in the social media giant's history. Meta is taking steps to pare costs following several quarters of disappointing earnings and a slide in revenue. The reduction is equal to about 13% of the workforce. The company will also extend its hiring freeze through the first quarter.

Source: The Times of India (10 November 2022).

EXHIBIT 7.8 AMAZON PLANS TO CUT 10K JOBS IN CO'S BIGGEST LAYOFF

Following Facebook and Twitter, Amazon plans to lay off about 10,000 people in corporate and technology jobs starting as soon as this week, people with knowledge of the matter said, in what would be the largest job cuts in the company's history.

The cuts will focus on Amazon's devices organization, including the voice-assistant Alexa, as well as at its retail division and in human resources, said the people, who spoke on condition of anonymity because they were not authorized to speak publicly.

The total number of layoffs remains fluid. But if it stays around 10,000, that would represent roughly 3% of Amazon's corporate employees and less than 1% of its global workforce of more than 1.5 million, which is primarily composed of hourly workers.

Source: The Times of India (15 November 2022).

2. Due to hard times and/or in order to increase their income, many employees are going for moonlighting in the IT sector. As a result of which many employers have terminated the services of such employees (see Exhibit 7.9).

EXHIBIT 7.9 WIPRO SACKS 300 STAFFERS FOR MOONLIGHTING ON SLY

The IT services industry is waging a war against moonlighting. Wipro chairman Rishad Premji said the company has fired 300 employees in the past few months for working for direct competitors while being on the rolls of Wipro.

Source: The Times of India (22 September 2022).

Most Tech companies like TCS, IBM India, Infosys, California-based Salesforce, etc., are rallying against moonlighting by their staff, though Tech Mahindra and some new-age companies like Swiggy and Cred have a more generous view of the phenomenon.[47]

3. These people will also face difficulty during the period of their unemployment. Hence, those people who have been either laid off or terminated or retrenched need some sort of social security like retaining allowance, unemployment allowance, lump sum compensation and so on.

There are some provisions of social security under the Industrial Disputes Act, 1947,[48] which provide for payment of compensation to workers in the event of lay-off or retrenchment. In the case of lay-off, a laid-off worker is entitled to payment at the rate of 50 per cent of total of the basic wage and DA, which should not be more than 45 days at a stretch during any period of 12 months. In the case of retrenchment, the worker has to be given one month's notice or wages in lieu thereof, and also 15 days average pay for every completed year of continued service. However, certain conditions apply in case of both lay-off and retrenchment. By amalgamating 3 Labour Laws into the Industrial Labour Code, 2020, the Central Government has taken some steps to secure the interest of workers in case of job loss or retrenchment of workers.

Other Steps

The other steps undertaken with regard to social security include the following:

1. The Seamen's Provident Fund Act, 1966.
2. The Assam Tea Plantations Provident Fund Scheme Act, 1955.
3. Unemployment Dole Scheme (introduced in Kerala in 1982).
4. Old Age Pension Scheme introduced by many state governments.

It is very much in the fitness of things if we follow the example of socialist countries whose avowed goal is to provide complete protection to every citizen from cradle to grave. In order to translate the above, the major hurdle is that of funds. In our country, at present, the major burden is on the shoulders of employers. Here, it may be suggested that the governments, both the central and state, should come forward and share a substantial part of the cost of social security benefits. The employees too should contribute according to their capacity to pay. Besides, the present fragmented character of our social security system also needs to be done away with. Moreover, whatever social security Acts are operational at present in our country, their implementation also needs improvement as many scrupulous employers, especially in small organizations, play mischief and do not allow the workers to take full advantage of these Acts. Finally, the lack of uniformity in the definitions of basic terms used in various social security Acts also needs to be overcome.

It is praiseworthy that the present government has initiated the process of classifying all 44 labour laws into four labour codes of which one will be that of social security. This is being done to bring uniformity of terms and definitions and remove anomalies.

Recent Biggest 'Labour Reforms'[49]

The total number of workers in India, including both in the organized and unorganized sectors, is more than 50 crores. However, the workers in the unorganized sector used to be a neglected lot. It is the first time that any Government has bothered for the workers in both the organized and unorganized sectors and their families and got the Labour Reforms Bill passed on 23 September 2022 in the Parliament. Hitherto, the entire workforce of the country was entangled in the web of labour legislation. In order to provide the working-class freedom from the aforesaid web, the Central Government has taken a revolutionary and historical step of codifying 29 labour laws into 4 Codes. It will help workers get security along with respect, health and other welfare measures which were overdue for long. Through these four Labour Codes, all workers of the organized and the unorganized sector will get the minimum wages and other benefits, including a large section of workers in the unorganized sector getting social security. Though the Second National Commission of Labour had recommended in 2002 that the then-existing multiple Labour Laws at the Central Level should be Codified in four or five Labour Codes, no serious step was taken in this direction from 2004 to 2014 and the topic of Labour Reforms had remained untouched even during the economic reforms carried out in 1991. Following detailed discussions at the level of the Ministry of Labour and Employment, Government of India, the Ministry uploaded all the draft Labour Codes on its website for stakeholders and public consultation. From 2015 to 2019, the Ministry of Labour and Employment organized nine tripartite discussions, involving Central Trade Unions, Employers' Associations and representatives of State Governments, inviting the opinions and suggestions of the aforesaid stakeholders on Labour Reforms. In addition, Parliament Standing Committee also examined all four Bills and finally made its recommendations to the Central Government. Prior to this, in order to give workers the benefit of portability through the Universal Account Number (UAN) so as to make it easier for the employees to access their EPF account and also enable them to withdraw their provident fund securely from anywhere in the country, the UAN mandate was brought into being on 1 October 2014. Besides, the system of 'inspector raj' was also removed and made the inspectors play the advisory role or act as facilitators for workers. In order to ensure 'workers' right to minimum wages, the Central Government amalgamated 4 Labour Laws in the wage code, 9 laws in the Social Security Code, 13 laws in the Occupational Safety, Health and Working Conditions Code, 2020, and 3 laws in the Industrial Relations Code.[50]

Major Labour Reforms Undertaken Since 2014

- For transparency and accountability, the usage of IT-enabled system for inspection has been made mandatory.
- The ceiling limit of gratuity has been increased from Rs 10 Lakhs to Rs 20 Lakhs on 29 March 2018.
- On 16 February 2017, the Payment of Wages Act enabled the payment of wages to employees by cheque or crediting it to their bank account.

- Maternity Benefit Amendment Act, 2017, which came into effect on 01 April 2017, increased the paid maternity leave from 12 weeks to 26 weeks.[51]
- The passing of the Labour Reforms Bill in 2020 will ensure the protection of the interest of workers like the right to minimum wages, social security, occupational safety, health and good working conditions, etc. Besides, provisions in the Industrial Relations Code in addition to providing several other benefits to workers will also enable the following:
- Faster justice for the workers through the Tribunal.
- Workers' disputes to be resolved within a year by the Tribunal.
- Industrial Tribunals to have two members to facilitate faster disposal of cases.
- In industrial establishments, a Trade Union having 51 per cent votes shall be recognized as the sole negotiating union which can make agreements with employers.
- In industrial establishments in which no trade union gets 51 per cent votes, a negotiating council of trade unions shall be constituted for making agreements with employer.[52]

Benefits of Codification

Codification will be useful for the workers in the following manner:

- 'Single Registration; Single License; Single Statement; Minimum Forms
- Common definitions
- Reduction of Committees
- Web-based surprise inspection
- Use of technology – Electronic registration and licensing.
- Reduction of compliance cost and disputes.'[53]

To conclude, it will be desirable to quote PM Narendra Modi, when regarding Labour Codes he said,

> We need to come out of the mindset that industry and labour are always in conflict with each other. Why not have a mechanism where both benefit equally? Since labour is a concurrent subject, the law gives flexibility to state governments to modify the codes further as per their unique situation and requirements. The right to strike has not been curtailed at all. In fact, trade unions have been conferred with a new right, enabling them to get statutory recognition. We have made employer-employee relations more systematic and symmetrical. The provision of a notice period gives an opportunity for amicable settlement of any grievance between employees and employers.[54]

He further stated,

> Until there are family sentiments among workers and employers, the feeling of belongingness does not arise. If the employer thinks that he feeds someone and if the labour thinks his sweat is running in employers' world, then I do not think that the business will work smoothly. However, if family sentiments exist, if the sorrow of a worker ruins the nights of the employer and a worker does not sleep in the night, or some loss for the factory, with the arising of such family sentiments, the journey of development cannot be stopped by anyone.[55]

These reforms initiated through Labour Codes are pro-worker as now the workers can avail themselves of all benefits and social security even if hired for a fixed term. These reforms will not only create huge employment but also protect the interest of workers by ensuring not only minimum wage reforms but also provision for social security for workers in the informal sector, and minimizing government interference. The reforms will ensure priority for the occupational safety of the workers and create a better working environment.

Recent Labour 'Reforms' and Social Security

Even after 75 years of Independence, around 90% of the total workers who work in the unorganized sector do not have access to all the social securities. However, through continuous reforms and by taking care of the interest of workers, the Modi government started the initiative of providing social security to old age workers in the unorganized sector. For this, the Pradhan Mantri Shram Yogi Man Dhan Yojana was started, in which provision was made for a pension benefit of Rs 3,000 per month after reaching the age of 60.[56]

In order to ensure social security to all 50 crore workers in the country, the Central Government has amalgamated 9 Labour Laws into the Social Security Code, 2020—thus, securing the right of workers for insurance, pension, gratuity, maternity benefits, etc. A comprehensive legal framework for Social Security has to be created so as to enable the workers to receive social security completely. Hence, a system would be institutionalized for the contributions received from employers and workers, in a phased manner. The main highlights of the Social Security Code, 2020, are as follows:

- Through a small contribution, the benefit of free treatment is available under hospitals and dispensaries of ESIC.
- The doors of ESIC will now be opened for the workers of all sectors along with the workers of the unorganized sector.
- Expansion of ESIC hospitals, dispensaries and branches up to the district level. This facility is to be increased from 566 districts to all 740 districts of the country.

- Even if a single worker is engaged in hazardous work, he would be given ESIC benefit.
- Opportunity to join ESIC for platform and gig workers engaged in new technology.
- Plantation workers get the benefit of ESIC.
- Institutions working in hazardous areas are to be compulsorily registered with ESIC.[57]

Expansion of Social Security

With the passing of the Labour Reforms Bill by the Parliament in 2020, the availability of social security benefits has now been expanded as follows:

- Benefit of pension scheme (EPFO) to all workers of organized, unorganized and self-employed sectors.
- Creation of social security fund for providing comprehensive social security to the unorganized sector.
- The requirement of minimum service has been removed for payment of gratuity in the case of fixed-term employees.
- Employees engaged on fixed terms get the same social security benefit as permanent employees.
- Creating a national database of workers of the unorganized sector through registration on Portal.
- Employers employing more than 20 workers to mandatorily report vacancies online.
- A Universal Account Number (UAN) for ESIC, EPFO and Unorganized Sector workers.
- Aadhaar-based Universal Account Number (UAN) to ensure seamless portability.[58]

Thus, the Social Security Code, 2020, focuses on the universalization of social security as now the Employees' State Insurance Corporation will extend to all workers medical care, sickness benefits, injury benefits, unemployment benefits, disablement and survivors' benefits and funeral expenses. Hitherto, the above benefits were available only to organized workers in 566 districts and were mandatory if more than 10 workers were working in an organization. As such only 3.5 crore employees and 13.5 crore members were covered under it. But as per Social Security Code, 2020, the benefits of social security will be extended to the entire country—740 districts. The scheme will be applicable to unorganized workers, including gig workers. There will be voluntary coverage by agreement of employees and employers even if the number of employees in an organization is less than 10 workers. There will be no minimum limit on the number of workers for hazardous or life-threatening occupations. Besides, the scheme is optional in

Plantations.[59] Besides, the provisions of the Employees Provident Funds Scheme, Employees' Pension Scheme and Employees' Deposit Linked Insurance Scheme which are monitored by the Employees Provident Fund Organisation and are hitherto applicable to government employees and organized workers in scheduled industries and are mandatory if more than 20 workers are employed in an organized and voluntary if less than 20 workers are employed, will now, after the implementation of Social Security Code, 2020, be applicable to all industries, and voluntary for an organization if employing less than 20 workers, and will also be applicable for all self-employed workers and any other class of workers including unorganized workers.[60]

These reforms provided under the Social Security Code, 2020, will be applicable to all workers even if hired for a fixed term. Besides, certain provisions in Labour Codes other than

Social Security Code, 2020, will also be supportive in providing some social security to workers directly or indirectly. For example, under the Industrial Relations (IR) Code, 2020, the following provisions will provide some help to the workers at the time of their unemployment:

- In case of job loss, a worker will get benefits under the Atal Bimit Vyakti Kalyan Yojna.
- Under the Atal Bimit Vyakti Kalyan Yojna, a worker of the organized sector who loses his job gets financial aid from the government. This is a type of unemployment allowance, the benefit of which is admissible to the workers covered under the ESI Scheme.
- At the time of retrenchment, a worker as per New Labour Code for New India 20 be provided 15 days' wages for re-skilling. The wages would be credited directly into the bank account of the worker so as to enable him to learn new skills.[61]

Management Strategy

While formulating its strategy with regard to fringe benefits, especially social security, the management should keep in view that wages are just one part of the total compensation—which the workers are entitled to for their contribution in the process of production. In order to enable the workers to lead a reasonably good life, they should also be extended social security and other fringe benefits. So far as mandatory social security is concerned, the employers are legally bound to provide the same to their workers and therefore, the management strategy should ensure that the social security measures as provided under various social security Acts must be provided in both letter and spirit. In addition to that, the management strategy should provide for voluntary social security, in consultation with worker's representatives. The strategy should also ensure that all labour reforms as envisaged under four Labour Codes should be implemented in the right spirit.

Chapter Review

1. Although employee benefits and services constitute a significant part of total compensation, no research study has yet been able to provide conclusive proof about their impact either on organization's performance or their ability to attract and retain employees or their effectiveness to motivate employees. Still, people have a favourable opinion about employee benefits and therefore, fringe benefits in one form or the other have been in vogue for a long period because fringe benefits are a great source of contentment to workers as these benefits supplement their income, make their lives comfortable, improve their status as also their standard of living. Since a contented worker is an asset to an organization, he is instrumental in the overall progress of the organization concerned. That is why today greater attention is being paid to fringe benefits by a good number of organizations.

2. The concept of fringe benefit is of recent origin. The benefits provided to the workforce of an organization apart from the negotiated wages are nowadays termed as either fringe benefits or non-wage benefits. These benefits are of great significance to workers as they reduce the gap between their nominal wages and real wages. Only those benefits which are computable in terms of money are not part of any contract indicating when the sum is payable, and of which the amount is not predetermined, fall under the category of fringe benefits. The main objectives of fringe benefits are to bridge the gap between money wages and real wages, attract and retain employees, seek the commitment of employees and so on. Besides, benefits are of great importance not only to employees but also to employers and society.

3. Intangible benefits are as important as tangible benefits and at times even more important than tangible benefits. The Second World War, the approach of trade unions, statutory requirements, the cost-effectiveness of benefits, paternalistic considerations and securing an edge over competitors have been the main factors responsible to realize the need for and promote the worth of employee benefits.

4. While framing benefit policies, the range of benefits, size of benefits, percentage of each benefit to the total compensation, options available, harmonization and so on should be clearly spelled out. In practice, benefits made available to employees differ from organization to organization and industry to industry. Planning and designing of benefits depend a great deal on the objectives of benefits envisioned by the management and the benefits package offered by the competitors. Options for choosing benefits packages in a cafeteria style, formulation of appropriate benefits programme, coverage of employees' financial considerations, compliance of statuary obligations and so on are some of the other issues to be taken care of under planning, designing and administration of benefits. There are three current approaches in the field of benefits, namely, innovative approach, flexibility and harmonization.

Age, sex, marital status, size of the family and so on are some of the main factors influencing choice of the benefits package.

5. It is desirable to review the benefits package from time to time and modify the same as and when required. However, communicating appropriately the benefits programme to the employees concerned is an important issue and demands adequate attention.

6. Payments included under fringe benefits can be categorized into: (a) Social security (b) Labour welfare benefits and (c) Bonus. Social Security which is one of the major constituents of fringe benefits is the security that society furnishes to a worker (or his dependents in case of his death) to sustain himself and his family in case he falls victim to any contingency of life. There is a greater need for social security for Indian industrial workers as they are poor, physically weak and highly exposed to contingencies of life. Social insurance and social assistance are the main forms of social security in our country. In Indian industries, social security is being provided mainly because of legal obligations. Employees' Compensation Act, 1923; ESI Act, 1948; Maternity Benefit Act, 1961; Employees' Provident Funds and Miscellaneous Provisions Act, 1952; Payment of Gratuity Act, 1972; and so on have been playing an important role in this direction. In other words, it is only the statutory provisions with regard to social security that have been playing an important role in the direction of making social security available to Indian workers. Very little has been done voluntarily either by employers or other agencies.

7. The initiation of the four 'Labour Reforms' which after amalgamation 29 Central Labour Laws have given rise to four Labour Codes will be extremely useful to the workers in both the organized and unorganized sectors across the country as they will ensure them right to minimum wages, social security, occupational safety, health, and good working conditions, etc.

DISCUSSION QUESTIONS

1. Discuss the objectives of social security and how social security is beneficial to employees.

2. Discuss the difference between social insurance and social assistance. Also, discuss whether commercial insurance should be included under the scope of social security or not.

3. Discuss the main provisions of social security under social security legislation in our country and what should be done to make them more meaningful.

4. Discuss the 'Biggest Labour Reforms' contained in the Labour Reforms Bill 2020.

5. Discuss the details of Social Security Code, 2019.

Individual and Group Activities

1. Individually or in a group of two members, visit a big organization and find out from the women employees if the Maternity Benefit Act, 1961, is being implemented both in letter and spirit in their organization and whether they are satisfied with the benefits available under the Act. Prepare a detailed report.
2. In a group of three members, visit a large manufacturing organization and find out from trade union leaders if the ESI Act, 1948, is being sincerely implemented in their organization. Take a note of their reaction towards the Act and prepare a brief report.
3. Individually visit a small organization to which the Employees' Compensation Act, 1923, is applicable. Discuss with the workers there if compensation for employment injury is paid to the injured workers as per provisions of the Act. Also, find out their observations on the Act.
4. In a group of two members, visit some big manufacturing organization and find out the reaction of trade union officials regarding 'Labour Reforms' initiated by Central Government.
5. Individually discuss with the HR officials of some big organization whether they visualize any difficulty in the implementation of Labour Codes in their organization.

APPLICATION CASE

John has been working as a welder in ABC Enterprise Ltd. manufacturing special nuts and bolts for a reputed company. Initially John was appointed as an Apprentice but by virtue of his hard work and quality work during the five years, he used to get appreciations from all concerned and rose to his present position. One day during the lunch hour, he went to the canteen of his organization and took lunch along with his three colleagues. After having lunch, all the four enjoyed themselves for some time under the shadow of a big tree just in front of the canteen. While three of his colleagues dispersed from there, John went to the rest shelter of his organization. As he felt sleepy, he saw a ceiling fan and slept on the bench which was placed just below the ceiling fan. Hardly five minutes had passed that the ceiling fan fell on John resulting in the fracture of his right-hand shoulder.

He was taken to the dispensary of the organization. The Medical Officer took the X-ray and found that the injury was very serious and therefore, John was referred to a Super Specialist Orthopaedician. After examining the X-Ray report, he conducted an operation on the shoulder of John. However, after about a fortnight, John found out that his right hand had no sensation and hence, he felt that he won't be able to work with the right hand anymore in future. John contacted his supervisor and approached the HR Department of his organization for claiming compensation, but the HR department refused to entertain his claim on the grounds that John was not working at the time of the accident. John approached the officials of the union of workers. One of the senior officials of the Union took John along with him to the HR department and pleaded that though John was not working at the time of the accident, it was his official lunch period and was relaxing in the official rest shelter. However, the HR department did not agree with the contention of the Union official.

Questions

1. Is the HR Department justified in refusing the compensation claim of John?
2. Is John justified in claiming the compensation? If yes, why?
3. What future course of action should be adopted by John?

Notes

1 R. C. Sharma, 'A Critical Study of Non-Wage Benefits in Sugar Factories of Haryana and Punjab' (unpublished PhD thesis, Kurukshetra University, 1973).
2 See Milkovich, Newman, and Venkata Ratnam, *Compensation*, 355.
3 *The Mckinsey Quarterly Chart Focus Newsletter*, June 2006, member edition.
4 For an exhaustive study, see R. C. Sharma, 'The Concept of Fringe Benefits in Indian Industry', *Indian Journal of Industrial Relations* 13, no. 2 (October 1977): 243–252; and R. C. Sharma, 'The Concept and Philosophy of Fringe Benefits', *Integrated Management* XIII, no. 3 (March 1978): 22–28.
5 The term 'fringe benefits' has been traced to a gifted regional chairman of the National War Labor Board in the United States. James C. Hill, 'Stabilization of Fringe Benefits', *Industrial and Labour Relations Review* 7, no. 2 (January 1954): 221–234.
6 D. J. Robertson, *The Economics of Wages* (London: Macmillan, 1961); W. J. Bowen, *The Wage Price Issue* (New Jersey, NJ: Princeton University Press, 1960); D. J. Robertson, *Fringe Benefits, Labour Costs and Social Security* (London: George Allen and Union, 1965).
7 See Sharma, *Industrial Relations*, 405.
8 R. Cockmar, 'Employee Benefits for Managers and Executives', in *Management of Salary and Wage*, ed. A. M. Pavery (Sussex: Grover Press, 1975), 73.
9 D. Belcher, 'Fringe Benefits: Do We Know Enough about Them?' in *Wage and Salary Administration*, eds. Langsner and Zollitsch (Cincinnati, OH: South-Western Publishing Company, 1961), 488.
10 Quoted in P. S. Rao, *Essentials of Human Resources Management and Industrial Relations* (Mumbai: Himalaya Publishing House, 2000), 423.
11 'Herzberg's Two Factor Theory', *Human Resource Management*, in J. M. Ivancevich, ed. (New Delhi: McGraw-Hill, 2008), 243–252.
12 See Paul Pigors and C. A. Myers, *Personnel Administration* (Tokyo: McGraw-Hill Kogakusha, 1977), 547.
13 Armstrong and Murlis, *Reward Management*, 415.
14 Ibid., 416.

15 Milkovich, Newman, and Venkata Ratnam, *Compensation*, 368–369.
16 Ibid.
17 Armstrong and Murlis, *Reward Management*, 443.
18 For details, see Ibid., 445.
19 Milkovich, Newman, and Venkata Ratnam, *Compensation*, 369.
20 R. H. Hodge, 'Pinning Down in Problematic Fringe', *The Personnel Function*, A Progressive Report, 113–115.
21 See Sharma, *Industrial Relations*, 417.
22 Substituted for 'Workmen's' by the Workmen's Compensation (Amendment) Act, 2009, and made effective from 18 January 2010.
23 For more details, see Sharma, *Industrial Relations*, 825–836.
24 Ministry of Labour & Employment, *Pocket Book of Labour Statistics*, 2013.
25 Ibid.
26 For more details, see Sharma, *Industrial Relations*, 836–857.
27 Labour Bureau, Ministry of Labour and Employment, Government of India, *Pocket Book of Labour Statistics*, 2013.
28 *The Economic Times*, 23 March 2018.
29 *The Economic Times*, 16 November 2018.
30 Ibid.
31 Ibid.
32 For details, see Sharma, *Industrial Relations*, 836–857.
33 Ministry of Labour & Employment, *Pocket Book of Labour Statistics*, 2013.
34 Ibid.
35 Ibid.
36 Ibid.
37 For details, see Sharma, *Industrial Relations*, 857–867.
38 For more details, see the Employees' Pension Scheme, 1995 in *The Employees' Provident Fund and Miscellaneous Provisions Act, 1952, Lexi Nexis, Gurgaon (2022–2023)*, 203–252.
39 Ibid.
40 Ibid., 185–202.
41 *The Economic Times*, 13 June 2018.
42 For details, see Sharma, *Industrial Relations*, 877–886.
43 Ministry of Labour & Employment, *Pocket Book of Labour Statistics*, 2013.
44 Ibid.
45 *The Economics Times*, 23 March 2018.
46 *Hindustan Times*, 2 January 2018.
47 For details, see *The Times of India*, 22 September 2022.
48 For details, see Sharma, *Industrial Relations*, 767–785.
49 For details, see *New Labour Code for New India*, Ministry of Information and Broadcasting, Government of India, New Delhi, 2021, 1–36.
50 Ibid., 8.
51 Ibid., 6.
52 Ibid., 20.
53 Ibid., 22.
54 Ibid., 21.
55 Ibid., 23.
56 Ibid., 5.
57 Ibid., 13.
58 Ibid., 14.
59 Ibid., 28.
60 Ibid.
61 Ibid., 19–20.

8

DESIGNING AND OPERATING FRINGE BENEFITS AND SERVICES, AND INTERNAL AUDIT OF COMPENSATION AND BENEFITS (II)

LEARNING OBJECTIVES

After studying this chapter, the reader should be able to:

1. Examine critically the various definitions of labour welfare as also its objectives and significance.
2. List and describe the principles of labour welfare.
3. Classify labour welfare work under different heads.
4. List and describe the statutory labour welfare work undertaken in our country.
5. List and describe the labour welfare work undertaken by employers and trade unions in Indian industries.
6. Explain the recent trends/development in the field of fringe benefits and services.
7. Explain the meaning of internal audit of compensation and benefits and also of related issues.
8. Understand and explain welfare measures initiated through the 'Labour Reforms Bill—2020'.
9. Understand and explain the labour welfare provisions contained in the Labour Codes.
10. Explain the details of Payment of Bonus Act, 1965.

DOI: 10.4324/9781032626123-8

Introduction

Labour welfare is the second important ingredient of fringe benefits, social security being the first and bonus the third. It's just not enough to take care of the social security of the workers because social security takes care of only contingent situations whereas labour welfare is concerned with the physical, mental and economic betterment of the workers on a regular basis, according to the requirement of workers. It may, therefore, differ from one set of workers to that of another set of workers. Since labour welfare activities lead not only to the betterment of workers but also of the employers (as it is assumed that labour activities add to the contentment of workers and enhance their productivity), more and more organizations have started paying their due attention to this regard.

Fringe Benefits and Current Practices (II)

As stated earlier, after social security which is the first important constituent of the fringe benefits, there come the labour welfare activities which are the second main constituent of fringe benefits.

Labour Welfare

The maintenance function of HRM aims at preserving and improving the physical, mental and economic conditions of the employees as it helps all the stakeholders of an organization. It is here that labour welfare comes into vogue. It is again, perhaps, for this reason that ever-increasing attention is being paid towards labour welfare activities in almost all organizations, though to different degrees.

Meaning and Definition

Since labour welfare has been defined in several ways, it has been understood in various ways in different countries. The Royal Commission on Labour has also remarked,

> The term 'welfare' as applied to the industrial workers is one which must necessarily be elastic, bearing a somewhat different interpretations in one country from another, according to the different social customs, the degree of industrialization and the educational development of the workers.[1]

Anyway, the *Oxford Dictionary* defines labour welfare as 'efforts to make life worth living for workmen'. According to the Labour Investigation Committee,

> anything done for the intellectual, physical, moral and economic betterment of the workers whether by employers, by government or by agencies over and

above which is laid down by law or what is normally expected as a part of contractual benefits for which the workers may have bargained.[2]

According to R. R. Hopking, 'welfare is fundamentally an attitude of mind on the part of management influencing the method by which welfare activities are undertaken'. The ILO has defined labour welfare as:

[W]orkers' welfare should be understood as meaning such services, facilities and amenities which may be established in, or in the vicinity of, undertakings to enable the persons employed in them to perform their work in healthy, congenial surroundings and to provide them with amenities conducive to good health and high morale.[3]

As a matter of fact, the term 'labour welfare' connotes anything that makes the conditions in the factory conducive to the happiness, health and prosperity of workers. The labour welfare operates to neutralize the harmful effects of large-scale industrialization and urbanization. Provisions of welfare amenities enable the workers to live a richer and more satisfactory life and contribute to their efficiency and productivity.

Objectives of Labour Welfare Work

The main objectives of welfare activities include the following:

1. To provide for economic betterment of the workers.
2. To improve their health.
3. To promote their intellectual betterment.
4. To infuse confidence and boost morale of workers.
5. To promote the goodwill of the organization.
6. To attract and retain good employees.
7. To increase productivity.
8. To maintain good human and industrial relations.
9. To treat workers as human beings first and workers thereafter.
10. To combat trade unionism.
11. To restrict government intervention.
12. To earn the loyalty of workers.
13. To reduce the rate of absenteeism and labour turnover.

Increased Focus on Employee Well-Being

Of late, organizations have started taking more interest in their employees' health and well-being (see Exhibits 8.1 and 8.2). All-round steps are being taken including family outreach, but an overarching health and wellness strategy is largely missing. A study found that in 2018, over 80 per cent of the organizations have taken at least one action in the following areas—health risk management; weight management, physical activity, nutrition; and mental health. While 61 per cent have taken at least one action to improve the financial well-being of employees in 2018, it is a matter of concern that almost half of the surveyed organizations still do not have a formally articulated health and well-being strategy.[4]

EXHIBIT 8.1 COMPANIES ARE INCREASING FOCUS ON EMPLOYEE WELL-BEING STUDY

Companies in India are beginning to take a more holistic view of employee health and wellness, going beyond physical well-being to include emotional and financial, according to the India Health and Well Being Study 2018 released by Willis Towers Watson, a leading global advisory, broking and solutions company.

Source: The Economic Times (27 November 2018).

EXHIBIT 8.2 COMPANIES ARE INCREASING FOCUS ON EMPLOYEE WELL-BEING

More companies need to acknowledge that the day-to-day well-being of employees and their overall workplace experience is a clear management of priority if they want to focus on the long-term productivity of individuals and the company at large. Our workspaces, which are in our control, are designed to develop these building blocks in a healthy way and for the long term. Organizations need to pay attention to sleep patterns, physical exercise, stress levels and diet.

Source: The Times of India (23 November 2022).

It is immensely encouraging to observe this increased focus on employee health and wellness. However, to translate this into all-round well-being enhanced productivity and ultimately improved financial performance, companies must develop a coherent and holistic health and wellness strategy encompassing all four aspects—physical, emotional, financial and family.

According to Gardner study, enterprises focused on work- and office-centric processes damage the productivity and well-being of employees. What is needed in the future of work is to have an employee-centric approach.

A toxic management, even in hybrid mode, can cause severe stress, which can reduce performance by as much as 33%, and employees are 54% likely to leave the current employment. The aim must be to reverse these undesired side effects and drive sustainable progress, a growth mindset and loyalty. For this, build a culture of employee-centricity that provides open communication and feedback mechanism, imbibes trust, assures psychological safety and inspires creativity and innovation.[5]

It is always good for the organization to start with employee well-being by having consideration for the physical, emotional, mental and financial well-being for the employees. Considering employees just as customers, redesign jobs, processes and workplaces on employee needs and requirements. Also, provide space and opportunities for growth of employees besides ensuring psychological safety by revamping feedback systems. Equally important is revamping compensation and rewards programmes.[6]

While a majority, 66 per cent, of employers have already taken or will take steps in the next three years to develop a mental health strategy, 59 per cent are planning to offer programmes to support chronic behavioural health conditions; currently offered by only 8 per cent of employers. Similarly, 63 per cent already have or are developing a strategy to improve financial well-being and 13 per cent are considering it in three years' time. Towards this, 50 per cent of companies are planning to deliver customized or personalized messages to help improve financial planning as compared to only 6 per cent today.[7]

The number of employers recognizing the role of the family in the overall well-being of an employee and in turn their productivity is noteworthy. It is heartening to see that almost one in four organizations is beginning to engage the employees' families in one way or another. Some of them are inviting family members to participate in various programmes and activities (27 per cent) organized by the companies; focusing communication to reach/involve family members (24 per cent) and redesigning employee assistance programmes to better address emotional and financial well-being for employees and their dependents (44 per cent).[8]

Significance of Labour Welfare in Indian Industries

An industrial worker in India is, by and large, a poor person and needs help for his economic, physical and intellectual betterment. Similarly, industrial units in India need a higher rate of productivity, quality workers, stability of manpower, industrial peace and so on. Labour welfare activities undertaken by an organization voluntarily, or even statutorily, are instrumental in the accomplishment of above aims and objectives, at least, to some extent.

Principles of Labour Welfare

Some of the main principles of labour welfare that should be kept in mind in the implementation of a labour welfare programme are as follows:

1. **Principle of self-help:** Labour welfare must aim at helping employees to help themselves.

2. **Principle of efficiency:** A welfare programme should also aim at increasing the efficiency of workers.
3. **Principle of democratic values:** Workers should be associated in the formulation, organization and implementation of a welfare programme.
4. **Principle of meeting the real needs of the worker:** A welfare programme should aim at fulfilling the real needs of workers.
5. **Principle of social responsibility:** Industry being a sub-system of the society as it draws its manpower from the society; it has an obligation towards its employees to look after their welfare.
6. **Principle of evaluation:** Welfare programmes must be evaluated periodically.
7. **Principle of re-personalization:** The welfare should aim at the overall development of the employees.
8. **Principle of confirming the benefit in which the group is more efficient than the individual:** The welfare programme should aim at benefiting the group instead of an individual.
9. **Principle of flexibility:** The benefit should be flexible enough so as to incorporate any desirable change at any stage.
10. **Principle of financial adequacy:** The welfare programme should be calculable and adequate financial provisions should be made for it.
11. **Principle of publicizing:** The welfare programme should be well publicized and communicated to all concerned.
12. **Principle of maintaining ego:** The employer should not assume a benevolent posture to indicate that it is due to generosity of the employer that a benefit has been given to workers.
13. **Principle of cafeteria approach:** A variety of packages suiting to different age groups, genders, family size, marital status and so on should be worked out and a worker should have an option of choosing any of these packages according to his preference or requirements.

Classification of Labour Welfare Work

Although there is no watertight classification of labour welfare work, yet for the sake of convenience, we may classify it into the following categories:

1. **Statutory welfare:** It refers to the welfare activities undertaken because of legislative compulsion. For example, it is mandatory, under the provisions of the Factories Act, 1948, for an employer to provide specified health (Sections 21–40) and welfare (Sections 42–50) facilities in a factory. Violation or non-adherence to these provisions may attract severe penalties under the relevant Act.
2. **Voluntary welfare:** According to many authors, real welfare work is that which is undertaken by an employer at his own sweet will and not under any legal pressure. That is why many employers undertake welfare activities such

as medical, recreation, transport, library, games and sports, education, housing, uniforms and picnics.

3. **Mutual welfare:** As stated earlier, trade unions or workers should also share a part of the responsibility of undertaking welfare activities. Hence, we come across some welfare facilities like newspapers/reading rooms, some games such as volleyball and kabaddi, part-time homoeopath doctor and so on being extended by some trade unions to their members.

According to another classification suggested by Broughtan, labour welfare activities can be grouped under two heads, namely (a) 'intramural welfare activities' which are undertaken within the premises of the factory, such as health, welfare and safety measures, healthy working conditions and canteen, and (b) 'extramural activities' which are undertaken outside the factory such as housing and medical facilities.

Labour Welfare Activities in Indian Industries

At the initial stages of the industrial revolution in our country, there were hardly any welfare activities undertaken by any agency except a little bit undertaken by outside agencies and that too were provided on humanitarian considerations. It was the First World War (1914–1918) and progress made by the industrial revolution that prompted both the government and the employers to come forward in this direction. The government had to take initiative because public (workers are also a part of the public) welfare is one of the major responsibilities of the government. The employers started coming forward because they also started realizing that welfare activities are not only in the interest of workers but also benefit the employers because welfare activities are instrumental in improving the health of the workers and making them feel satisfied which, in turn, helps in improving the efficiency and productivity of labour. Welfare activities also help in reducing the rate of absenteeism and labour turnover, infusing confidence and boosting the morale of the workers and improving human and industrial relations. All these things together help in improving the health of the organization—sometimes directly and sometimes indirectly. Hence, welfare activities should be well-planned and properly undertaken. The trade unions have also initiated welfare work, though at a very modest scale because their capacity to spend on welfare work is highly limited.

The welfare activities undertaken in our country can be studied under the following heads:

1. **Welfare activities undertaken by the Central government:** The government owes a great responsibility for looking after labour welfare as the workers constitute a significant part of people in general.

   a. **Directive Principles of State Policy:** The chapter on Directive Principles of State Policy (Articles 38–47) in our Constitution spells out the need for labour welfare as follows:

Article 38: State to secure a social order for the promotion of welfare of the people:

i. The State shall strive to develop a social system which will secure social, economic and political justice in all spheres of life.

ii. The State shall, in particular, strive to minimize the inequalities in income, and endeavour to eliminate inequalities in status, facilities and opportunities, not only amongst individuals but also amongst groups of people residing in different areas or engaged in different vocations.

Article 39: Certain principles of policy to be followed by the State:

i.   That the citizens, men and women equally, have the right to an adequate means of livelihood;

ii. That the ownership and control of the material resources of the community are so distributed as best to subserve the common good;

iii. That the operation of the economic system does not result in the concentration of wealth and means of production to the common detriment;

iv. That there is equal pay for equal work for both men and women;

v.   That the health and strength of workers, men and women and the tender age of children are not abused and that citizens are not forced by economic necessity to enter avocations unsuited to their age or strength;

vi. That children are given opportunities and facilities to develop in a healthy manner and in conditions of freedom and dignity and that childhood and youth are protected against exploitation and against moral and material abandonment.

Article 39A: Equal justice and free legal aid—The State shall secure that the operation of the legal system promotes justice, on a basis of equal opportunity, and shall, in particular, provide free legal aid, by suitable legislation or schemes or in any other way, to ensure that opportunities for securing justice are not denied to any citizen by reason of economic or other disabilities.

Article 40: Organization of village panchayats—The State shall take steps to organize village panchayats and endow them with such powers and authority as may be necessary to enable them to function as units of self-government.

Article 41: Right to work, to education and to public assistance in certain cases—The State shall, within the limits of its economic capacity and development, make effective provision for securing the right to work, to education and to public assistance in cases of unemployment, old age, sickness and disablement, and in other cases of undeserved want.

Article 42: Provision for just and humane conditions of work and maternity relief—The State shall make provision for securing just and humane conditions of work and for maternity relief.

Article 43: Living wage, etc., for workers—The State shall endeavour to secure, by suitable legislation or economic organization or in any other way, all workers, agricultural, industrial or otherwise, work, a living wage, conditions of work, ensuring a decent standard of life and full enjoyment of leisure and social and cultural opportunities, and in particular, the State shall endeavour to promote cottage industries on an individual or co-operative basis in rural areas.

Article 43A: Participation of workers in management of industries—The State shall take steps, by suitable legislation or in any other way, to secure the participation of workers in the management of undertakings, establishments or other organizations engaged in any industry.

Article 44: Uniform civil code for the citizens—The State shall endeavour to secure for the citizens a uniform civil code throughout the territory of India.

Article 45: Provision for free compulsory education for children—The State shall endeavour to provide, within a period of ten years from the commencement of this constitution, for free and compulsory education for all children until they complete the age of fourteen years.

Article 46: Promotion of educational and economic interest of Scheduled Castes, Scheduled Tribes and other weaker sections—The State shall promote with special care the educational and economic interests of the weaker sections of the people, and, in particular, of the Scheduled Castes and the Scheduled Tribes, and shall protect them from social injustice and all forms of exploitation.

Article 47: Duty of the State to raise the level of nutrition and the standard of living and to improve public health—The State shall regard the raising of the level of nutrition and the standard of living of its people and the improvement of public health as among its primary duties, and in particular, the State shall endeavour to bring about prohibition of the consumption except for medical purposes of intoxicating drinks and of drugs which are injurious to health.

Article 48: Organization of agriculture and animal husbandry—The State shall endeavour to organize agriculture and animal husbandry on modern and scientific lines and shall, in particular, take steps for preserving and improving the breeds, and prohibiting the slaughter of cows and calves and other milch and draught cattle.

Article 48A: Protection and improvement of environment and safeguarding of forests and wildlife—The State shall endeavour to protect and improve the environment and to safeguard the forests and wildlife of the country.

Article 49: Protection of monuments and places and objects of national importance—It shall be the obligation of the State to protect every monument or place or object of artistic or historic interest, declared by or under law made by Parliament to be of national importance, from spoliation, disfigurement, destruction, removal, disposal or export, as the case may be.

Article 50: Separation of judiciary from the executive—The State shall take steps to separate the judiciary from the executive in the public services of the State.

Thus, India being a welfare State, it is obligatory on the part of the Central government to promote the welfare of industrial workers. Hence, the Government of India has passed several Acts to ensure the welfare of the workers. Some of the main Acts are as follows:

b. **Factories Act, 1948:** Workers' well-being/welfare is closely related to their health, safety and welfare. Factories Act, 1948, has taken a good amount of care in this regard. The relevant provisions with regard to these aspects mentioned in the Factories Act, 1948, are as follows:

   i. Health provisions: The provisions pertaining to health are as follows:

   ○ *Cleanliness—Section 11(1):* Every factory shall be kept clean and free from any drain, privy or other nuisance.
      Disposal of wastes and effluent—Section 12(1): Effective arrangement shall be made in every factory for the treatment of wastes and effluents due to manufacturing process carried on therein, so as to render them innocuous and for their disposal.

   ○ *Ventilation and temperature—Sections 13(1), 13(1)(a), 13(1)(b):* Effective and suitable provisions shall be made in every factory for securing and maintaining in every room adequate ventilation by the circulation of fresh air, and such a temperature as will secure to workers therein reasonable conditions of comfort and prevent injury to health, etc.

   ○ *Dust and fume—Section 14(1):* In every factory in which, by reason of the manufacturing process carried on, there is given off any dust or fume or other impurity of such a nature and to such an extent as is likely to be injurious or offensive to the workers employed therein, or any dust in substantial quantities, effective measures shall be taken to prevent its inhalation and accumulation in any workroom, and if any exhaust appliance is necessary for this purpose, it shall be applied as near as possible to the point of origin of the dust, fume or other impurities, and such point shall be enclosed so far as possible.

   ○ *Artificial humidification—Section 15(1):* In respect of all factories in which the humidity of the air is artificially increased, the State Government may make rules: (a) prescribing standards of humidification and (b) regulating the methods used for artificially increasing the humidity of the air.

○ *Overcrowding—Section 16(I), 16(2):* No room in any factory shall be overcrowded to any extent injurious to the health of the workers employed therein. Without prejudice to the generality of sub-section(I), there shall be in every workroom of a factory in existence on the date of the commencement of this Act at least 9.9 m³ and of a factory built after the commencement of this Act at least 14.2 m³ of space for every worker employed therein.

○ *Lighting—Section 17(I):* In every part of the factory where workers are working or passing, there shall be provided and maintained sufficient and suitable lighting, natural or artificial, or both.

○ *Drinking water—Section 18(I), 18(2):* In every factory, effective arrangements shall be made to provide and maintain, at suitable points conveniently situated for all workers employed therein, a sufficient supply of wholesome drinking water. All such points shall be legibly marked 'drinking water' in a language understood by a majority of the workers employed in the factory, and no such point shall be situated within 6 m of any washing place, urinal, latrine, spittoon, open drain carrying sullage or effluent or any other source of contamination unless a shorter distance is approved in writing by the Chief Inspector. In every factory wherein more than 250 workers are ordinarily employed provisions shall be made for cold drinking water during hot weather by effective means and for distribution thereof.

○ *Latrine and urinals—Sections 19(Ia), 19(I), 19(2), 19(3):* In every factory, sufficient latrine and urinal accommodation of prescribed types shall be provided conveniently situated and accessible to workers at all times, while they are at the factory. Separate enclosed accommodation shall be provided for male and female workers. In every factory wherein more than 250 workers are ordinarily employed, all latrine and urinal accommodations shall be of prescribed sanitary types. The State Government may prescribe the number of latrines and urinals to be provided in any factory in proportion to the numbers of male and female workers ordinarily employed therein.

○ *Spittoons—Section 20(I), 20(2):* In every factory, there shall be provided a sufficient number of spittoons in convenient places and they shall be maintained in a clean and hygienic condition. The State Government may make rules prescribing the type and the number of spittoons to be provided and their location in any factory and provide for such further matters relating to their maintenance in a clean and hygienic condition.

ii. Safety Provisions: Safety at the workplace is very important for the welfare of the workers. It is good that the following provisions have been made in Chapter IV (Sections 21–41) for the safety of workers in the Factories Act, 1948.[9]

iii. Welfare Provisions: The relevant welfare provisions in the Factories Act, 1948, contained in Chapter V (Sections 42 to 50), are as follows:

- *Washing facilities—Section 42:* In every factory, adequate and suitable facilities for washing shall be provided and maintained for the use of the workers therein.

- *Facilities for storing and drying clothing—Section 43:* The State Government may, in respect of any factory or class or description of factories, make rules requiring the provision therein of suitable places for keeping clothing not worn during working hours and for the drying of wet clothing.

- *Facilities for sitting—Section 44(1):* In every factory, suitable arrangements for sitting shall be provided and maintained for all workers obliged to work in a standing position, in order that they may take advantage of any opportunities for rest which may occur in the course of their work.

- *First-aid appliances—Section 45:* There shall, in every factory, be provided and maintained so as to be readily accessible during all working hours, first-aid boxes or cupboards equipped with the prescribed contents, and the number of such boxes or cupboards to be provided and maintained shall not be less than one for every one hundred and fifty workers ordinarily employed at any one time in the factory.

- *Canteens—Section 46:* The State Government may make rules requiring that in any specified factory wherein more than 250 workers are ordinarily employed, a canteen or canteens shall be provided and maintained by the occupier for the use of the workers.

- *Shelters, rest rooms and lunch rooms—Section 47:* In every factory, wherein more than 150 workers are ordinarily employed, adequate and suitable shelters or rest rooms and a suitable lunch room, with provision for drinking water, where workers can eat meals brought by them, shall be provided and maintained for the use of the workers.

- *Crèches—Section 48:* In every factory, wherein more than thirty women workers are ordinarily employed, there shall be provided and maintained a suitable room or rooms for the use of children under the age of six years of such women.

- *Welfare officer—Section 49(1):* In every factory, wherein more than five hundred workers are ordinarily employed; the occupier shall employ in the factory such number of welfare officers as may be prescribed. (Refer to Annexure 7.1).

o *Power to make rules—Section 50:* The State Government may make rules to supplement this Chapter.

In addition, Section 67 of the Factories Act, 1948, deals with the employment of young persons and states that no child who has not completed his fourteenth year shall be required to work in any factory. Section 68 deals with the employment of children and adolescents and Sections 69 and 70 deal with the certificate of fitness granted to adolescents. There are some other Sections also under the Factories Act, 1948, which are related to the safety of workers.

Besides the aforementioned, the following officials/agencies have also been contributing towards labour welfare in one way or the other:

o Chief Inspector of Factories.
o Directorate General, Factory Advice Service and Labour Institute (DGFASLI).
o National Safety Council.
o Director General of Mines Safety.
o National Commission on Labour.

Not only that, but the Government of India has also sanctioned grants-in-aid for implementing water supply schemes to mine management in Maharashtra and Goa. Although most of the activities are administered directly by the welfare organizations under the Ministry of Labour & Employment, yet loans and subsidies are also provided to the state government, local authorities and to the employers for implementation of approved prototype schemes.

iv. Welfare Work under Statutory Funds:[10] In order to supplement the efforts of the employers and the state governments in providing welfare amenities to the workers, the Ministry of Labour & Employment administers the following welfare funds for beedi, cine and certain categories of non-coal mine workers, which are financed out of the proceeds of cess levied under the respective Cess/Fund Acts on manufactured beedis, feature films, export of mica, iron ore, manganese ore, chrome ore and so on.

o The Mica Mines Labour Welfare Fund Act, 1946.
o The Limestone and Dolomite Mines Labour Welfare Fund Act, 1972.
o The Iron Ore, Manganese Ore and Chrome Ore Mines Labour Welfare Fund Act, 1976.
o The Beedi Workers' Welfare Fund Act, 1976.
o The Cine Workers' Welfare Fund Act, 1981.

The Labour Welfare Organisation which administers these Funds is headed by a Director General (Labour Welfare)/Joint Secretary, Ministry of Labour & Employment assisted by the Welfare Commissioner (Headquarters) of Director's rank, who supervises nine Regional Welfare Commissioners for the purpose of administration of these Funds in the States.[11] Separate 'welfare funds' have also been formed for specified services such as posts and telegraphs, ports, dockyards and railways. The welfare measures financed out of these funds relate to provisions of medical, housing, drinking water, educational, recreational and family welfare facilities and so on.

2. **Welfare work undertaken by the state governments/union territories:**[12] The state governments have enacted several welfare-related Acts and have also set up welfare funds for different welfare activities.

Maharashtra and Uttar Pradesh's governments were pioneers in this field and still have more broad-based programmes of welfare as compared to other states. We come across model welfare centres in most of the states and the facilities provided in these centres usually consist of medical aid, educational and recreational facilities. In some states, vocational training is given to men and women. The Directorate General Labour Welfare looks after these activities on behalf of the State Government in Maharashtra. A special Labour Welfare Fund Act was passed in August 1965 in Uttar Pradesh, which provides for the provision of housing, general welfare and development. A brief account of some of the welfare activities of state governments/union territories is as follows:

So far as **Andhra Pradesh** is concerned, the Andhra Pradesh Labour Welfare Board implemented some welfare schemes like, scholarships, PH scholarship, medical aid, emergent economics ameliorative relief (FEAR), funeral expenses, daughter's marriage gift scheme, maternity benefit scheme, loss of limbs and family planning scheme.

It is the **Gujarat Labour Welfare Board**[13] that has been providing various welfare facilities to industrial workers and their dependents in Gujarat. Gujarat Unorganised Labour (Except Agriculture Labour) Welfare Board continues to implement various schemes to provide social security and safety net to the workers of urban areas, engaged in unorganized sectors. In order to enable the workers to avail benefits of social security and welfare schemes, 27,839 workers were registered and given unique ID numbers and identity cards during 2009–2010.[14]

The **Government of Meghalaya** has also initiated non-statutory labour welfare work. It has established five labour welfare centres in Meghalaya, which are providing basic elementary training in sewing, knitting and embroidery. These centres are usually located outside the precincts of the organization of workers. **The Government of Nagaland** has also established labour welfare training centres at Dimapur, Tuli (Mokokchung) and Wazeho

(Phek) imparting training in tailoring, knitting and embroidery to the family members and dependents of industrial workers so as to enable them to supplement their income by way of self-employment. This has helped in raising their standards of living.

The Goa Labour Welfare Board provides facilities such as training in embroidery, sewing, cutting and tailoring for the benefit of industrial workers and their families through the 17 labour welfare centres set up at different places in **Goa.**

In **Karnataka,** the statutory welfare facilities such as payment of wages, minimum wages, maternity benefit, employees' compensation and payment of gratuity are being extended in the state under the respective labour laws. In addition, 13 types of monetary benefits have been extended to the building and other construction workers by Karnataka Building and Other Construction Workers Welfare Board. Besides, the unorganized workers, namely head load workers, auto, taxi, lorry and bus drivers and conductors, small hotel workers, garage workers, tailors, washermen and so on are covered under the Swavalamban scheme.

In **Jammu division**, library facilities and other recreational facilities are being provided to industrial workers by the Labour Welfare Centre at Bari Brahmana. Besides, some accommodation in Labour Sarai is also provided to migratory labourers. In **Kashmir division**, study tours are conducted for the industrial workers from different industries to familiarize them with new working techniques and methods adopted by industrial workers of different states.

In **Andaman and Nicobar Islands,** six labour welfare centres are functioning in different parts of the Andaman and Nicobar Islands.

In **Maharashtra,** more than 280 welfare officers were appointed during the year 2009 in various factories in the state, who are doing a good job.

In **Tripura,** Tripura Building and Other Construction Workers Welfare Board constituted in July 2007 is continuously providing social security and welfare measures to the workers engaged in building and other construction work. Six Balwadi centres are run by the Labour Department in the tea and rubber plantations to impart primary education and to provide nutrition to the children of tea and rubber plantation workers in the age group of 3–6 years. About 600 students have actually been benefitted during the year 2009.[15]

So far as **Orissa** is concerned, in addition to statutory welfare facilities as provided under different labour enactments, non-statutory welfare facilities such as accommodation, dress allowance, soap allowance, transport allowance, leave and travel concession and education allowance have also been provided to the workers of different industries by virtue of bipartite and tripartite settlements as provided under Industrial Disputes Act, 1947.[16]

3. **Welfare work undertaken by the employers:**[17] Normally, the broad-based policy of the employers for providing welfare facilities comprises recreational

and educational facilities in large units. In the smaller units, employers usually conform to those facilities which are prescribed by law. In the case of some large-scale and well-organized industries such as jute and tea, welfare activities have been taken up on a joint basis. Individual mills have also set up a number of welfare centres as well as dispensaries for the benefit of their employees. Some details of welfare work undertaken by the employers are as follows:

In **Coal India Limited,** various statutory welfare facilities such as canteen, rest shelters and pithead baths are being provided to the coal miners. Non-statutory welfare measures have also been undertaken. Central cooperative and primary cooperative stores have been established to provide essential commodities and consumer goods at cheaper rates. Cooperative credit societies have also been functioning. Besides, Coal India Limited has started a scholarship scheme to encourage the children of its employees. Besides, good medical facilities are also provided to the workers and their families. There are 86 hospitals with 5,875 beds, 429 dispensaries, 673 ambulances and 1,646 doctors (including specialists) to look after the employees.[18] There are 12 Ayurvedic dispensaries that provide treatment to the workers through the indigenous system. Besides, Coal India Limited is also providing education facilities.

The **Chennai Port Trust** has been providing a number of welfare facilities. The Chennai Port and Dock Educational Trust Higher Secondary School has been functioning quite well since 1989. Many facilities are also being provided by the Trust. During 2009–2010, the Trust spent INR 47,297,602[19] crore on the welfare of the employees.

New Mangalore Port Trust, Kolkata Dock Labour Board, United Planters Association of Southern India, Visakhapatnam Port Trust, Mormugao Port Trust and Mumbai Port Trust have been doing a lot for the welfare of the workers.[20]

4. **Welfare work undertaken by trade unions:**[21] Trade unions can also undertake some labour welfare work, though the Indian unions, in general, have so far neither the will nor the ability to undertake the welfare work. The biggest limitation in the case of trade unions is the lack of funds. Hence, not much can be expected from such bodies. However, there are some good examples like the **Textile Labour Association, Ahmedabad, Tata Trust**, etc.

5. **Labour welfare work undertaken by voluntary social service agencies:**[22] It is worth mentioning that, of late, several voluntary social service agencies such as the Bombay Social League started by the Servants of India Society, the Seva Sadan Society, the Maternity and Infant Welfare Association and the Young Men's Christian Association (YMCA) have been doing a good job in the direction of welfare work. The activities of these organization comprise promotion of mass education through night schools, libraries and lectures, boy scouts' organization, promotion of public health, recreation and sports for

the working classes and so on. The Seva Sadan Societies in Pune and Bombay have undertaken social, educational and medical activities for women and children and have also trained social workers.

In advanced countries, voluntary agencies have played an important part in enforcement of social legislation through conferences, propaganda and fieldwork and in ensuring a high standard of compliance with law. Voluntary social services agencies can also follow suit in our country.

Recent Trends/Developments

Some of the happenings in the very recent past, especially during 2016, are as follows:

1. **Adoption leave:** A few companies like Accenture have started giving adoption leave to its employees (see Exhibit 8.3).

EXHIBIT 8.3 ADOPTION LEAVE

Changes were made on this front across many companies—most recently at Accenture—acknowledging an increasing trend of employees opting for adoption.

Source: The Economic Times (27 December 2016).

---

2. **Joining bonuses:** Joining bonuses went down, especially at start-ups (see Exhibit 8.4).

EXHIBIT 8.4 JOINING BONUSES

These went down, especially at start-ups with funds drying up. Such bonuses were offered to about 10 per cent of the staff, down from 30 to 40 per cent a year ago.

Source: The Economic Times (27 December 2016).

---

3. **Maternity leave:** Maternity leave has been extended from 12 weeks to 26 weeks (see Exhibit 8.5).

EXHIBIT 8.5 MATERNITY LEAVE

The Rajya Sabha passed amendments to the Maternity Benefit, Act 1961, increasing the period of *maternity leave* from 12 weeks to 26 weeks.

Source: The Economic Times (27 December 2016).

---

4. **Paternity leave:** Now many companies, e.g., TCS, Wipro, Zomato, etc., have started giving paternity leave (see Exhibit 8.6). The Central Government has already introduced it for their employees.

EXHIBIT 8.6 PATERNITY LEAVE

In a step towards making work cultures inclusive and progressive, more organisations are increasing their secondary caregiver parental leave. Some companies are now calling paternity leave 'partner-led' to ensure it is gender-neutral.

Source: The Times of India (5 November 2022).

---

5. **Yoga:** Of late, a good number of companies have started opting for yoga sessions (see Exhibit 8.7).

EXHIBIT 8.7 YOGA SESSIONS

An Assocham paper released this year noted that over 53 per cent of corporate companies were opting for *yoga sessions* at the workplace to boost employee productivity, reduce sick days and combat fatigue.

Source: The Economic Times (27 December 2016).

---

6. **Xmas gifts:** Despite the adverse impact of demonetizations of Rs 500 and 1000 notes, some start-ups offered several gifts to their employees (see Exhibit 8.8).

EXHIBIT 8.8 XMAS GIFTS

Despite the impact of demonetization, some start-ups are pampering staff this holiday season with *overseas getaways, road trips, bonuses, gifts* and even *happiness funds.*

Source: The Economic Times (27 December 2016).

---

7. **On-site acupuncture and improv classes:** Some companies, like Twitter, provide acupuncture and improv classes (see Exhibit 8.9).

EXHIBIT 8.9 ON-SITE ACUPUNCTURE AND IMPROV CLASSES

Twitter is well known for providing perks such as three-catered meals a day, but some lesser-known benefits include on-site acupuncture and improv classes.

Source: The Economic Times (20 June 2016).

---

8. **Death benefits:** It is good that some companies, like Google, provide the surviving spouse or partner of a deceased employee 50 per cent of their salary for a few years (see Exhibit 8.10).

EXHIBIT 8.10 DEATH BENEFIT

Google provides the surviving spouse or partner of a deceased employee 50 per cent of their salary for the next 10 years.

Source: The Economic Times (20 June 2016).

---

9. **Paid time off for volunteering and money for donation**: A new beginning has been made by some organizations, like Salesforce, whose employees are given paid volunteer time off and money to donate to a charity of their choice (see Exhibit 8.11).

EXHIBIT 8.11 PAID TIME OFF OR VOLUNTEERING AND MONEY FOR DONATION

Salesforce employees receive six days or paid volunteer time off a year, as well as $1,000 a year to donate to a charity of their choice.

Source: The Economic Times (20 June 2016).

---

10. **Partial reimbursement on student loan debt:** Some companies partially reimburse student loan debt (see Exhibit 8.12).

EXHIBIT 8.12 PARTIAL REIMBURSEMENT ON STUDENT LOAN DEBT

Employees are offered a $1,200-a-year reimbursement on student loan debt.

Source: The Economic Times (20 June 2016).

---

11. **Baby Cash:** Some companies provide cash to employees at the time of birth of baby (see Exhibit 8.13).

EXHIBIT 8.13 BABY CASH

Facebook provides $4,000 in 'Baby Cash' to employees with a new born.

Source: The Economic Times (20 June 2016).

---

12. **Egg freezing:** An initiative has been taken by Spotify to provide parental leave and so on for parents returning to the office, and reimbursing costs for egg freezing and fertility assistance (see Exhibit 8.14).

EXHIBIT 8.14 EGG FREEZING

Spotify provides six months of paid parental leave plus one month of flexible work options for parents returning to the office. The company also covers costs for *egg freezing* and *fertility assistance*.

Source: The Economic Times (20 June 2016).

13. **Gender reassignment:** Some companies, like Accenture, have started covering gender reassignment for its employees (see Exhibit 8.15).

EXHIBIT 8.15 GENDER REASSIGNMENT

Accenture covers *gender reassignment* for its employees as part of its commitment to LGBTQ right and diversity.

Source: The Economic Times (20 June 2016).

---

14. **Travel stipend:** An initiative has also been taken for giving employees an annual stipend to travel and stay in any listing of their company in the world (see Exhibit 8.16).

EXHIBIT 8.16 TRAVEL STIPEND

Airbnb gives its employees an annual stipend of $2,000 to travel and stay in any Airbnb listing anywhere in the world

Source: The Economic Times (20 June 2016).

---

15. **ESOPs:** Amidst concerns of a valuation bubble rising, ESOPs were slashed across the board at many of India's new-age companies.[23]
16. **Low-cost housing:** In order to provide low-cost housing, an organization has taken a highly appreciable initiative (see Exhibit 8.17).

In order to build low-cost houses, the government will collaborate with public sector banks, housing finance companies, state-owned construction firms like NBCC and there will be a tripartite agreement with member, bank/housing agency and EPFO.

The panel has suggested this scheme for low-income formal workers, who are EPFO subscribers and could not buy a house during their entire service period. At present, there are over 70 per cent EPFO subscribers whose basic wages are less than INR 15,000 per month.

EXHIBIT 8.17 EPFO PLANS TO INTRODUCE LOW-COST HOUSING SCHEME FOR ITS MEMBERS

The retirement fund body, Employees' Provident Fund Organisation (EPFO) is working on plans to provide *low-cost housing* to its five crore subscribers.

The Central Board of Trustees (CBT), EPFO's highest decision-making body, will consider the report of the expert committee on the same in a meeting scheduled for next month.

A committee set up by the EPFO last year had recommended a scheme to facilitate subscribers to buy houses where they will be allowed to give advance from their Provident Fund (PF) accumulation and also pledge their future PF contribution as EMI (equated monthly instalment) payments.

Source: Hindustan Times (23 May 2016).

---

17. **Flexi Timings:** These days flexi timings matter a lot (see Exhibit 8.18).

EXHIBIT 8.18 FLEXIBLE TIMING TOP PERK AT WORK: SURVEY

Source: The Economic Times (5 June 2018).

The then labour minister Bandaru Dattatreya had said in the Lok Sabha about the plan to provide housing scheme for EPFO subscribers.[24]

18. **Other initiatives:** Some other initiatives undertaken by Indian Inc. are as follows:
    a. **Flexible timings:** As per TimesJobs survey of over 700 employers, flexible timings matter the most for the employee (see Exhibit 8.18).
    b. **Deloitte** is readying a programme called 'EmoFit+' geared specifically towards the evolving needs of young parents. In addition to other facilities, it will provide counselling services for new mothers and fathers.[25]
    c. At **Infosys**, employers get[26] access to online and in-person interactions with specialists, annual medical camps, parenting sessions and counselling sessions.
    d. At **Mondelēz India Foods**, workshops[27] and sessions are conducted for new parents on topics like health of the child, health and financial wellness in perspective of becoming a new parent and changing priorities.

e. **Ericsson**, while offering crèche allowances and progressive maturity, paternity and adoption leave, also sends gift hampers after the birth of a child.

f. At **PepsiCo**, an automated system called 'MatCare4U' keeps consistent information flowing to women on maternity issues via email and SMS.

g. **Enhanced maternity leave:** A host of companies including PepsiCo, Godrej, PwC, GSK, Flipkart and KPMG allow women to take maternity leave for six months or more. Tata Sons provides a seven-month maternity leave.

h. **Part-time or flexible work options:** Allow employees to vary working arrangements based on personal needs, such as work from home, reduced working hours and sabbaticals.

i. **Returning moms' programme:** Offers a sustainable solution to women on prolonged maternity leave. Companies including EY and Genpact have second career programmes that help to skill and retain women in the workforce.

j. **Secure performance rating:** Helps new mothers in maintaining their high performance. Companies like Tata Sons, PwC, Ericsson India, Godrej and Citi have initiatives in place to let women retain their performance ratings, and also give women a greater choice to plan their return to work while managing personal needs.

k. **Cab and parking support:** Expectant mothers who self-drive are given priority parking at the office at companies such as Sony Pictures Networks India and PwC. Genpact has 'stork parking' at all its facilities, on-site and off-site day care centres at subsidized rates and reserved seating for expecting women in company transport vehicles.

l. **Day care facility/crèche allowance:** For working mothers who look for a safe and secure surrounding for their babies/kids when they themselves are at work. Companies such as Ericsson, Mondelēz, Genpact, EY and SAP Labs have various initiatives in place in this regard.

m. **Adoption and surrogacy leave:** Several companies have put in place parenting policies that formally cover alternative forms of parenthood such as adoption and surrogacy. Sony Pictures Networks India, SAP Labs, Ericsson, Tata Sons, KPMG, EY and Accenture are some companies that have adopted such policies.

n. **Men as advocates of gender diversity:** Companies like Accenture have policies in place with the aim to ensure that the workforce comes together in an inclusive manner.[28]

o. **Four-day work weeks:** A few organizations are floating a new possibility: A four-day workweek (see Exhibit 8.19).

EXHIBIT 8.19 FOUR-DAY WORK WEEKS

In recent months, adverse collection of employers, such as Japanese electronics maker Panasonic, fintech start-up Bolt and Government of Belgium, have recommended giving employees the option to work four days but get paid for five, Spain and Scotland are conducting their own trials of shorter weeks. They join a clutch of firms mainly in the tech sector that gravitated to a four-day format when the pandemic hit.

Source: The Times of India (4 December 2022).

p. **Small bedrooms to stay overnight:** Now some organizations have started providing bedrooms for employees to enable them to stay overnight (see Exhibit 8.20).

EXHIBIT 8.20 SMALL BEDROOMS TO STAY OVERNIGHT

Elon Musk has converted rooms at Twitter headquarters in San Francisco into small bedrooms, featuring unmade mattresses, drab curtains and giant work monitors, media reported. The beds are prepared for remaining 'hardcore' staffers to be able to stay overnight at office, reports Forbes.

Source: The Times of India (7 December 2022).

In one of its latest moves in the direction of providing social security, the Prime Minister's Office (PMO) gave approval to the labour ministry proposal on universal social security cover for 500 million workers, including those in the farm sector, seeking to start the process of putting in place a more secure welfare net a year before the General Election of 2019. The finance and labour ministries will work out the details of the scheme that will require nearly INR 2 lakh crore when fully rolled out for the lower 40 per cent of the country's total workforce. The remaining 60 per cent of the workforce was expected to make contributions out of their own pocket, either fully or partially.

Recent 'Labour Reforms' and Labour Welfare

In a tweet on the occasion of passing of the Labour Reforms Bill on 23rd September 2020 in the Parliament, PM Narendra Modi said

Long due and much awaited Labour reforms have been passed by the Parliament. The reforms will ensure wellbeing of our industrious workers and give a boost to economic growth. These reforms will contribute to a better working environment, which will accelerate the pace of economic growth. These reforms also seek to harness the power of technology for the betterment of the workers and industry both.[29]

By getting the Bills passed by the Parliament, 'the Central Government has made a headway towards changing the standard of living of workers in a fundamental manner. This will have a positive and far-reaching effect on workers. Employment creation and output of workers will also get enhanced.' Due to the passing of these four Labour Codes by the Parliament, the benefits of these Labour Codes would be available to workers both in organized and unorganized sectors. Hence, Employees' Provident Funds (EPF), Employees' Pension Scheme (EPS) and coverage of all types of medical benefits as per Employees' Insurance Act will be available to the workers of both the sectors, viz., the organized and the unorganized sector. With the amalgamation of 29 Labour Laws in the four Labour Codes, the working class is going to be benefited directly or indirectly as these Codes lead to economic, mental and physical betterment of the workers in both organized and unorganized sectors. For example, the amalgamation of the existing 13 labour Laws into one Code, viz., Occupational, Safety, Health and Working Conditions Code, 2020 (OSH Code 2020), will benefit the Inter-State Migrant Workers in the following manner:

- Many provisions in the OSH Code will ease the lives of the Inter-State Migrant Workers.
- Anomalies of the Inter-State Migrant Workers Act, 1979, have been exhaustively addressed in the OSH Code. For example, earlier only workers appointed by a contractor were recognized as Inter-State Migrant Workers but under the new provisions of the Code, workers can now be Aatmanirbhar as they can register themselves as Inter-State Migrant Workers on the national portal. This provision will enable the workers to get a legal identity which would allow them to get benefits of all social security schemes.
- A provision has been made for employers to provide travelling allowance annually to an Inter-State Migrant Worker for undertaking a to-and-fro journey to his native place.
- If a worker is engaged in building and other construction work in one State and moves to another State, benefit from the Building and other Construction Workers' Cess fund will be provided.
- It has been made mandatory to issue appointment letters to the workers.
- Similarly, free annual health check-up of the workers will be mandatory and is to be provided by the employers.
- After the amalgamation of 29 Labour laws into four Labour Codes, an Inter-State Migrant Worker would be entitled to get ration facility in the State he is

working in and the remaining members of his family would be able to avail of the ration facility in the State where they reside.

- There will be available mandatory helpline facility in every State for resolution of Inter-State Migrant Workers' grievances.
- National database will also be created for the Inter-State Migrant Workers.
- Now if a worker has worked even for 180 days, he shall be entitled to one-day leave for every 20 days of work done, instead of the requirement of 240 days earlier.

Besides, the aforesaid four Labour Codes will also lead to women empowerment in the following manner:

Women empowerment through the Labour Codes

- Women workers will have right to work in all types of establishments.
- Women will have the right to work at night with their consent and further that the employer will have to make necessary arrangements to provide safety and facilities to women workers at night.
- As per Maternity Benefit Act (amended) 2017, the paid Maternity leave for women workers has been increased from 12 to 26 weeks and crèche facility has been made mandatory in all establishments having 50 or more workers.

The Labour Codes (as per the Labour Codes Bill—2020) were to be implemented on 1 July 2022 in all the corporates and organizations under the registration of the Ministry of Corporate Affairs but due to multiple states not agreeing on the terms, the implementation of the above Codes have been postponed as of now. The Government has adopted a wait-and-watch policy because neither the trade unions nor the employers appear to be keen on the Labour Codes. With multiple states heading for assembly elections in 2023 and general elections in 2024 may be the other reasons, due to which the implementation of Labour Codes looks to be on the back burner. However, the Central Government has stepped up many schemes like Garib Kalyan, delivering of free food grains to the homes, etc., for the benefit of inter-state and the poor in the country.

Bonus

As mentioned earlier, in addition to social security and labour welfare activities which are the first and second constituents of fringe benefits, the third constituent of fringe benefit is bonus. There are three views about the concept of bonus. In the beginning, bonus was viewed as an *'ex-gratia'* payment and therefore, was considered derogatory from the point of view of employees. The second opinion about the concept of bonus is that once profits of an organization exceed a certain base, workers have a *right to share it* because they play an important role in earning profit for an organization. The opinion expressed by the Bonus commission, 1964, Government of India, is also almost the same. The third view about bonus is that bonus is a *deferred wage*. According to this point of view, since it is difficult to instantly measure exactly the contribution of a worker in the process of production, a worker is paid a roughly estimated amount, and at the end of the stipulated period his exact contribution is worked out and the difference between his exact contribution and the amount already paid to the worker as his wages should be paid to him as wages.[30] It is, therefore, necessary that the worker should be paid his due. Keeping in view the diverse opinions on the issue and avoid any confusion, the Payment of Bonus Act was passed in 1965 making bonus a *statutory right of workers* which can be claimed by them legitimately though under stated circumstances.

A few highlights of the Act are as follows:

The Payment of Bonus Act, 1965 (Repeated by the Code on Wages, 2019 with the Payment of Bonus Rules, 1975 as amended by (Amendment) Rules 2019[31]

The Act extends to the whole of India and applies to every factory (as defined in Clause (m) of Section 2 of the Factories Act, 1948), every other establishment in which 20 or more persons are employed on any day during an Accounting Year (the appropriate Government, by notification in the gazette, can reduce the limit of 20 persons). Every employee (other than apprentice) employed on salary or wage not exceeding INR 21,000 (earlier it was INR 10,000) per month doing any skilled or unskilled, manual, supervisory, managerial, administrative, technical or clerical work for hire or reward is entitled to a minimum bonus of 8.33% of the salary or wages earned by him or INR 100 whichever is higher, but not more than 20%, provided the employee has worked in the establishment for not less than 30 working days in that year.[32] An employee will be disqualified from receiving bonus in case he is dismissed from service for riotous or violent behaviour or fraud while on the premises of the establishment, and theft, misappropriation or sabotage of any property of the establishment. In case any financial loss is caused by the misconduct of the employee, the employer can deduct the loss from the bonus payable to the employee. The bonus should be paid in cash within a period of eight months from the close of the accounting year. The Act also spells out under section 15, the concept of 'set-on' and 'set-off' of allocable surplus.[33]

Internal Audit of Compensation and Benefits

Internal audit of compensation and benefits, including relational benefits, can bring not only transparency but also ensure that the process established in aligning and developing compensation packages is reliable, dependable and credible and that it is made as per law, internal regulations keeping in view the needs of employees. In order to make the compensation and benefit process efficient and effective in terms of risk management, control, delivery and proper governance, there should be internal audit of the system.

Planning and Definition of Internal Audit

Before moving further, it is essential to understand as to what internal audit is all about. As a matter of fact, internal audit is a method of independent and objective validation that results in enhanced value and improved operation and performance of an organization. It also facilitates the effects of related processes to accomplish the goals and objectives of the organization.

The Institution of Internal Auditors[34] defines internal auditing as an independent, objective assurance and consulting activity designed to add value and improve an organization's operation. It helps the organization accomplish its objectives by bringing a systematic and disciplined approach to evaluate and improve the effectiveness of risk management, control and governance process.

According to Kanello and Spathis,[35] internal auditing is a method of independent and objective validation, and it not only increases the value and improves the operation and performance of the organization but also facilitates the effects of related processes to accomplish the organization's goals.

Internal audit is also defined as a multi-step process aimed to determine whether current processes and procedures comply with pre-decided rules and regulations or differ in any way from the standard.

While conducting an internal audit on employee compensation and benefit, the audit can focus on the philosophy and structure of the compensation committee, compensation consultant's role and performance, pay and perks, and executive compensation. However, according to Wheeler,[36] wages can be audited from a number of dimensions such as record making, record keeping, minimum wage, overtime work, equal pay/non-discrimination issues, required deductions/withholding, other deductions, employee appraisals, vacations, holidays, personal leave, sick leave, other leaves, leaves of absence/disability, insurance benefits, pension benefits and deferred compensation. As a matter of fact, internal audit in HR compensation and benefits can be viewed as a process of determining if current processes and procedures of rewarding employees, including executives, synchronize with pre-laid down rules and regulations framed according to laws and statute of the organization and adopted by committee, or deviate from it in any way.

What Is Done in Internal Auditing?

Internal audit appraises the economy, efficiency and effectiveness of business operations and control, application of plans, procedures and policies. It conducts special checks. It also examines the functioning of accounting systems of the organization as well as of related controls, credibility of financial and operational information. Burnaby and Hass have rightly observed for enterprises that the audit activity monitors the adequacy and effectiveness of management's control framework and contributes to the integrity of corporate governance, risk evaluation, and financial, operating and IT systems.

It is obvious from the foregoing discussion that corporate governance, risk management and control are the three vital parts of the internal audit process. In order to enable internal audit functioning smoothly, International Standards for the Professional Practices of Internal Auditing (Standards) have been developed by the Institute of Internal Auditors for each part of the internal audit process. A few of the standards in this respect are as follows:

Standard 2110 (Related to governance)
Standard 2120 (Related to governance)
Standard 2130 (Related to governance)

Thus, the efficiency and effectiveness, that is, the performance of many functions, including HR function, can be improved through the process of internal audit. Over a period of time, there has been an overwhelming expansion in the scope.

Why Internal Audit of Compensation and Benefit Processes?

Of late, greater need for financial reporting, according and auditing which are instrumental in providing relevant information on the financial position and performance of an organization's business, is being felt across the corporate sector. According to Sabovic and Miletic,[37] this is due to the emergence of the financial crisis and the crisis in corporate governance. Internal audit is specifically an interesting area of auditing. The main task of internal audit is to support the management of the organization. The board, executive management, internal auditor and external auditor are the main participants in corporate governance extent and types of information being audited. Today, auditing has spread its wings to almost all the financial areas of management and has become a critical tool to assess an activity, including compensation and benefits; for example, HR auditing provides the baseline data that is helpful to improve HR performance.

In his framework of HR audit, Bargerstock[38] emphasized the following four phases through which audit unfolds:

1. Ranking Importance of the HRM Service Portfolio
2. HRM team Self-Evaluation
3. Measuring Current Service Level
4. Developing Action Plan

There is no doubt that the compensation and benefits process is very complex. It is for these reasons that compensation is an operational cost for the organization.

It constitutes as much as up to 60 per cent of total operational costs, though it may vary from organization to organization. All the same, it should not be forgotten that costs incurred on compensation and benefits are an investment in human capital that pays dividends all through it is made use of. Hence, such costs should be properly managed and duly audited to bring about improvement. Auditing of compensation and benefits is all the more important because it is a mechanism of corporate culture and also a vital source of employee motivation, and thereby affecting the performance of the organization through establishing a link between effort and reward. Here, Vroom's expectancy theory can be referred to[39] which states that motivation is a product of the values one seeks and one's expectations of the probability that a certain action will lead to those values, that is, before expanding a given level of effort, an employee would be asking,

> If to make a strong effort on their job, will a superior level of performance be achieved? And if I do achieve such an outstanding level of performance, what kinds of rewards or negative outcomes will occur? Besides, the employee also needs to know how valuable that outcome or performance level is to him/her.

Vroom calls this value of valence.[40] Besides, compensation and benefits are financial (tangible) and non-financial (intangible) rewards for employees and, therefore, they can be subject to many risks and frauds. They need to be thoroughly audited. It is also observed that in many cases there is little, and sometimes, even negative correlation with their contribution to the long-term performance of their organizations. Many executives have been generously paid even after their poor performances. Such lapses need to be identified through auditing and remedial steps must be taken. This sort of exercise will bring transparency to executive compensation and benefits. Not only this, all possibilities of improving compensation and benefits processes by providing insight and recommendations depending on analysis and assessment of data available must be explained and action taken. It will also ensure that the processes established in aligning and developing compensation and benefit packages are available. All this is possible only through internal auditing. Hence, internal auditing is necessary. Internal auditing assumes added significance at the stage when the organization is designing and recommending its own compensation and benefit packages. The structure and elements of aforesaid packages can be audited at this stage also, and in case of any inconsistency, corrective action can be undertaken.

Researchers have revealed that a productive working relationship is the strongest when a risk managing internal audit is paired with a strategic HRM function. Besides, an internal audit planning process is more strategic in the presence of same pairing.[41]

Auditors, both internal and external, should not only be objective but also independent in the implementation of audits, and many cultural aspects or dimensions can influence an auditor's assessment.[42]

There are many other reasons for doing internal audits in the area of HR compensations and benefits. Also, there are some researches done in the past that promote interest in and indicate the importance and benefits of internal audits in the contemporary production system. The request for cost efficiency, in terms of expenditures, and effectiveness, in terms of corporate governance, high performances and above-average profits, is typical for modern companies. All those requirements are also related to the HRM process, and inside of it, compensations for employees. Besides the reasons and importance, it is significant to analyse tasks, areas and risks that are linked to compensation internal audit.[43]

Compensation and Benefit Structure, and Internal Audit Tasks Involved

There are two reasons that indicate the importance of HRM procedures and policies, the first being that they present the expected level of employees' behaviour and standards for functioning of HR activities in the organization. In this regard, Savaneviciene and Stankeviciute (2010)[44] laid emphasis on the work of Dietz and Boon where the authors in 2005 identified 26 different practices that reflect the main objectives of most of the strategic HRM programmes used in more than 100 studies, of which top four are, in order of popularity: training and development, contingent pay and reward schemes, performance management (including appraisal) and careful recruitment and selection. The second reason is that these policies are standards which should be complied with and further that these policies are bases for conducting the internal control and internal audit. These policies are especially important in the areas of promotion and compensation, recruitment and selection, employee orientation, disciplinary action, evaluation and so on.

Since rewards impact employee satisfaction in the organization, it is essential to audit the processes of compensation and benefits as well as the main stages of it besides the structure of rewarding system. It will be quite relevant to mention here the basic stages of the compensation process which comprise job analysis, job evaluation, determining the structure of compensation and benefits, performance measurement, implementation of payment systems, feedback and monitoring.

Methods of Conducting Audit

There are several methods of conducting audits, including surveys, interviews, observations or a combination of the above and so on. However, the survey is the most popular approach.

Internal Audit of Compensation and Benefits: Risk Involved

Because of internal audit of compensation and benefit the organizations also carry several risks, such as compliance risk, employment market risk, reputation risk, operation risk and financial reports risk.

Another fact worth mentioning here is that only limited reviews of the justification of executive compensation and benefits are undertaken, and there are only a few organizations that get the compensation and benefits audited in the case of their executives.

Hence, in order to promote transparency and also to raise the market's trust and confidence in an organization, internal audit of executive compensation and benefits should be encouraged.

To sum up, internal audit is helpful in improving the efficiency and effectiveness of an organization. It is usually done through insight and recommendations which are based on the analysis of relevant data available from the organization with regard to compensations and benefits. Since compensation and reward systems constitute a very complex structure of activities and also of many types of compensation, they need appropriate management and control. Compensations and benefits cost the organization on the one hand and motivate and reward the employees on the other hand. The process of compensation and benefits also causes a lot of complexities which can be sorted out with the help of internal audit. For example, employment market risk, compliance risk, reputation risk, operation risk, financial reports risk and so on are the risks linked to HR compensation internal audit of compensation and benefit package.

Besides, internal audit is a support to HR management as well as to corporate grievance as a lot of information and data are collected in the process of audit which is very useful for the organization as a whole in terms of improvement of business processes related to compensation and benefits. The main areas with regard to compensation and benefit where internal audit should be conducted include overall plan, design, cash compensation, stock-based compensation, deferred compensation and various benefit-related areas like pension and other retirement contributions. Besides, executive compensation and benefit programmes are the grey areas for conducting internal audit as the executives are accountable for managing organization's business processes, functions and the organization as a whole. The audit of executive compensation and benefit programmes assumes added importance because many a time it is observed that there is no correlation or even negative correlation between their contribution made to the organization on the one hand and long-term performance of the organization on the other hand. Hence, it needs a thorough analysis through internal audit so that corrective steps may be initiated. Above all, an internal audit of compensation and benefits brings an element of transparency in the process.

Management's Strategy

The first and foremost vital thing for the management is to ensure that an employee benefit strategy should be an integral part of the total reward management strategy of the organization, and, more importantly, it should be supportive and instrumental in accomplishing the objectives of the organization concerned besides being in line with the values and culture of the organization. It should also add value to the base pay and performance-related pay policies of the organization and create an impression among the employees that the organization is genuinely concerned with the betterment of their working and living lives. It should also be instrumental not only in motivating the employees but also in infusing confidence among them as well as in boosting their morals, developing a sense of belongingness towards their organization and creating a feeling of commitment. The strategy should be formulated, as far as possible, in consultation with the employees so that the real needs of the employees can be identified and satisfied through the benefit strategy of the management.

The strategy should ensure that its implementation yields the desired results and that its implementation cost is more than that is compensated in terms of return by way of an increase in output of the organization through higher motivation, confidence, morale, commitment and sense of belongingness.

Besides, having adequate flexibility in operating the benefits package, tax implication with regard to various fringe benefits should also get appropriate attention, while formulating an employee benefit strategy. The importance of intangible benefits should not be overloaded and it should be ensured that the strategy should be innovative so as to secure an advantage over the employee benefit strategies of the competitors.

Chapter Review

1. Labour welfare which is another major constituent of fringe benefits. Broadly speaking, labour welfare is anything done for the intellectual, physical, moral and economic betterment of workers whether by employers, government or by other agencies over and above what is laid down by law or what is normally expected on the basis of contractual benefits for which the workers may have bargained for. Labour welfare has several objectives such as promoting economic, social, intellectual and physical betterment of workers, boosting their morale, infusing confidence and restricting union and government intervention. There are several principles of labour welfare such as principle of social responsibility, principle of self-help, principle of flexibility and principle of democratic values, which help in making a labour welfare programme effective. Labour welfare may be classified in statutory welfare, voluntary welfare and mutual welfare. Labour welfare is also classified as intramural and extramural welfare activities. Although most labour welfare work in Indian industries has been undertaken by the central government, state governments, employers, trade unions and some other agencies, it is primarily the central and state governments which have played an important role. However, there remains much to be done. Under the statutory welfare work, the Factories Act, 1948, which contains health provisions, safety provisions and welfare provisions, has made a significant

contribution. Besides, the Ministry of Labour & Employment administers several welfare Acts and a lot of welfare work has been undertaken under the auspices of these funds. The state governments have also been undertaking several welfare activities in their respective states. They have established welfare centres and welfare boards. A good number of employers, especially in jute, sugar and tea industries, have undertaken labour welfare activities. In coal mines, ports, plantations and so on, a good number of welfare activities have been undertaken. Mutual welfare work undertaken by trade unions has not been able to make any contribution worth mentioning. Their poor finances are mainly responsible for this phenomenon. As a matter of fact, all concerned should make a joint effort in a planned manner which will benefit all the stakeholders.

2. The passing of Labour Code Bill—2022 by the Parliament has enabled the amalgamation of 29 Central Labour Laws into four Labour Codes. This will promote a lot of labour welfare of workers in both the organized and unorganized sectors, including inter-state migratory workers. It will also lead to women worker empowerment.

3. Bonus, the third ingredient of 'Fringe Benefits', is now being paid as per the Payment of Bonus Act, 1965.

4. Internal audit of compensation and benefits is very important and should be conducted by all organizations.

5. While the management formulates its employees' benefits strategy, it should take the trade union into confidence and ensure that the benefits strategy is an integral part of the total management reward strategy. It should also create an impression that the management is genuinely concerned about the betterment of its employees and so on.

DISCUSSION QUESTIONS

1. Discuss the main definitions of labour welfare and main objectives of labour welfare work.
2. Discuss the classification of labour welfare work.
3. Discuss the steps taken by the Central Government to promote labour welfare, especially as per the Factories Act, 1948.
4. Discuss the labour welfare work undertaken voluntarily by employers in Indian industries.
5. Discuss the impact of Labour Codes on Labour Welfare.
6. Discuss the main provisions of the Payment of Bonus Act, 1965.
7. Discuss why benefits strategy should be an integral part of the total reward management strategy of an organization.

Individual and Group Activities

1. Individually discuss with the HR officials of a big organization and find out what voluntary welfare activities are undertaken by the employers in their organization. Also, find out from them whether the employees are satisfied with these activities. If not, what are their expectations?
2. Visit a big organization in a group of another two individuals and discuss with its trade union officials if the management of the organization has been implementing the statutory labour welfare requirements satisfactorily or not. If not, what is the take of the management in this regard?
3. Visit a large manufacturing organization, in a group of three members, and discuss with the union officials, what is the state of affairs with regard to the implementation of Labour Codes.
4. Visit individually the union officials of a big organization and find out the status of implementation of the Payment of Bonus Act, 1965.

In a group of two students, visit a big factory and find out the status of internal audit of compensation and benefits.

APPLICATION CASE

Fringe Benefits in Sugar Industry

Sugar industry enjoys a special status in Haryana and Punjab as the sugar industry draws its raw material, namely sugarcane, from the agriculture sector and the contribution of the agriculture sector constitutes a significant part of GDP of both the states. Hence, the significance of the sugar industry in these two states. Since fringe benefits or non-wage benefits play a very important role in enhancing the employee contentment and its consequent positive impact on the quality and quantity of the product coming out from the concerned factories, a positive state of the availability of fringe benefits in sugar factories in these two states under study will be of great importance to the health of sugar industry.

The sugar factories in Haryana and Punjab provide fringe benefits under three heads, namely

(a) social security benefits comprising compensation for employment injury, provident fund (including pension) and gratuity, (b) labour welfare benefits consisting of medical, educational and recreational benefits, canteen, uniform, housing and some other benefits in addition to retaining allowance and (c) bonus.

However, not much has been done by sugar factories in this regard and leave much to be desired, especially in the case of fringe benefits extended by the

employers on their own, that is, without any statutory obligation. The study reveals that social security benefits which are being provided by the sugar factories because of statutory obligations constitute 27.24 per cent of the total expenditure on fringe benefits as a whole and another 40.81 per cent of the total expenditure incurred on fringe benefits is spent as bonus which is also a statutory obligation. Thus, a total of
68.05 per cent of the total expenditure on all the fringe benefits is being incurred because of statutory requirements. Only 31.95 per cent of the total expenditure on all the fringe benefits taken together is incurred *voluntarily* on labour welfare, which is not a healthy trend and that is why the health of the sugar factories is not very sound. Thus, the expenditure on voluntary welfare activities needs to be increased substantially.

Source: The case study is based on the PhD thesis (unpublished) titled 'A Critical Study of Non-Wage Benefits to Workers in Sugar Factories of Haryana & Punjab' submitted by R. C. Sharma to the Kurukshetra University, Kurukshetra.

Questions

1. What types of fringe benefits are being extended to employees in the sugar factories of Haryana and Punjab?
2. Why does the expenditure on voluntary labour welfare needs substantial increase by the sugar factories in Haryana and Punjab?
3. Were you an authority to prepare a labour welfare plan for the sugar industry in Haryana and Punjab, what additions and attractions would you suggest?

Annexure

Duties, Status and Role of Labour Welfare Officer

The duties, status and role of labour welfare officer appointed under Section 49 of the Factories Act, 1948, have been specified in detail in the Model Rules called Welfare Officers (Recruitment and Conditions of Service) Rules, 1951, as modified in 1957.

Duty Chart of Labour Welfare Officer

Supervision of

1. Safety, health and welfare programmes and housing, recreation, sanitation services as provided under law or otherwise;
2. Working of joint committees;

3. Grant of leave with wages as provided and
4. Redressal of workers' grievances.

Counselling to workers in

1. Personal and family problems;
2. Adjusting to work environment and
3. Understanding rights and privileges.

Advisory functions to management in

1. Formulating labour and welfare policies, apprenticeship training programmes;
2. Meeting statutory obligation to workers and
3. Developing fringe benefits and workers' education and use of communication.

Liaison with workers

1. To understand various limitations under which they work;
2. To appreciate the need of harmonious industrial relations in the plant;
3. To interpret company policy to workers and
4. To persuade workers to come to a settlement in case of a dispute.

Liaison with management

1. To appreciate workers' viewpoints regarding various matters in the plant;
2. To intervene on behalf of workers in matters under consideration of the management;
3. To help different departmental heads to meet their obligations under the Acts;
4. To maintain harmonious industrial relations in the plant and
5. To suggest measures for promoting general well-being of the workers.

Work with workers and management

1. To maintain harmonious industrial relations in the plant;
2. For prompt redressal of grievances and quick settlement of disputes and
3. To improve productive efficiency of the enterprise.

Work with outside agencies

1. Factory inspectors, medical officers, other inspectors for securing proper enforcement of various Acts as applicable to the plant and
2. Other agencies in the community with a view to help workers to make use of community services.

It shall be observed from the duty chart that a labour welfare officer has direct responsibility for the administration of services pertaining to welfare and benefits, health and safety, joint committees, and leave with wages. He is also required to be concerned with the implementation of labour laws, proper working conditions, harmonious labour relations, industrial peace, plant productivity and workers' well-being. For this purpose, he must act as an advisor, counsellor, mediator and liaison man to both management and labour.

In order to ensure a proper discharge of the functions as stated above, the Model Rules lay down that a labour welfare officer should be a professionally trained person, given the status equivalent to the head of a department, and allowed to function as a 'neutral' person—a sort of buffer between management and workers.

Source: Welfare Officers (Recruitment Conditions of Service) Rules, 1951, Model Rules—Section 49, Factories Act, 1948.

Notes

1 Ministry of Labour & Employment, *Report of the Royal Commission on Labour in India*, 1931, 261.
2 Labour Investigation Committee, *Report of the Labour Investigation Committee* (New Delhi: Government of India, 1946), 245.
3 International Labour Organization, *Second Asian Conference*, Nuwara Eliya (Ceylone), January 1950, Report II, Provisions of Facilities for the Promotion of Workers Welfare (Geneva: ILO, 1949).
4 *The Economic Times*, 27 November 2018.
5 Quoted in *The Times of India*, 2 November 2022.
6 For details, see Ibid.
7 *The Economic Times*, 27 November 2018.
8 Ibid.
9 For details of safety measures under Sections 21–41, see Sharma, *Industrial Relations*, 653–658.
10 Ministry of Labour & Employment, *Indian Labour Year Book 2009–10* (Shimla/ Chandigarh: Labour Bureau, Ministry of Labour & Employment, Government of India, 2012).
11 Ibid.
12 Ibid.
13 Ibid.
14 Ibid.
15 Ibid.
16 Ibid.
17 Ibid.
18 Ibid.
19 Ibid.
20 Ibid.
21 Ibid.
22 Ibid.
23 *The Economic Times*, 27 February 2016.
24 *Hindustan Times*, 23 May 2016.
25 *The Economic Times*, 12 August 2016.
26 Ibid.

27 Ibid.

28 Ibid.

29 *New Labour Code for New India,* Ministry of Information & Broadcasting, Govt. of India, New Delhi, 2021, p. 0.

30 Sharma, *Industrial Relations and Labour Legislation,* 714.

31 For details, see *The Payment of Bonus Act, 1965 [Repealed by The Code on Wages, 2019 (29 of 2019)]* with *The Payment of Bonus Rules, 1975 as amended by (Amendment) Rules, 2019,-* Bare Act, LexisNexis, Gurgaon, 2020, 1–45.

32 Season workers who have worked for not less than 30 working days are also entitled to bonus; *J.K. Ginning & Pressing Factory V.P.O, Second Labour Court, (1991)* 62 FLR 207 (Bom).

33 *The Payment of Bonus Act, 1965 (Sec 15),* p. 15 and [sec4(a)], p. 6.

34 The Institute of Internal Auditors, *International Standards for the Professional Practice of Internal Auditing* (Florida, FL: Altamonte Springs, 2011) (Quoted by N. Berber, M. Pasula, M. Radosevic, D. Ikonov, and V. K. Vugdelija, 'Internal Audit of Compensation and Benefits: Tasks and Risks in Production Systems', *Inzinerine Ekonomika-Engineering Economics* 23, no. 4 [2012]: 414–424).

35 A. Kanellou and C. Spathis, 'Auditing in Enterprise System Environment: A Synthesis', *Journal of Enterprise Information Management* 24, no. 6 (2011): 494–519.

36 S. Wheeler, 'Human Resource Audit', in *Human Resource Development for the Food Industries,* ed. W. A. Gould (Maryland, MD: CTI Publications, 1994).

37 S. Sabovic and S. Miletic, 'The Impact of the Crisis in Financial Reporting, Accounting and Auditing', *Technics Technologies Education Management* 5, no. 3 (2010): 613–620.

38 A. S. Bargerstock, 'The HRM Effective Audit: A Tool for Managing Accountability in HRM', *Public Personnel Management* 29, no. 4 (2000): 517–527.

39 See Victor H. Vroom, *Work and Motivation* (New York, NY: John Wiley & Sons, 1964).

40 Sharma and Sharma, *Human Resource Management,* 449.

41 M. A. Hyland and D. A. Verreault, 'Developing a Strategic Internal Audit–Human Resource Management Relationship: A Model and Survey', *Managerial Auditing Journal* 18, no. 617 (2003): 465–477.

42 M. Moradi, M. Salehi, and A. Fakharabadi, 'An Investigation Cultural Factors' Affection on Auditors' Assessment Estimation of Internal Control and Control Risk Determination', *Technics Technologies Education Management* 6, no. 3 (2011): 698–210.

43 Berber, Pasula, Radosevic, Ikonov, and Vugdelija, 'Internal Audit of Compensation and Benefits', 418.

44 A. Savaneviciene and Stankeviciute, 'The Models Exploring the "Black Box" between HRM and Organizational Performance', *Inzinerine Ekonomika-Engineering Economics* 21, no. 4 (2010): 426–434.

9

DESIGNING AND OPERATING NON-FINANCIAL BENEFITS (INTRINSIC AND RELATIONAL REWARDS)

LEARNING OBJECTIVES

After studying this chapter, the reader should be able to:

1. Explain the types of non-financial benefits/rewards.
2. Enlist and explain the main non-financial benefits/rewards that motivate employees.
3. Explain the Heineken UK's approach to rewards.
4. Explain how understanding employee psychology may help an organization.
5. Explain the meaning and benefits of non-financial metrics.
6. Explain how dashboards and scorecards may be helpful to an organization in the accomplishment of its goals.
7. Explain the implications of intellectual capital assessment and also the market implications of human capital.
8. Explain the importance of non-financial recognition schemes and also the types of recognition schemes.
9. Enlist and explain the constituents of non-financial metrics and their benefits to an organization.

DOI: 10.4324/9781032626123-9

Introduction

While extrinsic which are usually tangible (financial) rewards, originate from something beyond the person, intrinsic and relational which are intangible (non-financial) rewards, originate from within the person. The intrinsic and relational rewards are mostly psychological and satisfy the emotional and intellectual demands of the employees and are instrumental in motivating the employees to use their talent and competencies in a better way and interact with others in a more positive and supportive way. They are concerned with recognition, work environment like quality of working life, work itself, learning and development, performance management, etc. They create a fulfilling workplace environment which leads to enhanced performance and creativity of the employees. These rewards relate to work situations as well as to the physical and psychological well-being of a company's employees.

Since non-financial benefits constitute a significant component of total compensation, they should be well-designed and effectively operated.

Role of Non-financial Benefits/Rewards on Employee Motivation

Financial versus non-financial benefits/rewards is an important, growing and alive controversy, that is, whether financial rewards are more important or non-financial rewards are more important. As a matter of fact, both financial and non-financial rewards for an employee play a vital role in meeting his needs. While financial rewards, in the present age, unquestionably boost up the employees' performance level in the sense that money makes the mare go, non-financial rewards in the form of promotion, job security, training, pleasant work environment and so on also contribute to the enhancement of motivation.[1] Even Jones and Butler admit that behavioural and social factors are missing from their model,[2] which shows the importance of non-financial rewards. Studying employee motivation dependence on non-financial benefits is very significant for managers at high levels in any organization in making decisions at the time of recruitment and promotions.[3]

There is no doubt that transactional rewards (financial rewards) as well as pay-for-performance programmes have their limitations. Hence, providing a wide variety of relational rewards is essential for the mutual and sustained growth of the individual and the organization he serves at. But not all employees will be motivated by just money. Hence, utilizing non-financial benefits/rewards enables an organization to reach and reward all the employees as these rewards do not involve money.

According to Joshi,[4] relational rewards relate to the work situation and to the physical and psychological well-being of the employees. These rewards satisfy emotional and intellectual demands, enabling the employee to make better use of their talents and promote interaction with others in a supportive manner. He further asserts that prominence to relational rewards in total reward strategy can be a powerful and flexible tool for motivating employees to achieve higher performance.[5]

However, of late, there has been a shift from sheer economics to behavioural sensitivities and, therefore, non-financial rewards have come into prominence. Employees do not leave their lives behind when they come to report for duty. They openly recognize their needs outside work. Today, there is an emphasis on valuing employees and growing engagement. Today, an opportunity is available to all organizations to provide all employees at all levels with a rewarding mixture of the elements of the non-functional reward system, whereby they can motivate their employees more effectively.

There is no doubt that non-financial rewards are much more difficult to clarify and their components are far more complex as compared to financial rewards because non-financial rewards have an almost infinite number of components that relate to the work situation and to the physical as well as psychological well-being of employees. Such non-financial or relational rewards meet emotional and intellectual demands of the employees as such benefits make employees feel good about themselves and make them content to a good extent.

Even if we go through the literature on compensation, it will be observed that the initial literature on it is mainly in terms of traditional (financial) rewards. Emphasis on relational (non-financial) rewards has come into prominence since the 1990s. Stone et al.[6] found that financial incentives are not always welcomed by employees and material incentives generally do not tend to satisfy basic psychological needs.

Of late, the monetary trend has been changed into non-monetary, and from extrinsic (financial) to intrinsic. Today, there is a gradual change from a manufacturing workplace to a work environment having a knowledge-driven nature. In this newly emerging environment, employees make greater use of their intellectual faculties within a problem-solving and decision-making framework. As such task assignments are mentally intensive, employees can derive intrinsic satisfaction and motivation in doing them.[7] Thus, the prominence of non-financial rewards in the total reward strategy may be a powerful and flexible tool for motivating employees, which will be instrumental in improving performance.

It is indeed difficult to say whether financial incentives are more important or non-financial incentives are more important. Some authors as well as practicing managers give more importance to financial incentives. They claim that money in itself has no value for man but in the context of the existing economic organization, money has become a means not only of satisfying the physical needs of daily life but also of obtaining social position and power. For this reason, financial incentives have assumed great importance. On getting money, man first turns his attention towards the things he needs—food, clothes, houses and so on. Then he satisfies the needs of health and education. Once these needs have been satisfied, he tries to obtain more and more luxuries. But some individuals continue to work even after having reached this stage because their social prestige and power increase with their bank balance. Individuals with this lust for money continue their search throughout their life as this search never ends. People who do not feel any specific need for power do not like to earn money once their needs and comforts have been taken care of. In the same way, economic loss has diverse effects. Loss of money deprives the poor man of his bread while the rich man loses his prestige, although he does not suffer from hunger. Despite this, the poor man suffers psychologically less on account of this loss because only his body is directly affected. On the other hand, the rich man suffers a blow to his social prestige and self-respect, which is a mental injury.

Money has become the means of satisfying many needs because it is the medium of exchange. If social position and power are not based on money in any society, then money will cease to be a powerful incentive. Money is the most important incentive in a society where a man's success is measured by the money he earns. But where this does not happen, money is not a powerful incentive. This analysis shows the importance of financial incentives. Financial incentives are offered in industries in two ways—either in the form of salary increase or in the form of occasional bonus. The financial incentives have the effect of increasing production and inducing the worker to work harder and better.

On the other hand, experts claim that 'man does not live by bread alone'. Hence, money cannot act as the only motivator. The workers, being human beings, need non-financial incentives more. Non-financial incentives satisfy their social, psychological and personal needs, and this satisfaction makes them happy and efficient. Nowadays, workers are more conscious as regards to their personality, behaviour of management, self-respect and self-satisfaction. These things cannot be provided by money only. Hence, non-financial incentives become a must. As a matter of fact, any one type of incentive cannot do in the absence of the other type of incentive. As both right and left foot are necessary for a man to walk smoothly, both types of incentives are necessary to establish industrial peace in the business.

The primary task of a manager is that of maintaining an organization that functions effectively. To do so, he must see that his subordinates work efficiently and produce results that are beneficial to the organization. Organizational goals can never be achieved without subordinates' willingness to put in their best efforts. Here arises the problem of motivation. 'The capacity to work' and 'willingness to work' are two different things. A man can be physically, mentally and technically fit to work but he may not be willing to work. Hence, the need for motivation. Motivating a worker is to create a need and a desire on the part of a worker to improve his present performance. Thus, performance is determined by two factors, namely, the level of ability to do certain work and the level of motivation. This can be expressed as follows:

$$\text{Performance} = \text{Ability} \times \text{Motivation}$$

Thus, motivation is the number one problem of management.

Non-financial rewards/benefits can be just as or even more motivating for employees than those involving traditional financial rewards. For example, research has revealed that those employees who are given positive recognition for their contribution towards the accomplishment of organizational objectives convey enhanced loyalty to the company, greater work-time productivity and proactively engage with their co-employees. It is so because employees want to feel that their work is valued. It is a matter of common knowledge that happy and motivated employees provide better customer service.

There is no doubt that every employee certainly appreciates more and more money (i.e., financial benefits), but it is also a fact that money cannot buy engagement and loyalty. Non- financial benefits/rewards motivate and engage employees in ways that financial benefits/rewards are incapable of doing. Not only this, non-financial benefits/rewards cost the organization little or no money but are significant in their impact on the motivation of employees. Non-monetary benefits are specifically crucial when a company continues to make cuts in employee compensation. Non-financial benefits/rewards, also known as relational rewards, are also instrumental in improving and monitoring good employer–employee relationship, which, in turn, is instrumental in retaining desired talent in the organization.

In order to feel motivated and contribute their best towards the accomplishment of the organization's objectives, employees must be made to feel valued, appreciated and their contribution welcomed. It is here that the non-financial benefits/rewards come into vogue.

In a survey conducted by Mckinsey & Company in 2009, praise and appreciation from immediate managers, attention from leaders and opportunities to lead projects or task forces were rated to be the top non-financial rewards. The least popular reward was stock or stock options. Not only this, the non-financial rewards were more popular than the leading financial rewards.

Types of Non-financial Benefits/Rewards

There are various types of non-financial benefits/rewards. Most types of non-financial benefits/rewards/incentives can also be categorized under the following four heads:

Rewards	Recognition	Flexibility	Opportunity
Prizes	Awarding in front of colleagues	Flexible scheduling	Promotion
Paid packing	More participation in decision-making	Paid personal days	Chance to lead teams
Gift cards	Dinner with high-ups of the organization	Flexible leave/holidays	Mentorship programme
Vouchers	New office	Telecommuting options	Paid training
Others	Others	Others	Others

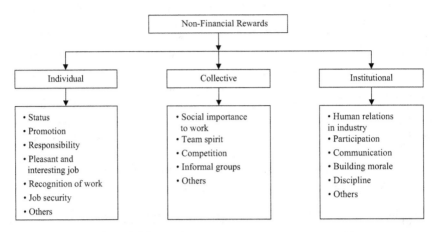

FIGURE 9.1   Non-financial Rewards

Individuals have various needs that they want to satisfy while working in the organization. People at comparatively higher levels of managerial hierarchy attach more importance to social–psychological needs which cannot be satisfied by money alone. Thus, management, in addition to the financial incentives, provides non-financial incentives to motivate people in the organization. The connotation of non-financial incentives does not mean that the organization has nothing to spend on these. However, the emphasis of non-financial incentives is to provide psychological and emotional satisfaction rather than financial satisfaction. For example, if an individual gets a promotion in the organization, it satisfies him psychologically more, that is, he gets better status, more challenging job, authority and so on than financially though he gets more pay also by the way of promotion. The non-financial incentives can be grouped into three parts as shown in Figure 8.1.

Individual Non-financial Benefits/Rewards/Incentives

These are incentives that motivate people on an individual basis. Various forms of individual motives are as follows:

1. **Status:** Status, in general terms, is the ranking of people in the society. In the organizational context, it means the ranking of positions, rights and duties in the formal organization structure. Good status motivates people to put in more work and do hard work.
2. **Promotion:** Promotion is defined as a movement to a position in which responsibilities and presumably prestige are increased. Promotion satisfies the needs of human beings in the organization from various angles such as money, prestige and status. The avenues of promotion, if they exist in the organization, play an important role in motivating the employees.

3. **Responsibility and challenge:** Many people prefer challenging and responsible jobs rather than monotonous and less responsible jobs. The management should provide such opportunities also by making the work challenging and more responsible.
4. **Making job pleasant and interesting:** The work should be made enjoyable and pleasant. If it is so designed, it will allow the employees to satisfy their natural instincts. This creates interest in the work and employees feel motivated.
5. **Recognition of work:** Most people have a need for a high evaluation of themselves. They want their work to be recognized by others. Recognition means acknowledgement with a sense of appreciation for work. When such appreciation is given to the work performed by employees, they feel motivated to perform work at a similar or higher level.
6. **Job security:** Job security and stability also play an important role in motivating people. If a job is secured, a worker will demonstrate more efficiency, will be highly motivated and give more production.

Collective Non-financial Rewards

Employees work in groups. Their efficiency, aspirations, behavioural norms and standards are affected by the group. If the group, in general, is efficient, an employee tends to become more efficient. Hence, group incentives are also important. Some of the collective non-financial incentives are as follows:

1. **Social importance of work:** People generally prefer a work that is socially acceptable. If society gives importance and praise to a work, people are likely to perform it. Sometimes, people prefer a job of high social importance even though the financial compensation would be less. The reason is simple. People have to live in society, and by performing a job of high social importance, they derive the satisfaction of being important in society.
2. **Team spirit:** The management should encourage team spirit, that is, to work in cooperation and coordination. Teamwork is a coordinated action by a cooperative small group in a regular contract wherein members contribute responsibly and enthusiastically towards task achievement. If there is a team spirit among the employees, they will try to put in maximum efforts to achieve the objectives.
3. **Competition:** Sometimes, for providing incentives to employees, competitions are organized between different individuals or different groups. There may be a case of self-competition where an individual tries to improve his earlier performance. When an individual performs very well because of any such competition, he should be given some advantages, not necessarily in terms of money, but it may be in terms of recognition, prestige, praise and so on. However, this method has a negative consequence also. Though all the

employees try to put in maximum effort, all of them cannot win. As a result, they may feel frustrated and their efficiency will go down. Hence, there is a need to have only healthy competition.

4. **Informal groups:** When people work together, they develop some sort of affiliation among themselves. These relationships are not officially pre-scribed, but created on the basis of certain factors, both personality factors of the employees and other social factors. The creation of these informal groups provides social satisfaction to employees at the workplace. People feel to achieve a sense of belongingness and security. Management should provide a way of creation of such informal groups as long as they are not detrimental to the organizational efficiency and objectives because, sometimes, the informal groups may go against the interest of the organization.

Institutional Non-financial Rewards

These rewards are related with the environmental factors in the organization. Conducive and congenial atmosphere of the organization motivates employees to produce better results. The following incentives fall under this category:

1. **Human relations in industry:** Human relations in the industry are related with the policy to be adopted in the organization to develop a sense of belong-ingness in the employees, improve their efficiency and treat them as human beings and not merely a factor of production. The emphasis is on providing greater satisfaction, both physiological and psychological, by creating such an environment in the organization where employees are able to work efficiently and pleasantly. In such an environment, employees are motivated to stay with the organization and also adopt productive behaviour.

2. **Participation:** The superior–subordinate relationship emphasizes that the superior takes the decisions and subordinates implement them. However, in such a decision-making process, subordinates do not feel very enthusiastic in implementing the decisions. As such, the subordinates should also be associ-ated with the decision-making process. This not only motivates subordinates to take prompt and proper action in decision implementation but also makes them responsible for anything that goes wrong.

3. **Communication:** Communication is the lifeblood of an organization. Complex nature and big size of organizations require greater specialization and division of work. Thus, for a particular goal, total activities are divided into parts and subparts to share information about their functioning among themselves. This is done through communication as it is the process of pass-ing ideas and understandings from one person or group to another person or group. A free and adequate flow of communication is necessary. This, besides providing a base for successful organizational functioning, provides satisfac-tion to individuals in the organization as they want to be informed properly about the matters concerning their interests. Thus, the free flow of communi-cation in the organization motivates employees properly.

4. **Building morale:** Though there are various definitions of morale, it can be defined as the attitudes of individuals and groups towards work environment and voluntary cooperation to the full extent of their ability in the best interest of the organization. Generally, a high level of morale results in high productivity. The high morale of employees depends on the various facilities provided to them to satisfy their physiological and psychological needs, the latter being more important. However, management should attempt to measure employees' morale. If the morale level is low, the factors should be analyzed and proper action is taken.

5. **Discipline:** Discipline, in essence, means obedience, application, behaviour and outward makes of respect shown by employees. It is employees' self-control to meet the organization's standards and objectives. Management has primary responsibility for developing and maintaining discipline. It maintains discipline by applying standards in a consistent, fair and flexible manner. This provides employees to behave in a particular direction as any employee whose behaviour is inconsistent with standards invites disciplinary action. Maintenance of proper discipline also motivates employees.

Planning the Non-financial Benefits/Rewards

Non-financial rewards/benefits have an emotional appeal to the employees. They get highly emotional when their contribution is recognized, appreciated and valued. They feel highly motivated, develop loyalty towards the organization and give their best to the organization. Non-financial rewards/benefits should promote competitive feeling and prompt the employees to enhance their performance. If it is so, such rewards/benefits become alluring and irresistible. Such rewards/benefits should be thoughtful and psychologically appealing to the employees, resulting in increased motivation. Awarding employees by way of appreciation in creative ways is one of the best ways for an organization not only to motivate but also to retain talented employees and give rise to a sustainable culture of success.

A Few Most Effective Non-financial Benefits/ Rewards to Motivate Employees

There are a large number of non-financial rewards/benefits that prove highly effective to motivate employees, which is the ultimate objective of rewards/benefits. However, the following non-financial rewards/benefits are highly effective in motivating employees:

1. **Recognizing their contribution:** Every employee wants his contribution to be recognized and appreciated by the organization. Recognition of contribution makes an employee feel proud and creates a feeling of ownership. Not only this, if the organization appreciates an employee's contribution, other employees also feel to make significant contributions so as to earn the same

appreciation and recognition of their contribution. Thus, it is a win-win situation for both the employee(s) and the management. An organization, therefore, should send a detailed email about the specific contribution made by any employee to all employees of the organization so that they also start craving for similar appreciation from the management. Social media can also be used in publishing information about the typical contribution made by any employee.

2. **Sending handwritten letter:** In order to make a worker feel more proud, another proposition is to pen a handwritten letter recognizing the contribution of an employee. Such a handwritten letter becomes a valuable possession for the employee and more often than not, he treats it as a treasure and usually proudly displays it on his desk or at any other prominent place so that it may attract the attention of peers and other employees.

3. **Providing employees to have lunch/dinner with the big wigs of the organization:** Offering an opportunity to have lunch with the CEO or any other VIP of the organization makes a worker feel proud. He feels that the organization cares about him beyond the office premises. It also provides him an opportunity for a good change in his routine work. He returns to his desk not only that very day but also in the following days.

   The lunch/dinner need not be lavish. It can be in the nearby café/canteen. It is just to give a feel to the employee making a significant contribution that he is cared for and recognized for his specific contribution. Such opportunities can be used to discuss matters other than work-related issues. Throwing a small department or company party is another way to motivate workers. Like their managers, the subordinates too feel stressed doing their routine work repeatedly. They get burned out and need some fun and change. Hence, throwing a small party for all the employees of the department or even for all the employees of the company is the best solution to motivate them. Such parties provide an opportunity for co-workers to become more than just colleagues as an emotional touch is also given by such work parties. Such parties also create team spirit in addition to making them just fun.

4. **Giving a personal touch and getting to know your employees:** In today's mechanized life, employees have to report for their duties every day, even at times when their presence is required—when somebody is ill at home or there is a family requirement or when there is a parents' meeting in the school of their children. They make a lot of sacrifices for the sake of their organization. All the time talking about business takes across the pleasure of work. There must be some occasions when something deeper can be talked about with the employees. This would establish that the management is interested not only in the contribution employees make towards the accomplishment of the objectives of the organization but also in their personal well-being. Their managers sometimes talk informally about their hobbies, the education of their children, specific interactions of the employees and so on. However, the

topics to be talked on should not be too personal lest it might get the employee to feel disturbed.

5. **Offering leadership role:** Playing a leadership role is, perhaps, highly motivating for an employee. Hence, whenever there comes an opportunity when the manager can provide an opportunity to an employee to play the leadership role provide it to the employee. It will make the employee feel extremely proud of himself and will feel very motivated. It may be possible as and when some new project comes up or there is an expansion in the current project or there is an assignment outside the organization for some work of the organization. The employee concerned should be given guidelines and instructions so that he completes the mission successfully and effectively. Some senior persons can act as mentors/advisors. Such things help in grooming them for leadership roles in the future.

6. **Associating employees in decision-making:** Employees feel proud if they are consulted or their advice is sought while decisions are being made on a new big project or some other office-related topic of great worth. Employees always like to be consulted to share their ideas and opinions with their high-ups to solve a particular problem. Let the boundaries regarding how rules are traditionally set be broken. Let the potential of the employees come out. That is how the employee can be motivated.

7. **Sitting down with the employee one-on-one:** Sitting down one-on-one with an employee is a great source of motivation for a worker. There is no doubt that group discussions and team meetings are good and useful, but talking with the boss on matters relevant to the employee on a one-on-one time basis is of particular importance in motivating an employee. There are many things that money cannot buy but talking with the employee on a one-on-one time basis can play an important role in dealing with those things. The boss can discuss with the employee what are his personal goals and how he (the boss) can help him in accomplishing those goals. Such an exercise will not only motivate the employee but also create a feeling of loyalty in the employees towards the organization.

8. **Sharing the gains of the organization with the employees:** In case the organization performs exceptionally well due to hard work put up by the team, or due to innovative ideas of the team members and the like, the reward should not go to managers or leaders of the team alone, it should be shared with all the team members. They should also feel that their efforts and hard work have been duly rewarded. There are many options for sharing such gains such as day(s) off for jobs well done, offering a spa package, picnic and fun making.

9. **Offering flexible schedule to high performers:** High performers not only work hard but also work, sometimes, for longer hours and at times avoid even family requirements. Hence, they should be allowed a flexible schedule. They may be allowed to work from home a few hours per week or to leave a bit

earlier on any working day of the week so that they can attend to any of their personal or family requirements. Flexi schedule will also help the high performers to maintain their work-life balance. At times, it also happens that the assigned work is completed before the office hours come to an end and the time so left is just whiled away by the employee. Just allow him to leave his office and sometimes he may work for more hours than the office hours. These are petty things but play an important role in motivating employees.

Heineken's Refreshing Approach to Reward

Heineken UK is leading in the cider and beer business in a mature market. It has a wider network and is not only going places but is also keen to go even further in the times to come, and is passionate about rendering excellent service and also about brands. Its core values comprise the following:

1. Passion for quality.
2. Respect.
3. Enjoyment of life.

Heineken UK took over Scottish & Newcastle Breweries in 2008 and thereafter, its employees started feeling undervalued and losing enjoyment, though at that juncture, the company needed its employees to be motivated and also engaged. The company, therefore, asked Hay Group for help after the takeover. At that stage, Heineken UK's employees had little understanding about reward, not to speak of trusting it.

Hay Group used its Total Reward Framework to find out what was happening in reward, that is, the then status of rewards in the company. Hay Group, therefore, worked with HR and the board of the company in order to develop a reward philosophy that had tight links to the board, HR and business strategy of the company.

During its continued partnership with the company, Hay Group helped in resulting out the strategy focusing on total reward and also on grading based on job families. Hay Group also endeavoured in improving the way the business talks about what it offers to its employees. All such efforts helped Heineken UK in not only attracting but also engaging the desired talent.

Why Did Heineken UK Get in Touch with Hay Group?

In 2010, Robin Pring joined Heineken UK as its HR director, followed by Anthony McNulty joining in 2011 as head of reward. Robin felt that reward policies and practices followed hitherto in Heineken UK and Scottish & Newcastle Breweries were not proving effective any longer and something needed to be done, especially in the areas of pay competitiveness, grading, paying for performance, reward communication, incentives and so on. She was more concerned with the reward strategy as it was not reflecting the brand value of the business and also of its HR and business strategies. In view of all this, she realized that the company needs an independent agency from outside the company that could build trust and challenge established thinking. She also wanted that this outside agency should also share its expertise and help in aligning reward to the brand. That is why she got in touch with Hay Group.

What Did Hay Group Do?

Hay Group started working in partnership with Robin, Anthony McNulty and their teams to work out an approach that may prove effective in the desired direction. They worked together and tried to find out the reasons for the success or future of reward strategies. There were many one-on-one interviews with the senior management team and had a heart-to-heart talk on the relevant issues. This was followed by conducting workshops not only with the managers but also with the employees so as to assess what they wanted to see more or less. Simultaneously, they consulted the internal reward team to know the present status and how consistently the current policies were being applied. Then, in order to compare Heineken UK's practices, they identified other major brand-led studies. This exercise enabled Heineken UK to identify what was needed to go ahead.

Findings

Hay Group finally shared its findings with the HR followed by with the board of the Heineken UK. It was pointed out that there existed mistrust based on misunderstandings about what employees got for working there and what the market would pay. For example, there was great confusion with regard to bonus which was felt to creating barriers in the business. Hay Group formulated a reward philosophy with the Heineken UK's board and taking along the HR team of the company worked on a detailed strategy. They identified what needs to be changed and in what order. Hay Group helped the company in designing and rolling out a job family-based consistent grade and pay structure. Consequently, the company is now in a better position with regard to organization design, base salary, variable pay and benefits, and the company is using its own portal, 'My Heineken', for the company's new recognition scheme reflecting corporate values, and also for its flexible reward choices.

Understanding the Employee Psychology

The study of mind and behaviour of job holders is what is referred to as employee psychology. It is concerned with why an employee behaves in a particular way while he is on the job. Thus, employee psychology gives an employer an insight into dealing with different employee personalities. Through employee psychology, an employer can classify employee behaviour into predictable patterns, which can be helpful in identifying the best way(s) to deal with individual employees. Employee psychology also helps in knowing what is it that motivates a particular employee on his identified job. For example, it helps in knowing what constituents of compensation and benefits both financial (extrinsic) and non-financial (intrinsic) affect his motivation and his subsequent work behaviour, and then the required steps may be taken to motivate the employees and keep them motivated. It helps in dealing with individual employees in a fashion that suits them.

The origin of employee psychology can be traced back to the publication of the book, in 1913, titled *Psychology and Industrial Efficiency*, authored by Hugo Munsterberg, a Harvard University Professor. It is based on the feedback received from executives as to what personal characteristics they desired most in their employees. He made use of the results so obtained for developing screening techniques and character assessment systems for employees.

Researchers in the realm of employee psychology conducted surveys to collect relevant data on a confidential basis so that the employees may divulge their honest feedback with regard to their attitudes and perceptions. However, so far as employers are concerned, they should focus on feedback from employees on things that work well for them. It is very important for employers to understand how their employees are extrinsically and intrinsically motivated because the former are driven by money, promotions and rewards while the latter are driven by recognition, appreciation, pride and so on. Having come to know what is it that motivates their employees, they can undertake the desired steps to ensure that the desired work behaviour happens in the organization, and that the employees perform their roles well and effectively.

It has also been observed that there has always been resistance to change because more often than not, change is painful. Organizational changes usually cause physiological pain in employees. But if the organizations learn the behavioural patterns of their employees, understanding their (employees') psychology, necessary adaptation measures can be applied to each employee when dealing with organizational changes. The employees too find it comfortable to adjust to changes. Usually every employee is interested in his growth and development through training and development programmes. It gives him a lot of psychic satisfaction. Understanding employee psychology can be instrumental in identifying what type of training and development programme would suit a particular employee and thereafter prepare customized training and development programmes for employees, which will not only satisfy employees but also result in improving the productivity of the organization. What is his take on relational benefits? We get the answer to this question after understanding the employee's psychology. How he reacts to financial benefits will indicate the employee's extrinsic motivation, hence, the necessity of understanding employee psychology.

Does the employee need positive reinforcement? For example, whether social praise in public, creative rewards and incentives are necessary for the employee or not will depend on the employee psychology also. It is also observed that after some time, positive reinforcement becomes ineffective or less effective as the employee becomes accustomed to that positive reinforcement. How much time it will take to be so depends to some extent on the employee psychology also. In such cases, withhold the reward (positive reinforcement) unless performance is continually improved upon.

Achievement theory also has psychological implications. In the control of desire to achieve best results, what is the psychology of the employee? Does he want a conducive work environment? Or is he usually inclined to take calculated risks and set attainable goals? Or does he need continuing recognition for his efforts? Thus, it is worth mentioning that understanding employee psychology is a very important phenomenon. We may talk of Herzberg's two-factor theory, or of goal setting theory, or of equity theory, everywhere employee psychology comes into picture.

Even at the time of recruitment and selection, psychological tools help the management a great deal in assessing whether the candidate will prove a fit employee if selected. His attitude, aptitude, personality, the level of confidence, morale and so on predict his suitability for the assignment. The management should find out whether the employee has job satisfaction. Whether the task design and assignments suit the bent of mind of the employee? What is it that he would like to perform or not perform? Whether the employee is in a learning mode or not? What are his aspirations? Whether he likes teamwork or not? Is he cooperative or not? Whether he is accommodative or not? Is he ambitious? Is he egoistic? Answers to a lot of such questions through understanding employee psychology can be instrumental in initiating desired steps which may prove beneficial to both the employee and the organization by way of improvement in the productivity of the organization. Employee psychology has a lot to say about leaders and leadership styles also.

Understanding what motivates an employee of a given enterprise is central to the work of many psychologists. Motivation at the workplace is an important factor for the management. For example, intrinsic motivation is one such factor which affects both the employees and the employer. Those employees who always have a desire to have effective performance behaviours for their own stake are stated to have intrinsic motivations. For example, those employees who prefer being at work and will be willing to do anything that helps the organization to flourish are intrinsically motivated most of the time. Further research studies have expanded equity theory which describes how workers assess their efforts and outcomes on the job by calculating a productive ratio, by classifying three types of equatorial behaviours as follows:

1. **Benevolent:** The benevolent employees psychologically feel guilty if they are over- rewarded, even if rewarded equally, when they compare themselves to peers or co-employees. Not only this, such benevolent employees may feel satisfied even if under-rewarded as compared to their co-employees.

2. **Equity sensitive:** Equity-sensitive employees want that everyone should be rewarded fairly. Hence, they feel guilty when over-rewarded and unhappy when under-rewarded.

3. **Entitled:** Entitled employees want to be over-rewarded if compared to their co-workers. If paid less, they feel unhappy. Hence, the management should remain alert and attentive with regard to the perceptions of its employees regarding their pay and rewards. The latest concept, known as the 'Pygmalion effect' states that those managers who expect high performance tend to get high performance and vice versa. Hence, management should understand not only their employees' psychology but also the aforesaid psychological concepts if management is keen to see its organization grow.

Employee psychology should be understood by the management both at employees' individual level because not all employees are alike and at the group level because group psychology also differs from group to group. It is necessary because the management has to make some decisions on the individual employee level and sometimes on the group level. It is so because what works for one employee may not necessarily work for another employee and so is the case with groups. Understanding employee psychology always helps management in making befitting decisions.

The management, after understanding the psychology of its employees, can also identify for whom recognition of their contribution is more important than the extrinsic reward, and take appropriate decisions. It is important because those employees who get praise and recognition frequently, become more productive and feel more engaged among their co-employees. Not only this, such employees continue with the organization for a long period. For today's employees, perks are no longer as important as the sense of achievement which gives them psychic satisfaction. Today, meaningful work has become a big driver of engagement and productivity. Employees today place a high premium on creativity, purpose of work, flexibility and so on. Such things provide greater psychological satisfaction to employees. Not only this, an empowered employee has a sense of ownership for his job and his engagement is significantly higher. Hence, employee psychology has a great role to play. Having understood employee psychology, it becomes easier to evoke emotional and functional commitment of the employees towards their organization and also align the employees with the vision of the organization.

Then employee psychology also reveals that most employees who work from home because of their flexi-hours are more productive than their office counterparts because the former with the help of cloud-based services can access the information and tools they need from anywhere with a solid internet facility and, therefore, feel more comfortable. Similarly, providing breaks also affects employees' psychology because after availing breaks they work more enthusiastically. Most employees want their contributions to be valued. Human psychology is such, and exceptions are limited ones.

The management should also find out, after understanding the employee psychology, the stages of psychological development and levels of consciousness. The stages or levels of development comprise service, making a difference, transformation, self-esteem, relationship and survival (it is because causes of happiness differ according to the level of development). The levels of consciousness the employees are operating from at any moment are dependent on the employees' level of psychological development, their general life circumstances and the specific life challenges being experienced by them.

Thus, it is obvious that understanding of employee psychology by the management serves the purpose of both the employee and the organization.

Non-financial Metrics

Though financial metrics play their own role, non-financial metrics in the realm of compensation and benefits to play no less important role as already discussed elsewhere in this text. Rather, at times, they play a more important role than the financial metrics.

Meaning and Benefits of Non-financial Metrics

The term, 'metrics', refers to measurement. There are financial metrics, employee satisfaction metrics, software performance metrics and so on. But metrics in each case discloses measure-specific characteristics of data sets such as employee satisfaction data and financial data. For instance, some organizations may use financial data in ways that signal misleading information. It is worth mentioning here that each financial and non-financial metrics conveys a unique message, which should be well understood and appreciated. Before we move forward, it is essential to know the meaning of non-financial metrics. As a matter of fact, non-financial metrics are quantitative measures that cannot be expressed in monetary units. While common financial metrics in the area of compensation and benefits include things such as salary, bonus, pension, gratuity and maternity leave, measures such as recognition, praise, job satisfaction, leaving and development, achievement and value addition in personality fall into the non-financial metrics.

Today, the board and executives of many organizations are really interested in non-financial performance measures, irrespective of the fact that their ability to manage these factors remains inadequate even now. It should also be noted that non-financial metrics may differ from one area of functional management to another area of functional management and so on.

Non-financial metrics can serve as a leading indicator of the future performance and can provide insight with regard to an organization's impact on its employees, society and other stakeholders. Such metrics can provide deeper insights into the inner workings of the organization, especially with regard to the human factor involved in the working of the organization. Non-financial metrics can be used to understand why certain results happened and what is needed to change in order to improve financial metrics. Some of the main constituents of non-financial metrics are taken up for discussion as follows:

Dashboards and Scorecards and In-Performance

With the continuing investment by organizations in business intelligence, analytical tools are getting more popular. Today, only performance reports, both financial and non-financial, are no longer enough. For the performance management to be effective, the numbers need to be accompanied by how and why so as to enable managers to know what is to be done next. Dashboard and scorecards are analytical tools that allow an organization to focus on the measurements that are vital for the business of the organization. If a simple definition of either of the two terms, namely, dashboards and scorecards, is to be sought from relevant people, most of them are likely to give the same response for both terms, that is, a customizable view of key performance indicators (KPIs) that offers actionable information to the organization concerned. However, these two terms are not the same. Hence, before implementing either of these two analytical tools, it is essential to understand what these terms are all about and how the two differ from each other.

Dashboards

So far as dashboards are concerned, they often provide at-a-glance views of KPIs relevant to a specific objective or business process. Dashboard is also known as 'report' or 'progress report'. Thus, like a dashboard in the car, a performance management dashboard displays various meters, gauges and lights that give instant up-to-date information on the current status of the business.

In this way, the dashboard metrics do not indicate whether the results are positive or negative. This will be decided by the user's own interpretation of the data displayed. It is a different story if the dashboard, customized with alarms or status colours, allows for a faster and more efficient understanding of the results.

Usually, a dashboard is displayed on a web page linked to a database for the report to be constantly updated. For example, a human dashboard may show numbers pertaining to employee recruitment, average cost per recruitment, open positions, retention, composition and so on. Another example may be of a marketing dashboard showing number of units sold, number of sold units returned, salesman employed, units sold per salesman and so on. The dashboard metrics are very user specific and tend to tell more about the status of performance.

Dashboards can be used in the case of financial and non-financial benefits reflecting the present status. For example, in the case of the cafeteria approach, the relevant details of non-financial benefit packages, the number of employees cadre-wise, department-wise, gender-wise, age-wise, region-wise and so on. Keeping in view the above current data, decisions can be made for the future.

Origin

Going back to the origin and history of dashboards, it may be mentioned that the early predecessors of today's modern business dashboards were first developed in the 1980s in the form of an executive information system, popularly known in those days as EISs. But due to the non-availability of complete and reliable information, it was soon felt that the approach was not practical. The concept of digital dashboards followed the study of decision support systems in the 1970s and in the 1990s, the Information Age quickened pace and data warehousing, and the online analytical processing enabled dashboards to function properly. However, the use of dashboards could not be popular until later in the 1990s. In the late 1990s, the concept of 'digital nervous system' was promoted by Microsoft and digital dashboards were considered as one leg of the system. In modern times, dashboards have become an important part of business performance management.

Main Purpose of Dashboards

Dashboards serve a lot of purposes. For example, the main purpose is to know performance at a glance. Just click and the relevant information is available. To seek current (often real time) data instantly is another main purpose. Since dashboards are almost linked to systems, current (often real time) data is easily and instantly available.

Advantages

As stated earlier, dashboards today have become a vital part of business performance management. It is because of the fact that digital dashboards allow the organization to monitor the contribution of the various departments towards the accomplishment of organizational goals and objectives. Today, digital dashboards help in capturing and reporting specific data points from all departments individually, thus providing a 'snapshot' of the performance of the organization. Digital dashboards are useful in more than one way as follows:

Digital dashboards measure both efficiencies and deficiencies, enabling the organization to take the desired action. They also save time as compared to running multiple reports and are instrumental in quick identification of data outliers and correlations. They have the ability to identify and correct negative trends, and also to generate detailed reports showing new trends besides making more informed decisions based on business intelligence. They make visual presentations of performance measures available and gain total visibility of all systems instantly. Above all, digital dashboards align strategies and organizational goals. The benefits of dashboards easily outweigh the costs associated with its implementation. They add real and immediate value to daily operations and managing performance.

Dashboards as a tool are very effective for managing daily or hourly performance and are, therefore, typically used by customer support managers and also by low- and middle-level operators who keep a watch on current data. For example, an inventory dashboard (hypothetical) may display the following:

Inventory Dashboard			
Part No.	*Actual*	*Plan*	*Variance*
1050A	3,453	3,500	1%
2201B	3,000	4,000	25%
3341C	60	100	40%
3399C	70	100	30%
4506A	2,341	2,250	4%
4509B	125	100	25%
7410A	130	100	30%
9040B	500	250	50%

Besides, most performance solutions include the capability to design dashboards. Dashboards provide easy and fast access to information for better decision-making. They are easily customizable for a variety of users. Besides being an enhanced analytical tool, dashboards lead to communication, prioritization and accountability.

Classification

Dashboards may be classified according to the role they play. Based on their premise, dashboards can be either strategic or analytical or operational. As far as strategic dashboards are concerned, they are supportive to managers at every level because they present the instant overview needed by managers to make important decisions, especially related to performance. The snapshots of data play are extremely responsible for managers. As far as dashboards for analytical purposes are concerned, they typically support interactions with the data and usually include comparisons, context and so on. Coming to dashboards for monitoring operations, they are helpful in monitoring activities and events that are subject to change constantly and, therefore, require attention and instant response. Hence, dashboards for monitoring operations are not designed in the manner in which dashboards that support strategic decision-making are designed.

Types of Dashboards

The digital dashboards that are ruling the roost today in the market are of three types, namely stand-alone software applications, desktop applications also called desktop widgets, and web browser-based applications. Then, there are specialized dashboards like a compact start-up scorecard dashboard suitable for smaller organizations that track main activities across a lot of domains. As against this, there are specialized dashboards that track almost all corporate functions such as HR, recruitment, security, project management and IT.

Scorecards

Scorecards are also analytical tools allowing managers to focus on the measurements that are important for their business. Scorecards measure performance periodical results against predetermined goals and enable users to gauge how their performance stands against expectations. They are usually used by upper-level managers and are sometimes linked to systems. Scorecards also provide easy and fast access to updated information, which helps in making better decisions. They can be customized according to the requirements of a variety of users. They are of great use in increasing communication, prioritization as also accountability.

Dashboards and Scorecards

Dashboards and balance scorecards are not mutually exclusive. They have been linked together as if they are interchangeable. But in reality, this is not the case. Although both of them usually display vital information, the difference between the two is that of format. While dashboards provide calculated direction, scorecards can open the quality of an operation.

Though both dashboards and scorecards are analytical tools and, therefore, like other best analytical tools, they are often used in combination. Both can be combined into a hybrid tool. While scorecards can include graphics to improve readability, dashboard metrics can provide some tie-in to business objectives.

Intellectual Capital Assessment and Market Implications of Human Capital

Of late, there is a growing interest in measuring, reporting and managing intellectual capital because of the strategic value of intangibles in creating wealth and conferring competitive advantages to organizations and also to countries. Despite the fact that in the current social and economic context (knowledge economy), knowledge and information are core competencies, there is still a dearth of academic works related to intellectual capital, especially at the macro level. The two main journals in this regard are the *Journal of Intellectual Capital* and the *Journal of Knowledge Management*, though in recent decades, intangibles that make up intellectual capital have become the most important resource for wealth creation. Therefore, more research should have taken place and more research work should have been published so far.

It is worth mentioning that the first studies on intellectual capital were conducted at the level of firms (micro level) and intended to explain the market value of the firms. It was later on, starting in the 2000s, that researchers, governments and international agencies came forward to develop new works for measuring and managing intellectual capital at the macro level.

In the context of fast technological changes, wealth creation at the micro level depends primarily on capabilities and entrepreneurial strategies, though growth potential is determined by an organization's resources including both tangible and intangible, the latter being the main source of capacity to innovate. Of course, today intangible sources like intellectual capital are viewed as the main source of wealth, prosperity and economic growth.

Meaning and Definition of Intellectual Capital

Before going forward, it will be in the fitness of things to know what intellectual capital is all about. Intellectual capital basically refers to knowledge and information, that is, where in an organization or country production and distribution are directly based on the use of knowledge and information. As a matter of fact, intellectual capital refers to business-related intangibles. Hence, knowledge, experience, skills, procedures, database, intellectual property rights, firm's routines, research and development and so on all together constitute intellectual capital of an organization. It may be mentioned here that intangibles related to business are called intellectual capital. Intellectual capital is also said to be the combination of organizational resources and activities including entrepreneurial, human and relational assets. Some researchers view intellectual capital as comprising human capital, which is embodied in people; relational capital, which is related to relationships with suppliers, partners, or customers; and structural capital, which refers to intangibles comprising modified and stored knowledge. Thus, it is seen that researchers have differed with regard to the meaning of intellectual capital in one way or the other. That is why the models to evaluate intangibles have followed different paths.

Motivation to Study Knowledge

Now the question arises as to why to study knowledge in firms (i.e. at the micro level). The answer is that motivation to do this erupts from the variations noted between the book value and the market value of firms. Providing more accurate and precise information to stakeholders is another reason to study knowledge in firms. It is also because of the fact that intangibles constitute the base of competitive advantage.

Intellectual Capital Models

The relevant literature on intellectual capital and related issues presents a number of models to evaluate intangibles at the macro level (country level) which differ from those developed to evaluate intangibles at the micro level (firm level). Two main lines were closer to intellectual capital at the micro level, known as academic models, and the other developed by international organizations and business schools, known as international models. The latter models take into account the value of intangibles in order to measure development, innovative capacity and competitiveness. The main difference between these two main lines is with regard to the treatment given to intangibles. The international organization models take tangibles and intangibles together in all steps of the evaluation, whereas the academic models view academic models as the most important factor in wealth creation and therefore, intangible assets are evaluated independently of tangibles. One thing to be noted is that academic models mainly use human capital and structural capital components, for explicit evaluation of intellectual capital, though some models also include relational capital, renewal capital or market capital. Besides, based on the objectives and conceptual framework, the academic models determine national intellectual capital directly and a few models also determine national wealth as a way to predict future performance, whereas the international organization models stress directly on the capacity for growth and do not identify either the intellectual capital or intellectual capital constituents. Again, it is primarily non-financial indicators that are used for academic models and further that financial indicators are used to provide information with regard to capital or invested in intangibles. As against this, it is the high proportion of financial indicators that are used in international organizational models.

Although assessing intangibles is a complex job, some models have received wide acceptance, mainly the international organization models, though the consensus on the evaluation models or indicators is still far from achieved.

At the macro level, intellectual capital is still at its infancy stage, confirming that in order to build a more acceptable framework for national intellectual capital, more efforts will have to be made. The study of relevant literature offers several models to measure intellectual capital at the macro level, using different methods to identify intangibles. Because of the large number of methods used in different models to measure intangibles, it becomes difficult to categorize them. Yet, the same can be divided into categories according to two important features, namely, the type of asset evaluated and the very purpose of the model.

Some macro models which are more related to the intellectual taxonomy were developed for organizations as most of them originated in studies of intellectual capital at the organization level.

Recognition

It is unfortunate that despite five to six decades of organizational research establishing that employees are motivated by more than just money alone, most organizations still continue to depend exclusively on financial rewards. No doubt, every employee generally wants more money but the result of such an assumption reflects overemphasizing the importance of financial rewards. There are a lot of alternative motivators capable of affecting employee behaviour and level of motivation too. Gratton has rightly remarked,

> while motivation is determined by both monetary and non-monetary factors, money has come to play an overly important role in our thinking about the cause of behaviour. In most companies, very limited time and effort are spent on considering non-monetary sources of motivation.[8]

At times, non-monetary rewards play a more important role and their impact is everlasting or at least continue for a long period. For example, if the organization rewards an employee in cash for his act of bravery, it may not be the right proposition because after the cash is consumed, he is likely to forget the recognition in the long run and further that an act of bravery should not be weighed in terms of money. It deserves much more than that. It is for this reason that the remark made by Hanson et al. (2002) is worth appreciating which reads:

> We would never think of promising a cash bonus for every act of courage under fire. In fact, the thought of remuneration for such deeds actually cheapens them. On the other hand, try to get a teenager to clean his room without some contract about what is in it for him.[9]

Here, it may also be pointed out that there is also a negative point against offering tangible benefits or cash benefits. According to Armstrong and Murlis,

> More complex recognition programmes—those organization-wide schemes that offer a fat cheque or generous prize—can work well if well designed, but they can all too easily miss the boat by focusing on the few they may alienate the money.[10]

Most researches conducted so far also reveal that for most people, money is not the prime motivator in employment. Most employees place tangible (financial) benefits after interesting and enjoyable work, job satisfaction and a feeling of accomplishment. As a matter of fact, appropriate recognition generates both job satisfaction and a feeling of accomplishment.

Here, it may be pointed out that there is a difference between reward and recognition. While rewards are promised from the outset, recognition is accorded in a post hoc manner. Failing to reduce the aforesaid difference, many organizations endeavour to motivate employees forgetting the essential nature of human motivation. They implement motivation schemes that not only prove ineffective but also end up disrupting the very goals they are trying to accomplish. A word of caution here: recognition will not motivate the demotivated employee but can reinforce the motivated, and encourage and reassure those who are trying to succeed.[11]

Defining the Concept of Non-financial Recognition

The primary objective of non-financial recognition is to motivate the employee at no cost or negligible cost. Non-financial recognition is a sort of non-cash award. It is given to recognize high-level performance or any other significant achievement of a predetermined target. Non-cash award does not necessarily mean that it should have no financial value. Recognition should give a feeling of pride to the receiver so that the recipient should feel motivated for a long period, which is possible when the act of recognition is substantially more memorable than a cash award. Instead of cash awards, the non-financial recognition scheme should have provisions for offering a gift or the like.

As per the non-financial recognition scheme, first of all individual employees or teams are identified, whose achievement is to be recognized and, therefore, deserve praise or acknowledgement. It is also to be noted that there is no uniformity in the non-financial recognition scheme. Their scope and size may differ from industry to industry, from organization to organization and also from time to time. There can be so many options for recognizing employees' distinguished achievements.

Theoretical Background

There is a lot of overlap between the concepts of reward and recognition. While reward is given in return for doing something as required, or compensation for services thus performing certain behaviour becoming a means by which to get reward and making the reward act as an incentive. Hence, in order to get reward, an employee has to do something. As against this, recognition is conferred for doing something special and attracting the notice of others. For example, doing something that reduces the cost of production significantly or doing something innovative. Thus, as stated earlier also recognition is afforded in a post hoc manner; reward is promised from the very outset. Hence, there is a difference between the two. Recognition is required to enhance intrinsic motivation, whereas financial reward affects extrinsic motivation and has little influence on intrinsic motivation. It can, therefore, be said that employees do work for money, but they work even more for measuring their lives. While F.W. Taylor's concept of 'economic man', which was management's thinking around 1912, relates to reward and Maslow's fourth level of need, namely esteem, it was a combination of self-respect and the need for esteem and appreciation by others, and, therefore, relates to recognition. It can, therefore, be well said that employees' goals or intentions play an important role in determining behaviour.

Types of Recognition Schemes

According to Armstrong and Murlis, recognition schemes may be formal or informal, financial or non-financial, and private or public. The most important aspect is that recognition is meaningful to the individual recipient (and colleague), as this is how it will most positively impact motivation. Thus, there are various types of recognition schemes. Some of the main types are as follows:

1. **Day-to-day recognition:** Simply speaking, recognition is private, usually non-financial, and happens on a day-to-day basis, either orally or on a short note. This is cost-free. It encourages employees, and should be done frequently and not just as an annual feature. It is genuinely felt positive back to the employee or the team as the case may be for the work well done. However, the most effective recognition is one that is given by the immediate boss, that is, it should be manager led and not the company initiated. It should be a natural part of routine work and a part of organizational culture.

2. **Formal recognition:** Formal recognition has fewer high-value rewards and is highly structured, leaving little scope for discretion. Such recognition has provisions to provide employees with tangible means of recognition so that these may have impact on the motivation of employees for a longer period. Such tangible means of recognition may be in the form of gifts, meals out, trips abroad, weekend day(s) at health spas, vouchers and so on. Similarly, team awards may be in the form of trips to a foreign country, picnics, outings, parties and so on. Such formal recognition schemes are usually centrally driven and follow the process and procedure laid down for the purpose or even devolved to line managers, authorizing them to recognize individuals/ teams and allocating a budget to cover the cost, if any.

    Such formal recognitions come in handy at the time of promotion, whereas an opportunity arises for the recipient of recognition. Formal recognition enables the employees concerned to meet people of high profile. They also get appreciation not only from their juniors and peers but also from their seniors. However, it should also be noted that formal recognition can be effective in achieving the desired objective if the formal awards/recognition is given to the right employees and is being felt fair by other employees. Besides, it should be in proportion to the achievement. Formal recognition may become demotivating if the above-mentioned points are not taken care of.

3. **Informal recognition:** Informal recognition is more common and popular in large-scale organizations employing a large number of employees, most of whom get low salary, and where the number of recipients of informal awards/ recognition is likely to be great. It also sounds good if instead of giving a gift of INR 100,000 to one employee, 1,000 employees are given a gift of INR 100 each. Instant awards can also be given to employees for doing something unusual, which may be in the interest of the organization or for doing an excellent job. No system should attach the tag of 'winner' to any employee. Kohn also argues strongly against any system that creates a 'winner' because 'for each person who wins, there are many others who have lost'.[12] Giving informal recognition does not amount to compensating the employee; it is

rather a small token for a large amount of thanks. Informal awards/recognition may also be in the form of public recognition, and, therefore, may be displayed on notice boards or published in house journals/magazines/newsletters or through an intranet. Such steps bring to the notice of all other employees the achievement of the recipient of the informal award/recognition, and that too at virtually no cost. Informal recognition may be in the following forms:

a. Letter of appreciation to the employee by a high-up in the organization and a copy of it to his boss.
b. Running trophy.
c. Hotel package.
d. Airline tickets.
e. Bottle of champagne.
f. Charity donation.
g. Chauffeur-driven car for a short period, say, a month or so.
h. Cinema tickets.
i. Basket of fruits.
j. Air miles.
k. Conference/seminar participation/registration fee.
l. Dinner for family along with taxi and a babysitter.
m. Food hamper.
n. Some working days off.
o. Gold coffee mug.
p. Car parking for a year or so.
q. Tie pin, watch and brooch.
r. Funny gifts.
s. Pen and pencil set.
t. Personalized items.
u. Shopping vouchers.
v. Company shares.
w. Ticket to a concert.
x. Others.

The award/recognition so given should appear meaningful to the recipient. It should give a feeling to the recipient that his contribution is being realized and valued by the company.

4. **Financial recognition:** The impact of financial awards/recognition is usually short-lived. Not only this, the recipient more often thinks that the award received by him is not comparable to the amount of big contribution made by him because he knows the worth of cash offered to him as against a certificate of appreciation given to him, which will always remain invaluable. Its worth cannot be gauged.

Examples: There cannot be uniformity in the ways informal awards or recognition are given to recipient employees. They may differ from one rank of employees to another rank of employees, or from one type of contribution to another type of contribution, or from one occasion to another occasion, or from one organization to another organization and so on. In case a particular item or gift is of no use at all to the recipient, it may not have the desired effect on the motivation of the employee. For example, offering a 'makeup pack' to an employee who does not use it at all, will not serve the purpose of earning his goodwill or motivating him. In whatever form the informal reward/recognition is given to an employee, it should be meaningful to him. Examples of non-cash awards/recognitions may include the following:

a. Certificate of appreciation.
b. Bouquet delivered at workplace in the presence of co-employees.
c. Books.
d. T-shirt.

Advantages of Recognition

Recognition, first of all, does not cost the organization anything and even if it does, it is negligible. It is almost a free tool for motivating employees. Recognition for a good job done well by an employee can be accomplished by uttering a few words of appreciation such as thanks, sending an SMS or an email and writing a simple letter recognizing the contribution made by the employee. Neither it takes time nor it costs anything except a few seconds or minutes. But, it wins the heart of the employee. Recognition is a very powerful motivator. Employees want their achievements to be appreciated (see Exhibit 8.1) which gives them psychic satisfaction, which, in turn, boosts their morale and motivates them to give their best to the organization.

EXHIBIT 8.1 EMPLOYEE RECOGNITION

Employee recognition is no recent invention by any standards, but its implication for organizations is most definitely moving to higher grounds. After a comprehensive research study, Jean M. Twenge of San Diego State University and Stacy M. Campbell of

Kennesaw State University concluded that Gen Yers have personality traits such as high self-esteem...unrealistically high expectations, a high need for praise.... Their recommendations: organizations should upscale their recognition and praise programmes to appeal to the psyche of this new brave workforce.

Source: Human Capital (February 2014, p. 8).

The importance of recognition can be defined as a key part of the value set of the organization and this would be reinforced by education, training and performance appraisals.[13]

Designing a Recognition Scheme

In order to be an effective scheme, it is necessary to follow the relevant principles. So it is, obviously, the case of designing an effective recognition scheme. Hence, while designing a recognition scheme, the following points should be kept into consideration:

1. **Simplicity:** For a scheme to be successful, it is essential that it should be simple, that is, easy to understand. It should be comprehensible by all concerned, especially those who are going to be benefitted by it. The beneficiaries should be able to understand in clear-cut terms what type of behaviour or what values are going to be rewarded under the scheme.
2. **Alignment of awards with culture:** It is a matter of common knowledge that most employees leave an organization not because those employees do not like the organization but because they do not like their managers. In case the good behaviour and contribution of the employees is not recognized, they prefer to leave the organization. Whatever good behaviour is displayed by the employees or whatever significant contribution they make, most managers simply overlook these by saying that it is their duty to behave in that fashion or contribute in that way. Everything starts with a small beginning. In case an organization does not recognize the accomplishment of the employee thinking that it is not extraordinary, the employees may not feel motivated to do better in the future. Hence, an achievement even if it may not be very big should also be recognized, and suitably praised and rewarded.
3. **Let it happen:** According to Armstrong and Murlis,[14] the difficulty arises when the recognition scheme is to be integrated with other business initiatives, both within HR and in other areas of the business. Sound implementation is vital. It is, therefore, necessary that the scheme should first be well communicated and it should also be ensured that the employees are aware of it and further that their interest is maintained in the scheme so that they may like to take advantage of it. There is no point that everybody is talking and appreciating the scheme in the first few months of its initiation but it is found that at the end of the year or so nobody is awarded. Another case may be that the notice of 'best worker of the month' is displayed in the first two months and thereafter no such notice is displayed for months together. Therefore, it is necessary that organization should follow up the scheme properly and make it happen.

4. **Take care of taxes:** The organization should also ensure that the rewards should not attract any tax on the same, otherwise it will be shocking to them when later on they find that they have to pay tax on the reward received by them. If they are supposed to pay any tax, the organization should own the liability of paying the tax.

5. **Types of the behaviour to be recognized:** Only that type of behaviour or contribution should be recognized and rewarded which falls in the 'most cherished' category of the reward, that is, which the organization values most and is highlighted in the scheme(s). On the one hand, there are some organizations that may have recognition schemes that acknowledge or recognize inputs like ideas, on the other hand, there are many organizations that acknowledge or recognize outputs. There are organizations which recognize social behaviours like teamwork. There are yet some other organizations that acknowledge 'business benefits' like higher output.

    Although there is no hard and fast rule for giving recognition, the following may be worth considering for recognition:
    a. Extraordinary contribution.
    b. Excellent teamwork.
    c. Action or behaviour beyond the call of duty.
    d. Excellent customer service.
    e. Innovative ideas.

6. **Organizational benefits:** Although there is no uniformity in the goals to be accomplished for which non-financial recognition schemes are implemented by organizations, some of the benefits that organization expect by implementing non-financial recognition schemes are as follows:
    a. Motivate high performers.
    b. Acknowledge extraordinary performance.
    c. Reinforce desired behaviours.
    d. Improve customer service.
    e. Recognize distinguished achievement.
    f. Support a culture change.
    g. Boost morale.
    h. Support line managers.
    i. Encourage loyalty.
    j. Infuse confidence.
    k. Support organizational value.
    l. Increase retention.
    m. Attract talent.
    n. Increase goodwill and reputation of the organization.

Problems Involved in the Non-financial Recognition Schemes

There are several problems involved in the success of non-financial recognition schemes, some of the main ones are as follows:

1. The scope of the scheme(s) may be too narrow or too wide. In the former case, the employees may start thinking that they have little chance to get awards. Hence, they may not attach any importance to the scheme(s). In the latter case, because of the large number of awards, the schemes may decrease their credibility. The schemes, therefore, should be such that employees feel that they are fair and that they have a chance to take advantage of the scheme(s).
2. The value of the reward should be according to the expectations of the employees, that is, it should be meaningful for them. Hence, employees should be associated while awards or way of recognition is being finalized at the formulation stage of the schemes.
3. In case, the recipients of the award/recognition find later on that they will have to pay tax on the awards, they become rather demotivating. Hence, this aspect should also be kept in view by the organization.
4. The credibility of the schemes is very important. If they are not, they will not be effective. In case the criteria for choosing the employees who are to be rewarded or recognized for their contribution/achievement are not reliable and dependable, the scheme will not be a success. Hence, standards/criteria should be laid down in the schemes on the basis of which recipients will be chosen.
5. In case there are fraudulent nominations, the schemes will not be successful.
6. External economic environments may also come in the way of success of non-financial recognition schemes.[15] For example, if the organization is retrenching some of its employees, the schemes in question may not be effective and may be perceived by employees as empty attempts to appease employees.
7. In case the momentum of the schemes is not maintained, they may lose their charm. They should be reviewed periodically and updated according to the liking of the employees.

Thus, in order to ensure that non-financial recognition schemes prove effective, the first thing to be taken care of is striking a balance between the extrinsic and the intrinsic rewards so that the psychological contract enlisted between the employee and the employer could be reinforced. The rewards received by the employees should be meaningful to them and should generate a feeling among them that their contribution is valued by the organization. Besides, the employees should be associated while non-financial recognition schemes are formulated, implemented and reviewed.

Praise

Personal acknowledgement by the boss for performing well verbally is perhaps the simplest and the most fundamental non-financial recognition. Simply saying, 'thank you' is cost free but has an immediate impact on the motivation of the employee. Hence, it should become a habit to thank the employee every time he performs his job well. Praise satisfies the ego of an employee to a great extent and prompts him to put in more and more efforts in his job to earn further praise (see Exhibit 8.2).

EXHIBIT 8.2 CRAVING FOR APPRECIATION

Psychologist and philosopher William James pens a letter to his class at Radcliffe College, with the quote: 'The deepest principle of human nature is the craving to be appreciated.' He succinctly captures the essence of human motivation and its core connection to the power of recognition. He is probably clueless that an entire body of work will be built on this simple thought and it will continue to be relevant even centuries later, especially in the organizational context.

Source: Human Capital (February 2014, p. 8).

When an employee is praised, other employees too start craving for it and, therefore, they also begin to work harder so that their efforts may also be praised by their bosses or by any other senior people who matter in the organization. Thus, praise is another non-financial reward which should be made use of as frequently as possible whenever it is required.

Learning and Development

Usually, every employee is keen on his self-growth and development. Hence, creating a conducive environment for learning and development enables an employee to fulfil the inherent urge for self-growth and, therefore, becomes a source of motivation. Employees have a great sense of satisfaction when they find that the organization cares for their growth and development, and through which their worth will go up not only in the organization but also in the market. It will also be recognized by the organization. Hence, creating an enabling environment for learning and development is another way of non-financial benefits rewards and also a great source of motivating employees.

Achievement

Every employee wants to achieve something new even if he has to go the extra mile because he knows that it is the achievement of something of great value to the organization that will bring laurels to him and will open for him the door for promotion. Not only this, achievement gives a personal satisfaction and makes him feel proud of himself. It also fulfils the fourth and fifth stages of his needs as per Maslow's Need Theory. Hence, the organization should create a work environment which is conducive for employees to achieve something significant. As such achievement also constitutes a type of non-financial benefits and rewards.

Value Addition in Personality

Anything done by the organization which adds to the personality of the employee is another type of non-financial benefit and reward. For example, if the organization arranges classes for improving communication skills or distributes some material to them which is helpful in improving their vocabulary or soft skills, it will be greatly appreciated by the employees as it results in a value addition to their personality. Hence, value addition in personality is also a type of non-financial reward and benefit.

Others

There may be other types of non-financial benefits and rewards which may be appealing and motivating to employees, for example, arranging religious discourses.

Chapter Review

1. Both financial or transactional or extrinsic rewards and non-financial or relational or intrinsic rewards are instrumental in motivating employees. Both are important in their own places. But, of late, especially since the 1990s, there has been a shift from sheer economics to behavioural sensitivities. It is because money cannot buy engagement and loyalty, and that non-financial benefits cost the organization little or no money.
2. Non-financial rewards can be categorized in more than one way. According to one classification, these can be divided into three categories, namely (a) individual non-financial rewards such as recognition, job satisfaction, status and security of job, (b) collective non-financial rewards such as assigning social importance to work, encouraging healthy competition and encouraging informal groups and (c) institutional non-financial rewards such as encouraging workers' participation in management, free flow of communication, building morale and promoting good human relations.
3. Non-financial rewards/benefits have an emotional appeal to the employees. For example, if anybody's contribution is recognized and appreciated, he is likely to get emotional satisfaction. There are several non-financial rewards to motivate employees such as recognizing employees' contribution, sending handwritten letters of appreciation, providing employees the opportunity to have lunch/dinner with the big wigs of the organization, giving a personal touch and getting to know one's employees, offering subordinates leadership role, associating employees in decision-making, sitting down with the employee one-on-one, sharing a part of gains of the organization with the employees and offering flexible schedule to high performers.
4. Heineken UK, whose core values comprise passion for quality, respect and enjoyment of life, got in touch with Hay Group to work out a future reward strategy. They could identify what needs to be changed and in what order.

Accordingly, with the help of Hay Group, Heineken UK designed and rolled out a job family-based consistent grade and pay structure and benefits plan.

5. Internal audit of compensation and benefits yields fruitful results and many shortcomings in the system can be overcome because internal audit is a method of independent and objective validations that results in enhanced value and improved operation and performance of an organization. Internal audit appraises the economy, efficiency and effectiveness of business operations, and controls the application of plans, procedures and policies.

6. Internal audit of compensation and benefits supports management in several ways because it tells whether current processes are being followed in both letter and spirit and further whether they are proving effective or not. If not, remedial steps may be taken to overcome the problems.

   There are several methods of audit, including surveys, interviews, observations or a combination of two or more of the above. However, a survey is the most popular method. Because of internal audit, an organization runs several risks such as compliance risks, employment market risks, reputation risk, operating risks and financial reporting risks. But in order to promote transparency and also to raise the market's trust and confidence in an organization, internal audit of executive compensation should be encouraged.

7. It is necessary to understand employee psychology which is the study of the mind and behaviour of job holders. It helps the organization to know what motivates an employee. It, therefore, helps both the employer and the employee. Non-financial metrics play an important role in the realm of compensation and benefits. It can be used to understand why certain results happened and what is needed to change in order to improve financial metrics. However, it should be simple and the design should be appropriate.

8. Dashboards and scorecards are analytical tools that allow an organization to focus on the measurements that are vital for the business of the organization. Dashboards often provide at a glance views of KPIs relevant to a specific objective or business process. They are just like 'report' or 'progress report'. They reflect the present status of a business. So far as the classification of dashboards on the basis of the role they play is concerned, they can be either strategic, analytical or operational. So far as types of dashboards are concerned, the digital dashboards that are ruling the roost today in the market are of three types, namely, stand-alone software applications, desktop applications and web browser-based applications. Then, there are specialized dashboards such as a compact start-up scorecard dashboard and specialized dashboards that track almost all corporate functions.

9. Scoreboards too are analytical tools allowing managers to focus on the measurements that are important for their business. While dashboards provide calculated direction, scorecards can open the quality of an operation.

10. Today intangible sources like intellectual capital are viewed as the main source of wealth, prosperity and economic growth. Intellectual capital refers to knowledge and information. There are a number of models of intellectual capital.

11. Recognition is a vital non-financial source of motivating employees, which is given for a high level of performance. Recognition schemes may be formal or informal, financial or non-financial and private or public. The various types of recognition include day-to-day recognition, formal recognition, informal recognition and financial recognition.

12. Non-financial metrics are the measures which cannot be expressed in monetary units. These include things such as recognition, praise, learning and development, achievement and value addition in personality.

13. So far as designing a recognition scheme is concerned, it is necessary that in order to be effective, it should have certain features such as simplicity, alignment of awards with culture, letting it happen, taking care of taxes, types of behaviour to be recognized and benefits to organization. However, there are many problems also involved in non-financial recognition.

14. Praise, learning and development, achievement, value addition in personality and so on are some of the other constituents of non-financial metrics.

DISCUSSION QUESTIONS

1. Discuss the role that non-financial benefits/rewards play in motivating employees.

2. Discuss the main types of non-financial benefits/rewards.

3. Discuss the findings of Hay Group with regard to Heineken UK in the context of approach towards rewards.

4. Discuss the meaning of internal audit of compensation and non-financial benefits, and also point out audit tasks and risks involved in the context of compensation and benefits structure.

5. Discuss the meaning of employee psychology and how understanding employee psychology may help an organization.

6. Discuss the meaning and benefits of non-financial metrics, and also point out its constituents.

7. Discuss the importance of non-financial recognition schemes and also various types of recognition schemes.

8. Discuss the purpose and role of dashboards and scorecards in enabling an organization to achieve its goals.

9. Discuss the meaning and models of intellectual capital.

10. Discuss the implications of intellectual capital assessment and also market implications of human capital.

Individual and Group Activities

1. As an individual visit some big organizations and discuss with its HR officials the types of non-financial benefits/rewards usually given to their employees. Also, find out if these are serving the desired purpose.
2. In a group of two, find out from the HR officials of some big organizations the purpose and benefits of internal audit of compensation and benefits. Also, find out the audit tasks and risks involved with regard to the compensation and benefits structure.
3. As an individual, visit some organizations and find out from the HR officials if there has been any effort on their part to understand employee psychology. If yes, how far this effort has yielded the desired results?
4. In a group of three, discuss with HR officials of some big organizations their non-financial metrics and its constituents.
5. As an individual, visit some manufacturing organizations and find out from the officials of their production department if they are using dashboards and scorecards. If yes, how far these have been proven instrumental in furthering their production effort?

APPLICATION CASE

Jacob is heading a company as its CEO. The company has a 10 per cent market share and is well known for its quality goods and instant delivery. It is one of the 10 most popular companies producing the same product, that is, dry motor batteries. The raw materials and technology being used by the company are of high quality and most of its employees including technocrats and executives are highly competent. With all these features, the company should have earned reasonably good profits but this has not been happening for the last few years.

In the last board meeting, the issue came up for discussion, and everyone was wondering why financial results were not coming up to expectations. Almost everyone participated in the discussion, but no concrete solution could be found. Towards the end of the meeting, the HR manager was asked about his opinion on the issue. After a minute's pause, he put forward his views.

He informed that while the salary and financial rewards being given to the employees were comparable to those being given to their counterparts in the market, that is, everything was perfect so far as external alignment with respect to compensation and financial rewards was concerned. There appeared to be good internal alignment in this respect. Everything was fine up to this. He said that he had nothing to say with regard to compensation and financial rewards. The company was taking good care of that aspect. He changed his tone a bit now and expressed his inner feelings in a choked voice. He told the other members of the board that nothing was alright about the relational benefits and rewards. He informed that while the employees were well paid and getting good financial benefits and services, money alone could not fulfil all types of needs of employees. They crave for praise, recognition, appreciation and the like, which are the potential sources of intrinsic motivation. He said that the line staff appeared to be extremely miser in this respect. He further said that though human relations were not bad in the company, he had never heard any supervisory staff say 'thank you for the job well done' or the like. Financially, the employees were well off but relationally or intrinsically satisfying aspect was missing to a great extent. He further told that though their productivity rate was quite alright, it was likely to go up further if the employees felt intrinsically, psychologically or relationally more satisfied.

The board agreed with the contention of the HR manager and asked him to take the necessary steps in this direction.

Questions

1. What has been wrong with the company because of which the employees are not making full use of their potential?
2. What steps should the HR manager take now to improve the situation?
3. Do you think that it will be proper for the board to appreciate the HR manager recognize his pragmatic thinking and bestow on him some significant non-financial awards? Yes or no, why? Give arguments.

Notes

1 A. Ahmed et al., 'Role of Non-financial Benefits on Motivation of Employees', *Proc., 5th International Statistical Conference* 17 (23–25 January 2009): 115.
2 Jones and Butler (1992), quoted in ibid., 115.
3 Ibid., 116.
4 P. Joshi, 'Relational Rewards: Creating Fulfilling Workplace Environment', *International Journal of Engineering and Management Research* 6, no. 4 (July–August 2016): 1.
5 Ibid.
6 Stone et al. (2010), quoted in ibid., 2.
7 Ibid., 4.
8 L. Gratton, 'More than Money', *People Management* 10, no. 2 (29 January 2004): 23.
9 F. Hanson, M. Smith, and R. Hansen, 'Rewards and Recognition in Employee Motivation', *Compensation and Benefit Review* 34, no. 5 (October 2002): 64–71.
10 Armstrong and Murlis, *Reward Management*, 371.
11 Ibid.
12 A. Kohn, 'Why Incentive Plans Cannot Work', *Harvard Business Review* 6 (September–October 1993): 54–63.
13 Armstrong and Murlis, *Handbook of Reward Management*, 37.
14 Armstong and Murlis, *Reward Management*, 377.
15 E. Tahmincioglu, 'Gifts that Gall', *Workforce Magazine*, April 2004, 43–46.

10

COMPENSATION AND REWARD MANAGEMENT POLICY, PROCESSES, PROCEDURES AND SOME OTHER ISSUES

LEARNING OBJECTIVES

After studying this chapter, the reader should be able to:

1. Explain the meaning and objectives of reward management and reward management policy.
2. Enlist and explain the main reward management processes and procedures with special reference to compa-ratio analysis.
3. Explain the concept of pay reviews, especially the individual reviews, and procedures for grading jobs and pay rate fixation.
4. Explain how to control payroll costs and the main methods of controlling payroll costs.
5. Explain how to evaluate reward processes.
6. Enlist and explain recent and future trends in reward management.
7. Explain the concept of 'total reward'.
8. Explain the issues involved in boardroom pay and what is the current thinking in this regard.
9. Enlist and explain the guiding principles for boardroom remuneration.
10. Explain the concept of deferred bonus schemes.

DOI: 10.4324/9781032626123-10

Introduction

Compensating/rewarding employees appropriately for their contribution is both a science and an art. It is, therefore, essential to have adequate knowledge about compensation/reward management policies, processes, procedures and other related issues.

Reward Policy

First, it is important to know what reward management is all about. As a matter of fact, reward management refers to the formulation and implementation of policies, processes and strategies that aim at rewarding the employees of an organization fairly, equitably and consistently, keeping in view their value to the organization. Reward management takes care of analyzing and controlling remuneration, compensation and other benefits for the employee of an organization. It, therefore, generates and operates officially a reward structure for the organization concerned, which deals with issues such as pay policy, processes, practices, W&S admin and total reward.

The reward policies are strongly influenced by the principles as well as the philosophy of reward the organization believes in. Though the concept of reward management is easily comprehensible theoretically, when put into practice, it may not go according to the expected results. An organization may create a reward system expecting to reward a particular behaviour but end up rewarding another one.

Objectives

The following are the objectives of reward policies:

1. To recognize the contribution of employees.
2. To motivate employees to work towards accomplishing strategic goals set by the organization.
3. To suggest training and development programmes to meet increased job responsibility.
4. To reward fairly, that is, keeping in view the value of individuals to the organization.
5. To reward equitably.
6. To reward consistently.
7. To provide guidelines for the implementation of reward strategies as well as the design and management of reward processes.
8. To attract employees.
9. To reduce employee turnover.
10. To build a better employment deal.
11. To retain employees.

12. To increase employees' willingness to work wholeheartedly in the organization.
13. To enhance employees' productivity.
14. To create a better work environment.

Objectives can also be grouped under three heads, namely organizational objectives, collective objectives and individual objectives.

Reward Policy and Level of Awards

According to Armstrong and Murlis, the policy on the level of rewards indicates whether the company is a high payer, is content to pay median or average rates of pay or even, exceptionally, accepts that it must pay below the average.[1] Policies on the level of rewards should also take care of employee benefits such as health care, holidays, perks and transportation.

Reward Policy, and Market Rate and Equity

Reward policy should ensure that rewards are market-driven rather than equitable. In order to attract and retain employees who are in demand and whose market rates are high, an organization will have to take liberty with internal equity so as to keep pace with the market. The organization will have to compensate the aforesaid employees as per the market rate because of market pressures and thus be market driven. Otherwise, the organization may not be able to attract and/or retain such employees.

In the case of the kind of people mentioned above, market considerations will impact the levels of pay in an organization. It may, however, allow for the use of market supplements, that is, additional payments to the rate for a job as determined by job evaluation (internal equity), which reflects market rates.[2]

It may be laid down in the policy that these additional payments may be reviewed regularly. However, those who have already been granted such payments should be allowed to continue with them but may be adjusted at the time of pay progression to buy them close to the corporate jobs. Market pay and market supplements should have no gender bias and be objectively justified.

Reward Policy Regarding Attracting the Candidates

Keeping in view the value of the high quality of candidates to the organization or the urgency of the requirement, the policy may have a provision of 'golden hellos', that is, offering recruitment bonuses. It will be even better if the attraction strategy is based on a competitive remuneration package including 'golden hellos'. Factors such as career prospects, training and development opportunities, working environment, intrinsic interest in the work and work-life balance policies can also be included in the policy so that their package may be made competitive at market rates.

Reward and Retention of Employees

Cappelli has rightly stated that it is the market, not the company, that will ultimately determine the movement of employees.[3] Indeed, it is difficult to counter the pull of the market. Since an organization cannot shield its employees from attractive opportunities and aggressive recruiters, it can definitely influence who leaves and when. The organization can conduct risk analysis to quantify the seriousness of losing key people or of key jobs becoming vacant.

Reward Policy and Business Performance Rewards

The reward policy should incorporate and clarify the link between business performance and pay. It should mention the extent of the impact of results on pay. The policy should also spell out how profit-sharing or gainsharing plans would operate (see Chapter 5).

Reward Policy and Talent Management

Talent management refers to the organization's approach towards attraction and retention of good quality people which may not be tackled with money alone. Talent management relates to linking HR policies and practices together to make them mutually supportive in action. It should also be kept in consideration that talent management is concerned with key personnel of the organization. It is equally concerned with other employees also as everybody has a talent for which he is paid, though the former category of personnel should be given preference over the latter category of personnel. There is a need to have a cohesive view as to how talent management processes should mesh together so as to accomplish the overall objective of acquiring and retaining talent by using a number of interdependent policies and practices. Reward policy should be encouraging in this regard.

Reward Policy and Contingent Rewards

Reward policy should make it clear whether the organization intends to pay for competence, contribution, performance or skill. If yes, under what circumstances and how much. For example, whether a bonus is to be paid for exceptional performance or not. If yes, what should be the lower and upper limits of bonus in respect to basic pay? Similarly, the policy should point out its approach towards individual, team or organizational performance regarding contingent rewards.

Reward Policy and Total Rewards

Reward policy should also specify the stand of the organization on contingent rewards and other forms of non-monetary rewards. Whether it has any preferential treatment for either of the two or believes in a balance approach.

Reward Policy and Assimilation of Current Employees in Revised Pay Structure

The reward policy should also spell out how existing employees would be assimilated into the new or substantially revised pay structure, that is, where they would be placed in their new grades and how they are going to be adjusted if their current rate is below or above the new scale

for their new job, that is, the 'green circling' and 'red circling', respectively. In case, their current rate is above the new pay structure (i.e., red circling), the current rate of pay should be protected and similarly in the case of green circling, the policy should specify when it would be increased so as to fit in the new scale.

Rewards Policy and Transparency

It is in the interest of all concerned if the rewards policy is duly communicated and well publicized. The employees should have a feeling that the organization has nothing to hide from its employees in this regard. Secrecy in this regard on the part of management creates misunderstanding, suspicion and hostile attitude on the part of employees. It should appear to the employees that the management is committed as there is no attempt on the part of management towards keeping secrecy about pay and rewards. If secrecy is maintained, it may lead to a bad psychological contract between the two, namely, the management and the employees. It should not be forgotten that reward processes are powerful media for informing the employees about the company's values as well as the company's expectations in upholding those values and accomplishing its objectives and goals. Hence, a clear-cut message should go to the employees about the implications of different rewards and how they are going to be affected.

Rewards Policy and Employees Involvement

It is always advisable that employees should be involved in the design, formulation and implementation of reward policies. After this is done, the policy is expected to yield the desired results. Employees will have no grievance or less grievances because they themselves become parties to reward policy and, therefore, are under a moral obligation to cooperate in the implementation of the policy.

Rewards Policy and Flexibility

Since a lot of changes take place from time to time regarding the functioning of the organization, there should be enough scope to assimilate changes as and when there is a need for the same. Rigidity may create complications and sometimes lead to poor relations between the employees and the management.

Reward Policy and the Line Managers

Line managers have an important role to play in administering the reward policy. The policy should spell out the role of line managers in the implementation of reward policy, that is, the level of decisions they can make in this direction. The policy should also clarify how the guidance is to be given to line managers. If need be, some set of training and counselling can be extended to them.

It is obvious that employees are not providing their services for free and that the companies are also not charity institutions. That is why there is a contractual obligation between the two, spelling out how much work is to be done by the employees and how much is to be paid, both monetarily and non-monetarily, by the company for that work. It is, therefore, essential that reward policies should also keep in view the intrinsic needs of the employees such as recognition and tolerably good treatment by superiors as such things are the foundation of reward policies.

There is no doubt that pay increases, allowances, bonuses and so on, which are monetary in nature, are major sources of motivation in the case of employees because these extrinsic rewards are instrumental in meeting their basic requirements. Therefore, the organizations should offer graded pay hikes and bonuses on comparable levels without any discrimination based on gender and so on. Reward policies should ensure the fit between the employee and the role performed by him. Similarly, the reward policy should incentivize intrinsic needs. It should maintain a perfect balance between extrinsic and intrinsic rewards as both play a vital role in motivating the workers and prompting them to give their best to the organization. There is a long list of non-monetary rewards from which an organization can choose such benefits keeping in view their suitability to the employees.

A reward policy should be well designed and effective, only then it can help in creating a work environment where employees feel recognized and appreciated for their efforts and contribution, and serve to attract, motivate and retain people.

Reward policy should ensure that recognition and reward should be aligned with the values of the organization. Hence, it should identify what is to be rewarded. For example, the organization can reward employees' performance over and above job requirements, clients' appreciation of services rendered to them, contribution to the team's success, ongoing excellence in performance and so on.

Reward policy should ensure that recognition and reward should become a part of the culture of the organization. The policy should initiate formal recognition programmes, encourage supervisors and managers to be courteous towards their subordinates and so on. Provisions should be made in the policy for both cash and non-cash rewards. Employees should be consulted as to what kinds of rewards should be instituted. There should also be budgetary provisions for rewards. There should also be a provision in the policy for establishing processes for nominating and awarding individual employees or teams as per the circumstances prevailing in the organization. For rewarding big achievements carrying rewards of considerable value, final approval is to be sought from senior management or the committee constituted for the purpose. However, informal recognition may be given by anyone to anyone across the organization.

Reward Policy and Culture of Success

The success of a new organization depends, to a great extent, on teamwork. If the team is well knit and its members are dedicated and cooperative, the organization is likely to be effective. Hence, reward policy should be such as may encourage and support teamwork. The reward policy of start-up organizations should have provisions for performance rewards for both the teamwork and the individual employees, and there should be consistency in their implementation. There should also be provisions for effective performance management and setting internal equities. In a new organization or start-up, the rewards management in the initial stage is in the hands of an individual who may or may not have exposure to it. If he does not have, as happens in most cases, he usually takes reward management as an administrative system where he may not take a broad view of its various objectives and, therefore, may develop reward policies, which may not be appropriate in the wider interest of the organization. If it is so, there may be dissents and may even cause unhealthy competition among employees or their teams. Hence, reward policies should be conducive to create a culture of success for the organization.

Intending and Preparing for Growth

The basic intention of reward policy in the case of start-ups or large organizations should be to develop. For example, it is difficult for a start-up to have a pension scheme in its early years. 'How and when it should be introduced' can be discussed with the expert professionals/consultants. Similarly, expert advice can be obtained regarding introducing ESOP. Again, performance rewards should be given only when key milestones in the business plan are achieved. The reward policy regarding start-up organizations should keep the above points in consideration.

Involving Investors and Auditors

The new organization moving forward strongly and promising to grow will seek investment from providers of venture capital and, therefore, will be attaching a lot of weightages to long-term share schemes and other substantial incentives to top management personnel so that they may be fully committed and dedicated. The reward policy should be a high-risk reward policy.

Similarly, the auditors, advocates and others providing professional consultancy should also be taken care of in the reward policy because they provide advice, which plays an important role in the success of the organization.

Reward Policies for New Start-Up and High-Growth Organizations

Priority for reward is usually low on the priority list in the case of genuine start-up organizations as they are more concerned with the creation of long-term wealth. Even if there exists anything like a reward, it is mostly personalized and not systematic. However, if there exists any systematic approach to reward, it has been found that it is substantially impacted by the earlier experience and/ or prejudice of those who have introduced this approach. They usually ignore that part of it which appears demotivating to them and follow the rest. They might have also picked up some features from the reward policies they have come across earlier. They choose benefits like pensions that serve the purpose of some top people in the organization but cannot be applicable to other groups of employees in a maturing company. In such a case, the justification may be that in the case of unsatisfactory performance of the company, it is the high-powered cadre who is sacrificed quickly as compared to any group of people in the company.

Objectives of Start-Up Organizations' Reward Policy

The main objectives of reward policy in the case of start-up organizations are as follows:

1. To attract talent and keep it enthused in the direction of growing the organization.
2. To compensate those who have taken the risk to join a new company, the future of which is not yet certain.
3. To keep the base salary under control and supplement it with rewards which can be easily withdrawn in case of an emergency.
4. To keep the base salary at the market rate but attract rare skills by providing rewards.
5. To make the awardees aware that in the beginning only the minimum can be awarded, but when the company stabilizes the minimum can be improved, and a balance between the base salary and rewards may be initiated.
6. To celebrate the success of achieving key milestones in the business plan by offering bonuses or one-time non-cash rewards.
7. To seek rare skill by providing one-time favour at the top of the market.

Reward Policy and Joint Ventures

There may be another category of 'start-up', namely, a joint venture set up by two organizations designed to leverage a new technology, a new product and so on. A joint venture may need a different type of reward policy that may be quite challenging because the reward policies of these two organizations may be quite different as we come across in the case of acquisitions and mergers. Now the problem would be how to protect the interest of both the organizations. Whether the entitlements of individuals of these two organizations be retained or there should be a new reward policy based on the new agreements. Besides, joint ventures involve a greater amount of risk as compared to employment in established partner organizations. However, in order to carry forward the growth of the joint venture, it may be essential to have an aggressive reward policy. There may also be a question of whether long-term rewards should be based on the performance of the joint venture or partly on the performance of the parent organization. The reward policy is to take care of such controversial issues in the very early stages of the joint venture lest it may be difficult to solve the problem at later stages. Again, a joint venture, because of its different nature, may need certain specialists from outside. Obviously, their remuneration package may have to be different from what already exists in partner organizations. Such issues need to be taken care of in the reward policy.

Reward Management Processes

Developing and Introducing Reward Processes

Since it is not simple to develop and introduce reward management processes on its own for the organization, it is always advisable to use consultants in this regard. But why? The answer is not far to seek. First, the consultants are experts in their own field. They might have come across different situations and may have exposure to relevant techniques. They have their own understanding of various problems and exposure in analytical techniques. Hence, they can better guide in developing and introducing various reward management processes. Not only this, consultants are above local politics and personal interests. Therefore, they will be more objective, independent and under no pressure. Consultants can also take advantage of ideas already developed or are in the process of development in the organization but might have been facing resistance from vested interests or confronting the challenges of the change process. Besides, once the job is assigned to consultants, the management can concentrate on its routine problems due to having more time by entrusting job reward management processes to consultants. Now the next question arises, 'how to choose consultants'?

Choosing Consultants

Selection of consultants depends on the objectives of the reward management. Hence, both objectives and terms of reference should be well defined as these will form the basis of selecting the consultants. In case, the objectives are not clear, a special committee can be constituted to critically examine the issue and identify, in clear-cut terms, the objectives and terms of reference. Having done this now is the time to look at professional registers, which can provide enough guidance about the whereabouts of various consultants. Feedback from organizations, which have already used the services of consultants, can also be obtained. In case the organization is sure and certain about the expertise and other details of the consultant that serve its purpose well, it is all right. Otherwise, you may approach a few consultancy firms, discuss with them what you want and assess their capabilities to render the desired services and take a decision. In this regard, the organization will also have to decide whether it chooses a big consultancy firm that has all the resources at its disposal or a smaller specialist firm which will be good to investigate the organization's specific problem(s). Then, what are their fees and how much the organization can afford? What is their reputation and standing in the market? The cost of their proposal, the value they will provide to the organization and other things. Before taking a final decision, examine the proposals of the consulting firms and find out whether they have understood the requirements of the organization clearly and explicitly, and what benefits they will achieve for the organization.

It is only after looking into the above that the organization may make up its mind and enter into an agreement or contract, mentioning all relevant details, for example, if any modification is required, the stipulated period within which the project is to be completed, penalty for delay, fees to be paid, and any other relevant terms and conditions.

Help to Be Rendered by Consultants

There are several areas in which consultants can help the organizations. For example, the consultants can help in preparing reward strategies; correlating reward and performance management and career development; in tax implications of remuneration policies; in designing and formulating incentive/bonus (premium) plans; in proper pension schemes; in developing profit-sharing, gain sharing and ESOP schemes; in developing/revising pay structures; in conducting salary and reward surveys; in advising salary levels; in creating total reward packages; and so on.

How to Use Consultants?

The consulting firm(s) work in partnership with its/their clients and discuss various relevant issues at length such as what is/are the problem(s), what new problem(s) is/are likely to emerge and what can be the probable solution(s). It should also be ensured that the consultants would finish their job within the stipulated period and the agreed costs unless there are unforeseen circumstances. There should be progress that should be regularly checked. The organization should seek the preliminary findings and the probable solutions to the problems and give their feedback to the consultants. In case there is any alternate proposal, it should be discussed jointly, and a decision should be made.

It is necessary to develop trust between the organization and the consultants; ensure that the consultants have a genuine concern for the organization and there is a built partnership between the consultants and the firm. There should be regular discussions between the consultants and the executives concerned about the firm. The consultants should aim at making use of the potential of the employees of the organizations to their full. The consultants must understand the business strategy of the organization as well as the HR strategy and take care of the overall health of the organization. For example, when it comes to rewards, the consultants must know what the reward strategy of the organization is, does it need any modification, what are processes that should be involved in it and how well can it be implemented.

Reward Management Procedures

Reward management procedures which are needed by an organization to monitor the implementation of reward management policies and payroll costs are usually concerned with the following.

Monitoring the Implementation of Pay Policies and Practices

The pay policies and practices that need monitoring, in particular, relate to the pay structure with special reference to internal and external relativities, managing rewards, impact of grade drift, the implementation of pay progression policies, pay-for-performance, and impact of performance management (all these aspects have already been discussed in earlier chapters). However, in this regard, a few issues also need discussion, which are as follows:

1. **Compa-ratio analysis:** Compa-ratio, a short form of comparative ratio, establishes differences between policy and practice by measuring the relationship between actual and policy rates of pay as a percentage, in a graded pay structure. According to Armstrong and Murlis,[4] the policy value used is the reference point in the grade structure which represents the target rate for a fully competent individual in any job in the grade. This reference point is aligned to market rates in accordance with the organization's market stance policy. However, the reference point may be either at the mid-point in a symmetrical range (e.g., 100 per cent in an 80–120 per cent range), or at the top of the scale in an incremental structure.

Since, of late, organizations have started positioning the reference points at other points in the range, the same need not necessarily be placed at the mid-point.

Compa-ratios are popular for the simple reason that they answer in short to the question, 'how high or low is an organization paying its personnel relative to its policies on pay levels'? A method of calculating compa-ratios can be expressed as follows:

$$\text{Compa-ratio analysis} = 100 \times \frac{\text{Actual rate of pay}}{\text{Reference point rate of pay}}.$$

While a compa-ratio of 100 per cent indicates that actual and policy rates are the same, less than 100 per cent means that pay is below the reference point. And a greater than 100 per cent indicates that pay is more than a reference point.

Compa-ratios are of three types, namely, the individual compa-ratio, the group compa- ratio and the average compa-ratio.[5]

2. **Attrition:** Payroll costs go down on account of attrition because it happens when employees enter jobs at lower rates of pay than the previous incumbents or the employees find their pay rates in their existing organizations lower than the market rates and leave the organization. It is also said that attrition is instrumental in absorbing the pay increases within a range and that fixed incremental systems can be entirely self-financing due to attrition but normally this does not happen in practice. The formula to calculate attrition can be expressed as:

Total percentage increase in payroll arising from general or individual pay increases – Total percentage increase in average rate of pay

3. **Monitoring internal relativities:** At times, differentials may exist vertically within departments or between categories of employees. For monitoring, the study should be conducted to examine critically the differentials built into the pay structure. The study should also analyse the differences between the average rates of pay at different levels. If the findings of the study point that changes in pay increases are not in proportion to the changes in role or according to the impact of pay review, and therefore appear to be unfair, then the matter can be further looked into the reasons leading to the present state and if needed, remedial steps should be initiated.

Similarly, the pay rate between the pay of the CEO and that of the lowest paid employee should also be analyzed and if it is found that it has changed more than it should be, it should also be considered. For other jobs too, this exercise can be undertaken (also see Chapter 3).

4. **Monitoring external relativities:** An organization must make a choice whether it wants its pay levels to be above the market or less than the market or to match with the market. For the purpose of knowing market rates, the

organization can conduct salary surveys or can consult some relevant publications. Special attention should be paid to the market relativities of key jobs in various occupations or even job families. Necessary steps can be initiated to bring about changes in the existing pay rates of the organization as per the pay philosophy of the organization and the internal relativities (also see Chapter 6).

5. **Market place matching:** An organization has to make a decision with regard to the point in the review period when the aim will be to achieve the chosen competitive stance and to project the point in the review period where it intends to reach its competitive status. The three basic approaches to making this projection include: lead/lag, lag/lead, lead/lead[6]; the last approach, namely lead/lead, is considered to be the most competitive. All the same, it is expensive too.

Pay Reviews

For implementing the organization's reward policies as also for improving performance, continuous motivation and retention of employees, pay reviews are important means. The ways in which pay reviews are conducted and the outcome for employees reflect these policies and the culture of the organization. Hence, pay review should be able to meet the reasonable expectations of the employees about their reward vis-à-vis their performance and contribution, though budgetary constraints and trade unions too will play a role. Anyway, while planning and conducting a pay review, the following things should be kept into consideration (also see Chapter 6).

1. **General reviews:** When due to general market rate movements or increases in the cost of living or union agreements, an across-the-board pay hike is given to employees, which is referred to as a 'general review'. A general review may be conducted at the same time as individual reviews, or separately, as in the latter case the employees will be more motivated by distinct performance-related payments. However, organizations prefer review responding to market rate increases and assert that thereafter there is no need of conducting cost of living reviews.

2. **Structural reviews:** When changes in pay ranges due to increases in the market rates or cost of living take place, it is called a structural review. According to Armstrong and Murlis,[7] in a graded structure, a general market rate means that there had been a change in the pay policy line, which could be represented by the percentage difference between the old and new range reference points. If the existing differentials are to be maintained, this would mean a percentage increase for all grades.

In case there is a policy decision to change the pattern of differentials as a reaction to changes either in the organization structure or levels of responsibility, a structural review may be conducted. In case the existing range sizes have to be retained, the range's minimum and maximum would have to be increased by the same percentage as the reference point. However, the structural review should not be taken as implying that individual pay hikes should necessarily correspond with general hikes to 'range reference points' or 'maxima'.

3. **Individual reviews:** PRP or special achievement or even sustained performance bonuses are usually determined by individual reviews. The individual reviews are conducted by reference to performance ratings. The following are the main concerns of individual reviews:

    a. **Timing of reviews:** Individual reviews may either be conducted separately or can be integrated with general reviews as stated earlier. They may be conducted once or twice a year. However, the date of the review can vary as per the convenience of the organization. Some organizations conduct such reviews in periods of high inflation while some others conduct it when the organization is growing rapidly, and yet some other organizations conduct it when employee turnover is exceptionally high. There are also examples when a few organizations prefer to conduct individual reviews on the date of their employee's birthday or on the date of the employee's last promotion.

    b. **Individual review budget:** It is always better to express the performance review budget in terms of a percentage increase to the payroll that can be allowed for performance-related hikes. How much should be the size of the review budget will be influenced by several factors. For example, how much amount the organization can afford to pay based on payroll costs, and profit and budgeted revenues are important to determine the size of the review budget. The size of the review budget is also influenced by what the organization thinks it should do to remove a discrepancy between pay practice and pay policy. Again, the size of the review budget is affected by the policies of the organization on pay progression.

    c. **Individual review guidelines:** In order to maintain consistency and equity between departments and still allowing some amount of discretion, though in limits, and to manage the distribution of rewards within their departments, it is desirable to have some guidelines for managers. There may be guidelines with regard to rating practices like methods of rating fairly and observing consistency in the distribution of rewards. The important guidelines on linking pay hikes to ratings are as follows, though all the time budgetary limits have to be kept in view:

i. Guidelines on average and minimum/maximum pay increase: Such guidelines should indicate the average performance awards with limits on the maximum and minimum pay increases. Within the maximum and minimum limits, the managers have freedom to exercise their discretion in line with guidelines (also see Chapter 6).

ii. Guidelines on reward and rating: These guidelines relate performance pay hikes or bonuses, if applicable, to the ratings by the use of a scale. For example, for a rating of 'outstanding' performance, the percentage increase may be 12 per cent or so and for an 'effective' rating it may be 10 per cent and so on. There can be a provision of non-eligibility for an increase if the rating for performance is 'unsatisfactory'. Guidelines enable managers to maintain a consistent relationship between the rating and the reward. As per this approach, the managers must ensure that pay decisions are properly and fairly linked to performance and their own whims should not come in the way of aforesaid linking.

iii. Forced choice distribution guidelines: Such guidelines refer to the way different performance ratings and awards should be distributed among employees. It is done by defining the percentage of who should be rated at what level. For example, 5 per cent of employees may be given a rating of 'outstanding' and they get pay increases of 10 per cent, another 15 per cent be given the rating 'very satisfactory' and they are given a pay rise of 8 per cent, another 65 per cent be given a rating of 'satisfactory' and they are given pay rise of 5 per cent, and the remaining 15 per cent be given the rating of 'developing' and a pay rise of 3 per cent.

   The major defect of this approach is that the managers are forced to distribute the employees into a predetermined percentage of categories, which at times may not be desirable.

iv. Pay modelling: Today software packages for pay systems are available which enable organizations with formal pay structures and performance rating procedures to relate pay hikes exactly to the ratings they use. The size of the hike is determined by a formula that allocates money as per points.

v. Choice of method: An organization should study the aforesaid methods and choose anyone depending on its objectives. However, as far as possible, the benefits of consistency and uniformity should be available to employees.

vi. Dealing with market rates: The organization should deal with the increase in market rates that influence specific occupations or job families.

Planning and Implementing Pay Reviews

There may be negotiated pay reviews and non-negotiated pay reviews as follows:

Negotiated Pay Reviews

The steps required to plan and implement negotiated pay reviews may be as follows:

Step 1. Obtaining and analyzing data on pay agreements and market rate movements.

Step 2. Agreeing on target settlements, which can be comfortably affordable and comparable.

Step 3. Ensuring that the above does not affect any other unit or balance power between the employees or their trade unions and the management.

Step 4. Preparing a brief of the negotiations.

Step 5. Negotiating to have the best settlement as per targets.

Step 6. Entering into an agreement.

Step 7. Implementing the agreement.

Non-negotiated Pay Reviews

In the case of non-negotiated reviews, Armstrong and Murlis[8] have suggested the following steps:

Step 1. Obtaining and analyzing data.

Step 2. Preparing and obtaining agreements so that guidelines may be reviewed.

Step 3. Providing review managers with data, guidelines, budgets and timetables.

Step 4. Advising and supporting as and when required.

Step 5. Setting up peer review processes.

Step 6. Achieving acceptable proposals regarding pay policies, review guidelines and budget.

Step 7. Summarize the cost proposals.

Step 8. Obtaining approval.

Step 9. Updating payroll.

Step 10. General letters from managers to employees.

Step 11. Inform employees.

Procedures for Grading Jobs and Pay Rates Fixation

1. **Job grading:** It can be done only after an appropriate job evaluation exercise has been conducted by a duly constituted team which itself may be having an

expert in job evaluation or it must be assisted by a job evaluation expert from either inside or outside the organization. The steps that should be taken to control grade drift are discussed in Chapter 4 of this book.

2. **Fixing payroll on appointment:** There is a practice of allowing managers to have a big say in pay offers, but they should make use of this big say within the ambit of pay policies of the organization, also subject to the approval of the authority concerned. Policy guidelines should clearly spell out the conditions under which pay offers can be made above the minimum of the range. It is usually observed that pay policies permit offers to be made up to the reference point subject to the competence of the incumbent because offering pay above the reference point will leave little scope for expansion. Such pay offers are sometimes made because of market compulsions.

3. **Promotion hikes:** It is obvious that some pay hikes are given at the time of promotion which may vary between 5 and 10 per cent but the promotee, as far as possible, and should not be given above the reference point in the pay range of his new job. It enables the organization to have enough scope for performance-related hikes.

4. **Dealing with anomalies:** Despite all monitoring and controlling, anomalies do occur which should be dealt with during a pay review. In order to rectify anomalies, at times, it may need higher level hikes for those employees who are underpaid compared to their performance, or efforts put in, or time spent on the job. While it is easy to correct anomalies in the case of an underpaid employee in the fixed incremental structure, it will be difficult to do so in the case of an overpaid employee. It has also to be ensured that the cost incurred on anomaly correction is not substantial. It can be done if review managers are encouraged to fine-tune their pay recommendations. If needed, necessary guidance can be provided to managers.

Controlling Payroll Costs

1. **Pay review budgets:** Control is exercised through the review budgets to a great extent, but all the same managers are also required to use their own judgement and work as per pay policy. Pay review budgets spell out the overall increase in the payroll that the managers are allowed to recommend for their departments to take care of the cost of performance–competence-related awards. Since this is the basic principle of control, managers should be required not to cross the limit of budgetary provisions and be made account-able for any lapse.

    Though whatever is said above is very important, still additional control is required to ensure that no anomalies and drift occur in the distribution of pay in grades or bands.

    It can also be a fruitful exercise if the managers are given a pay review budget at the very beginning of the financial year and asked to plan how they are going to use it effectively, and the whole of this exercise is monitored by a superior or an expert.

It should also be remembered that pay review budgets are not meant to control the payroll costs emerging from new hiring, promotions or transfers. They are normally concerned with performance–competence pay awards. That is why some companies workout budgets which take control of increases caused due to promotions or upgrading and so on (also see Chapter 6).

2. **Total payroll budgeting:** Payroll costs depend on the number of people employed on different jobs and their rates of pay; pay hikes caused due to general and individual pay revenues; amount offered to new appointees; extra pay earned by promotees or on upgrading; and so on. According to Armstrong and Murlis, the total payroll budget is based on present payroll costs adjusted for forecast changes in the number and mixture of those employed in the budget centre and the forecast cost of general and individual pay increases. While preparing budgets, guidelines are issued to managers regarding what they should allow for an individual and general pay review pay hikes. The managers are supposed to keep themselves within these guidelines while conducting pay reviews and preparing budgets. In case the financial performance of the organization is good, then more funds can be made available to finance performance or competence-related hike. The budget guidelines can state the limit under which extra pay costs due to such hikes can be incorporated into the budget.

In case managers anticipate additional staff or promotions, which may be above the guidelines, they can make a case for the additional costs in the proposed budgets, though they will have to justify these additional costs in terms of the value anticipated to be added to the organization. Efforts should be made to prove that the additional costs are self-financing. However, the managers expect to maintain or exceed the present level of output by dropping some employees and thus reducing the cost of pay rolls. They can make out a case for the cash so saved due to the reduced number of employees, either to finance the performance–competence-related or career development-related increases. The cash available on account of reduced costs due to dropping some employees can also be used to reward staff for their additional contribution.

Here is a word of caution. Since these extra increases may cause internal inequities, these awards must be proved fully justified in terms of extra value added to the organization. This needs rigorous exercise. It is advisable that payroll budgets should be fixed during the year as a reaction to new projects or changes in the levels of activities. It is better if the organizations have interim forecasts once or twice a year to enable managers to review their original budget or end it if required.

Budget expenditure should be controlled by regular reports by analyzing differences. However, managers should be answerable to explain them. Such budget expenditure control exercises help in effective control over payroll costs. Still, there may be a need for adequate support consultants or an expert from the HR department of the organization.

3. **Control:** It becomes easier to control payroll costs and pay policies if there exists a well-defined and clearly understood pay structure in the organization. Similarly, clearly defined pay review guidelines and budgets help a lot in controlling payroll costs and pay policies. Other things that help in this direction are the existence of a systematic process to monitor and implement pay policies and costs against budget, well-laid out procedures of grading jobs and fixing pay rates, the well-defined authority of the managers that they can exercise at each level for deciding rates of pay as well as pay hikes. It will be still better if there is an expert HR person to support and guide the reviewing managers (also see Chapter 6).

   a. **Control of grade drift:** It is not uncommon to come across cases where employees want to be upgraded without a justifiable increase in their job size, which is usually called grade drifting. It can be controlled to a great extent by providing and using a competent and strong evaluation panel which is fully trained in job measurement on a formal basis. If needed, there must be a provision for getting guidance in such matters wherever necessary. Such job panels should also have the authority to ask questions and ask for justification on any claims that an increase in responsibility justifies the regrading. Not only this, there should be rigorous comparisons with well-established benchmark jobs and further that there may be re-evaluation of such jobs. It is also common to see that managers ask for regrading jobs on account of market rate pressures, threats of leaving the job by the employee(s) or difficulties in hiring suitable substitutes. Such demands should not be met easily because these can be tackled on other platforms.

   b. **Developing ownership without losing control:** It is advisable that if line managers take ownership of reward practice, that is, empowering them, they should take the responsibility of making decisions on pay-related matters also though within the framework of related guidelines. In order to make the right decisions within the framework of guidelines and the proper implementation of guidelines, it will be good if the key reward issues and processes such as job evaluation, performance management, performance rating, paying for performance, competence or skill and so on are discussed and agreed with managers, team leaders and other employees. It should also be ensured that new freedoms and related responsibilities are clearly understood by all concerned. Team leaders and managers should be properly trained in making appropriate decisions regarding rewards. Besides, managers should realize that though they may have a reasonable amount of independence, still be interdependent on other sister units and therefore their decisions may impact them. Hence, they should make thoughtful decisions. Not only this but reward management processes should also be periodically audited departmentally to ensure that proper procedures are being followed and policies appropriately implemented.

In addition to the above points, computerized HR information systems should be developed so that unnecessary reporting, filling out forms and so on are avoided.

c. **Control information:** In order to generate control information, the best way is perhaps to make use of computers. However, some jobs such as control data on costs against budget and outcome of the pay reviews are better done if presented manually. For this, data sheets and other forms can be worked out and filled out manually.

d. **Salary planning:** Since individuals have their own abilities, aptitudes, needs, skills and performance, planning and administration should take care of these. Of course, the organization too has its own needs and the same needs to be fulfilled. The planning should, therefore, adopt the integrated approach. However, salary planning should view employees as individuals who are always concerned about their careers. Salary planning should ensure that incentives and rewards are instrumental in enhancing the skills, abilities, competencies and performance of the employees so that career opportunities also get secured and promoted wherever necessary.

Besides, in a pay system, progression rates differ according to the performance of employees leading to some anomalies. These anomalies emerge because sometimes performance suddenly goes up and sometimes it goes down, and employees are, therefore, underpaid or overpaid accordingly. Hence, under such circumstances, employees should be treated individually, and anomalies corrected accordingly. Pay planning must take care of this aspect because in this direction reward processes are to be handled very cautiously and effectively (also see Chapter 6).

Evaluation of Reward Processes

1. **Need:** It may not be very difficult to initiate reward processes in an organization but it is quite difficult to ensure that the same are functioning effectively. It is here that the evaluation of reward processes comes into vogue. Hence, organizations need to constantly evaluate whether the reward processes are serving the desired purpose or not. For example, despite high salary and other benefits being extended to the employees, there is a lack of motivation among employees. In such a situation, organizations should check whether the reward systems are in place and effective to motivate the employees. Hence, the necessity of evaluation of reward processes. Next, if the attrition rate is high or employees are migrating to other organizations, then the

organizations concerned should go for an evaluation of reward processes. Next, if despite good reward systems, organizations are not performing well in the market place, they should go for an evaluation of reward processes. One of the simplest ways out for such organizations is to get feedback from their employees to find out whether the employees are happy with the current reward processes, that is, they are getting reward matching with performance or contributions.

Since the bottom line of any organizational process is whether it is effective in achieving the objectives for which it is instituted, it is desirable to get the evaluation of rewarded processes conducted at periodical intervals.

2. **Methods of evaluation of reward process:** Among the several methods of evaluation of reward processes, one of them is to get satisfaction surveys and assessments done in a confidential manner. In this regard, blind surveys, in which the identity of employees is kept confidential, can be conducted to know what the opinion of employees about the effectiveness of reward processes is. The other method can be exit interviews, which are conducted at the time when an employee exits the organization. At that time, the employee is under no pressure, and he can reveal his feelings candidly.

   Not only employees but the organization can also explain their perspective about the effectiveness of reward processes. Organizations can conduct market rate surveys and also can get consultants engaged to set their reward processes evaluated. The plus point of getting an external survey of reward processes conducted is that it is likely to be objective and unbiased. Another method can be that the organization can assess whether the rewards match the performance or contributions of the employees, that is, whether the high performers are being suitably rewarded.

3. **Role of organizational politics:** In many organizations, rewards are given to the favourite of some managers, resulting in frustration among high performers. In this regard, it can be said that there should be a balancing act between the competing interests for rewards on the one side and the desirability of rewarding talent on the other. Although it is true that partiality in rewarding the employees cannot be eliminated altogether, an all-out effort should be made to get the reward processes evaluated.

Recent and Future Trends in Reward Management

By and large, reward management strategy in our country has been the extension of business strategy of the organization. Trends in reward practices can only be forecasted in the light of predictions on how business strategies and programmes flowing from them are likely to develop.[9] Therefore, changes in reward management are the outcomes of changes in business strategies and practices which themselves have been in response to changes in the competitive environment.

Of course, one of the recent changes in the reward management approach is that of 'total reward'.

Armstrong and Murlis[10] have pointed out the following trends in reward management:

1. **Total reward:** The concept of 'total reward', which emerged during the late 1990s, focuses on the importance of considering all the aspects of reward as an integrated and coherent whole. The basic reason for the emergence of the concept of total reward might be that it takes into consideration the combined effect of the whole range of reward measures on commitment, job engagement and, above all, motivation. It has attracted the attention of organizations towards non-financial rewards, including intrinsic rewards through financial rewards, that is, extrinsic rewards too motivate but relatively to a lesser degree. The concept takes care of talent management including attracting, maintaining and retaining talent.

    The concept of total reward recognizes the importance of the concept of employee value proposition (EVP) which has drawn the attention of people worldwide from all corners, including industries, banking, calculation, health care, tourisms and so on. Total reward concept appreciated EVP because the latter is instrumental, to a great extent, in attracting and retaining talent which is crucial to the survival and growth of any business. EVP answers the question: 'Why should an employee join a particular organization'?—that is, the value that an employee gets in return for working at a particular organization. That is why every organization endeavours to build a unique brand of itself. Coming back to total reward management, no doubt, as stated earlier, the traditional elements of reward management such as pay and benefits play their own role, but total reward takes into account the impact of intangible and intrinsic aspects of rewards. These examples of such intrinsic rewards comprise a lot of things such as working environment, leadership style, recognition, care of the staff and other environmental factors.

    It is therefore implied that all elements of employment experienced should be aligned.

2. **Broad banding:** Broad banding has become a recent trend in the world of reward management. Broad banding refers to collapsing a number of grades into a smaller number of broad grades with wide ranges. Since the late 1990s, many organizations have gone into it without understanding it comprehensively. For example, they have not been able to appreciate the difference between, say, a 4-banded structure with zones in a band and a 12-graded structure. They have also not been able to appreciate the point of unstructured broad bands if, practically, they simply consist of spot rates. It has also been observed that broad-banded structures are more difficult to manage than narrow-graded structures, despite claiming that they would be easier. Another problem is that broad banding leads to building greater expectations

of substantial pay opportunities, which in most cases do not get fulfilled. Again, it is not that simple to explain to the employees the working of the broad banding and how employees are going to be impacted by it. Not only this, but it is also difficult to justify objectively the decisions on movements within bands than in any other type of grade and pay structures.

The recent trend is to develop broad-graded structures with just 6–10 grades because these are managed like the traditional narrow-graded structure using reference points, zones and compa-ratios. These are also associated with career family structures.

3. **Job evaluation:** Around the late 1990s, many organizations had abandoned job evaluation, but it re-emerged in the 2000s, though playing a supporting role instead of a driver's role in decisions related to grading. It is because organizations started realizing that because of additional importance being attached to equal pay, internal equity is important, hence job evaluation.

4. **Career and job family structures:** Another recent development in the realm of reward management is the use of career and job family structures. According to Armstrong and Murlis,[11] a career family structure is one in which separate job families are identified and defined but a common grade and pay structure applies to all families. As a matter of fact, a typical career family structure divides a broad-graded structure into several families, each of which, according to Armstrong and Murlis,[12] contains levels that are defined by reference to key activities, and competence of knowledge and skill requirements. In this way, they define career paths within and between families. It is because of this that it is viewed as part of an integrated approach to HRM. In career families, it is the continuous development that is attached to the first preference, pay considerations come later.

5. **Greater realism about the role of reward:** Reward creates a lot of expectations among employees who are later disillusioned because in most cases not all their expectations are met. It should be clearly realized that reward management is not the strategic lever for change. However, reward supports cultural changes, which is why it is surviving and flourishing too.

6. **Line management capability:** Another trend emerging in reward management is about devolving more authority to line managers in matters of pay decision-making. But doubts are also being expressed in the capability of line managers to make such decisions fairly, consistently and at the same time falling in line with policy guidelines. Since line managers remain in direct touch with their subordinates and know a lot about their work behaviour and performance, they should be assigned a part of the responsibility in pay decision-making. At the same time, it is also advisable that line managers be given adequate training so that they may discharge their responsibilities appropriately.

7. **Flexible benefits:** Though the concept of flexible benefits is not a new one, the novelty of this trend is that it is being now adopted by more and more

organizations. Flexible benefits not only fulfil the increasingly varied needs of a diverse workforce that we now come across more visibly but also enhance the perceived value of the package by targeting expenditure into areas chosen by employees. The concept of flexible benefits is concerned with first finding out what employees want through surveys or otherwise and then tailoring the reward offer accordingly. It serves the greater interest of employees because they opt for whatever meets their needs and forego what is not wanted by them. However, this approach may not always be in the best interests of an employer because it is not always possible to meet all the needs of employees. However, it is always good to balance the needs of the employees to the extent possible and simultaneously reinforce the values of the employer through reward.

8. **Equal pay:** The trend of equal pay has also come into prominence since the 2000s because of the findings and recommendations of various committees and commissions. The trend has necessitated not only the introduction of analytical job evaluation but also of conducting equal pay reviews and audits. In our country, the trend has got momentum in public sector undertakings and making its way into the private sector by and by.

9. **Contribution-related pay:** Contribution-related pay is another recent trend coming into vogue as an alternative to competence–performance-related pay. Contribution-related pay is, as a matter of fact, a combination of PRP and competence-related pay as contribution-related pay rewards employees for both their inputs (competence) and outputs (performance), thus making a holistic process.

Some Other Trends

In addition to the above recent trends in reward management pointed out by Armstrong and Murlis, other trends are also noticeable which are as follows:

1. **Transformation of leadership:** Though delegation of authority follows a formal hierarchical structure with clear lines of accountability, the digitalized world of today has come across larger success with networked organizations, which often enable individuals to initiate leadership, sometimes even without formal authority, especially where work relationships are numerous. Today, leadership is not so much about leading employees as it is about orchestrating the ecosystem of work. And such types of employees are being rewarded suitably. In future, leadership will require agile thinking, global operating skills, communication skills and interpersonal skills.

2. **More personalized and transparent rewards:** Another trend making its roads into corporate and other sectors is a more personalized and transparent management of total rewards. Since a job-based pay structure is also coming into prominence which allows employees to more easily compare their pay to those offered to others, personalized rewards are also getting popularity.

Earlier, disclosing pay and benefits openly was not considered desirable, but today with the advancement of social media and digital platforms, it has become easier to get details of everyone's pay and benefits. Today, in certain countries, it has become a statutory requirement to publically disclose the details of executive pay. There is now a trend towards transparency about rewards.

Again, today the concept of contribution-related pay is replacing the concept of PRP because of the changing business models and shifting nature of work which are now challenging the individual performance definition and the role of basic pay.

Today, the concept of 'guaranteed jobs' is also losing ground and organizations are looking to redefine what a career means. Besides, career security is being enabled through career development.

3. **Targeted recruitment driven by social media and cognitive assessment:** Today, digital tools such as social media and cognitive assessment are playing an important role in the area of recruitment of employees. Cognitive technologies include self-learning, predictive algorithms and natural language processing. Cognitive assessment can be used in HRM in several ways like machine learning platforms matching candidates to jobs through a fit score based on skills and career experiences. As far as social media is concerned, 'social listening' makes it easy to get an organization's and competitors' publicly available reviews which can serve the purpose of reputation checks. Artificial intelligence (AI) reduces the man-hours needed for HR recruitment. Employees having expertise in the use of digital tools, cognitive assessment and AI are being suitably rewarded by organizations.

4. **Leveraging employee analytics to improve organizational performance:** Another recent trend in future reward management is to use employee analytics and predictive models which enable HR management to identify, recruit, develop and retain the right talent more effectively so that organizational performance can be improved. Data analytics is also instrumental in identifying employees who intend to leave the organization in the near future. The organization can, therefore, take steps to convince them to continue with the organization by taking remedial steps. The employees engaged in people analytics should be suitably rewarded.

5. **Redefining HRM:** Today, organizations are putting people analytics at the core and data analytics is making roads into routine HR processes consistently. Besides, the predictive power of people analytics is being used to improve decision-making. Then, HR operations are changing due to the use of highly sophisticated automation tools and standardized processes. Consequently, the level of service and employee experience is getting raised. Again, the role of a business partner is being replaced with a new talent value leader, usually called TVL. Besides, HR professionals being freed up by functional changes

in HR operations can devote more time to strategic work. Due to all this, new roles such as robot trainer, talent and AI integrator, cyber ecosystem designer, people analytics professionals and virtual cultural architect are emerging. Hence, HRM is being redefined these days and is likely to continue so in the future as well.

6. **Improving the employee experience by applying product design thinking:** Today, added importance is being attached to human factors. That is why it is being said, 'staff first, customers second and shareholders third'. It is so because, in today's digital era, talent and ideas, instead of capital, have become critical to the success of an organization. It is being realized that an organization is primarily composed of its employees, customers and products. It is alright that financially sound organizations have an edge over others to hire talent by offering more pay but today most talents are attaching more importance to other factors beyond profit like employee experience. Hence, organizations are not hesitating in adapting product design in order to improve employee experience. This will shift focus from HR programmes or process to the employee. This is a new phenomenon in reward management.

7. **Working for more hours:** Today, most organizations expect that their professional-level employees work for more hours than they did earlier.

In addition to the aforesaid trends, some other trends in reward management are as follows:

1. In order to attract, retain and engage employees, organizations have started to have in place an approach to talent management and reward, irrespective of economic environment.
2. Adapting programmes to changing conditions and environment.
3. Defining different employment experiences for different employee segments.
4. Aligning talent management and reward programmes.
5. Most organizations formally identify job performers and relatively a smaller number of organizations identify critical-skill employees or high-potential employees.
6. Not all high-performing employees are rewarded.
7. A smaller number of organizations plan team pay.
8. More flexibility in benefit packages.
9. Some organizations are introducing broad-banded pay structures.
10. Establishing well-developed career management programmes.
11. Establishment of well-designed implementation of performance management processes.
12. Line managers make pay decisions to some extent.
13. Treating employees as stakeholders.

14. Flexible benefit schemes.
15. Developing more integrated pay structures.
16. Use of variable pay.
17. More rigorous examination of cost-effectiveness of PRP.
18. Integration of reward, and other HR processes and practices.
19. Alignment of pay strategy more effectively with business strategy.

Boardroom Pay

Usually, boardroom pay and pay hikes, which are usually high, invite criticism because the pay and pay hikes in the case of rank-and-file employees are normally kept at a minimum or so. That is why, of late, major institutional shareholders have shown their interest in linking boardroom rewards with corporate performance and success. In the past, in most cases, directors used to be mere 'rubber stamps' on the decisions made by the top management. It was so because, in many cases, directors used to be either retired corporate executives, relatives of shareholders, suppliers, advocates and so on. Today, shareholders are critical of high director compensation and, therefore, the scenario is changing as most employees and shareholders feel that the boardroom pay is not keeping pace with the success of organizations.

There has been no uniform pattern regarding boardroom remuneration. It differs from industry to industry and organization to organization. In most cases, the principles of boardroom remuneration are not followed.

Guiding Principles for Boardroom Remuneration

The guiding principles for boardroom remuneration are as follows:

1. Pay policies and practices for executive directors should be able to attract and retain talent of high order who may increase shareholder values.
2. Their pay should be as per the pay philosophy and strategy of the organization.
3. Their pay should be so tailored as to match the competitive environment, management style and culture of the organization.
4. Their pay should create a culture of pay-for-performance and add to shareholder values.
5. Their pay should be based on their individual needs and not at the cost of organization's goals and objectives.
6. Their pay schemes should be simple to be understood and explicitly communicated.
7. Pay philosophy, design of the scheme and pay levels should have the approval of and be monitored by independent non-executive directors.
8. Their pay processes should become part of the overall management process.

Individual Remuneration Package

Most of the work and practices on individual pay packages of directors of companies originated from the United States of America and Australia, followed by other countries. Often organizations find it difficult to promote an individual to the board level from within the organization. Also, they find pay negotiations tough from those who are picked up from outside the organization. Not only this, the demand for pay package may be one which is competitive not only nationally but also globally. The latter mostly occurs in the case of pay packages offered at the top of major multinationals and international organizations. This is because of the following reasons:

1. Today, the market rates of people at the top of organizations are not secret. People are aware of them. Hence, they try to catch up with remuneration based on market rates. Directors expect to get a substantial rise in remuneration to make it worth moving from their present location. Hence, they prove very expensive if recruited from outside the organization.
2. Similarly, in case people are already in a good position and if approached by search consultants and so on, realize that they are in a better state to negotiate major improvements package for themselves.
3. People already settled in their positions would like to shift to new organizations as directors only if they get a very high salary as the price for their moving to new organizations where they carry the risk of proving themselves worth the job. Hence, they ask for high compensation to cover the aforesaid risk.
4. People expect a substantial rise in their pay package if they know that they are going to a 'sleepy' organization where they will have to wake up to a not so alert and dynamic workforce as it should be.
5. People also get in touch with their own consultants and remuneration specialists to find out what would be a bad deal for themselves to join elsewhere as director or so.

In view of the high expectations of people enticed to join at the top in an organization, the organization too should be flexible. They should, therefore, be willing to offer a tailor-made remuneration package to fit individual requirements. Organizations should be able to defend themselves appropriately if the package of a newly appointed director creates internal inequities. Organizations should also have a clear idea as to which item of pay they are willing to negotiate. They should also have an idea about the maximum they can offer to the newly appointed candidate.

Ensuring Stay for Due Term

Normally boardroom people are appointed for a fixed term, say, 1–3 years or so. But it has also been experienced that in some cases the directors or people at the top quit even before the completion of their term. In order to cover such uncertainties, the penalty clause can be incorporated in the written contract itself at the time of appointment. In addition, the following options are available to tempt the people at the top of the organization to continue for the whole term or for a longer stay if so required.

Share Option Plans

In share option plans, options are awarded to people at the top that they will be offered the aforesaid number of shares of the company if long-term performance conditions are met by them. Some other conditions can be that they will be entitled to a certain amount of shares if the company's earnings per share remains above the rate of inflation for a given period and if they continue with the company for that period.

Performance Share Schemes

Under such schemes, top executives are provisionally awarded shares. However, the release of shares is subject to the company's performance over a certain period, say, three years or so. Release of shares is also conditioned that they should have continued with the organization till the end of the stipulated period.

Deferred Bonus Schemes

Under deferred bonus schemes, a part of the top executive's annual bonus is deferred for a certain period, say, two years. The deferred amount is converted into shares, each of which is matched with an extra free share subject to the condition that the executive continues with the organization till the expiry of the stipulated period.

Corporate Governance and Boardroom Pay

Corporate governance and boardroom pay may differ from country to country and from organization to organization.

Chapter Review

1. Reward management refers to the formulation and implementation of policies, processes and strategies that aim at rewarding the employees of an organization fairly, equitably and consistently keeping in view their value to the organization. Reward management, therefore, generates and operates officially a reward structure for the organization concerned, which deals with issues such as pay policy, processes, practices, W&S admin and total reward. However, reward policies are strongly influenced by the principles as well as the philosophy of reward the organization behaves.

2. There are several objectives of reward policies such as recognizing the contribution of employees, motivating them, and attracting and retaining employees. Reward policy should ensure that rewards are market driven. At times, an organization must take liability with the internal equity to keep pace with the market and be able to attract candidates who are in short supply. In order to attract rare candidates, the attraction strategy is based on a competitive remuneration package including 'golden hellos'. Then, in order to retain the desired talent in the organization, it is the market, not the company that will ultimately determine the movement of employees. The reward policy should also clarify the link between business performance and pay. Talent management relates to linking HR policies and practices to both attracting and retaining people. Reward policies should make it clear whether employees are to be paid for competence, contribution, performance or skills. Reward policies should also specify the stand on contingent rewards and other forms of non-monetary rewards. They should also clarify the organization's stand on the assimilation of current employees in the revised pay structure, employee involvement, role of line managers, transparency and flexibility.

3. Reward policies should keep into consideration the intrinsic needs of employees. Reward policies should maintain a perfect balance between extrinsic and intrinsic needs. The policies should be well-designed and effective. They should attach due importance to recognition and should make recognition and reward a part of the culture of the organization.

4. In case of new organizations/start-ups, reward policies should keep into consideration how to develop in future and should involve investors, auditors, consultants and professorial as and when required. There are several objectives of reward policies of start-ups such as attracting-retaining desired talent and salary control. In some cases, the reward policies for new, start-up and high-growth organizations must be a little bit different, and so is the case with joint ventures.

5. There are several reward management processes such as developing and introducing reward processes. While choosing consultants, the objectives of reward management should be kept into consideration. Consultants render help in several areas like preparing reward strategies. Similarly, there are several reward management procedures such as monitoring the implementation of pay policies and practices with the help of compa-ratio analysis, attrition and monitoring internal and external relativities and reviews.

6. Regarding planning and implementing pay reviews, there may be negotiated pay reviews and non-negotiated pay reviews. As far as procedures for grading jobs and pay rates fixation are concerned, there may be job grading, fixing payroll on appointments, promotion hikes and dealing with anomalies.

7. As far as controlling payroll costs are concerned, this can be done through pay review budgets and total payroll budgeting. Controls can be exercised through control of grade drift, developing ownership without losing control, control information and salary planning.

8. Evaluation of reward processes is very important and should, therefore, be conducted periodically. There are several methods of evaluation of reward processes such as satisfaction surveys, interviews and taking help from consultants. Partiality in rewarding should be kept aside.

9. Regarding recent and future trends in reward management, the concept of 'total reward', which emerged in the 1990s, takes into consideration both the extrinsic and the intrinsic rewards. Intangible rewards will remain in the limelight. Then comes broad branding, which is a recent trend. Job evaluation was abandoned by many organizations in the late 1990s, but it continued to play a supporting role. Career and job family structures are a recent development. Delegating more authority to line managers is also becoming an important demand and an emerging trend. Flexible benefits are a new concept and are getting momentum. Equal pay is also getting into prominence since the 2000s. Contribution-related pay is also a recent trend and attracting the attention of more and more organizations. Other trends include transformation of leadership, more transparent and personalized rewards, targeted recruitment driven by social media and cognitive assessment, leveraging employee analytics to improve organizational performance, redefining HRM, improving the employee experience by applying product design thinking, working for more hours by executives and many others.

10. Boardroom pay and the related pay hikes do not synchronize with contribution. Hence, a lot of criticism. Principles of the boardroom are not being properly followed, which are many in number. Individual remuneration package in the case of directors of the company is very difficult as in most cases they are appointed from outside the organization. The issues to be kept into consideration while appointing new directors and fixing their pay should include ensuring their stay for full terms, share option plans, performance share schemes, deferred bonus schemes and the like.

DISCUSSION QUESTIONS

1. Discuss the concept, meaning and objectives of reward management.
2. Discuss the concept, meaning and objectives of reward management policy.
3. Discuss the main reward management processes and procedures, especially the compa-ratio analysis.
4. Discuss what is meant by pay reviews, especially the individual review and procedures for grading jobs, and how pay rates are fixed.
5. Discuss the various methods of controlling payroll costs.
6. Discuss how to evaluate reward processes.
7. Discuss the recent and future trends in reward management.
8. Discuss the concept of total rewards.

9. Discuss the issues involved in boardroom pay and also the principles for boardroom remuneration.
10. Discuss the concept of bonus and the implications of deferred bonus schemes.

Individual and Group Activities

1. Individually visit some big organizations and discuss with HR officials there about the objectives of their reward management and reward management policy and prepare a brief report.
2. In a group of two, discuss with the HR officials of a big manufacturing organization their reward management processes and procedures, especially pay review and how jobs are graded in their organization.
3. In a group of two, pay a visit to some service organization and find out from its HR and finance officials how they control payroll costs.
4. Individually discuss with HR officials of some big organizations the recent and future trends in reward management, especially with regard to 'total reward'.
5. In a group of two, visit some large-scale organizations and find out how the HR officials determine the remuneration of their boardroom directors.

APPLICATION CASE

While auditing the annual accounts of sugar mills, it was pointed out by the internal auditors that the payroll costs were too high to be borne with by the sugar mills in future. They especially cited the case of the board of directors. In the last three years, despite the fact that one of the directors was being paid at a much higher rate than the competitors companies were paying their directors, he left the company just after the completion of half of the term he was supposed to complete. Another director completed his term but had attended just one-fourth of the meetings held by the board of directors during his tenure of stay. The overall performance of the sugar mills was pathetic and the dues to be paid to sugarcane suppliers had accumulated substantially. Even the wages of workers of the sugar mills were not being paid regularly and on time. Hence, their trade union had also been raising hue and cry. It appeared that most top officials were also warned about the future of the sugar mills. Their grievances were that they were not getting proper guidelines from the board.

In the General Body Meeting of the sugar mills, these issues were raised and it was decided to constitute a high-powered committee, consisting of the finance manager and the general manager of the sugar mills, a renowned consultant from outside the sugar mills, and the general secretary of the trade union of the mills. The committee was especially asked to examine the remuneration of directors. The committee was asked to submit its report within 15 days as the fresh crushing season was to start shortly.

The committee used to meet almost every working day. It made several observations. With regard to remuneration and related issues pertaining to directors, it was observed that despite the fact that directors are appointed for a fixed term, most of them leave without completing their term—thus disturbing the functioning of the board. There was not available any stock option plan which could have tempted the director not to leave before the completion of their term. There was no correlation between their remuneration and performance of the sugar mills, and there was no term or condition to this effect in their letter of appointment. There was also no deferred bonus scheme that could have tempted the directors to give their best and complete their term of appointment.

The report of the committee was submitted in time to the officials detailed by the general body in its meeting when the decision was taken to constitute the committee.

Questions

1. Do you think that constituting a committee by the general body to investigate the problem was justified? Yes or no, why? Give arguments.
2. Do you agree with the observations of the committee? Have you got any other suggestions?
3. What do you suggest for monitoring and controlling the remuneration of directors/boardroom?

Notes

1 Armstrong and Murlis, *Reward Management*, 41.
2 Ibid., 42.
3 P. Cappelli, 'A Market Driven Approach to Meeting Talent', *Harvard Business Review* 78, no. 1 (January–February 2000): 3–11.
4 Armstrong and Murlis, *Handbook of Reward Management*, 529.
5 For details, see ibid., 529–530.
6 Ibid., 535.
7 Ibid., 535.
8 Ibid., 540.
9 Armstrong and Murlis, *Reward Management*, 587.
10 Ibid.
11 Ibid., 598.
12 Ibid.

11

TAX PLANNING AND THE INCOME TAX ACT, 1961

LEARNING OBJECTIVES

After studying this chapter, the reader should be able to:

1. Understand the objectives of tax planning.
2. Explain the various types of tax planning.
3. Explain deductions to be made while computing total income (Sections 80 A to 80 VV).
4. Explain fringe benefits (Section 115W to 115WM).
5. Explain the tax authorities (Section 116 to 138).

Introduction

Think of the mighty empires, powerful dynasties and the era of emperors and monarchs. Once mighty powerful and in command, they have all faded into oblivion to rest in a few pages of their history. What they have left for the succeeding generations is their legacy. The most conspicuous part of the legacy is the system of Taxation. It would be fruitful to study in detail Acharya Chanakya's celebrated treatise: the *Arthashashtra*. Written about 2,000 years back, it is a fountainhead of wisdom regarding the determination, imposition, collection and utilization of taxes.

As in the past, so in the present, the tax collected by the Government of the day is utilized for maintaining an army, police, running of railways, provision

DOI: 10.4324/9781032626123-11

of basic amenities to the citizens like water, electricity, education, health care, creation of infrastructure like national highways, airports, seaports, etc., among others.

As a matter of fact, a Tax is an income of the Government and an expenditure of the citizens and all others mandated by law to pay the Tax. Therefore, while, on the one hand, a tax system should be so designed that it evokes maximum compliance by the taxpayers and therefore be instrumental in generating maximum revenue for the government, it should also, on the other hand, enable the taxpayers to budget and plan for their tax liability appropriately. In the taxation regime, therefore, there is no room for presumption and nothing can be taken to be implied. Everything needs to be properly planned. This implies that the tax an individual or a corporate has to pay is a matter of planning for them. It is here that tax planning comes into vogue.

Tax planning is a very wide and broad subject. It requires specialized knowledge to deal with multifarious aspects of Tax. Chartered Accountants, Cost Accountants, Advocates and experts in taxation matters are qualified professionals who are authorized to render their services in and out of court of law regarding all aspects of Tax.

In the above backdrop, it is necessary to understand the term which here means 'Income Tax'. It can be defined as an annual tax on the income of a taxpayer.

Meaning and Definition of Tax Planning

Tax is a burden and a liability imposed on the taxpayer by the government as per prevailing law. Tax planning per se is an exercise involving the reduction of a determined tax burden/liability as per law. It also includes the utilization of deductions, exemptions and other benefits offered by the government. Tax Planning, therefore, means an understanding, analysis and interpretation of a taxpayer's financial status at each time so that he may take full advantage of relevant deductions, exemptions and other benefits as per provisions of the existing Income Tax legislation.

Such legislation may comprise a number of considerations like taxable income in the total income, the timing of incomes received and expenditures incurred, investments made, etc.

Objectives of Tax Planning

The primary objective of tax planning is the timely discharge of tax liability and compliance with the provisions of the Income Tax Act, 1961 (as amended), keeping in view the interest of a taxpayer.

It aims at reducing tax liability, optimally utilizing the deductions, exemptions and other benefits and thus, achieving tax efficiency.

Why Tax Planning?

One of the biggest benefits of tax planning is that after availing the permissible deductions,

exemptions and other benefits, whatever money is saved can be utilized for making investments. It enables investing tax exempted money and generating a flow of white money in the economy, thus contributing to the economic development of the country and aiding in the economic stability of the taxpayer. Another significant benefit is the avoidance of time-consuming, multi-layered, costly and cumbersome litigation outcome which is uncertain.

Types of Tax Planning

It can be classified into the following:

- **Short-range tax planning**—Under this method, tax planning is thought of and executed at the end of the financial year. Investors resort to this planning to search for ways to limit their tax liability legally when the financial year comes to an end. As such, the taxpayer has no option but to comply with the existing legal tax provisions. This method does not take partake long-term commitments. However, it can still promote substantial tax savings.
- **Long-range tax planning**—This plan is chalked out at the beginning of the fiscal year and exercises options about various deductions, exemptions, benefits, etc. The taxpayer follows this plan throughout the year. It can prove useful in the long run.
- **Permissive tax planning**—Tax planning falls under the provisions of the law in force. Tax planning in India offers several provisions such as deductions, exemptions, contributions and incentives. For example, Section 80C of the Income Tax Act, 1961 (as amended) offers several types of deductions on various tax-saving instruments.
- **Purposive tax planning**—Tax planning with a specific objective. It involves using tax-saver instruments with a specific purpose in mind. This ensures that a taxpayer obtains optimal benefits from his/her investments.

Income Tax Act, 1961 (as Amended) (ITA)

In the ITA, a taxpayer would find many options to minimize his/her tax liability. For example, under Sections 80C, 80D, 80E and 80G certain deductions/exemptions for depositing or investing money in Public Provident Funds, 5 Year Bank Deposits, National Saving Scheme, Equity-Linked Saving Schemes, Tax Saving Fixed Deposit; Premiums paid for Health Insurance Policies; Education Loans; Donations to Charitable Organisations respectively; etc., are allowed.

In his tax planning, a taxpayer should resort to '**Tax Avoidance**' which pertains to reducing or negating tax liability in a legally permissible way. The basic features of Tax Avoidance are, as under:

- It is not tax evasion and carries no public disgrace with it.
- It is an act valid in law and cannot be treated as fictitious merely on the basis of some underlying motive supposedly resulting in lower payment of tax.
- There is no mala fide intention or motive involved in tax avoidance.
- It is sound law and certainly not bad morality.

Tax Avoidance got the seal of approval from the Supreme Court of India in a case: Union of India versus Azadi Bachao Andolan [2003] 263 ITR 706/132 Taxman 373.

However, while a taxpayer is working out his tax planning, he should not resort to '**Tax Evasion**' which involves any act, method and/or attempt in contravention of law to avoid discharge of tax liability can be termed as Tax Evasion. The basic features of Tax Evasion are, as under:

- It is an attempt to evade tax liability with the help of unfair means/methods.
- It is a tax omission.
- It is unlawful and entails punishment specified under the law.
- It is an intentional attempt to avoid payment of tax after the liability has arisen.

Difference between Tax Planning and Tax Management

Here, planning is not the same thing as management. Both are different from each other. Basic differences between the two are, as under:

- Tax Planning pertains to reduce the tax liability to minimum.
  Tax Management pertains to complying with the provisions of the law.
- Tax Planning is futuristic in its approach.
  Tax Management relates to past actions (filing of income returns, assessment proceedings, rectification, revision, appeal, future corrective actions, etc.)
- Tax Planning is very wide in its scope and includes tax management.
  Tax Management is limited and specific in its scope (filing of income returns, drafting of appeals, deduction of tax at source, updating records from time to time, etc.).
- The benefits arising from Tax Planning are substantial, particularly in the long run.

As a result of effective Tax Management, imposition of penalty and penal interest, prosecution, etc., are avoided.

Tax Planning and Income Tax Act, 1961 (as Amended) (ITA)

In order to have proper tax planning, the understanding of the following as defined in the ITA is desirable:

- Assessment Year.
- Previous Year.
- Person.
- Assessee.
- Resident of India.
- Income.
- Gross Income.
- Total Income.
- Exemption and Deduction.
- Charitable Purpose.

The above is just a brief and a panoramic view of the gamut of income tax in our country. One has to fully understand the provisions of Income Tax Act, 1961 (ITA), keep himself/herself abreast of the frequent amendments made in the ITA, Notifications issued by the Government of India from time to time, Changes in taxation announced every year by our Finance Minister during the Budget session of Parliament.

Thus, tax planning is vital for every taxpayer as it results in minimizing tax liability. The money so saved can be further invested which may be in the interest of both taxpayer and government as well as the economy at large.

Income Tax Act, 1961 (as Amended) (ITA): A Brief

Introduction

Great Indian Sanskrit scholar of ancient times Kalidas in his epic poem Raghuvansh wrote, 'It was only for the good of his subjects that he collected taxes from them, just as the Sun draws moisture from the Earth to give it back a thousandfold.'

ITA stems its origin from the taxation system formulated and implemented during British rule in India. For the first time, Income Tax was introduced by Sir James Wilson in the year 1860, to meet the losses suffered by the Government on account of Military Mutiny in the year 1857. Several amendments were made to it from time to time. In the years 1886, 1918 and 1922, new Income Tax Acts were passed. The 1922 Act remained in force up to the Assessment Year 1961-62.

The ITA was enacted by the Parliament and brought into force on 1st April 1961. Several amendments have been made to it from time to time. Amendments to the ITA are announced in Parliament during the presentation of the Union Budget every year.

Constitutional Provisions: Article 265 of the Constitution of India and Entry 82 of List I of the Seventh Schedule therein are relevant. According to the former, no tax can be levied or collected except by the authority of law. The letter pertains to income tax.

The said List I is the Union List where the Central Government is empowered to determine, demand and collect the income tax.

Direct Tax and Indirect Tax: These are the two types of taxes in India. The Income Tax, Corporate Tax and Wealth Tax are the direct taxes. VAT, Service Tax, Excise Duties, Import Duties, etc. are examples of Indirect Tax.

Income in General: In general and ordinary parlance, income simply means Money that an individual or business receives in exchange for providing a good or a service or through investing capital. However, a detailed and elaborate definition of Income as defined in the ITA is dealt with herein below.

Income Tax Act, 1961 (ITA)

Income Tax Act, 1961 (as amended), with its 23 Chapters, 298 Sections, 14 Schedules and Appendix appended to it, is amongst the bulkiest Acts of India. It provides for scope and machinery for the levy of income tax. The ITA is supported by the Income Tax Rules, 1961 to give effect to the provisions of ITA. Circulars and Notifications are issued by the Central Board of Direct Taxes (CBDT) and sometimes by the Ministry of Finance, Government of India dealing with various aspects of income tax. Stated briefly, important provisions of ITA are, as under:

Territorial Jurisdiction: The ITA extends to the whole of India.

Tax: It is in the nature of the exaction of money by public authority for public purpose as mandated by law.

Income Tax: It is a mandatory annual financial charge/tax levied on both types of income: earned (wages, salaries, commission, etc.) and unearned (dividends, interests, rents, etc.). It is a tax on the total income of a person called the Assessed of the Previous Year relevant to the Assessment Year at the rates prescribed in the relevant Finance Act.

Advance Tax: In ITA, there is a provision for advance tax; it means the advance tax payable in accordance with the provisions of Chapter XVII-C.

Charging Section: Section 4 of ITA is the basic charging section according to which income tax is chargeable on the total income of any person.

Assessment Year, Section 2(9): It is a period of 12 months starting from the 1st day of April every year and ending on the 31st day of March of the next year. In an Assessment Year, the income of the Assessed during the Previous Year is fixed at the rate prescribed by the relevant Finance Act. It is, therefore, also called the Tax Year.

Previous Year, Sections 2 (34) and 3: Previous Year is the financial year immediately preceding the Assessment Year. Income earned in one financial year is taxed in the next financial year. The year in which income is earned is also called the Previous Year.

Person, Section 2(31): The term 'person' includes:
  a. an individual;

b.   a Hindu Undivided Family;

c.   a Company;

d.   a Firm;

e.   an Association of Persons or a Body of Persons whether incorporated or not; a local authority; and

f.   every artificial juridical person not falling within any of the preceding categories.

The above are the categories of persons chargeable to tax under the ITA. The above definition is inclusive and not exhaustive. Therefore, any person, not falling in the above-mentioned categories, may still fall within the definition of 'person' and be liable to tax.

Assessee, Section 2 (7): 'Assessee' means a person by whom income tax or any other sum of money payable under the ITA and it includes:

a.   every person in respect of whom any proceeding under the Act has been taken for the assessment of his income or loss or the amount of refund due to him;

b.   a person who is assessable in respect of income or loss of another person or who is deemed to be an assessee; or

c.   an assessee in default under the provisions of the ITA.

A minor child is treated as a separate assessee in respect of any income generated out of activities performed by him like singing in radio jingles, acting in films, tuition income, delivering newspapers, etc. However, income from investments, capital gains on securities by a minor child, would be taxable in the hands of the parent having the higher income (mostly the father), unless such assets have been acquired from the minor's sources of income.

Assessment, Section 2(8): An assessment is a procedure to determine the taxable income of an assessee and the tax payable by him. Section 2(8) of ITA gives an inclusive definition of assessment. 'An assessment' includes reassessment.

Income, Section 2 (4): Though income tax is a tax on income, the ITA does not provide any exhaustive definition of it. Instead, the term 'income' has been defined in the widest sense by giving an inclusive definition. It includes not only the income in its natural and general sense but also the incomes specified in Section 2(4).

Broadly, the term 'income' includes the following:

i.   Profits and gains;

ii.   Dividend;

iii.   Voluntary contributions received by certain institutions;

iv.   Receipts by employees the value of any benefit or perquisite, whether convertible into money or not;

v.   Incomes from business (Section 28);

vi.   Any capital gains chargeable under Section 45;

    vii. Any sum earlier allowed as a deduction and chargeable to income tax under Section 59;

    viii. Any winnings from lotteries, crossword puzzles, races including horse games and other games of any sort or from gambling or betting of any form or nature whatsoever;

    ix. Any contribution received from employees towards any provident fund or superannuation fund or Employees State Insurance Act, 1948, or any other fund for the welfare of such employees;

    x. Any sum received under a Keyman insurance policy including the sum allocated by way of bonus on such policy; and

    xi. Any sum of money or value of the property as a gift—Section 56 (2) and Shares of closely held companies transferred to another company or firm are covered in the definition of gift except in the case of transfer of such shares for recognition of business by amalgamation or demerger, etc.

Agricultural Income, Section 2(1A): Agricultural income is exempt under the ITA. However, while computing tax on non-agricultural income; agricultural income is also taken into consideration. Agricultural income is computed in the same manner as is done to compute business income.

Residence in India, Section 6(3): ITA recognizes and classifies a taxable person under three categories, as under:

1. Resident in India
2. Resident not ordinarily resident
3. Non-resident

Residential Status of a Company, Section 6 (3): A Company is said to be resident in India in any Previous Year if either of the following conditions is fulfilled:

1. If the company is an Indian company or
2. If the place of effective management during that year is in India.

    'The Place of Effective Management' is the place where all the important and key managerial and commercial decisions for the conduct of business are made.

Best Judgment Assessment, Section 115WF: It is an assessment of income tax done by the Assessing Officer even though the said Officer may not be fully aware of the circumstances of the assessee or there may not be cooperation from the assessee. While making such an assessment, the said Officer is not expected to act dishonestly, capriciously or with mala fide intention.

Deductions to Be Made in Computing in Computing Total Income, Sections 80A to 80 VV: ITA allows deduction in respect of certain payments (Insurance Premium, Deposits under the National Savings Scheme, donations to charitable institutions, among others), in respect of certain incomes (Profits and gains from newly established industrial undertakings, hotel business, housing projects, outside India, export business, etc.) and deduction in case of a person with a disability. For example;

Section 80C of ITA is the friendliest and it offers Deposits in Public Provident Funds, 5-Year Bank Deposits, National Savings Certificates, Equity Linked Saving Schemes, and Tax Saving Fixed Deposits, among others.

Section 80D of ITA offers deductions to a taxpayer on the premium paid towards Health Insurance Policies for Self, Children, Spouse and parents, if covered under the insurance plan. Certain deductions are also allowed for parents in the Senior Citizen bracket.

Section 80E of ITA offers tax deductions on the interest paid for an Education Loan. This deduction can be claimed for a certain number of years starting from the date of repayment and as notified by the Government. There is no upper limit on the deductible amount. This means that a taxpayer can claim the entire amount paid as interest from the taxable income.

80G of ITA: A taxpayer donating to a charitable organization and public charitable trust is eligible for claiming exemption from payment of income tax and such organizations and trusts are eligible for exemption from payment of tax on their income.

House rent allowance is a conspicuous relief under ITA. A taxpayer can claim an exemption on the cost incurred to stay in rented accommodation. The taxpayer is mandated to furnish a rent receipt provided by the landlord.

Double Taxation Relief, Section 90 to 91: This deals with agreements with foreign countries, specified territories, and the adoption of agreements by the Central Government between specified associations and with countries with which no agreement exists.

Avoidance of Tax, Sections 92 to 94A: These are the special provisions in the ITA which deal with avoidance of tax which means reducing or negating the tax liability.

Determination of Tax in Certain Special Cases, Sections 110 to 115BBD: It includes tax on short and long-term capital gains, dividends, royalty, winning lotteries, income from Global Depository Receipts, non-resident sportsman or sports associations, anonymous donations, etc.

Special Provisions, Sections 115C to 115JF: These provisions pertain to certain incomes of Non-Residents, Companies and Limited Liability Partnerships.

Special Provisions, Sections 115K to 115VZC: These provisions pertain to tax on Distributed Income, Income Received from Venture Capital Companies and Funds, and Income of Shipping Companies.

Fringe Benefits, Sections 115W to 115WM: These provisions pertain to income tax on Fringe Benefits, procedure for filing returns in respect of Fringe Benefits, assessment of tax and payment of tax in respect thereof.

Income Tax Authorities, Sections 116 to 138: For the purposes of ITA, there shall be the following authorities:

1. Central Board of Direct Taxes (CBDT).
2. Directors General of Income Tax or Chief Commissioners of Income Tax
3. Directors of Income Tax or Commissioners of Income Tax or Commissioners of Income Tax (Appeals).
4. Additional Directors of Income Tax or Additional Commissioners of Income Tax or Additional Commissioners of Income Tax (Appeals).
5. Joint Directors of Income Tax or Joint Commissioners of Income tax.
6. Deputy Directors of Income Tax or Deputy Commissioners of Income Tax or Deputy Commissioners of Income Tax (Appeals).
7. Assistant Directors of Income Tax or Assistant Commissioners of Income Tax.
8. Income Tax Officers.
9. Tax Recovery Officers.
10. Inspectors of Income Tax.

The Central Government may appoint such persons as it thinks fit to be income tax authorities and also appoint such executive or ministerial staff as may be necessary to assist it in the execution of its functions.

Jurisdiction: The Income tax authorities shall execute the powers assigned to such authorities under the ITA and it may have regard to any one or more of the following criteria:

1. Territorial area.
2. Persons or classes of persons.
3. Incomes or classes of incomes.
4. Cases or classes of cases.

Powers: Authorities from the Assessing Officer to Chief Commissioner and the **Dispute Resolution Panel** under Section 144C of ITA shall have the same powers as are vested in a Court under the Code of Civil Procedure, 1908 when trying a suit in respect of the following matters:

1. Discovery and inspection.
2. Enforcing attendance of any person and examining him on oath.
3. Compelling the production books of accounts and other documents.
4. Issuing Commissions.

The above powers are inclusive of powers of Search, Seizure, Survey, Call for information, Collect information, Inspect the Registers of Companies and Application of seized or requisitioned assets.

Proceedings before Income Tax Authorities to Be Judicial Proceedings: The proceedings shall be deemed to be judicial proceedings within the meaning of Sections 193 and 228 and for the purposes of Section 196 of the Indian Penal Code, 1860 and every income tax authority shall be deemed to be a Civil Court for the purposes of Section 195, but not for the purposes of Chapter XXVI of the Code of Criminal Procedure, 1973.

Procedure for Assessment, Sections 139 to 158BI: These provisions pertain to Return of income, Permanent Account Number, procedure for assessment, special provision for avoiding repetitive appeals and special procedure for assessment of search cases.

Liability in Special Cases, Sections 159 to 167: These provisions pertain to Legal Representatives; Representative assesses (General provisions, Special cases and Miscellaneous provisions).

Collection and Recovery of Tax, Sections 190 to 234D: These provisions pertain to direct payment; advance payment, deduction at source (salary, dividends, winnings from lotteries, crossword puzzle, horse race, insurance premium, etc.), collection at source, recovery of tax in pursuance of an agreement with foreign countries, recovery of penalties, fines, interests, recovery by suit, tax payable under provisional assessment, etc.

Refunds, Sections 237 to 245: These provisions deal with Refunds, refunds on appeal, interest on delayed refunds, set off of refunds against tax remaining payable, etc.

Settlement of Cases: Decisions to Be by Majority, Section 245A to 245M: These provisions, among others, deal with the settlement of cases. The Central Government shall constitute a Commission called the Income-tax **Settlement Commission** which shall consist of a Chairman and other members appointed by the Central Government who shall be persons of ability, integrity and possessing knowledge and experience of dealing with direct taxes and business accounts.

An assessee at any stage of a case relating to him makes an application to the Settlement Commission to have the case settled. In case, Members are equally divided in their opinion, they shall state the points/s of difference and make a reference to the Chairman. The Chairman shall either hear the point/s himself or refer the case for hearing on such point/s by one or more Members of the Settlement Commission and such point/s shall be decided according to the opinion of the majority of the Members of the Settlement Commission who have heard the case, including those who first heard it.

Advance Ruling, Sections 245N to 245V: These provisions, among others, pertain to a determination by the Authority in relation to the tax liability which has been undertaken or proposed to be undertaken by a non-resident applicant or a resident applicant with the said non-resident and, a determination by the Authority an issue relating to computation of total income which is pending before the Appellate Tribunal. Such determination shall include any question of law or of fact. The Authority shall be a Civil Court and shall have the powers of a Civil Court and be subject to the provisions of ITA. The Authority shall also have the power to regulate its own procedure in all matters arising out of the exercise of its powers under the ITA.

Appeals and Revision, Sections 246 to 255: Broadly, the provisions under the ITA are, as under:

1. Assessee.......... Assessment, Reassessment or Recompilation by the Assessing Officer.......... Appeal to Deputy Commissioner (Appeals).......... aggrieved.......... Commissioner (Appeals).
2. Assessee.......... confirm, reduce, enhance or annulment of assessment Order passed by the Joint Commissioner.......... aggrieved.......... Commissioner (Appeals).
3. Assessee.......... order of Deputy Director (Appeals), Commissioner (Appeals) or Assessing Officer.......... aggrieved.......... Appellate Tribunal.

Appellate Tribunal shall be deemed to be a Civil Court as described aforesaid and any proceeding before the Appellate Tribunal shall be deemed to be a judicial proceeding as described aforesaid.

The appeals are required to be filed within the time along with the fee prescribed under the ITA.

Statement of the Case to the High Court, Section 256: Pertaining to an order under Section 254 (passed before 1/10/1998) of the ITA, the assessee or the Commissioner may by an application in the prescribed form and within the prescribed time require the Appellate Tribunal to refer to the High Court any question of law arising out of such order.

Statement of the Case to the Supreme Court in Certain Cases, Section 257: If on an application made against an order (under Section 254 passed before 1/10/1998), under Section 256, the Appellate Tribunal is of the opinion that there is conflict in the decisions of the High Courts in respect to any particular question of law, the Appellate Tribunal may draw up a statement of the case and refer it to the Supreme Court direct through its President.

Appeal to the High Court, Section 260A: From every order passed by the Appellate Tribunal (before the date of establishment of the National Tax Tribunal), an appeal shall lie to the High Court, if the High Court is satisfied that the case involves a substantial question of law and the appeal shall be heard by not less than two Judges.

Appeal to the Supreme Court, Section 261: From any judgment of the High Court delivered (before the establishment of the National Tax Tribunal) on a reference made under Section 256 (against an order under Section 254 before 1/10/1998 or an appeal made to High Court in respect of an order passed under Section 254 on or after that date) in any case which the High Court certifies to be fit one for appeal to the Supreme Court.

Revision of Orders Prejudicial to Revenue, Section 263: The Commissioner may call for and examine the record of any proceeding under the ITA and if he considers that the order passed by the Assessing Officer is erroneous in so far as it is prejudicial to the interests of the revenue, he may, as deemed fit, cause an inquiry to be made and, pass an order as the circumstances of the case justify, enhancing or modifying the assessment or cancelling the assessment and directing fresh assessment.

Tax to Be Paid, Section 265: Notwithstanding that a reference has been made to the High Court or the Supreme Court or an appeal has been preferred to the Supreme Court, tax shall be payable in accordance with the assessment made in the case.

Penalties Imposable, Sections 271 to 275: These provisions, among others, pertain to failures on the part of an assessee to comply with different provisions of the ITA and the penalties imposable thereon. Failure to: Furnish returns, Comply with notices, Maintain books of accounts, Get accounts audited, Collect tax at source, Concealment of income and particulars of fringe benefits, False estimate of or failure to pay advance tax attract different penalties from payment of Rs 5,000 to Rs 1,50,000, three times the amount of tax, 2 per cent of the value of the international transaction and 10 per cent of the undisclosed income. The penalty may be for each failure and default. In case of continuing offences, the penalty may be imposed for each day of failure and default.

There are provisions in the ITA for the reduction of and waiver of penalty in certain cases and grant of immunity from penalty. In cases, the assessment proves that there was reasonable cause for a particular failure, the penalty may not be imposed. The penalties can be imposed within the times specified in the ITA for each penalty.

Offences and Prosecutions, Sections 275A to 280: These provisions, among others, pertain to offences and prosecutions. Depending on the nature and type of offence, there may be simple or rigorous imprisonment from three months to seven years. The imprisonment may be with or without a fine.

In case of offences by Companies, every person who at the time offence was committed was in charge of and was responsible to the company for the conduct of the business of the company as well as the company shall be deemed to be guilty of the offence and shall be proceeded against and punished accordingly.

In case of offences by Hindu undivided families, it shall be the 'karta' thereof who shall be deemed to be guilty of an offence and shall be liable to be proceeded against and punished accordingly.

In case of prosecution, the court shall presume the existence of a culpable mental state on the part of the accused but it shall be a defence for the accused to prove that he had no such mental state with respect to the act charged as an offence in that prosecution.

Miscellaneous, Sections 281 to 298: This is the last part of the ITA. Important Sections are, as under:

Bar of Suits in Civil Court, Section 293: No suit shall be brought in any Civil Court to set aside or modify any order made under the ITA and no prosecution, suit or other proceedings shall lie against any officer of the Government for anything done in good faith or intended to be done under the ITA.

Power to Make Rules, Section 295: The Board under the ITA and subject to the control of the Central Government, by notification in the Gazette of India may make rules for the whole or any part of India for carrying out the purposes of ITA.

Power to Remove Difficulties, Section 298: If any difficulty arises in giving effect to the provisions of ITA, the Central Government may, by general or special order, do anything not inconsistent with such provisions and that appears to it to be necessary and expedient for the purpose of removing the difficulty.

The Schedules: There are 14n Schedules in the ITA which pertain to certain specifications for giving effect to the provisions of the ITA. Some of the Schedules, as it appears in the ITA, are omitted.

Appendix 1: It contains the text of the provisions of allied Acts referred to in the ITA.

Conclusion: In India, Progressive Rate Structure is followed as is clear from the different rates of income tax levied on different amounts of income. The tax structure has been designed in such a manner that all relevant ability indices are considered. In other words, the more the income; the more the income tax thereon. It is, therefore, desirable to have tax planning and a fair amount of knowledge about relevant provisions of the Income Tax Act, 1961 as amended up to date.

Chapter Review

1. Tax planning is a very wide and a broad subject, requiring specialized knowledge to deal with multi-furious aspects of tax.

2. Tax planning is an exercise involving reduction of a determined tax burden/liability as per law. It also includes utilization of deductions, exemptions and other benefits offered by Government. The primary objective of tax planning is the timely discharge of tax liability and compliance of the Income Tax Act, 1961 (as amended up to date), keeping in view the interest of a taxpayer. It aims at reducing the tax liability, optimally utilizing the deductions, exemptions, and other benefits and thus, achieve tax efficiency and making investments/better utilization of the money so saved.

3. Tax planning can be classified into short-range tax planning, long-range tax planning, permissive tax planning and purposive tax planning.

4. In order to have proper tax planning, it is necessary to know and understand the Income Tax Act, 1961 (ITA) as amended to date.

5. However, the Income Tax Act, 1961, which is amongst the bulkiest Acts of India, is supported by Income Tax Rules, 1961, to give effect to the provisions of ITA. Income tax is a mandatory annual tax levied on both types of incomes, earned (wages, salaries, commission, etc.) and unearned (dividends, interest, rents, etc.).

6. All the relevant terms of ITA have been duly defined. Deductions to be made in computing total income are contained in Sections 80A to 80VV. Double taxation relief is mentioned in Sections 92 to 94A.

7. Provisions pertaining to certain incomes of non-residents, companies and limited liability partnerships are contained in Special Provisions (Sections 115 to 115 JF). Sections 115 W to 115 WM contain provisions pertaining to Fringe Benefits, the procedure for filing returns in respect of fringe benefits, assessment of tax and payment of tax in respect thereof. Various Income Tax Authorities are included in Sections 116 to 138. Provisions pertaining to Refunds, Refund on Appeal, interest on delayed refunds, set off of refunds against tax remaining payable, etc., are included in Sections 237 to 245. Whereas Penalties imposable are contained in Sections 271 to 275, Sections 275A to 280 deal with Offences and Prosecutions. Finally, Sections 281 to 298 deal with Miscellaneous issues.

DISCUSSION QUESTIONS

1. Discuss the concept and definitions of tax planning.
2. Discuss the classification of tax planning.
3. Discuss the permissible deductions while computing income tax for a particular financial year.
4. Discuss what are the fringe benefits the value of which is taxable under the ITA, 1961 (as amended up to date).
5. Discuss why should not all the tax exemptions to be abolished and rates of income tax on various slabs of income be reduced.

Individual and Group Activities

1. Individually visit a small organization and discuss with some employees there whether they do tax planning or not. If not, why? Prepare a brief report.
2. Individually visit a big manufacturing organization and discuss with a few employees if they file income tax returns and also what are the difficulties, they come across in doing so.
3. In a group of two, visit some big organization and discuss with the trade union officials there if they are aware of the provisions of tax exemptions contained in the Income Tax Act, 1961. If yes, what are those?
4. Visit, as an individual, some organizations employing more than 200 employees and talk to any ten of the employees. Find out the difficulties they come across in getting refund from the Income Tax Department.
5. In a group of three, visit a service rendering organization and find out from any ten of the employees what suggestions they have to make in order to improve Income Tax Act, 1961 (as amended up to date).

APPLICATION CASE

Ravindra has been working as a Purchase Officer in a tractor manufacturing organization for the last ten years and has been filing his annual income tax returns regularly. His total income from his monthly salary worked out to be INR 15,00,000 in the financial year 2021–2012. Since his work performance was quite good, he will get an employee stock option for INR 2,00,000 during the year 2021–2022. As per the policy of the organization, he is entitled to an annual bonus which is likely to be around INR 1,00,000. He has gone on a family tour for which he spent INR 1,50,000. He also earned an interest on his fixed deposit which is likely to be INR 52,000. He is also entitled to Capital gain to a tune of INR 18,000 on his mutual fund investment. On acquiring the age of 60 as on 25th February 2023 he will stand retired and will be getting gratuity for INR 15,00,000 and INR 1,27,000 for unavailed earned leave.

Questions

1. Compute his taxable income.
2. Which of the amounts he will or is entitled to earn, as mentioned in the case, are taxable and which are not taxable?
3. Can he file a revised income tax after 30 June 2023 if he finds later that he forgot to claim a particular exempted income in his IT Return for the assessment year 2022–2023?

Appendix

Income-Tax Rate Chart for the Financial Year 2022–2023 (Asst. Year 2023–2024)

For Individuals & Women

Total Income Slab	Rate of Income Tax	Surcharge	Health & Edn. Cess
Up to INR 2,50,000	Nil	Nil	Nil
INR 2,50,001 to INR 5,00,000	5%	Nil	4%
INR 5,00,000 to INR Rs.10,00,000	INR 12500 + 20%	Nil	4%
INR 10,00,001 and above	INR 1,12,500 + 30%	Nil	4%
INR 50 Lakhs & above	INR 13,12,500 + 30%	10%	4%
INR 1 Crore & above	INR 28,12,500 + 30%	15%	4%

For resident Senior Citizens (60 Years and above)

If a citizen attains 60th year during the Financial Year, He is a Senior Citizen for that Financial Year.

Total Income Slab	Rate of Income Tax	Surcharge	Health & Edn. Cess
Up to INR 3,00,000	Nil	Nil	Nil
INR 3,00,001 to INR 5,00,000	5%	Nil	4%
INR 5,00,000 to INR 10,00,000	INR 10000 + 20%	Nil	4%
INR10,00,001 and above	INR 1,10,000 + 30%	Nil	4%

For Sr. Citizens.......... for Income up to INR 3,00,000/- ...... There is no tax.

For resident Super Senior Citizens (80 Years and above)

If a citizen attains the 80th year during the Financial Year, He/She is a Super Senior Citizen for that Financial Year.

Total Income Slab	Rate of Income Tax	Surcharge	Health & Edn. Cess
Up to INR 5,00,000	Nil	Nil	Nil
INR 5,00,000 to INR 10,00,000	20%	Nil	4%
INR 10,00,001 and above	INR 1,00,000 + 30%	Nil	4%

For Super Senior Citizen, for Income up to INR 5,00,000/- there is no tax

For anyone, If the total taxable income does not exceed INR 5,00,000/- (i.e., after claiming allowable deductions including Section 80), 100% tax or INR 12,500/- whichever is less can be claimed as rebate u/s 87A. (No tax payable on a total income up to INR 5,00,000/-.)

Section 194P .... w.e.f. 01.04.2021

Those attained 75 years of age and their source of income is Pension and interest only ... No need to file 'Income Tax Return' as per Section 194P of Income-tax Act, 1961.

Allowable Deductions from Gross Salary

1. Under Section 16 (IA) of Intact, 1961—Standard Deduction of INR 50,000/-.
2. Under Section 16 (iii) of IT Act, 1961—Professional Tax paid.
3. House Rent Allowance (HRA) as per calculation under Section 10(13A)— Section 10 (13A) ... House Rent Allowance.

Least of the following is exempted.

- Actual House Rent Allowance received.
- Rent paid in excess of 1/10th of salary.
- 50 % of Salary...for cities Delhi/Mumbai/Kolkata/Chennai 40% of salary ...for any other place.

Those who are not in receipt of HRA can claim deduction up to INR 5,000/- p.m. for rent paid, u/s 80 GG.

Salary means Pay + D.A.

For claiming H.R.A., one has to produce the rent receipt

Employees drawing H.R.A. up to INR 3,000/- are exempted from producing rent receipts.

If the rent paid exceeds INR 1 Lac per annum, for claiming H.R.A. deduction, one has to produce the PAN and address of the Owner of the house.

If anyone is paying rent, more than INR 50,000/- p.m., must deduct income-tax @ 5% from the rent and to pay the remaining to the owner of the house. The amount so deducted must be paid to the Central Government A/c immediately. No need to obtain TAN for rent purposes. Section 194IB

If the Government Employee is staying in the city where his own house is situated, the total HRA drawn is taxable. It is immaterial whether he is staying in that house or not.

Deductions under Section 80

Deduction u/s 80D—For Individual/HUF...... **contribution towards Medical Insurance Premiums**—Self plus family ... INR25,000:: Self plus family plus parents ... INR 50,000 :: (INR 50,000/- for Criticizes) *Preventive Health Checkup for self/family restricted to INR 5,000/-p.a.*

Deduction u/s 80DD—Medical Treatment/maintenance of handicapped dependents—For Individual/HUF, up to INR 75,000/-- (Certificate from Medical Authority be produced) (INR 1,25,000/- for severe disability i.e. if the disability is 80% or more)

Deduction u/s 80DDB—Medical Treatment of specified disease of himself or dependent or member of a family—For Individual/HUF, Amount actually paid or INR 40,000/- whichever is less. (INR 1,00,000/- for Criticizes)

Deduction u/s 80E—interest paid on Education Loan availed from a Financial Institution or an approved Charitable Institution – No Limit (Only for 8 Years)

Deduction u/s 80EEA—Maximum of INR 1,50,000/-. Interest paid on loan taken for a residential house property Loan availed during the period 01.04.19 to 31.03.22.

Allowed, where the assessee does not own a house, and Stamp duty not to exceed INR 45 Lac.

Deduction u/s 80EEB—Maximum of INR 1,50,000/-. Interest paid on loan taken for purchase of an Electric Vehicle purchased during the period 01.04.2019 to 31.03.2023.

Deduction u/s 80G—Donation, if exceeding INR 2,000/- must be made in cheque only (80G.5D). 100% exemption >>>>Donations made to PM/CM relief fund, National Defense Fund, PM Cares Fund.

50% exemption >>>>Donations made to approved charitable institutions Donation made up to 10% of Gross total income is allowed as an exemption.

Deduction u/s 80GG—U/s10 (13A)—For an individual/self-employed person, who is not in receipt of HRA. House Rent paid by the employee for his residential accommodation –INR 5,000/-p.m.

Deduction u/s 80TTA—Only for individuals and HUF...... Exempted up to INR 10,000/-, interest received on Savings Bank A/cs of Bank/Post Office/ Coop Societies.

Deduction u/s 80TTB—Only for Criticizes Exempted up to INR 50,000/-, interest received on Bank/Post Office deposits.

Deduction u/s 80 U—A resident individual suffering from disability—Amount of deduction INR 75,000/- (INR 1,25,000/- for severe disability). The assessee shall furnish a certificate from Neurologist or a from a Civil Surgeon or from Chief Medical Officer in a Government Hospital.

Disability means … 40% or more … Severe disability means …. 80% or more.

Income from House Property

If anyone owns a house and gave it on rent, the received must be shown as income from House Property.

If any loan is availed for the construction of that house, then the interest paid on that loan up to a maximum of INR 2,00,000/- is allowed as a deduction.

Note:

1. Employee must furnish a statement in Form 12BB providing details of other income, viz., house property or claims of deduction under Chapter VIA to the employer.
2. No TDS is to be deducted on disability pension to ex-servicemen.
3. Interest on borrowed capital for construction of a house under House Property Income is INR 2,00,000/- p.a.
4. Salary for Income tax purpose means Salary received or accrued. In case any Salary is drawn in advance, the same is taxable in the year of receipt.
5. While in service, the total E.L. Encashment and Tuition Reimbursement Fee for children are totally taxable for that year.

TAX on GPF Contribution ... Section 10(11) and 10(12) of IT. Act, 1961 Rule 9D of Income-tax Rules, 1962

The maximum non-taxable limit is INR 5,00,000/- for Government Employees and INR 2,50,000/- for non-Government employees.

For example, if a government employee, for the F.Y. 2022–23, is contributing INR 55,000/- per month, the total contribution for that year is INR 6,60,000/- (INR 55,000/- × 12 Months). The non-taxable limit is INR 5,00,000/-. Hence an amount of INR 1,60,000/- (INR 6,60,000 – INR 5,00,000/-) is taxable. The interest earned on INR 1,60,000/- is also taxable. Hence INR 1,60,000/- + INR 1,893/- (INR 1,60,000/- × 7.21% (GPF rate of int.) = INR 1,61,893/- is taxable for the F.Y. 2022–23.

New Tax Rates (Section 115BAC)—Alternate to existing Tax Slab Rates.... No Deductions are allowed under

New Tax Slabs. The Gross income is subject to Tax and that is the Taxable Income only. The following table shows the new slab rates as per Section 115BAC.

Annual Income	New Income Tax Slab Rate
Nil to INR 2.5 Lac	Exempt
Above INR 2.5 Lac to INR 5 Lac	5%
Above INR 5 Lac to INR 7.5 Lac	10%
Above INR 7.5 Lac to INR 10 Lac	15%
Above INR 10 Lac to INR 12.5 Lac	20%
Above INR 12.5 Lac to INR 15 Lac	25%
Above INR 15 Lac	30%

Allowed Deductions: Transport Allowance (Allowance for attending the office) and investment in New Pension Scheme u/s 80CCD. New Tax Regime is useful for high income groups with less savings.

At the Time of Retirement

1. For Govt. Employees all the benefits received at the time of retirement are tax free.
2. Death cum Retirement Gratuity up to INR 20,00,000/- ... Section 10(10).
3. Commutation of Pension ... Section 10(10A).
4. Encashment of Earned Leave at credit etc. ... Section 10(10AA).
5. Payment from Provident Fund Account ... Section 10(11).

Capital Gain Tax

Income tax is payable on the sale of any Capital Asset if it results in profit. If anyone purchases one residential house/open plot and keeps it for a period of 2 years or more and sells it/re-sells it, one must pay tax on selling that property.

Some examples of Capital Assets:

1. Sale of Plots.
2. Sale of Houses/Apartments.
3. Compulsory acquisition of the assets under any law.

Tax must be paid in the year in which the transfer took place. For example, for the sale of one apartment the advance was taken on 12.12.2021 (F.Y.2021–22) and the total amount was paid on 10.04.2022 (F.Y.2022–23) then tax is to be paid during the F.Y. 2022–23 only. In the case of compulsory acquisition of any land by the State Government or Central Government, the tax must be paid in the year in which the compensation was received.

The rate of tax is different for 'Short Term Capital Gain' and 'Long Term Capital Gain'.

Short-Term Capital Gain ... If any land or building is held in your hands for a period of 24 months. *'Land or Building purchased on 01.01.2020 and sold on December 2021'.*

Long-Term Capital Gain ... If any land or building is held in your hands for more than a period of 24 months. *'Land or Building purchased on 01.01.2020 and sold on January 2022'.*

How to Calculate

Sale Price .... INR xxxxxxx
Less: Indexed purchase price ...... INR xxxxxxx
Less: Indexed improvement price...... INR xxxxxxx
Less: Transfer expenses like Brokerage/Commission ...... INR xxxxxxx ......
INR xxxxxxx Capital Gain on which tax @ 20% payable ...... INR xxxxxxx

Our purchase price will be calculated for today's price. That is called indexed cost of acquisition or indexed purchase price.

Any improvement made to the property also can be deducted with an indexed price.

For example, we purchased a property for INR 10,00,000/- during the year 2008 and is being sold in 2022, the price of INR 10,00,000/- may be INR 22,00,000/- today as per calculation. Hence the purchase price we show as INR 22,00,000/-

TDS (Tax Deducted at Source)

• When to deduct TAX? ... At the time of making payment, PAN must be produced.

- TDS without PAN is @ 20% or applicable rate whichever is higher TDS deducted is a Government Money. Hence be remitted into Govt. A/c within the time. Otherwise, interest will be levied. In some cases, prosecution will be launched.

TDS for Foreign Remittances

- Especially on sending money for Children on Educational loans etc. For remittance overseas under Liberalized Remittance Scheme (LRS)..........
- If the foreign remittance exceeds INR 7 Lac during the Financial Year through Authorized Banking Channel Tax will be collected @ 5% on the remittance exceeding INR 7 Lac.
- For example, if you are sending 12 Lac, an amount of INR 25,000/- will be collected as Tax. (INR 12,00,000 – INR 7,00,000 = INR 5,00,000 × 5% = INR 25,000/-).

12

INTERNATIONAL REMUNERATION

LEARNING OBJECTIVES

After studying this chapter, the reader should be able to:

1. Explain the meaning of international remuneration, sources of staffing foreign subsidiaries and types of international organizations, and their aims and objectives.
2. Enlist and explain factors affecting international remuneration and also various approaches to international remuneration.
3. Explain the concept and meaning of expatriate compensation and also the constituents of expatriate compensation.
4. Enlist and explain what expats demand if posted in remote locations.
5. Enlist and explain the various approaches to determine expats' pay.
6. Explain the balance sheet approach to determine an expat's pay.
7. Explain how the remuneration of third country nationals is determined.
8. Explain how the remuneration of local country nationals is determined.
9. Enlist and explain the stages through which a company has to pass before finally becoming a global company.
10. Explain how compensation is determined during various stages of growth of a company finally becoming a global company.

DOI: 10.4324/9781032626123-12

Introduction

Understanding how to develop and optimize the design of total reward programmes within global organizations is a much sought-after skill in the arena of HRM. International/global remuneration is a complicated issue as it has many dimensions to be taken care of.

Globalization is the outcome of two major trends, namely (a) internationalization of marketing, and (b) endeavour to reduce the costs of production. Internationalization of marketing has been possible because of the revolution in communication which has enabled demand for goods and services to go upward all over the world due to ever-increasing standards of living. Consequently, a good number of companies now see their marketplace as not only their country or continent but also the whole world. Endeavour to reduce the costs of production is due to locating the production facilities where labour is available at cheaper rates. These two trends have caused a good number of companies to have their plants and offices in different countries.

Global international remuneration refers to payment or compensation received by foreign employees and people working at overseas locations for their employment or services rendered by them. Global remuneration involves several international issues like differences in cost of living, variables in working environments, international law, etc. It, therefore, includes base pay, different types of allowances, housing, transportation assistance, health care, children's education, and so on.

Staffing the Global Organizations

Staffing a global organization appropriately is critical to the success of an international organization. International organizations operating overseas may use any one or more than one of the following sources (see Figure 12.1) for staffing:

1. **Home-country or parent-country nationals (PCNs):** Multinational corporations (MNCs) may employ the citizens of the country in which the

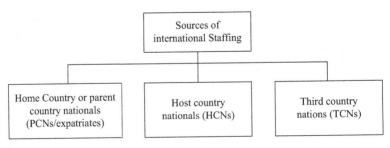

FIGURE 12.1   Sources of Staffing International Organizations

multinational company has its headquarters. They are not the citizens of the host country. For example, an American working for America-based General Motors' subsidiary in India is a home-country national and an expatriate. Hence, home-country nationals are usually appointed as managers, subsidiary heads, experts, and heads of some key functions. For example, in India, Maruti has more than 15 Japanese heading key functional areas such as finance and production. PCNs are preferred because they know better about the functioning of the parent company and can also better ensure proper linkage between the foreign subsidiary and the headquarters. PCNs are also helpful in developing global capabilities in the organization. But it should also be kept in view that PCNs are expensive and not aware of the culture of the country where the subsidiary is located. PCNs are usually preferred when the subsidiary is in its initial stage and when the host country does not have the required expertise. PCNs are also helpful in ensuring that the foreign subsidiary complies with the philosophy and policies of headquarters.

2. **Host-country nationals (HCNs):** Many people do not want to work in a foreign country. Besides, the cost of using expatriates is far greater than the cost of using HCNs. They are well versed in local languages and dialects. They are also familiar with the local customs, norms, culture and so on. Hence, international companies prefer appointing HCNs, especially at the middle and lower management levels. At times, even some home-country governments also pressurize international companies for the nationalization of local management. By appointing locals (HCNs), MNCs earn goodwill from local people. Sometimes, it is difficult to bring PCNs to the country where the subsidiary is located. For example, TCS has recruited many people in Latin America including some in senior positions as well. The main shortcoming of HCNs is that they have a local rather than a global view about the operations of the subsidiary. At times, HCNs do not appreciate the needs of headquarters. However, HCNs are most suitable if the required technical expertise is available in them and when the subsidiary is well established. They may also be helpful in establishing a wide network for market as well as, for business expansion.

3. **Third-country nationals (TCNs):** TCNs are citizens of a country other than the parent or the host country. For example, a Chinese who works in an Indian subsidiary of an organization having its headquarters in the United States of America is a TCN. It has been observed that usually TCNs are less costly than PCNs and have a considerable amount of international experience. However, it is not easy to get such competent and experienced people because of their short supply and also they pose greater challenges in terms of cross-cultural diversity management. All the same, TCNs usually prove their technical expertise.

It has usually been observed that when an organization is in its early stage of global expansion, it depends mostly on PCNs/expatriates to give shape to operations and other vital activities, especially if the subsidiary is being set up in a developing country or relatively less developed economy, and by and by it starts picking up people from the host country. TCNs are appointed when a typical talent or expertise is needed and the same is not conveniently available in the host countries and the like.

Types of International Organizations

Before we go forward, it will be in the fitness of things to know the types of international organizations, which are as follows:

1. **International corporations:** International corporations are the companies that are built on their existing capabilities to penetrate overseas markets. Such companies adopt their products to overseas markets without making changes in their normal operations. Procter & Gamble and General Electric Co. are some of the examples that followed this approach to penetrate European markets.

2. **Multinational corporations:** An MNC has operations in many different countries, but each is viewed as a relatively separate enterprise supplying its products for the geographical region surrounding the country of operation of the unit. Thus, each separate enterprise within MNC is responsible for adapting the company's products to the local culture, but the most vital control remains either with the company's home offices or in the hands of an expatriate from the home country. The majority of the employees including managers are usually from the host country.[1] Xerox and Philips can be quoted as examples in this regard.

3. **Global corporation (GC):** A GC is so structured that the national boundaries disappear. It hires the best people for jobs, irrespective of national origin. It sees the world as its labour source as well as its marketplace. Hence, it locates an operation wherever it can achieve its objectives and goals in the most cost-effective manner. For example, McDonald's, Coca-Cola and Nestle believe in a world market for their products. A GC maintains control over its global operations through a centralized home office. It is the expertise of an employee in his area that matters most for a GC instead of his national affiliation. Its employees are often moved across national boundaries to meet the current needs of the organization.[2]

4. **Transnational corporations (TNCs):** A TNC is an ideal type but hardly exists. It provides autonomy to independent country operations and brings these separate operations into an integrated whole through a networked structure like Unilever. A TNC is a fine blend of local responsiveness of an MNC and the efficiency of a GC.

Anyway, irrespective of any of the forms discussed above, an organization that conducts business overseas is usually known as an international organization. It must face a major challenge of locating and nurturing HR required for implementing a global strategy.

Aims and Objectives of International Remuneration

Though there are several aims and objectives of international remuneration, the following are the main ones:

1. **Attracting the desired and talented people:** One of the main objectives of international remuneration is to attract talented people who have the desired skills, expertise, experience and qualifications, and are willing to accept international assignments. It is possible only when they are offered attractive pay and benefits.
2. **Retaining talented employees on their current international assignments:** It is always desirable to retain talented people on their current international assignments so that international organizations may take advantage of their experience and expertise. Otherwise, going for a fresh recruitment proves a costly proposition.
3. **Reducing grievances:** In case employees on international assignments are paid adequate compensation for their assignments, they will have less grievances and, therefore, will feel more motivated, and their confidence and morale will be at a higher level as compared to a level that would have been had their compensation package been inadequate. The base pay, variable pay and different types of allowances and benefits of expatriates should, therefore, be determined at appropriate level.
4. **Enabling the employees and their families to adapt themselves to the socio-cultural environment of the host country:** While determining international remuneration, care should be taken to extend all those facilities that will enable the employees on foreign assignments and their families to adapt themselves to the cultural and social environment of the host country. For example, the fee for club membership, as applicable in the host country, should be included in the pay package.
5. **Enabling the employees to move from one subsidiary to another subsidiary:** In case an expatriate is transferred from one foreign subsidiary to another foreign subsidiary in a different host country or from subsidiary to home country or from home country to host country, several issues come up, especially regarding pay package and lot of expenses to be incurred by expats. In case an international remuneration package takes care of all the relevant expenses and if the desired benefit is extended to employees according to the requirements of the new place of posting, they may feel comfortable and accept the change of place/country/assignment.

6. **Improving and maintaining employee motivation:** Employees' motivation depends to a great extent on their pay package. It should, therefore, be good enough to make employees feel motivated, resulting in their enhanced contribution towards their assignment.

7. **Maintaining internal and external equities:** An expatriate's pay package should be worked out in a fashion that it does not disturb either the internal equity or external equity, otherwise a host of problems would emerge which would be difficult to handle. Hence, the pay package should be comparable to the pay packages of employees at headquarters in the same rank, and that of the host country subsidiaries.

8. **Maintaining balance between employees' pay and their performance:** International remuneration should be in proportion to the performance of an employee on foreign assignment, otherwise it will be difficult to sustain the subsidiary.

9. **Perception of fairness:** The international remuneration package should be such that it may be perceived by the employees as fair and just. Only then and then alone will the employees give their best to their organization.

10. **Aligning compensation with the strategy of the organization:** An international remuneration package should be in alignment with the strategy of the subsidiary and be instrumental in contributing enough towards the accomplishment of strategic objectives and goals of the subsidiary located in the host country.

11. The other objectives may include establishing that the package is both competitive and is always better than other packages, improving organizational performance, etc.

Factors Affecting the Design of International Remuneration

International remuneration is affected by a host of factors which are as follows:

1. Statutory obligations of the host country have to be met by every person entrusted with international assignments abroad. Hence, his pay package should take care of the additional expenses to be incurred by him.

2. State of technology used in the host country also affects the international remuneration. In case state-of-the-art technology is being used in the host country, which requires highly sophisticated skills, the pay package needs to be relatively substantial.

3. Socio-cultural factors also come into the picture while determining international pay package. In certain host countries, the standard of living may be very high, or people are highly conscious or believe in leading a luxurious life, or there may be regional differences and so on. In such cases, the international remuneration needs to be properly addressed. Otherwise, expatriates may develop an inferiority complex in the host country. This may affect their work performance.

Besides, regional practices and government controls may also affect international remuneration. For example, the host country's taxation policy, especially the income tax rules and regulations, affects international remuneration a great deal. Similarly, the Central Government or state government's policies and practices followed in the host country also impact international remuneration as the same also have to be followed by people on international assignments. Labour policy of the host country has also to be followed.

The Union's approach, especially about lower international assignments, may also affect international remuneration. Economic trends prevalent in the host country also affect international remuneration.

Approaches to International Remuneration

There are several approaches to international remuneration right from the traditional approach to the contemporary approach, which are as follows:

Regarding base pay, there is the 'traditional approach (or home country based)' in which base pay for international assignments may be determined on the basis of how it is worked out in the home country, that is, it is home-country based. It may be considered fair. Base pay can also be worked out as per the 'balance sheet approach' (discussed at length in the following pages). The other way out is that base pay for international assignments may be headquarter based. This also appears to be appropriate because in the case of expatriates, if they are to be repatriated, their base pay may remain undisturbed. However, in all the above cases, expatriates expect that their base pay should be more because of the typical nature of international assignments. Then, there is also a 'local approach', also known as the 'host country-based approach'. As per this approach, the base pay should be as per rates applicable for similar assignments in the host country because internal and external equities should not be disturbed. However, this may not sound fair if the expatriate is from a developed country where the base pay is usually more than that of the host country of the expatriate. Then, there is another approach known as the 'global market approach' according to which base pay for international assignments should be global market-based. It may appeal to all concerned though it may be burdensome if the expatriate is from a developing country, where base pay rates are relatively much less as compared to the global market-based rates of base pay.

Since, as stated above, the nature of international assignments is typical and usually demands higher skills, experience, expertise, qualifications and so on, and further that they involve greater risk, physical discomfort and so on; the expectations of people who are entrusted with international assignments are greater. There is also a 'contemporary approach' which includes premium and allowances and takes care of the typical nature and requirements of international assignments. As per the contemporary approach, international remuneration should take care of typical aspects of international assignments. For example, the pay package of the people taking up international assignments should include hardship pay as they usually confront more hardships. They may also be subject to more risk and hazards. Hence, their pay package should include risk/hazard pay. Another way out is that they should be paid for the cost-of-living adjustments so that there is no grudge on account of the difference in the cost of living between the host and home countries. In case housing facilities are costly in the host country, their pay package should include housing assistance. Similarly, their pay package should include educational assistance which may cover up the expenses incurred on the education of their children in the host country. Their pay package should also include the cost of any other expenditure that expatriates may have to incur in the host country because of its typical environment there. Besides, the expatriates must visit their home country periodically, say, quarterly, half-yearly or annually, for which they need to be granted paid home leaves (see Exhibit 10.1). Then, there is also a variable/incentives compensation approach which has provisions for short-term or long-term incentives usually based on their performance. There should also be a provision for variable pay which is directly dependent on their contribution towards the goals and objectives of the organization. Thus, appointing expatriates in foreign subsidiaries is a costly proposition as they expect a lot of other things (see Exhibit 12.1).

EXHIBIT 12.1 WHAT EXPATS DEMAND TO LOCATE TO REMOTE LOCATIONS

A review visit before signing up. This is a must.	Gym and club facility (some say tennis courts in particular).	Shopping malls, recreation and international schooling for children.

In many cases they want to opt for boarding schools for their kids in locations like Singapore for which they need separate compensation.

If a spouse joins, they need adequate safety in township, spouse clubs and foreign language training.

Contract-break protection, ease of forex conversion and tax filing help from Big4.   Medical and accidents insurance and air ambulance.

Source: The Economic Times (8 January 2019).

Some other approaches may include 'negotiation or bargaining' approach in which international remuneration is determined through mutual negotiations between the employees and the employer. According to another approach, viz., 'lumpsum' approach, the total international remuneration package covers the money value of all kinds of allowances and benefits in addition to the base salary. Then there is another approach known as the 'cluster approach' according to which the international organizations segment the countries/cities into clusters based on the cost of living and some other factors such as danger and hardships issues that affect the remuneration package, following the determination the same compensation package for each job within the same cluster of cities. As per another approach, viz., the 'buffet' approach, the total salary level is by the organization, and the employee is given an option to decide the cash component and benefits component in the global or international package. As per the 'mutual investment' approach, international remuneration is based on the concept of national pay scales within a country. As per another approach, namely, 'double home country salary and living compensation at the host country' approach, the expatriate gets double of the best salary that a best candidate gets in the home country for a similar job plus living host country compensation.

Which of the aforesaid approaches is better is difficult to decide. It should be chosen based on the typical nature/circumstances of the international assignment concerned.

Expatriates' Compensation

Concept and Definition

As mentioned earlier, expatriates are the present employees or new hires from the home country of the company posted in the host country. For example, if a manufacturing company whose home country is the United Kingdom, appoints any of its present employees or new hire belonging to the United Kingdom, at its new office in New Delhi would be treated as an expatriate by its new office. But why should the MNC located in the United Kingdom prefer to send its employees to any other country? It may be for several reasons. For example, the host country may not have the desired knowledge and skills or they may be in short supply; or its current employee may not be fully conversant with the functioning of the company, which is necessary for coordinating various activities abroad; or the company may feel like exposing and developing its executives to have the perspective required in order to be a good executive and perfect fit in the new global economy. Such executives may include those who have recently joined the company and have just started their careers in the company. There is also another possibility that the executive(s) may be at a later stage of his/their career and the company wants him/them to be groomed so that he/they may become fit to join a higher level of job at its local sites or elsewhere it may deem fit. Normally, expatriates are sent to a host country for a temporary assignment, that is, a short-term assignment, say for a period less than one year, though some countries like the United States of America prefer to post expatriates in new foreign countries for a period of two to three years, whereas some countries do so for a still longer period, say five years or so. Japan is one such example. Since temporary assignments are for a period of about one year or so, pay and benefits remain almost the same as they were getting earlier plus some additional pay or benefit to cover the living cost. However, in order to attract and retain expatriates, the companies make the package a little bit tempting. Because of the typical nature of expatriates' jobs, their pay is also determined in a different way. However, first, it is necessary to know the meaning and definition of an expatriate. As a matter of fact, an international assignment compensation plan has to appropriately balance rewarding and motivating expatriates while keeping costs under control for corporate headquarters in the home country.

Hiring expatriate professionals has never been as difficult for corporate India as it is now. Apart from hefty pay cheques, prospective 'foreign hands' expect companies to specially take care of their personal safety, comfort and superfluity.[3]

As an increasing number of companies in India, both domestic and global multinationals, have their businesses in small cities and towns, hiring an expatriate is becoming a tough negotiation.

India, once reckoned to be one of the much sought-after destinations that added to the repertoire of experience of international talent, is maybe losing its charm or is becoming pricier for companies. For those who are willing to risk a few years in India often ask for the moon—from air ambulance to personal bodyguards, gym and foreign language training institute for spouses, tennis courts and club facilities—even at remote plant sites. Here, we concede the example of a senior Japanese engineer who before taking up the assignment in

India not only wanted to visit the site but also sought to meet local administrators such as the district collector, NGOs, suppliers and water contractors to understand the ease of functioning at the location. 'Such kind of demand would never be made when one is going to Europe or even South America. It arises from the concerns about bottlenecks in functioning smoothly in the country.'[4]

Among the demands expats make to move into industrial regions are international schooling or boarding schools for their kids in locations like Singapore for which they need 'separate compensation'. A review visit of the local area before signing up is a must. If the spouse joins, they need adequate safety in the township, gym, spouse clubs and foreign language training so that spouses can use this time to learn new languages and vocations. Medical and accident insurance are a must with key man protection against environment and safety incidents.[5]

For example, when foreign subsidiaries in India do not have expertise in a particular field locally, they look forward to talent from abroad; however, expats ask a lot more questions than a local hire. Things become still difficult in hiring expatriates if they have to be appointed in a second-rung town as today in India many of the industrial activities are moving to second-rung cities such as Nashik, Udaipur, Vadodara and Aurangabad where finding many of the facilities asked for by the expatriates are difficult to be arranged (see Exhibit 12.2).

India's financial, commercial and entertainment capital, Mumbai, tops global rankings for expat salaries, according to a survey conducted by HSBC International. Foreigners moving to the Indian

---

EXHIBIT 12.2 TO WORK IN INDIA, EXPATS ASK FOR THE MOON

Not every company can afford to have such infrastructure in remote locations and for them it is tough ask to hire expats for niche roles for which homegrown talent is not available.

Source: The Economic Times (8 January 2019).

EXHIBIT 12.3 EXPAT SALARY: MUMBAI NO. 1

An average Mumbai's expat salary is more than twice the global average of the top 10 and select European cities.

The HSBC Expat Explorer survey was completed by 27,587 expats from 159 countries and territories. With a minimum sample of 90 expat respondents required, 52 cities were included in the analysis.

	Rank	($,000s)
Mumbai	1	217.2
San Francisco	2	207.2
Zurich	3	206.9
Shanghai	4	202.2
Geneva	5	184.9
New York City	6	182.2
Los Angeles	7	161.1
Jakarta	8	152.6
Hong Kong	9	148.4
Paris	10	139.6
London	26	107.9
Global Average		99.9
Dublin	37	91.4
Berlin	42	84.2
Prague	46	68.7
Birmingham	50	62

Source: The Economic Times (27 February 2019).

The subcontinent's most populous city reported average annual earnings of $217,165, which is more than double the global expat average of $99,903 (see Exhibit 10.3). Expat's salary is higher because Mumbai is more expensive for expats than many other global cities (see Exhibit 12.4).

Constituents of Compensation of Expatriate

As stated in the foregoing paragraph, the package of expatriates is usually tempting. It may comprise the following:

1. **Base pay:** It is the basic constituent of an expatriate's pay. The minimum base pay should not be less than that of a person doing the same job in their home country, otherwise, usually nobody would prefer to move from their home country to their host country. In this regard, one way nobody would prefer to move from home country to host country. In this regard, one way out is to work out the figure through the job evaluation method, which is a universally recognized method. Having worked out the base pay through the job evaluation method as prevalent in the home country, some additions can be made to it as the person concerned has to move from home country to a host country where the conditions may be quite different. Another way to determine the base pay of an expatriate is to identify the market worth of the job for which software is available in which by feeding the title of the job, location of the country, the company, industry, size and so on, base salary figures can be obtained. By taking the performance level of the person as also his experience, a decision for determining base pay can be taken.

EXHIBIT 12.4 MUMBAI MORE EXPENSIVE FOR EXPATS

Cities	Cost of Living Ranking
Mumbai	55
Melbourne	58
Frankfurt	68
Buenos Aires	76
Stockholm	89
Atlanta	95

- Reason for jump in Mumbai's ranking is continued surge in prices of food, alcohol and domestic supplies.
- Hong Kong is ranked as the world's costliest city to live for expatriates.

- Inflation, among the highest in Indian cities surveyed remained at 5.57 per cent.
- 93 per cent of companies compensate through a cost-of-living allowance for their expatriate assignee.

This increase in prices of goods in our cities, viewed along with the exchange rate, has a direct impact on the Indian assignee compensation when using a balance sheet approach, and making overseas assignment costs sometimes greater and smaller.

Source: The Economic Times (25 June 2018).

However, difficulties may emerge if the base pay determined as above does not match the base pay because in certain host countries, the base pay may be considerably less than what has been determined in the home country or if the base pay of that particular job in the home country is considerably higher than that of what has been worked out for that job in the home country. If an expatriate is working at a higher base pay in the host country and if he is to be repatriated to the home country, then the problem will arise as to how the base pay will be redetermined, which is also not easy to solve. Another problem in determining the base pay of an expatriate is that in most countries dependable wage data may not be available because wage data of base pay prevalent in the host country plays an important role in determining the base pay of expatriates. It is expected in the times to come that the availability of wage data will not be as difficult as it is today.

2. **Variable pay:** Another constituent of expatriate pay is variable pay. Although it is a different story that most expatriates may like it, at the same time, they do not like it to be a substantial part of their total compensation. However, it is getting very popular nowadays. In most countries, several types of variable pay plans are operational. In the case of the expatriate variable pay, the same can be based on any variable pay plan of the host country, preferably of the country where the organization/industry is based in which the expatriate is posted. However, it may be a little difficult to have a clear-cut idea about the goals, performance standards and exact performance of the expatriate as his supervisor is usually in the home country, whereas he is performing in the host country. So far as the form of variable pay is concerned, it is usually paid in the form of short-term bonuses usually dependent on the performance of the expatriate or due to the profit earned because of the contributions made by the individuals, including the expatriates, team or organization. The other common form of payment of variable pay is a long-term one. It is usually Employee Stock Ownership Plan (ESOP). The headquarters of the company located in the host country may make a suitable decision in this regard depending on its convenience.

3. **Bonuses:** The third constituent of expatriate remuneration is the 'bonuses' which are usually in addition to performance bonuses of variable pay. It can be paid in different forms. For example, it can be paid as a lump sum amount at the very beginning of the assignment, the intention being to make some amount of cash available to the expatriates to cover their expenses which are usually high at the time of joining. Some organizations pay bonuses in the form of a percentage added to the base pay of an expatriate. Though there is no hard and fast rule, this may vary between 10 and 30 per cent of the base pay of an expatriate. With the passage of time, expatriates consider this amount as a part of their base pay. But this is stopped on their repatriation; they take it as a cut in their base pay and start getting demotivated. In between the two approaches, there is a third approval adopted by some organizations, which is via media of the aforesaid two approaches. In it, the organizations prepare the schedule of bonus payments according to which payments are weighted from the beginning of their assignment and are then paid before the expatriates are sent back to their home country.

4. **Allowances:** Another substantial chunk of expatriate compensation is the *allowances*. Since an expatriate has to establish his family, if there is any, in a new environment, new culture and new circumstances, he has to incur different types of expenses to adapt himself/his family. Hence, normally organizations come forward to help the expatriate by offering him help in finding appropriate housing, medical help, school for his children and so on. The main allowances in this regard are as follows:

    a. The major allowance falling in this category is *cost-of-living allowance*, which intends to enable an expatriate to cover the difference in the cost of living, in order to maintain his normal standard of living, between the home country and the host country. In case the expatriate moves from a developing country to a developed country, the cost-of-living allowance constitutes a significant amount. But if the expatriate is shifted from an advanced country to a developing country, where the cost of living is low, normally the expatriate is not penalized.

    b. *Automobile allowance* is also a popular constituent of an expatriate's pay. In case a car is not provided by the home-country organization of the expatriate on his posting in the host country, he is provided automobile allowances as he not only needs to purchase a vehicle but also to get it registered, maintain it and bear the fuel expenses, and so on. Some organizations provide driver allowance also as it is always advisable to have the driver from the host country as he is aware of the local driving rules and location of different places and so on.

    c. Another constituent of an expatriate's pay may be *education allowance*. Because of language and other problems, the children of expatriates must be admitted to reputed private schools where the medium of instruction is English or any other language of the expatriate, if available, they must pay higher fees as compared to government schools of the host country where fees charged are relatively significantly low. Not only this, but an expatriate also has to incur expenses in visiting and identifying the school which will suit his children the most. For all these inconveniences, both financial and non-financial, the expatriates are usually compensated by the home-country organization by paying education allowance.

d. *Hardship allowances* are the other form of allowance paid to expatriates. In order to make expatriates feel comfortable in the host country where living conditions are not good, expatriates are offered hardship allowances. For example, there may be physical hardships due to typical climate at the place of posting in the host country, like excessive cold or heat, or other difficulties experienced in getting proper food, housing and so on. Some of the factors usually taken into consideration while determining hardship allowances, according to Armstrong and Murlis,[6] are as follows:

  i. An excessively hot or cold climate.
  ii. Health hazards.
  iii. Poor communications.
  iv. Isolation.
  v. Language difficulties.
  vi. Daily possibility of burglary, kidnap, mugging and so on.
  vii. Scarcities of food.
  viii. Poor amenities.
  ix. Political risk.
  x. Force majeure, floods, typhoons, earthquakes and so on.

e. Another form of allowance may be *risk allowance*. In certain places, there is a law-and-order problem, traffic congestion or accident-prone areas, or disease-prone areas due to poor hygienic conditions, or non-availability of medical aid and so on. If an expatriate is posted at such a place in the host country, he is to be compensated.

f. There may be some other allowances which may be found necessary to be paid to an expatriate according to the typical nature of the job, or status of the expatriate, or place of posting or the host country. Such allowances may include club membership allowances, uniform allowance, picnic allowance and so on. Other allowances, according to Armstrong and Murlis,[7] may include separation allowance, clothing allowance, added responsibility allowance (position allowance) and relocation allowance.

Payment of Taxes

It is another consideration at the time of determining an expatriate's pay. For example, income tax rules vary from country to country. In some countries, income tax rates are very low, say, 5–10 per cent, and in some countries, they go up even to 40–50 per cent. An expatriate needs to be compensated for all the taxes that he is liable to pay as per the rules of the host country, especially where the rates of such taxes are high. Some organizations pay the taxes of expatriates that they are liable to pay to both the host and home countries. The rate and structure of income tax, which are levied on expatriates working in a particular country, vary from country to country and therefore, the home country gathers all the relevant information from host country consultants about the income tax levied in host countries. A comparative study of the amount of income tax payable in the host country and in the home country is made to make required adjustments in the concerned expatriate's pay. For example, in some countries, if the income tax is more in the host country than the home country, then the expatriate has a tax credit which can be carried back for two years or so and forward, say five years or so. Again, if the tax in the home country is greater than the host country, the difference is paid by the expatriate in the home country. An effort is made by the home country organizations that expatriates are 'no worse off' in the host country. It is as per the policy of 'keeping the expatriate whole'.

Thus, a home-country organization, according to Armstrong and Murlis,[8] may safeguard expatriates from fiscal penalization by the following methods:

1. **Tax protection:** If an expatriate receives a gross salary while working at a location where the tax rates are low, the employer is not required to make any adjustment. However, if the tax rates in the host country are higher than in the employer's home country, the difference is reimbursed to expatriates.
2. **Tax equalization:** In a more favoured tax system called 'tax equalization', the home-country employer reimburses tax excesses to those expatriates who are in high-tax host countries, but if in the host country, the tax rates are zero or less than the home country, then deductions are made from the total remuneration of such expatriates.
3. **Net payments:** In this system, payment of net salary is made to the expatriate and therefore, it ensures expatriate's fiscal equity across the world but removes the onus of tax administration from the employee in countries that have no equivalent of the Pay as You Earn (PAYE) system; of course, it is expensive to operate this system.
4. **Purchasing power of money:** The purchasing power of a manager makes a lot of difference, especially if it varies substantially between the home country and the host country. The primary objective of determining an expatriate's pay is to make him reasonably comfortable and if any factor affects his living negatively, the organization of the home country should ensure that the expatriate is compensated for that. In this regard, the exchange rate plays an important role. Hence, this must be kept into consideration while determining an expatriate's pay. Not only this, during certain periods, it keeps on fluctuating, sometimes very significantly. If such fluctuation affects the living of an expatriate, it should be compensated by adjusting his pay or allowances accordingly. Similarly, in some countries, during some periods, the rate of

inflation goes very high making it difficult for an expatriate to maintain his standard of living if the income of the expatriate is not increased accordingly. The expatriate should be compensated for the extra amount being spent by him in the host country due to inflation and so on, and the amount of his savings that he is sending to his family in the home country in case he has not moved his family to the host country.

5. **Fringe benefits:** These are the other constituents of an expatriate's pay. Since the provision of fringe benefits affects the lives of expatriates in the host country, home organizations take it into consideration while determining an expatriate's pay. Fringe benefits available in the host country and the home country may be different and sometimes differ widely. The list of benefits in the two countries should, therefore, be investigated sincerely and a decision be made as to what sort of changes or adjustments need to be made by the home-country organizations. In certain countries, there is a long list of certain benefits that are statutorily mandatory to be extended to the employees, otherwise, they may attract legal penalties. Such benefits must be attached priority by the home-country organizations as the expatriate is subject to receive the required benefits of the host country. For example, statutorily required benefits in India include social security benefits as covered under various acts[9] such as Employees' Compensation Act, 1923; ESI, 1948; Employees' Provident Funds and Miscellaneous Provisions Act, 1952; Maternity Benefit Act, 1961; and Payment of Gratuity Act, 1972, and similar is the case with welfare benefits as covered under various acts.[10] As such, expatriates may be required to pay for social security programmes in both the host and the home countries because social security programmes are there in almost all countries though they differ widely from one country to another country. Some countries have entered into agreements whereby expatriates are not required to pay for such programmes in the host country.

Another benefit, known as rest and relaxation leave, carries significance, especially in hardship assignments. In such cases, expatriates are sent for a short period to safe and familiar places where they can relax and come back fresh to take up their assignments with more vigour and enthusiasm.

6. *Pay for time not worked* is another benefit popular in almost all countries in the case of expatriates. Under this type of benefit, various types of leaves and holidays are included. In every host country, there are some public holidays, which are applicable in the case of expatriates also and, therefore, must be granted to them. Then 'get ready time', especially in the case of female staff who prefer to spend some time in getting ready to start their work, 'warm-up time', 'shaking hands', 'tea/coffee breaks', 'lunch time' and so on, are also availed by expatriates, during which they do not work but are paid. Similarly,

expatriates are also granted home leaves with full pay so that they can visit their home country and use their vacation there. Besides, in most cases, expatriates are also reimbursed the travelling costs incurred by them in visiting their home country during home leave. All such things cost the home-country organizations a lot.

7. In addition to the above benefits, expatriates are also granted certain benefits, which are at the sole discretion of the home-country organizations. Such benefits are called discretionary benefits. For example, most home-country organizations have health insurance programmes for their employees abroad, which also cost a lot to them. Similarly, the home-country organizations may have relevant plans for the expatriates when they come back from foreign assignments and are entitled to superannuation plan benefits. Many home-country organizations reimburse the medical bills of expatriates which they pay in the host country. There can be some other expenses that expatriates incur in the host country depending on the nature of their assignment or the environment of the host country, and the home-country organizations may like to bear the same at their own end.

8. Less common benefits associated with the expatriate assignment, according to Armstrong and Murlis,[11] may include servants (which still represent affluence, power and status though the practice has been given up in many countries), club subscription, rest and recuperation.

Thus, it is to be noticed that expatriate pay includes not only the base pay but also different types of other benefits and privileges, as covered under the aforesaid discussion, which the home-country organizations must bear at their own costs.

Approaches to Determine an Expatriate's Pay

How to determine an expatriate's pay depends on the approach the home-country organization adopts for the purpose. Among the several approaches discussed earlier in this very chapter, the employer can follow any one or a combination of more than one of the already earlier discussed approaches, for determining an expatriate's remuneration. However, the main approaches to determining an expatriate's remuneration are provided below.

The Balance Sheet Approach

It is a very common and popular way of determining an expatriate's pay. One of the two-fold purposes of the balance sheet approach is keeping the 'expatriates whole', that is, how is his standard of living in the host country, and the second purpose is controlling the costs involved in the whole exercise. Milkovich, Newmann and Ratnam[12] have pointed out the following three objectives:

1. Ensure mobility of people to global assignments as cost-effectively as possible.
2. Ensure that expatriates neither gain nor lose financially.
3. Minimize adjustments required of expatriates and their dependents.

It is worth mentioning here that none of the above objectives is related to performance. Thus, it is a costly proposition to send an employee, and his family, overseas on an international assignment. The first step in the balance sheet approach is to determine the base rate for the job, which can be done through the job evaluation process being used by the home-country organization. The other option is to take a decision keeping in view the market rate for the job. Though not essential, the base rate for the job so arrived at may be divided into certain categories such as taxes, goods and services, housing and utilities, and discretionary income. The aforesaid categories reflect living costs in the home country of the expatriate. The second step involves estimating the costs the expatriate is likely to incur on the above categories in the host country. In case the costs so worked out for the host country are more than such costs incurred in the home country, the difference is the allowance that should be paid to the expatriate. As per the balance sheet approach, the following format can be used to calculate the above:

Category of Expenditure	Costs Incurred in the Home Country	Costs Incurred in the Host Country	Differentials
Total cost of living			

The differential amount should be paid to the expatriate otherwise he/she may decline the offer of appointment. Though this is a good approach, at the same time, it is mechanical in nature and leaves no scope for the expatriate to go further for any negotiation, which he would have otherwise preferred.

Armstrong and Murlis[13] have pointed out the following three components of the balance sheet approach:

1. National home salary.
2. Spendable income.
3. Allowances.

Flexible Compensation Approach

The flexible compensation approach, also known as the cafeteria approach, is another approach for determining an expatriate's pay with flexibility as the main feature. It takes care of the needs and desires of an expatriate as there is a scope for adjustment. For example, if an expatriate prefers a spacious house with good furniture and fittings, he may need more money for meeting expenditure on the count of housing, but since he does not yet have any children, he may not need any money for schooling of children.

Negotiation Approach

It is a simple approach as per which the two, namely the management of the home-country organization and the would-be expatriate, negotiate and reach a decision regarding compensation which is acceptable to both. The main shortcoming of this approach is that if a good number of employees are sent overseas for international assignments, it will be difficult to negotiate with each of them individually as it is a time-consuming process to work out mutually agreed compensation for every expatriate.

Localization Approach

It is another approach to decide compensation and is usually used in the case of determining compensation of new employees. As per this approach, the compensation for overseas assignments should be as it is in the host country, though some adjustments can be made if the costs on a particular category are substantially higher than in the home country. This plan is getting popular day by day.

Lump Summing Approach

It is yet another approach whereby a lump sum amount is given to the expatriate, which he can spend as he likes. According to Armstrong and Murlis,[14] there are three main expatriate remuneration systems that are now prevalent as described below:

1. Balance sheet or build-up (home based).
2. Local market rate (host based).
3. Hybrid (usually a combination of home-based and host-based pay systems).

TCNs' Compensation

Besides expatriate compensation discussed above, there is another section of international employees whose compensation is as important to be discussed as that of expatriates. This section of international employees comprises the employees that the home-country organization transfers from one host country to another host country, who are known as TCNs. For example, an Indian international organization transfers its employee presently posted in a foreign subsidiary located in Hong Kong to its another subsidiary located in London. Although the process of working out compensation package for TCNs is the same, some differences are there which should be taken care of as follows:

The first question that arises in this direction is that of equalization of compensation to which country. In this regard, it may be said that if an employee is working in a particular host country and if he is transferred to another host country, then he should be paid the same amount as that of a local country national (LCN, i.e., of another host country to which the employee is transferred from his previous host country). This is also known as 'host-country equalization'. However, his salary will not be reduced from his present status. Another possibility may be that of 'headquarters equalization' as per which all TCNs are treated as if they are citizens of the headquarters country and, therefore, all employees working in a country are paid the same compensation package. This system helps in maintaining internal consistency. Of course, as different countries follow different taxation policies, which may disturb internal consistency because the compensation package due to different rates of taxes may be below or above the TCN's current one. The other possibility may be that of 'home-country equalization', in which the TCNs are paid their regular home-country compensation:

However, if the housing accommodation is costly in the host country, a housing allowance is

added to the pay package so that the cost of living could be maintained. The fourth possibility may be that of modified 'home-country equalization', under which for calculating the cost of living, the home-country approach discussed above is followed but for calculating base pay, the headquarters approach, also discussed above, is used. In case the organization makes use of the split pay system, the home-country equalization approach is perhaps the best approach. However, according to Milkovich et al.,[15] equalizing pay may not motivate an employee to move to another country, particularly if the new location has less personal appeal. Hence, in order to encourage the employees to move to the host country, many home-country organizations offer some form of financial incentive or bonus too. For example, home-country organizations may give relocation bonuses to tempt people to take up expatriate assignments in the host country. However, if an expatriate himself is keen to get international experience, relocation allowance can be ignored or, at least, the amount of it can be reduced.

Now the question arises: How to determine the amount of various constituents of remuneration in the case of TCNs? The reply to this question is as follows:

1. **Base pay:** It is not easy to determine the base pay, which is a vital component of a TCN's pay package. Suppose, a TCN is from a developing country where, obviously, pay rates are very low as compared to pay rates of a similar type of job of a person employed in an advanced country. In case his base pay is determined according to the value of the job in his home country, it means his pay will be very low if transferred to a high-wage country. Not only this, it's also very difficult to know the compensation rates of his job in his home country if it is a developing country because such details are usually not available

in most developing countries. Even if available, their dependability carries a question mark. Another problem is that if a TNC is working in a developed country and is transferred to a job in a developing country, his salary would be much more than another employee already working in a developing country. Hence, while determining the base pay of a TNC, all such factors should be taken into consideration.

2. **Variable pay:** Another constituent of TNC's compensation is also a controversial issue. Variable pay is usually either performance-based or is paid in the form of bonuses. While in some countries like the United States of America, individual performance-based pay is common, in some countries it may not be the case. Similarly, the issue of bonuses is viewed differently by different countries. While in some countries, bonuses are performance related, in other countries it is paid because one is the employee of the organization and his individual performance does not matter. Besides, in some countries, the bonus is considered a 'deferred wage'. In yet some countries, the bonus is viewed as an 'ex-gratia' payment which is paid solely at the discretion of the employer. Again, in some countries or cultures, the security of job is more important, and they do not attach much importance to PRP. Hence, these factors are kept into consideration while determining base pay.

3. **Allowances:** They too constitute an important part of TCN's pay package, as these constitute a considerable part of TCN's package. It may be pointed out here that the amount to be paid for different allowances may be determined as it is done in the case of expatriate pay already discussed earlier.

4. **Taxes:** They affect the 'carry home pay' of TCN's a great deal because of the variation in the rate of taxes payable in different host countries. Hence, while determining the compensation package of a TCN, the rates of taxes prevalent in the host country to which he is to be transferred or posted should be considered. In case, these are higher than the home country of the TCN or his current place of posting, the difference may be paid to the TCN.

5. **Benefits:** They are another segment of a TCN's compensation package as is the case with other types of international employees. Benefits differ from country to country. For example, in certain countries there exists a national health system and, therefore, the employee's health is taken care of by that country, whereas in other countries it may not be the case. It is, therefore, advisable that if a TCN is transferred from a country where the national health system is operational to a country where such a system does not exist, his compensation package should be inflated with the amount which the TCN is supposed to pay for private health insurance in the host country. Hence, while determining the compensation package of TCNs, either the benefits already being availed by him at his current place of posting should be made available to him in the host country or their expected cost may be added to their compensation package.

Compensation Determination during Various Stages of Growth of a Company Finally Becoming Global Company

With the advent of globalization, many companies have started moving from one stage to another. For example, initially a company may expand its business outside its home country mainly in respect of its trade. To meet its human requirement for expanding its trade outside the country and to have its sales office there, the organization may need only a few expatriates overseas, but they may be mostly at the clerical level or so. It is known as the 'expert stage'. Later, the home-country company may start its manufacturing process overseas for which it may need some technology resources outside the home country. Moving from having sales offices in host countries to having production facilities indicates that the company is becoming an MNC. This is known as the 'international stage'. When MNCs grow and start moving to more and more host countries, they reflect the features of a TNC. When a TNC loses its connection to any specific country and starts reflecting the features of an international organization, it is called the 'transnational stage'. Here, determining the compensation becomes more complex. With further growth of the company, its primary business focus spreads across the world. Its management then starts making its geographic business decisions as if the same is being taken for a borderless world. There remains no real home country for such a company and, therefore, it starts hiring, training and developing staff from any part of the world, wherever the desired talent is available. Political boundaries cease to be meaningful for such a company and hence, its operations and markets are determined by economic decisions. Such a company at this stage is also known as in a global stage and needs an advanced integrated type of compensation scheme.

It becomes easier to determine base pay for different stages. Similarly, wage structure also differs from country to country. A job evaluation plan from the home country is usually applied to the local situation but the difficulty is that job factors used to create a wage structure in the home country may not necessarily be the same in the target country. Again, the demand for supply of labour affects the wage structure in different countries as the demand for and supply of manpower differs from country to country. Then, the wage spread is also not the same in all countries. In some countries, the wage spread from top executives to entry-level employees is as large as 1,000 to 1 while in some other countries it is as low as 20 to 1.

Coming to 'bonus' also which are very common across the world, in some countries a bonus is considered as the '13th month' pay, while in others it may be considered an ex-gratia payment, in others as a deferred wage and in yet some other countries like India it is considered as statutory payments.

LCNs' Pay

There is a great variation in the wage level of different countries due to the state of their country's economy, its culture and laws. There are several practices of determining the wage levels being followed across the world and many of them differ widely from country to country. For example, negotiations and collective bargaining play an important role in determining LCN's compensation. Some countries exercise control over wages through their income and tax policies and enacting laws. On-going rates in the country also play an important role. Some others constitute wage boards to set wage rates. Culture too affects pay practices in several ways, and so on (see Chapter 3).

In view of the above, there is a great variation in the base pay of different countries, which is considerably affected by the differences in countries' prosperity, internal business factors, social factors and purchasing power of money. For example, prosperous countries usually pay more as compared to poor countries. In some countries, the influence of government policies, laws and unions play an important role in the determination of base pay. Availability of wage data and cultural norms also exercise a great influence on the determination of base pay. Similarly, regarding bonuses, in some countries, it is viewed as an ex-gratia payment; in some countries, it is called 'deferred wage', while in some countries it must be determined and paid as per legal provisions. For example, in India it is determined and paid as per provisions of the Payment of Bonus Act, 1965. Hence, there is a great variation in the determination of bonus also in the case of LCNs.

As far as variable pay in the case of LCN is concerned, in some countries like the United States of America, it is very popular while in some other countries it is not so where profit-sharing may be popular, and so on. So is the case with stock options. Similarly, pay-for-performance is very popular in countries like the United States of America but may not be so in many other countries, the reason being that performance is usually evaluated by managers depending on their whims instead of measuring it scientifically or mechanically.

Then comes the allowances, the meaning of which differs from what it is in the case of LCNs than in the case of expatriates. In most countries, allowances are paid as additions to base pay and given for several reasons. In some countries, they constitute a significant part of their base pay and may go up to 25 per cent or even more. Allowances differ widely from country to country. For example, there are 56 separate allowances that can be claimed by an employee, subject to conditions laid down for the purpose in the Metal Trades Association Agreement in Australia. However, allowances paid are categorized under certain heads based on the position of the employees, behaviour and so on.

Benefits too differ a great deal from country to country. Some benefits may be very popular in one country but be totally missing in another country because benefits are extended to meet the local requirements and to provide psychic comfort to the employee which may differ from country to country. Statutory benefits also vary from country to country though a few are common in all countries. For example, in India, there are legal provisions for extending certain benefits as per Employees' Compensation Act, 1923; ESI Act, 1948; Employees' Provident Funds and Miscellaneous Provisions Act, 1952; Payment of Bonus Act, 1965; Payment of

Gratuity Act, 1972; Industrial Dispute Act, 1947; Industrial Employment (Standing Orders) Act, 1946; Maternity Benefit Act, 1961; and so on. Again, how much financial burden for implementing the required benefits will be borne by whom, that is, the government, employer, employees or a combination of two or more of them. Time off is another benefit which may be available to the employees in the form of holidays and vacations. The number of national holidays may also differ from country to country. Working hours, though usually 8 hours per day or 40 hours per week, is a common phenomenon, but in certain countries, it is up to 48 hours a week also. For example, in India, it is 48 hours per week. Similarly, in some countries, it is 5 days a week, in some countries it is 6 days a week and so on. The rates of overtime also differ from country to country. In some countries, it is one and a half times more than the rate of standard hour; it is twice the standard hour rate in other countries. Again, while severance pay is common in most countries, it is not paid at all in some other countries. The base amount of severance pay also differs from country to country. Occupation and age are the other factors that play their own role in the case of severance pay. Discretionary benefits, as the name suggests, vary from country to country because they are based on the needs, customs and culture of respective countries. Transport allowance or a vehicle in lieu thereof, meals, loans and taxes too differ from country to country. Executive perks also differ in variety, quality and frequency from country to country. Thus, it is noticed that there is a great variation in LCNs' compensation. It must be decided to keep in view the factors stated above.

Chapter Review

1. With the advent of globalization, most big companies now see their marketplace as not only their country or continent but the whole world. Their foreign subsidiaries have to be staffed and, therefore, be appropriately compensated for their contribution.
2. So far as staffing the foreign subsidiaries is concerned, there are three major sources, namely,
   (a) parent country (home country) nationals (PCNs/expatriates), (b) HCNs and (c) TCNs. There are many types of international organizations such as international corporations, MNCs, GCs and TNCs. The major objectives of international remuneration include: attracting and retaining the desired talent, minimizing grievances, enabling the employees and their families to adapt themselves to the new socio-cultural environment, enabling the employees to move from one subsidiary to another subsidiary as and when required, improving their motivation, maintaining internal and external equities, balancing pay and performance, perception of fairness and aligning compensation with the strategy of the organization.
3. As far as factors affecting the design of international remuneration are concerned, they are several in number, the main being the statutory obligations, state of technology used in the organization, socio-cultural factors, taxation

policy, regional practices, government controls, unions' approaches and other economic trends in the host country.

4. Coming to the approaches of international remuneration, there are several approaches. For example, regarding the base pay, there is a traditional approach (or home country-based approach), a balance sheet approach, a local (or host country) country-based approach, global market approach, contemporary approach, variable/incentive compensation approach and so on.

5. As far as the expectations of expatriates are concerned, the expats destined for remote locations expect certain things such as a review visit before signing up the contract, gym and club facility, shopping malls, boarding school facility for their children, safety for women, spouse clubs, foreign language training, contract break up protection, tax filing facility and ease of forex conversion.

6. Coming to the concept and definitions of expatriate compensation, it may be pointed out that an international assignment compensation plan is expected to appropriately balance rewarding and motivating expatriates while keeping costs under control for corporate headquarters in the home country. In case expats have to take up assignments in small cities/towns abroad, their demands for so many things go up. Expats' expectations in terms of salary are quite high compared to many other countries.

7. The main constituents of expat's compensation comprise base pay, variable pay, bonuses, cost of living allowance, automobile allowance, education allowance, hardship allowance, risk allowance and a number of other allowances depending on the nature of assignment and location of the city/country, such as clothing allowance, separation allowance, responsibility allowance, relocation allowance, payment of taxes and purchasing power of money, and fringe benefits such as pay for time not worked, servant allowance and other discretionary benefits.

8. There are many approaches to decide an expat's pay. For example, the balance sheet approach which has three components, namely, national home salary, spendable salary and allowances. Other approaches include the flexible compensation approach, the negotiation approach, the localization approach, the lump summing approach and so on.

9. As far as TCN's compensation, which refers to the employees that the home-country organization transfers from one host country to another host country, is concerned, it has several dimensions. For example, whether the compensation of the TCN should follow host-country equalization or headquarters equalization, or home-country equalization so that if he is transferred back to his home country, there may be no problem in adjusting his pay. The major constituents of TCN remuneration are base pay, variable pay, required allowances, taxes, required benefits and so on.

10. So far as compensation determination during various stages of growth of a company finally becoming a global company is concerned, it may be pointed

out that after globalization many companies have started moving from one stage to another such as moving to expert stage, to international stage, to transnational stage where determination of compensation becomes more complex and a host of factors have to be kept in view while determining pay, especially the base pay. Deciding bonus is also to be paid, which in some countries is known as 13th month pay.

11. Coming to LCNs' pay, the base pay is determined in different ways depending on the practices prevalent in a particular country. It may be according to collective bargaining, wage board, government regulations, direct negotiations and so on. Variable pay differs from country to country. For example, it is not in practice in some countries. Similarly, pay for performance is not a universal practice. Bonus too is determined on different patterns in different countries. So is the case with allowances and benefits, which differ from country to country. However, statutory benefits are to be given as per country's legal requirements.

All said and done, there is a great variation in LCNs' remuneration.

DISCUSSION QUESTIONS

1. Discuss the meaning of international remuneration, the sources of staffing of international organizations as also the types of international organizations.
2. Discuss the factors that affect international remuneration.
3. Discuss the various aspects of expatriates' remuneration and also the constituents of expats' remuneration.
4. Discuss the specific demands of expats if to be posted in small cities/towns or remote places.
5. Discuss the various approaches to determine the remuneration of expatriates.
6. Discuss the balance sheet approach in the context of determining expat's remuneration.
7. Discuss how the remuneration of TCNs is determined.
8. Discuss how LCNs' remuneration is determined.
9. Discuss the stages through which a company has to go through in order to become a global company.
10. Discuss how the remuneration is determined during various stages of a company finally becoming a global company.

Individual and Group Activities

1. Individually, visit the headquarters of some international corporations and find out what are the sources they tap to recruit staff for foreign subsidiaries.
2. In a group of two, discuss with some senior officials of some international corporations as to what the constituents of their expatriates' remuneration are and what the specific demands of expatriates are in case they are to be assigned some job abroad in a remote location.
3. In a group of two, visit some international corporations and discuss what approach they follow in determining the expats' remuneration.
4. In a group of two, visit some international corporations and discuss with the officials concerned there, how they determine the remuneration of TCNs.
5. Individually talk to some officials of an international corporation and find out how they determine the remuneration of LCNs.

APPLICATION CASE

Mr A. K. Sharma, after doing his master's in business administration (marketing) from IIM, Bangalore, started a start-up at Mumbai. He has also a bachelor's degree in mechanical engineering from IIT, Kharagpur. Over a period of five years, his start-up made tremendous progress and he started expanding his business outside India in respect of trade. For exporting its trade outside India, his company established an office in China. To meet human requirements for its China office, there was a requirement of only a few expatriates. It is known as the export stage. Later on, the home-country company (i.e., Mr Sharma's company) started its manufacturing process overseas for which he needed some technology resources outside the home country (India)—thus the company became an MNC. Such a stage is known as the international stage. Here, determining the compensation becomes more complex. The company grew further and started moving to more and more host countries. It, therefore, started reflecting the features of a TNC. By and by, his corporation started losing its connection to political and geographical boundaries, it became meaningless to any specific country and, hence, started reflecting the features of global organization. At this stage, there develops a need for an advanced integrated type of compensation.

About a few months back, the home-country corporation transferred one employee from its foreign subsidiary located in China to another foreign subsidiary located in the United States without effecting any change in his remuneration. The employee started feeling disturbed both economically and culturally. It was due to the fact that the principle of equalization was not followed in respect of his remuneration. His remuneration should have been changed based on the principle of 'host-country equalization'. His remuneration was not made equal to what another person doing the same type of assignment in the United States was getting. First, his basic pay was not increased substantially as the salaries in the United States are very high. His variable pay and bonus were also not revised to what are prevalent in the United States. His allowances were also not revised so as to have some synchronization with the allowance paid in the United States. No adjustment with regard to taxes was made, though tax rates in the United States are comparatively higher as compared to China. In the case of benefits too, no change was effected. Benefits available for foreign assignments in the United States are different than what is available in China. Hence, economic disturbances were bound to happen in the case of the employee transferred from China to the United States. The work performance of the employee transferred to foreign subsidiary located in the United States was adversely affected and, therefore, the United States located foreign subsidiary refused the case in question to headquarters located in Mumbai (India) for necessary pay review.

Questions

1. What are the stages that Mr Sharma's start-up had to pass through before it became a global corporation? Discuss the features of each stage.
2. Why did the work performance of the employee transferred from a foreign subsidiary located in China to the one located in the United States decline? What went wrong? Identify the factors responsible for this.
3. Suppose, you were asked to look into the pay review of the transferred employee in question, what would you do?

Notes

1 See Ivancevich, *Human Resource Management*, 101.
2 See D. J. Cherrington and L. Z. Middleton, 'An Introduction to Global Business Issues', *HR Magazine*, June 1995, 124–130.
3 *The Economic Times*, 8 January 2019.
4 Ibid.
5 Ibid.
6 Armstrong and Murlis, *Reward Management*, 512.
7 Ibid.
8 Ibid., 519–520.
9 For applicability, scope and other details, see Sharma, *Industrial Relations*, 825–895.
10 For details, see Sharma and Sharma, *Human Resource Management*, 388–426.
11 Armstrong and Murlis, *Reward Management*, 518.
12 Milkovich, Newman, and Venkata Ratnam, *Compensation*, 488.
13 Armstrong and Murlis, *Reward Management*, 510.
14 Ibid., 507.
15 Milkovich, Newman and Venkata Ratnam, *Compensation*, 489.

GLOSSARY

360-degree feedback: In it, ratings are collected 'all around' an employee, from supervisors, subordinates, peers and internal and external customers.

Adjudication: It refers to legal machinery as provided in the Industrial Disputes Act, 1947, to resolve industrial disputes.

Arbitration: It refers to the scenario when the parties involved in an industrial dispute mutually agree to refer the disputes to an arbitrator for its settlement.

Assessee: It means a person by whom income tax or any other sum of money payable under the ITA.

Assessment year: It is the period of 12 months starting from the 1st day of April every year and ending on the 31st day of March of the next year. In an assessment year, the income of the previous year (financial year) of the tax-payer (assessee) is assessed for the purpose of income tax payment.

Attendance bonus: It is given to employees who have maintained perfect attendance for a period of time, usually a full year or full quarter, in the form of cash.

Attrition: It refers to employees leaving the organization.

Balance sheet approach: As per this approach of determining remunera-tion of an expatriate, if the costs of expenditure on various items incurred by an expatriate in the host country is more than the costs incurred on such expenditure in the home country, then the difference should be paid to him by the company because the total of two sides of a balance sheet is always equal.

Basic pay/basic compensation: It is the basic cash compensation paid by the employer for the work performed by the employee. It tends to reflect the value of the work itself and ignores differences in individual compensations.

Boardroom pay: It refers to the pay received by the members of the board of directors.

Bonus: It is a lump sum payment to an employee in recognition of good achieve-ment. Some people consider it as an ex gratia payment, some others view it as a deferred wage and some others consider it as a statutory payment.

Bonus (premium) schemes: In these schemes, a worker is induced to produce more by correlating earnings to output and simultaneously assuring minimum wage.

Bottom-up budgeting: In this budgeting starts from the recommendations made by the managers for pay increases of their subordinates to the top management for its modification or approval so as to have proper control over salary costs.

Broad-banded structures: These comprise a multi-graded structure into less number of bands, say, four or five bands, but have wide pay bands. Progression is linked to competence and contribution.

Broad banding: It refers to collapsing a number of grades into a smaller number of broad grades with wide ranges.

Broad-graded structures: These structures are controlled through thresholds or zones. Broader grades are defined clearly, and better control can be exercised over grade drift.

Career and job family structure: This structure is one in which separate job families are identified and defined but a common grade and pay structure applies to all families.

Career family structures: These have a number of different career 'families'. In these structures, jobs in the corresponding levels across each of the career families are within the same size range. The pay ranges in corresponding levels across the career families are the same.

Career planning: It is a deliberate process through which an employee gets aware about his personal skills, interests, knowledge, motivation and other characteristics and establishes action plans to attain specific goals.

Central tendency: It refers to the phenomenon where the rater rates all or almost all his personnel as average.

Christmas bonus: It is usually a small amount paid to reward loyalty and enable the employees to meet the extra costs of the season.

Clothing bonus: It is paid to the staff who need to buy special clothing for work when the company does not provide uniforms.

Compa-ratio analysis: It refers to an index that helps assess how managers actually pay employees in relation to the mid-point of the pay range established for jobs. It estimates how well actual practices correspond to the intended policy. It is calculated as average rates actually paid divided by the range mid-point.

Compensable factors: It refers to those job factors for which compensation should be paid to the job holders.

Compensation: It includes all forms of financial returns and tangible services and benefits employees receive as part of an employment relationship.

Compensation management: Compensation management is concerned with the design, development, implementation, maintenance, communication and evaluation of compensation processes which deal with working out relative worth of all jobs in an organization, designing and monitoring of pay structures, paying for skills, competence or performance, performance management, employee benefits, reward management procedures and the like.

Compensation philosophy: It is a formal statement that spells out the organization's stand or position with regard to employee compensation.

Compensation policy: A compensation policy provides guidelines for the implementation of compensation strategy as also for working out design and management of compensation processes.

Compensation strategy: It provides specific directions on how the organization will develop and design programmes that will ensure that it rewards the behaviour and performance outcomes that support the achievement of the business goals.

Competence: It refers to adequacy of knowledge and skills that enable an employee to act in a wide variety of situations. It is a combination of knowledge, ability, skills and commitment that makes an employee to act effectively in a job or situation.

Competence–performance-related pay: It is a combination of competence-related pay and PRP. It rewards employees for both their inputs (competence) and outputs (performance), thus making a holistic process.

Competency: It describes the 'behaviour' needed to perform a role with competence. It, therefore, refers to basic knowledge and abilities employees must acquire or demonstrate in a competency-based plan in order to successfully perform the work, satisfy customers and achieve business objectives.

Competency-based pay: It is a compensation approach that links pay to the depth and scope of competencies that are relevant to doing the work. It involves paying for the development and application of essential skills, behaviours and actions that support high levels of individual, team or organizational performance.

Conciliation machinery, adjudication machinery and arbitration: These are the main provisions under the Industrial Disputes Act, 1947, to resolve industrial disputes.

Contingent pay: It consists of payments related to individual performances, contribution, competence or skill or to team or organization performance.

Contingent rewards: It refers to rewards related to individual performance, contribution, competence or skill, or to team or organizational performance.

Contribution-related pay: It refers to a pay system in which employees are paid for their contribution and competence.

Dashboards: These are analytical tools that allow an organization to focus on the measurements that are vital for the business of the organization. They display various meters, gauges and lights that give instant up-to-date information on the current status of a business.

Dearness allowance: It protects the wage earners' real income by neutralizing the increased cost of living due to increase in prices.

Deductions to be made in computing total income: It means the deductions allowed under ITA in respect of certain payments (insurance premiums, deposits under the National Saving Scheme, donations to Charitable institutions, etc.), in respect of certain incomes (profits and gains from new established industrial undertakings, hotel business, housing projects outside India, export business, etc.), deductions in case of a person with disability, etc.

Deferred bonus scheme: This approach provides payment of bonus to an employee at some future time as reward for work performed now.

Differential piece rate plan: It refers to plans in which differential piece rates are set for different amounts of output.

Disablement benefit: It is paid in cash and in instalments to the insured person on fulfilling certain conditions.

Discretionary benefits: These are the benefits which are at the discretion of the employer—whether to give or not to give to his employee.

Draws: It is a sort of advance, also known as a 'predetermined draw', given to salesmen. At the end of each pay period, whatever is left after adjusting the amount of draw goes to the salesmen.

Embedded controls: These controls are inherent in the design of techniques such as job analysis, job evaluation and SBP, which are also instrumental in regulating managers' pay decisions by guiding what managers are able to do and what they cannot do.

Employee motivation: It is an inner urge in an employee to put in his best efforts to achieve the desired results.

Employee psychology: To study the mind and behaviour of job holders is what is referred to as employee psychology.

Employees' Deposit Linked Insurance Scheme, 1976: This scheme is applicable to all eligible factories/establishments with effect from August 1976. All members of the employees' provident fund scheme are required to become members of this scheme.

Employees' Pension Scheme, 1995: The scheme provides a number of benefits to the members and their families such as monthly member pension, disablement pension, widow/widower pension, children pension, orphan pension, disabled children/orphan pension, nominee pension, pension to dependant parents and withdrawal benefit.

Employees' Provident Fund Scheme: Under this scheme, the member's and the employer's contributions along with interest are payable to the member of the scheme at the time of his retirement or leaving the service, as per rules.

Employment costs: These are salary-related costs which include recruitment expenses, basic salary, employment taxes, benefits, space, equipment and so on.

Expatriates: These are the people who are sent by the home-country organizations to foreign subsidiaries to take care of the assignments entrusted to them.

Expatriate compensation: It refers to the compensation payable to expatriates for performing the assigned task in the foreign subsidiaries.

External alignments: It refers to pay structures worked out by competitors for different skills, jobs or competencies in their own organizations. An organization has to align its pay structure to that of its competitors.

External equity/relativities: It refers to pay structures worked out by competitors for different skills, jobs or competencies in their own organizations. An organization has to align its pay structure to that of its competitors.

External relativities: While fixing pay/grade of an individual, attention should be paid to market relativities of key jobs in the various occupations or even job families, that is, what the competitors are paying for the same type of jobs should be kept in view.

Extramural welfare activities: Welfare activities which are undertaken outside the factory such as housing and medical are known as extramural activities.

Fair wage: It is a wage above the minimum wage but somewhat below the living wage, depending on the capacity of the organization to pay.

Fringe benefits: The benefits provided to the workforce apart from the negotiated wages are nowadays termed as either fringe benefits or supplementary benefits or non-wage benefits. These benefits reduce the gap between the nominal wages and the real wages of the workers.

Gainsharing: It is a commitment to employee involvement that ties additional pay to improvement in workforce performance.

General reviews: When due to general market ratio movement or increase in the cost of living or union agreements an across-the-board pay hike is given to employees, it is referred to as 'general review'.

Global corporations: A global corporation is structured so that the national boundaries disappear. It hires the best people for jobs, irrespective of national origin.

Golden handcuffs: Also called 'retention payments', these are payments made to retain people in the organization and are made in the form of lump sum payments or in the form of guaranteed bonuses.

Golden handshakes: These are commonly negotiated rewards as part of the 'compromise agreements' used to enable senior executives who may no longer be fit to continue with the organization and, therefore, enable them to depart with dignity, pursue 'other interest' or even 'spend more time with their family'.

Golden hellos: Often called 'recruitment bonuses', these are payments made to tempt much sought-after individuals or specialists to join the company at particular positions.

Graded salary structure: It has a sequence of salary grades, each having a defined minimum and maximum. A well-designed salary structure should ensure that all jobs of the organization are allocated into a salary grade within the structure.

Grievance: A feeling by an individual that some injustice has been done to him.

Hardship allowance: It is paid to make expatriates feel comfortable in the host country where living conditions are not good.

Halo effect: Halo effect exists where the rater is influenced by ratee's one or two outstandingly good (or bad) performance and he evaluates the entire performance accordingly.

Honoraria: These are lump sum payments made to recognize specific contributions or expertise. These are psychologically more satisfying.

Host-country nationals: These are the nationals of the country where foreign subsidiary is located.

Human capital: It is the education, experience, knowledge, abilities and skills required to perform the work that constitutes human capital.

Incentive plans: (see bonus [premium] schemes).

Informal groups: These groups come up spontaneously to fulfil those needs of employees which are not fulfilled by formal groups.

Intellectual capital: It refers to business-related intangibles such as knowledge, experience, skills, procedures, database and intellectual property rights of an organization.

Internal alignment: It refers to the maintenance of internal equity with regard to pay relationship among different jobs or competencies or skills or all taken together within the organization.

Internal audit: It is a multi-stepped process aimed at determining whether current processes and procedures comply with pre-decided rules and regulations, and standards.

Internal equities/relativities: It refers to the maintenance of internal equity with regard to pay relationships among different jobs or competencies or skills or all taken together, within the organization.

International corporations: It refers to the companies that are built on their existing capabilities to penetrate overseas markets. They adopt their products to overseas markets without making changes in their normal operations.

International remuneration: It refers to the remuneration paid to the employees of foreign subsidiaries for performing tasks assigned to them abroad or at international organizations.

Intramural welfare activities: Welfare activities which are undertaken within the premises of the factory, such as health, welfare and safety measures, healthy working conditions and canteen, are known as intramural activities.

Intrinsic/relational/non-monetary rewards: These are non-quantifiable rewards employees get from their employers, such as recognition, appreciation and job satisfaction.

Job analysis: It is a process of determining the duties and skill requirements of a job and the kind of person who should be hired for it.

Job description: A job description is a written statement of what the worker actually does, how he does it, what the working conditions are and so on. It represents a written summary of the job as an identifiable organizational unit.

Job evaluation: Job evaluation establishes the relative value of jobs based on their contents, independent of link to the market.

Job family structures: In these structures, there is a separate grade and pay structure for a different category of job family containing similar jobs. Job families comprise jobs in an occupation or function but involve different levels of knowledge, responsibility, skill or competence.

Job grading: It is done after job evaluation is conducted and grades are allocated according to the worth of the job as found out by job evaluation.

Job pricing: Job pricing is attaching a price tag to each job and creating a wage structure that equitably relates jobs to their calculated values.

Job specification: A written explanation of the knowledge, skills, abilities, traits and other characteristics (KSAOs) necessary for effective performance on a given job.

Knowledge-based pay systems: In these systems, pay is linked to additional knowledge related to the same job (depth), for example, teachers, scientists or to a number of different jobs (breadth), for example, technicians.

Labour costs: These are costs incurred on employing people who are to be paid wages, benefits and so on.

Labour grades: Labour grades are established, each grade representing a range of point values, with one wage rate or range for the entire grade.

Labour welfare: Labour welfare is anything done for the intellectual, physical, moral and economic betterment of the workers whether by employers, government or agencies over and above what is laid down by law or what is normally expected on the past of contractual benefits for which the workers may have bargained.

Lay-off: Lay-off refers to a situation where an employer, for reasons beyond his control, is unable to offer employment temporarily.

Layoff/retrenchment compensation: Under the Industrial Disputes Act, 1947, a worker who is laid off or retrenched is entitled to payment as per the rules.

Living wage: It represents the highest level of wages including all amenities which a citizen living in the modern civilized society is entitled to and expects when the economy of the country is sufficiently advanced and the employer is able to meet the expanding aspirations of his workers.

Management by objectives: In the MBO programme, there is a special provision for mutual goal setting and appraisal of progress by both the appraiser and the appraisee(s).

Managerial compensation: It is proportional to the results or goals already settled for managers and, therefore, variable and motivating.

Minimum wages: It is the amount of remuneration which may be sufficient to enable a worker to live in reasonable comforts, having regard to all obligations to which an average worker would ordinarily be subjected to.

Multi-graded structures: Also called a narrow-graded structure, it has narrow pay ranges, for example, 20–40 per cent. It consists of a sequence of job grades (maybe 10 or more) into which jobs of broadly equivalent value are placed. Grades may be defined by grade definitions or profiles.

Multinational corporations: An MNC has operations in different countries but each is viewed as a relatively separate enterprise supplying its products for the geographical region surrounding the country of operation of the unit.

Negative salary reviews: These are reviews containing negative feedback about the work performance and so on of the reviewee.

Negotiated pay review: In it, target settlements are agreed which are comfortably affordable and comparable, based on analysis of data on pay agreements and market rate movement, and an agreement is reached.

Nominal/money wage: It refers to the monetary form of wage payment.

Nominal wages: Nominal wages are the wages which are paid in the form of money and are, therefore, also called money wages.

Non-financial benefits/rewards: These are rewards which do not cost or cost very little to the employers.

Non-financial metrics: These are quantitative measures that cannot be expressed in monetary units such as recognition, praise and job satisfaction.

Non-financial recognition: It is a sort of non-cash award which is given to employees at no cost or negligible cost to recognize high level of performance or any other significant achievement.

Overtime payments: It is the amount paid to an employee who works for more than a specified number of hours in a week; the additional hours are called overtime. Overtime is paid at a higher rate per hour than for regular hours, usually one to two times the rate of regular hours.

Ownership plans: Also known as stock option plans, in these plans, stock options are offered to employees in the form of company stocks, and thus employees become partners in the company.

Paired comparison technique: In this technique, each job is compared with every other job, one at a time, and thus ranked in order of their merit, and wage rates are fixed accordingly.

Parent-country nationals: It refers to the nationals of the country where the parent country is located.

Pay for excellence: It is paid when an employee meets, rather 'overachieve', their targets or for performing excellently well.

Pay for person: Attached to the person, these are structures based on skills that pay individuals for all the skills they possess irrespective of the fact whether the work they do requires all or just a few of those particular skills.

Pay for time not worked: It refers to the pay paid to an employee for the period for which he does not work such as holiday, leave and lunch hours. It is a sort of fringe benefit.

Pay review: Pay review is conducted to implement an organization's reward policies and also for improving performance, continuation of motivation and retention of employees. Pay reviews should also meet the expectations of employees and at the same time should be within the budget.

Pay review budget: It spells out the overall increase in the payroll which the managers are allowed to recommend for their departments.

Pay spines: These are a series of incremental 'pay points' covering all jobs. Such pay spine increments vary between 2.5 per cent and 3.0 per cent. Pay spine increments may be standardized from the top to the bottom of the spine.

Payment by results: (see piece rate method).

Payment for qualifications: It is usually a lump sum payment given to achievers of higher qualifications such as MBA and PhD just to recognize their added value to the organization.

Payment of Gratuity Act, 1972: As per the Act, all the employees (including managers and supervisors) engaged in the eligible establishments are legally entitled to gratuity at the rate of 15 days' wages multiplied by the number of completed years of service, subject to fulfilment of certain conditions laid down under the Act.

Peer appraisal: It means appraisal of an employee by his peers.

Performance appraisal: Performance appraisal is a systematic, periodic and so far as humanly possible, impartial rating of an employee's excellence in matters pertaining to his present job and to his potential for a better job.

Performance management: Performance management is a process that consolidates goal setting, performance appraisal and development into a single, common system so as to ensure that the employee's performance is supporting the aims of the organization.

Performance-related pay: It aims at providing incentives and rewards which will improve the performance of the organization by improving individual performance. In it, payments are made as per the performance/contribution made.

Phillips NV Holland Model: This model includes a 5-point scale ranging from excellent to insufficient and provides for evaluation of employees on the few qualities, namely conceptual effectiveness, operational effectiveness, interpersonal effectiveness and achievement motivation.

Philips Hi-Lo Matrix: In it, a 2×2 matrix is used to evaluate performance and potential in a single process.

Piece rate method: Under this method, wages are paid on the basis of the quantum of output, that is, the number of units produced × predetermined rate per unit.

Praise: It is personal acknowledgement given verbally by the boss for performing well.

Previous year: It is the financial year immediately preceding the assessment year.

Problem children: The employees who have low grades in both performance and potential.

Profit-related pay: It is a form of profit-sharing used in the United Kingdom and, therefore, varies according to the profitability of the organization.

Profit-sharing: In it, an employer pays to the eligible employees, as an addition to their normal remuneration, additional sums in the form of cash or shares in the company related to the profits of the business.

Promotion: Promotion refers to the advancement to positions of increased responsibilities, higher pay and better status.

Psychological contract: It refers to the relationship between an employer and his employee where there exists unwritten and mutual expectations—what an employee expects from his employers and vice versa.

Psychometric tests: Such tests try to capture the abilities of the employee on several fronts such as aptitude, logic deduction and inference.

Real wage: It represents the actual exchange value of money wage, that is, the purchasing power of money wage.

Recognition: Recognition of one's contribution by the organization generates both job satisfaction and a feeling of accomplishment, and motivates an employee.

Red circle rates: When some current rates generally show up as distinctly out of line, such 'over' rates are red circled and are temporarily regarded as personal rates, to be protected as long as present employees remain in these jobs and are eliminated as soon as the employees concerned leave their jobs.

Review appraisal: Conducted by the immediate supervisors/departmental heads, such tests provide insights into the potential of the employee.

Reward management: It is related to the formulation and implementation of strategies and policies that aim at rewarding employees fairly, equitably and consistently in accordance with their value to the organization. Reward management deals with the design, implementation and maintenance of reward processes and practices that are geared to the improvement of individual, team and organizational performance.

Reward management policy: These are guidelines for effective execution of reward management.

Salary budget: It is a statement in quantitative/financial terms of the planned allocation and use of resources so as to meet the operational requirements of the organization. It involves forecasting the levels of activity indicating the number of different categories of employees that are required for the period of the budget.

Salary control: It is an exercise to control salary costs by controlling the number of people employed by following a top-down or bottom-up budgeting approach and embedded controls.

Salary costs: These include base salary and salary-related costs beyond base salary. Salary costs usually constitute 50 to 70 per cent of the total cost of production.

Salary planning: It is an integral part of the budgetary process of the organization and it is in the salary planning process that it is decided what is it that the organization wants to do and how it is going to get it done.

Salary progression curves: These refer to an increase in salary resulting from the movement up an incremental scale, pay range or band.

Salary reviews: These are carried out to award the best-performing employees and keep them motivated so as to enable them to give their best to the organization.

Salary structure: It comprises grades or ranges and salary levels for a single job or group of jobs. A salary structure or a salary range structure is a hierarchical group of jobs and salary ranges within an organization.

Salary surveys: These are conducted to collect information with regard to rates of salaries paid and benefits extended to the employees by other employers in the market for various jobs.

Sales force incentives: These are programmes that serve a good purpose in motivating sales personnel by providing incentives in the form of cash, merchandise, tips or gifts depending on how much the organization can afford.

Scorecards: An analytical tool that measures performance periodical results against predetermined goals and enables users to gauge how their performance stands against standards.

Self-assessment: In it, the manager himself assesses his performance and work behaviour. It should be taken as complementary to the appraisal done by the superiors.

Self-rating: It means appraisal by the employee himself.

Shift pay: It is a way of paying a premium to employees who work in a shift that has less desirable hours a business must operate.

Short-range tax planning: It is thought of and executed at the end of the financial year so as to search for ways to limit their tax liability legally when the financial year comes to an end.

Skill-based pay: It is a compensation system that provides employees with additional pay in exchange for formal certificates of an employee's knowledge, mastery of skills and/or competencies.

Social assistance: It is a purely government affair and, therefore, financed exclusively by the government and benefits are granted on fulfilling prescribed conditions, though benefits are claimed as a matter of right.

Social insurance: It aims at the maintenance of minimum standard of living of the employee during the period of contingency of life.

Social security: It is the security that the society (all the agencies concerned) provides to a worker to enable him to sustain himself and his family in case he falls victim to any contingency of life.

Spendable salary: It is a disposable salary, which the employee can spend as he desires. It is usually the salary which is left in the hands of the employee after all sorts of deductions are made from the salary.

Spot rates: A spot rate is a rate for a job or an individual that is not fitted into a job grade or band in a conventional grade structure and does not allow any scope for pay progression. At times, spot rates may be attached to a person instead of a job.

Stars: Those employees who are very good in both performance and potential.

State-of-the-art technology: It refers to the latest and sophisticated technology presently available.

Statutory obligations: It refers to the obligations which have to be discharged because of legal compulsions.

Statutory minimum wage: It is the amount of remuneration fixed according to the provisions of the Minimum Wages Act, 1948.

Stock options plans: (see ownership plans).

Straight piece rate plan: In this system, a worker is paid more or less depending on his actual output.

Straight piece work plan: It is like a straight piece rate plan with the exception that in it hourly earnings are guaranteed.

Structural review: When changes to pay ranges due to an increase in the market rates or cost of living take place, it is called structural review.

Supplementary compensation: These are benefits for time not worked, such as vacation, holidays and sick pay.

Take-home salary: It refers to the amount of salary left to the employee after making authorized deductions such as income tax, provident funds and life insurance premium.

Tax management: It relates to past actions (filing of income tax returns, assessment proceedings, rectification, appeal, future corrective actions, etc.

Tax planning: It means an understanding, analysis and interpretation of a taxpayer's financial status in a given time so that he may take full advantage of relevant deductions, exemption and other benefits as per provisions of the existing Income Tax Act, 1961 (as amended up to date).

Team-based pay/rewards/systems: These are payments or other forms of non-financial rewards provided to members of a defined team, which are linked to the performance of that team.

Team spirit: It relates to cooperation extended to teammates.

Third-country nationals: These are the citizens of a country other than the parent or host country.

Thirteen-month bonus: Thirteen- or even 14-month payments are more common in the United Kingdom and Europe and are paid either at Christmas or in the summer to reward loyalty and meet the extra costs of the season.

Time wages: As per this method, an employee is paid on the basis of time worked, that is, hourly, daily, weekly or monthly, irrespective of the quantity of work.

Toll payroll budgeting: It is based on present payroll costs adjusted for forecast changes in the number and mixture of those employed in the budget centre, and the forecast cost of general and individual pay increases.

Total compensation/rewards: In addition to compensation and benefits which are tangible, there are intangible rewards also such as appreciation, recognition, work-life balance and development opportunities—all taken together constitute total compensation.

Transfers: Transfers refer to reassignments to similar positions in other parts of the organization or to a different place at which the plant/office of the organization is located. There is no change in salary or status and so on.

Transnational corporation: It is a fine blend of local responsiveness of an MNC and the efficiency of a global corporation. It provides autonomy to independent country operations and brings these separate operations into an integral whole through a networked structure.

Unilateral wage fixation: In it only one party, that is, the employer fixes wages.

Variable/differential pay: It refers to payments related to individual performance, contribution, competence or skill, or team or organizational performance.

Wage board: It is a tripartite body constituted by the government for an industry for fixing wage structure of employees.

INDEX

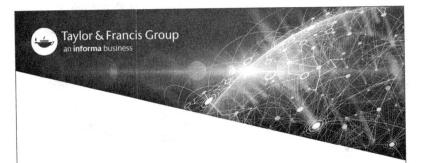

Printed in the United States
by Baker & Taylor Publisher Services